WOLVERINE

FIRST CUTS

WRITERS
CHRIS YOST & **CHRIS CLAREMONT**
with **JOHN BYRNE**

PENCILERS
MARK TEXEIRA, JOHN BYRNE,
FRANK MILLER & **SAL BUSCEMA**
with **MARSHALL ROGERS**

INKERS
MARK TEXEIRA,
RICARDO VILLAMONTE,
TERRY AUSTIN,
JOSEF RUBINSTEIN
& **STEVE LEIALOHA**
with **RANDY EMBERLIN**

COLORISTS
JOHN RAUCH,
GLYNIS WEIN
& **BEN SEAN**
with **BOB SHAREN**

LETTERERS
TODD KLEIN,
TOM ORZECHOWSKI,
JOHN COSTANZA,
JOE ROSEN,
DIANA ALBERS
& **CLEM ROBINS**

ASSISTANT EDITORS
DANIEL KETCHUM,
JIM SALICRUP & **JO DUFFY**

EDITORS
NICK LOWE, ROGER STERN,
LOUISE JONES & **AL MILGROM**
with **MICHAEL HIGGINS**

BONUS HANDBOOK PAGES
HEAD WRITER/COORDINATOR: **MIKE O'SULLIVAN**
OFFICIAL HANDBOOK OF THE MARVEL UNIVERSE OVERSEER: **JEFF CHRISTIANSEN**
WRITERS: **SEAN MCQUAID, MIKE O'SULLIVAN, MARKUS RAYMOND** & **STUART VANDAL**
with **RONALD BYRD, JEFF CHRISTIANSEN, ANTHONY FLAMINI** & **ERIC MOREELS**
PRODUCTION: **JOE FRONTIRRE**
SPECIAL THANKS TO WWW.G-MART.COM AND JEPH YORK

COLLECTION EDITOR: **MARK D. BEAZLEY**
ASSISTANT EDITORS: **ALEX STARBUCK** & **NELSON RIBEIRO**
EDITOR, SPECIAL PROJECTS: **JENNIFER GRÜNWALD**
SENIOR EDITOR, SPECIAL PROJECTS: **JEFF YOUNGQUIST**
RESEARCH & LAYOUT: **JEPH YORK**   PRODUCTION: **COLORTEK** & **JOE FRONTIRRE**
BOOK DESIGNER: **RODOLFO MURAGUCHI**
SVP OF PRINT & DIGITAL PUBLISHING SALES: **DAVID GABRIEL**

EDITOR IN CHIEF: **AXEL ALONSO**   CHIEF CREATIVE OFFICER: **JOE QUESADA**
PUBLISHER: **DAN BUCKLEY**   EXECUTIVE PRODUCER: **ALAN FINE**

WOLVERINE: FIRST CUTS. Contains material originally published in magazine form as X-MEN
P #83-85. First printing 2013. ISBN# 978-0-7851-8427-0. Published by MARVEL WORLDW
020. Copyright © 1979, 1982, 1987, 2009 and 2013 Marvel Characters, Inc. All rights r
e trademarks of Marvel Characters, Inc. No similarity between any of the names, characte
ny such similarity which may exist is purely coincidental. **Printed in the U.S.A.** ALAN FINE,
President - Print, Animation & Digital Divisions; JOE QUESADA, Chief Creative Officer; TOM
reator & Content Development; DAVID GABRIEL, SVP of Print & Digital Publishing Sales; JIM O
perations Manager; ALEX MORALES, Publishing Operations Manager; STAN LEE, Chairman E
Marvel Partnerships, at ndisla@marvel.com. For Marvel subscription inquiries, please call

VEL COMICS, WOLVERINE #1-2 and MARVEL TEAM-
PUBLICATION: 135 West 50th Street, New York, NY
es and likenesses thereof, and all related indicia
g or dead person or institution is intended, and
Marvel Characters B.V.; DAN BUCKLEY, Publisher
Procurement, Publishing; C.B. CEBULSKI, SVP of
of Publishing Technology; SUSAN CRESPI, Editorial
Marvel.com, please contact Niza Disla, Director
3 by R.R. DONNELLEY, INC., SALEM, VA, USA.

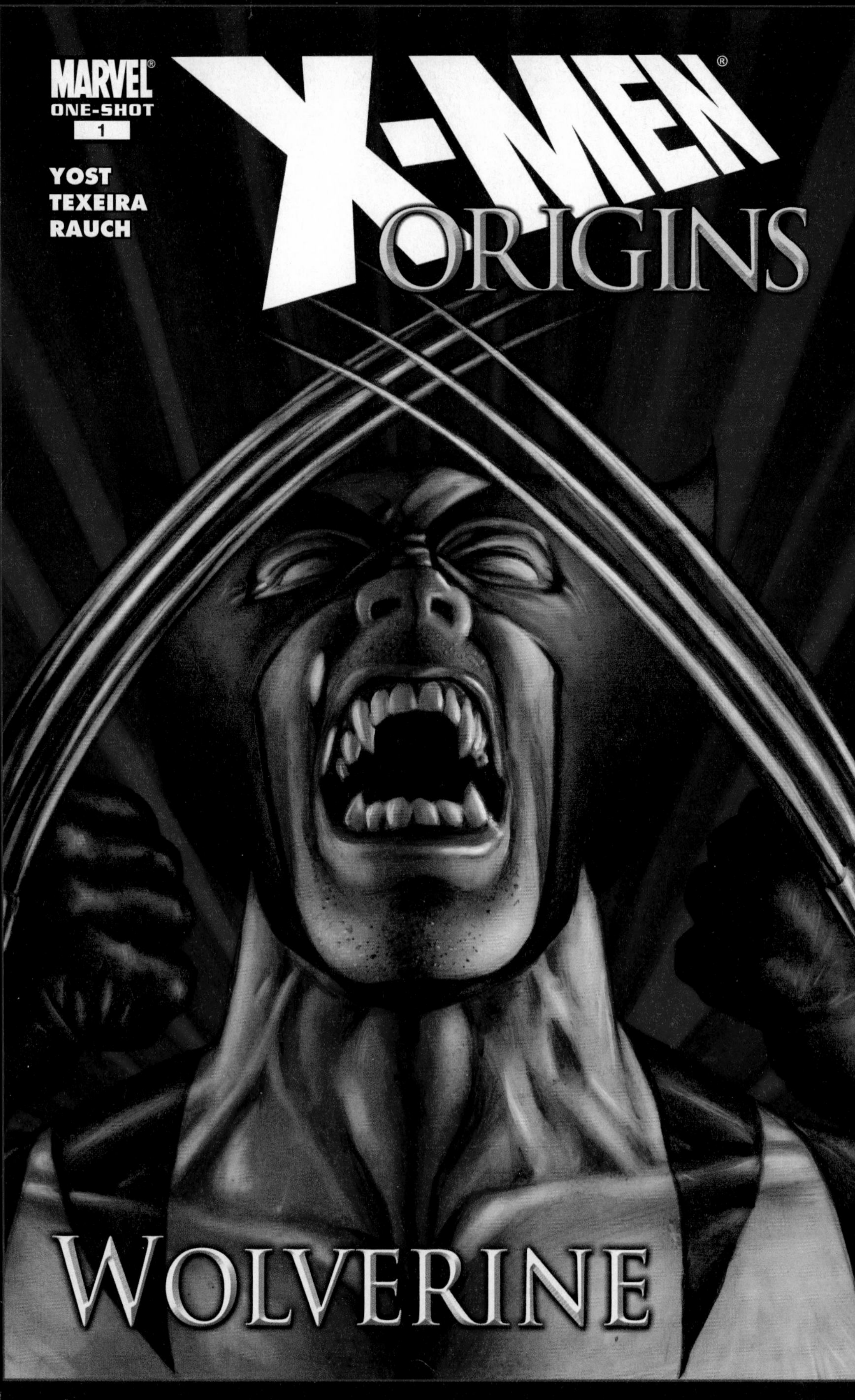

MARVEL
ONE-SHOT
1
YOST
TEXEIRA
RAUCH
X-MEN
ORIGINS
WOLVERINE

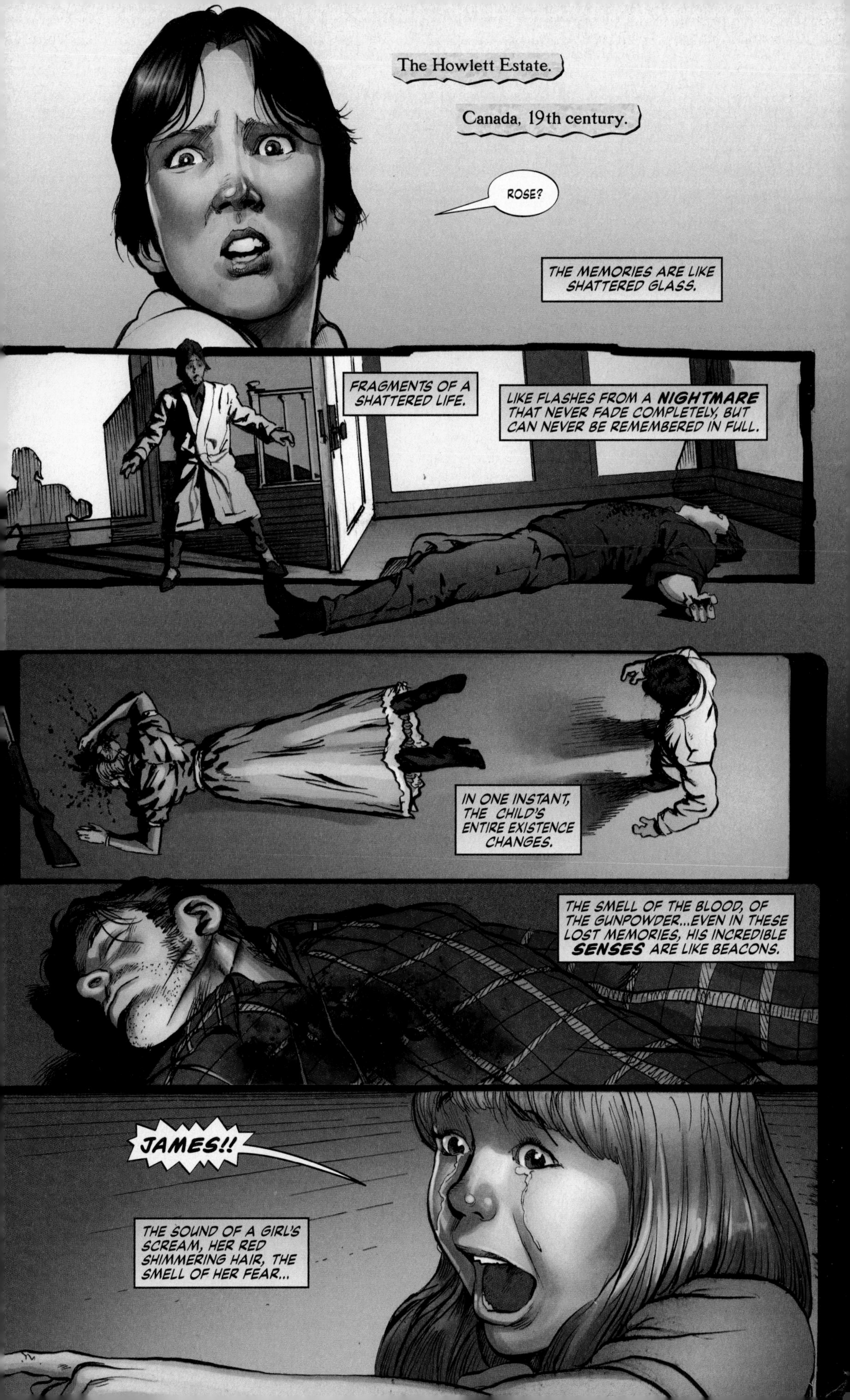
The Howlett Estate.
Canada, 19th century.
ROSE?
THE MEMORIES ARE LIKE SHATTERED GLASS.
FRAGMENTS OF A SHATTERED LIFE.
LIKE FLASHES FROM A NIGHTMARE THAT NEVER FADE COMPLETELY, BUT CAN NEVER BE REMEMBERED IN FULL.
IN ONE INSTANT, THE CHILD'S ENTIRE EXISTENCE CHANGES.
THE SMELL OF THE BLOOD, OF THE GUNPOWDER...EVEN IN THESE LOST MEMORIES, HIS INCREDIBLE SENSES ARE LIKE BEACONS.
JAMES!!
THE SOUND OF A GIRL'S SCREAM, HER RED SHIMMERING HAIR, THE SMELL OF HER FEAR...

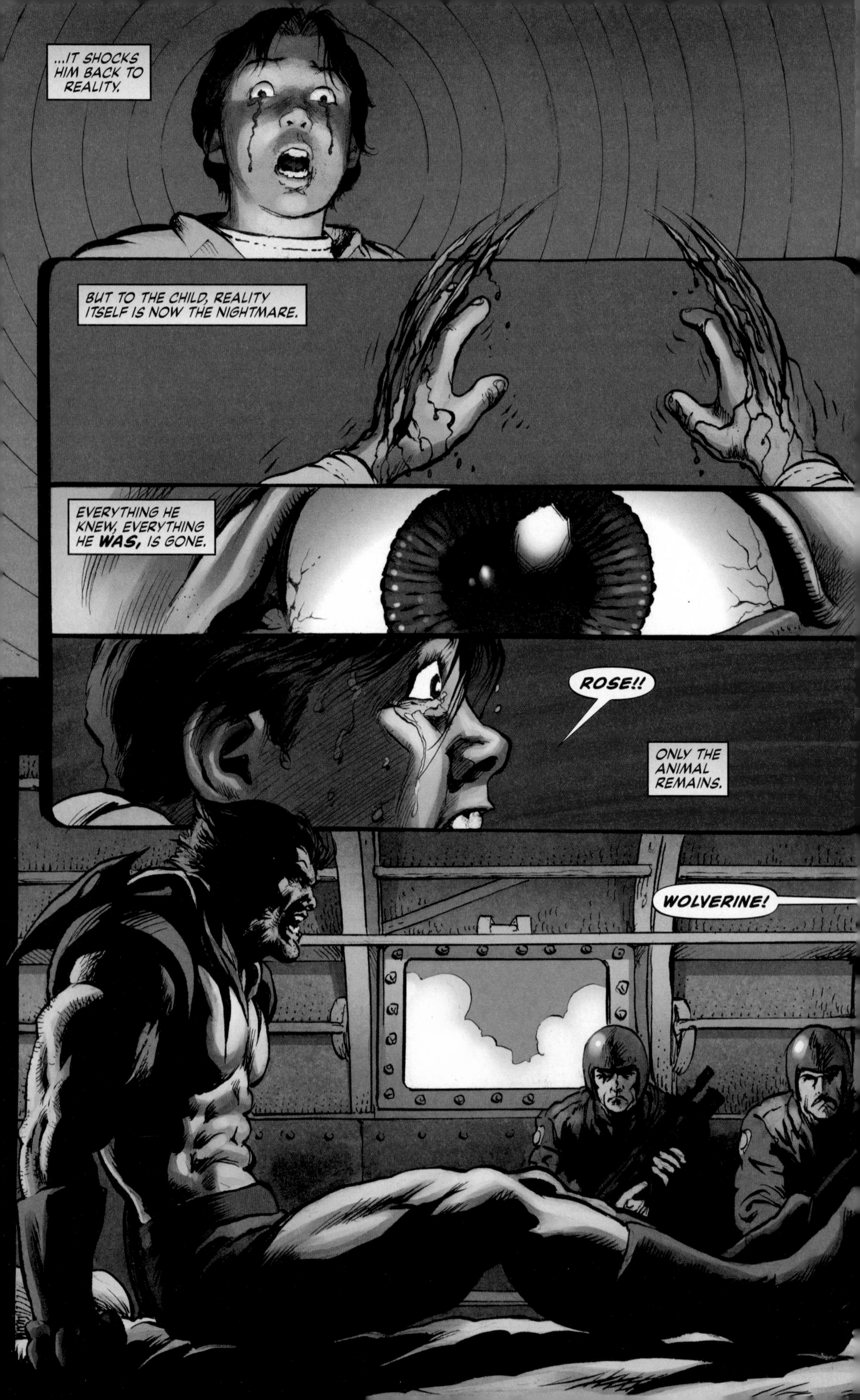
...IT SHOCKS HIM BACK TO REALITY.
BUT TO THE CHILD, REALITY ITSELF IS NOW THE NIGHTMARE.
EVERYTHING HE KNEW, EVERYTHING HE **WAS,** IS GONE.
ROSE!!
ONLY THE ANIMAL REMAINS.
WOLVERINE!

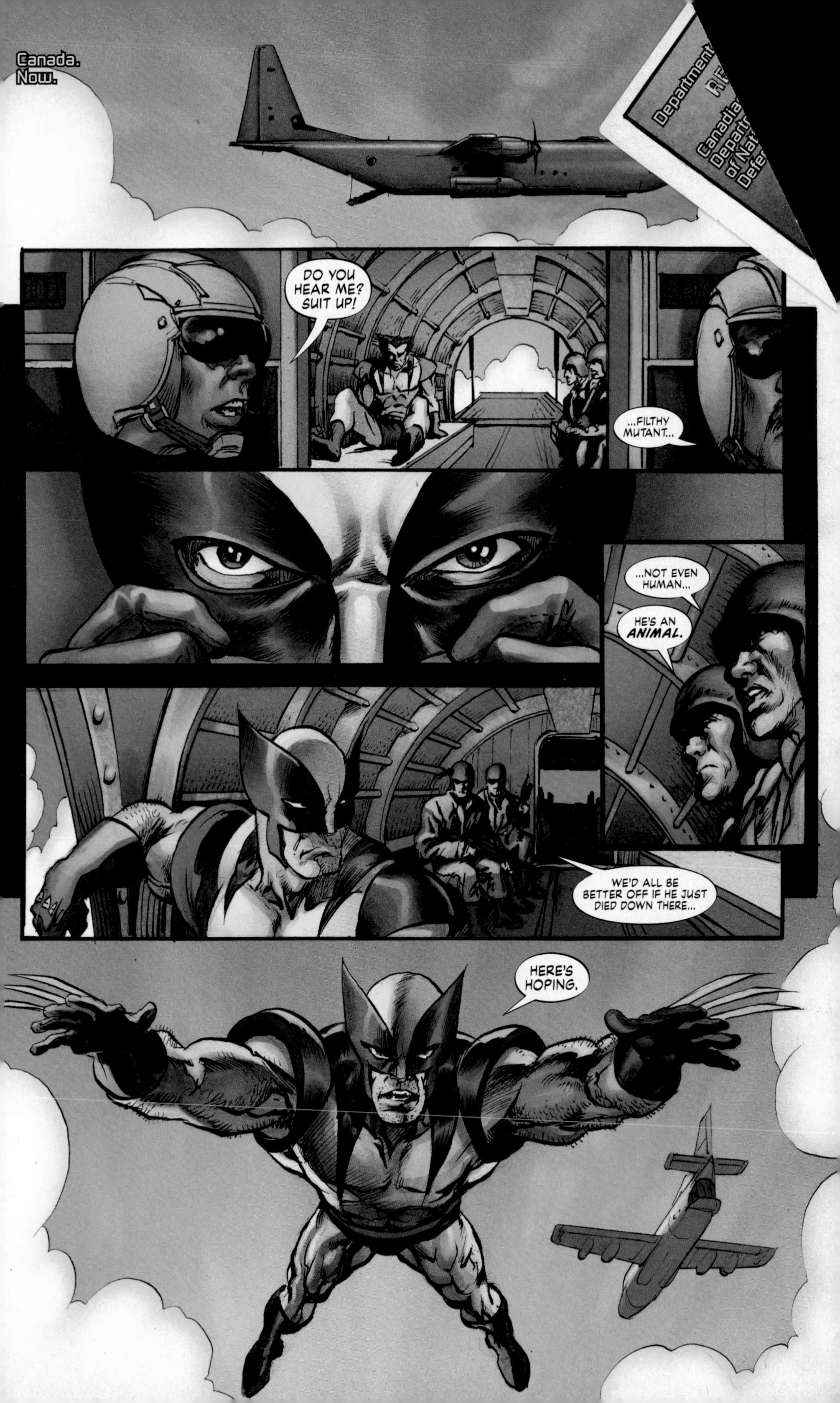
Canada.
Now.
Department
DO YOU HEAR ME? SUIT UP!
...FILTHY MUTANT...
...NOT EVEN HUMAN...
HE'S AN ANIMAL.
WE'D ALL BE BETTER OFF IF HE JUST DIED DOWN THERE...
HERE'S HOPING.

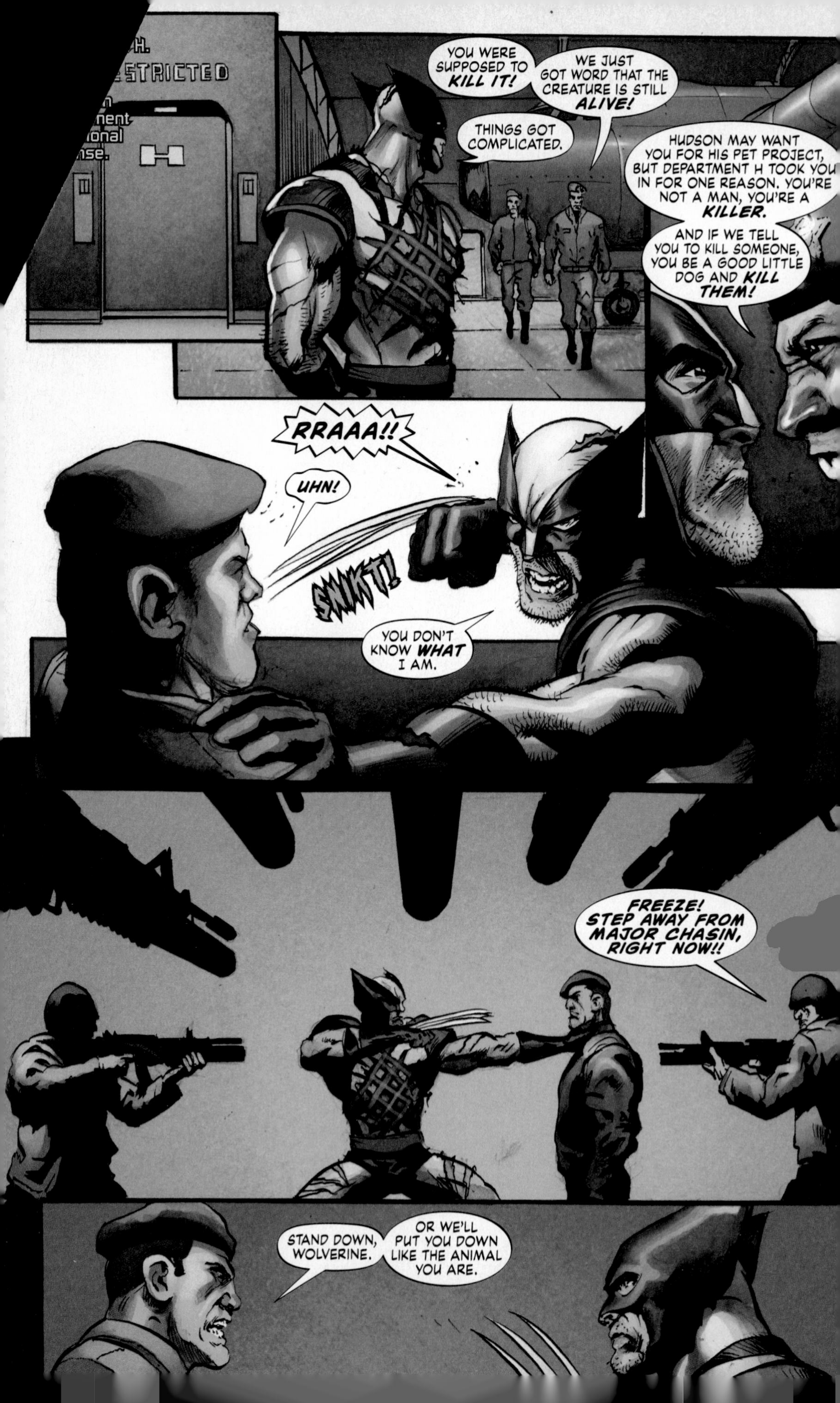
H.
RESTRICTED
YOU WERE SUPPOSED TO KILL IT!
WE JUST GOT WORD THAT THE CREATURE IS STILL ALIVE!
THINGS GOT COMPLICATED.
HUDSON MAY WANT YOU FOR HIS PET PROJECT, BUT DEPARTMENT H TOOK YOU IN FOR ONE REASON. YOU'RE NOT A MAN, YOU'RE A KILLER.
AND IF WE TELL YOU TO KILL SOMEONE, YOU BE A GOOD LITTLE DOG AND KILL THEM!
RRAAA!!
UHN!
SNIKT!
YOU DON'T KNOW WHAT I AM.
FREEZE! STEP AWAY FROM MAJOR CHASIN, RIGHT NOW!!
STAND DOWN, WOLVERINE.
OR WE'LL PUT YOU DOWN LIKE THE ANIMAL YOU ARE.

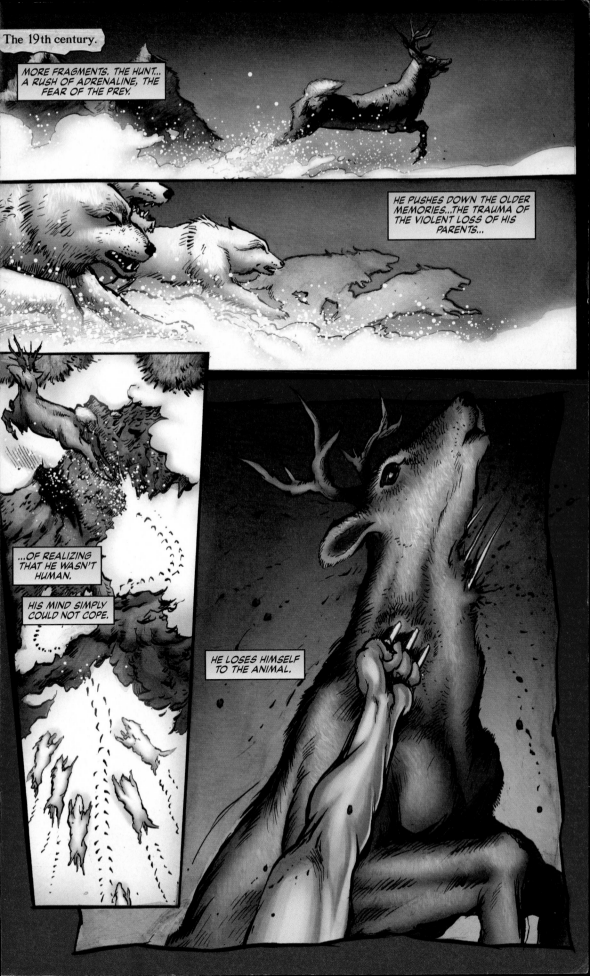

The 19th century.

MORE FRAGMENTS. THE HUNT... A RUSH OF ADRENALINE, THE FEAR OF THE PREY.

HE PUSHES DOWN THE OLDER MEMORIES...THE TRAUMA OF THE VIOLENT LOSS OF HIS PARENTS...

...OF REALIZING THAT HE WASN'T HUMAN.

HIS MIND SIMPLY COULD NOT COPE.

HE LOSES HIMSELF TO THE ANIMAL.

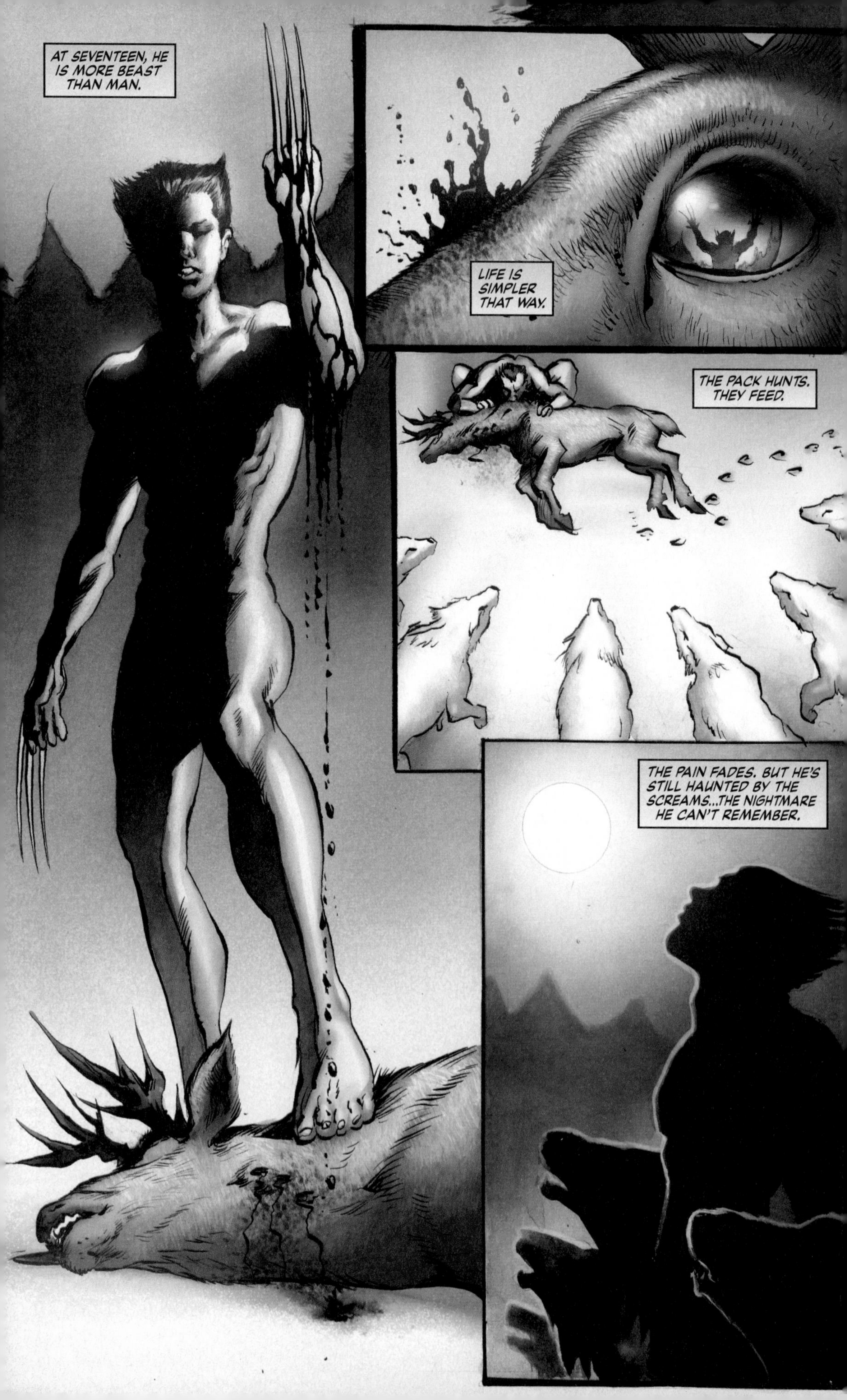

AT SEVENTEEN, HE IS MORE BEAST THAN MAN.
LIFE IS SIMPLER THAT WAY.
THE PACK HUNTS. THEY FEED.
THE PAIN FADES. BUT HE'S STILL HAUNTED BY THE SCREAMS...THE NIGHTMARE HE CAN'T REMEMBER.

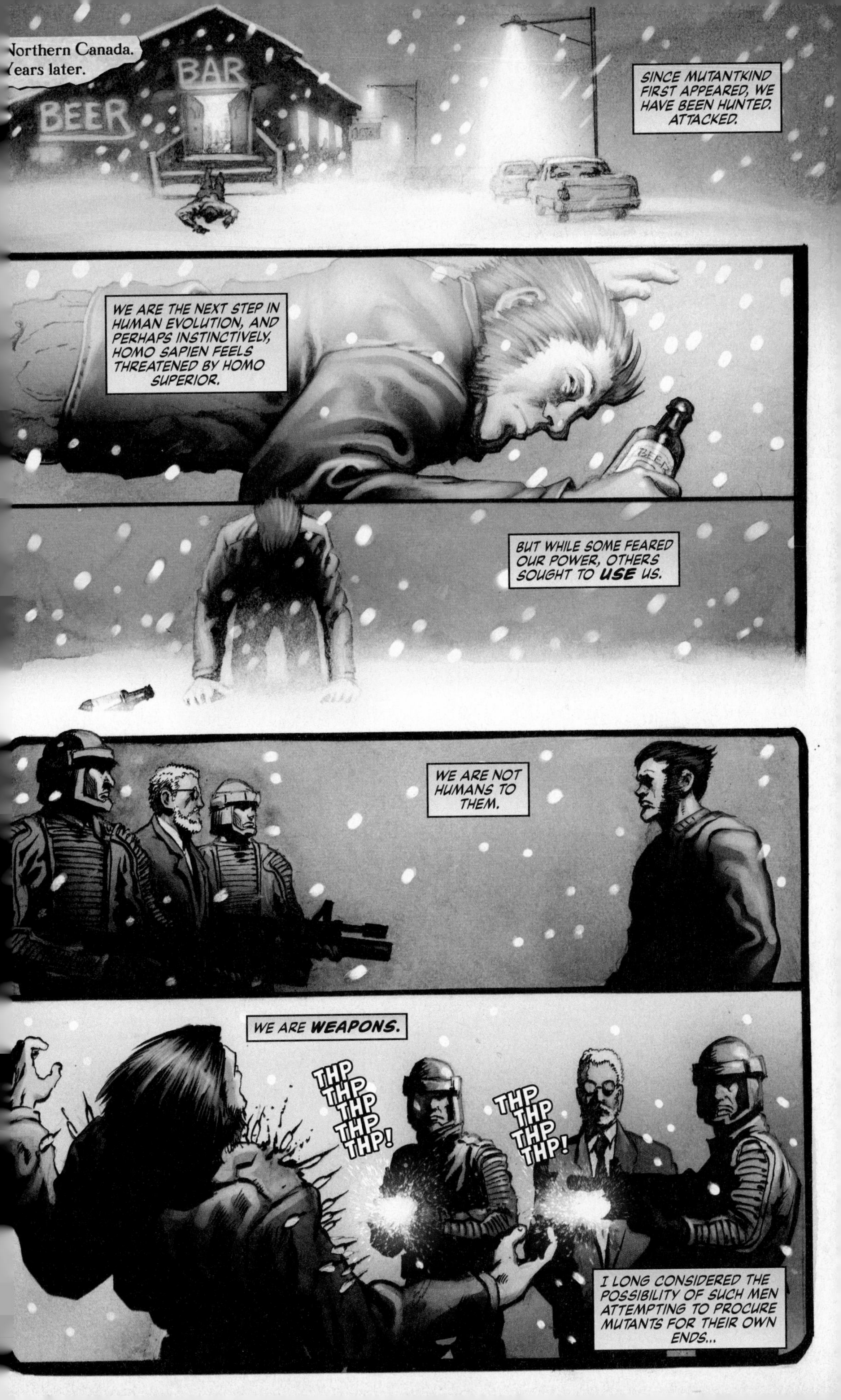

Northern Canada. Years later.
BAR
BEER
SINCE MUTANTKIND FIRST APPEARED, WE HAVE BEEN HUNTED. ATTACKED.
WE ARE THE NEXT STEP IN HUMAN EVOLUTION, AND PERHAPS INSTINCTIVELY, HOMO SAPIEN FEELS THREATENED BY HOMO SUPERIOR.
BEER
BUT WHILE SOME FEARED OUR POWER, OTHERS SOUGHT TO USE US.
WE ARE NOT HUMANS TO THEM.
WE ARE WEAPONS.
THP THP THP THP THP!
THP THP THP THP!
I LONG CONSIDERED THE POSSIBILITY OF SUCH MEN ATTEMPTING TO PROCURE MUTANTS FOR THEIR OWN ENDS...

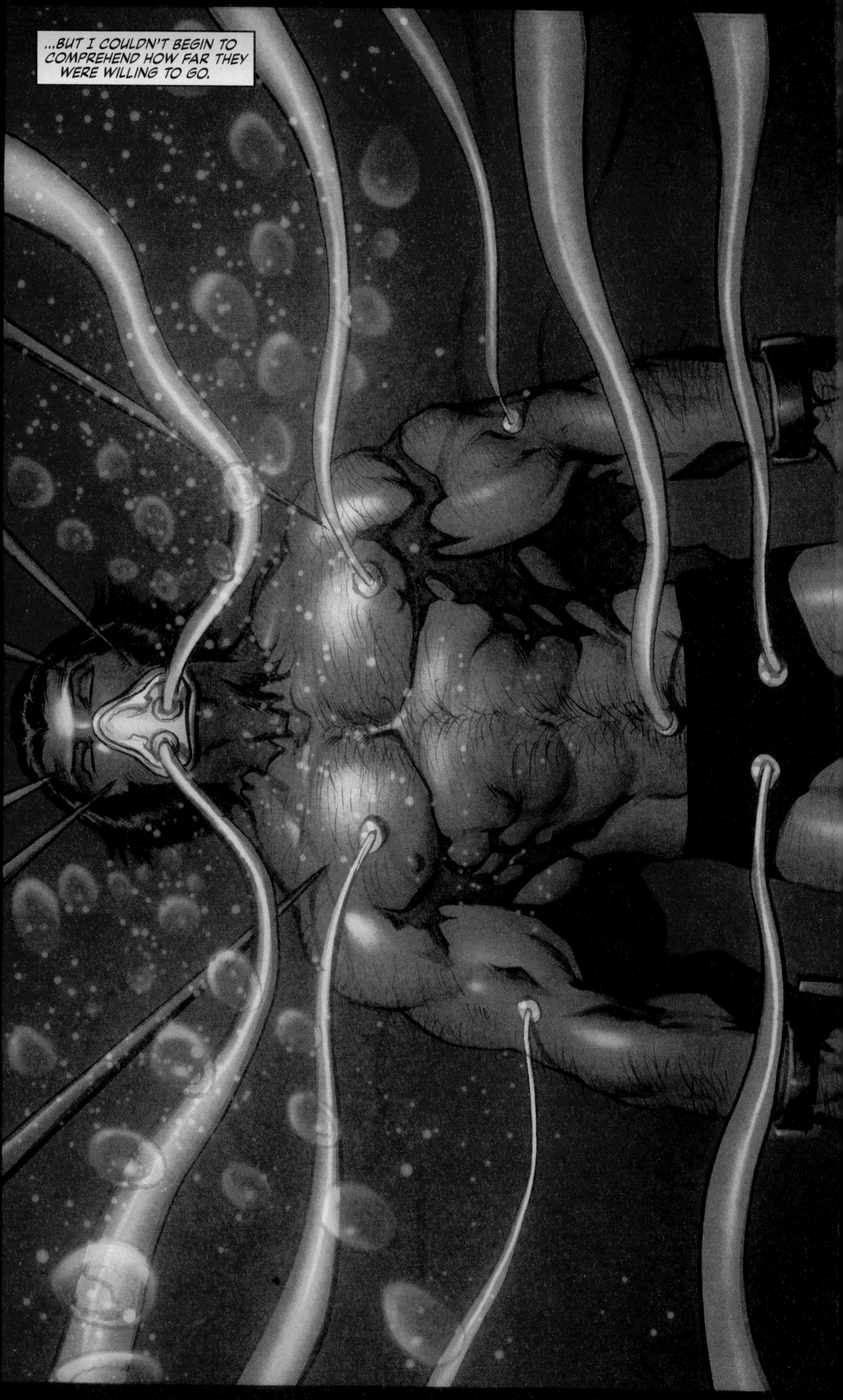
...BUT I COULDN'T BEGIN TO COMPREHEND HOW FAR THEY WERE WILLING TO GO.

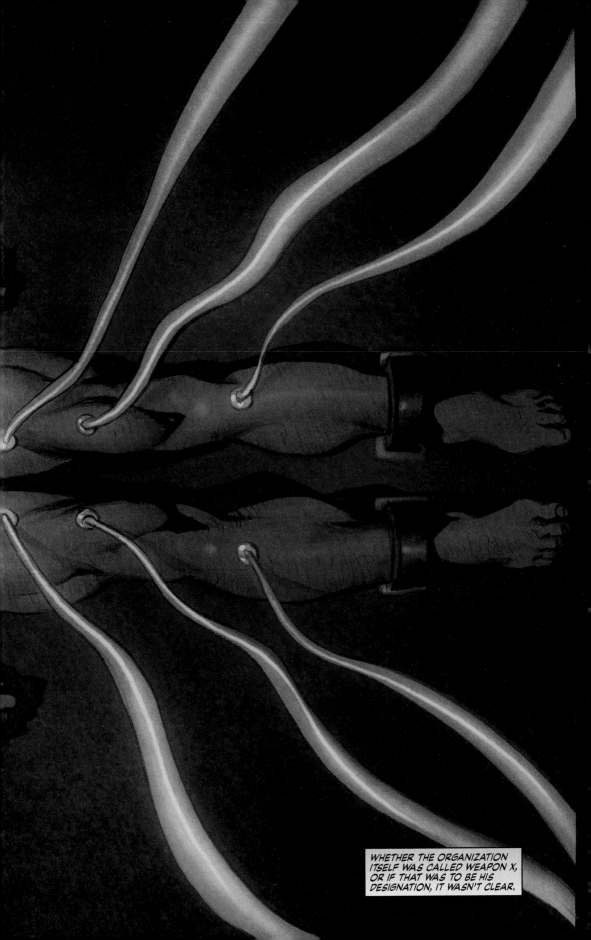

WHETHER THE ORGANIZATION
ITSELF WAS CALLED WEAPON X,
OR IF THAT WAS TO BE HIS
DESIGNATION, IT WASN'T CLEAR.

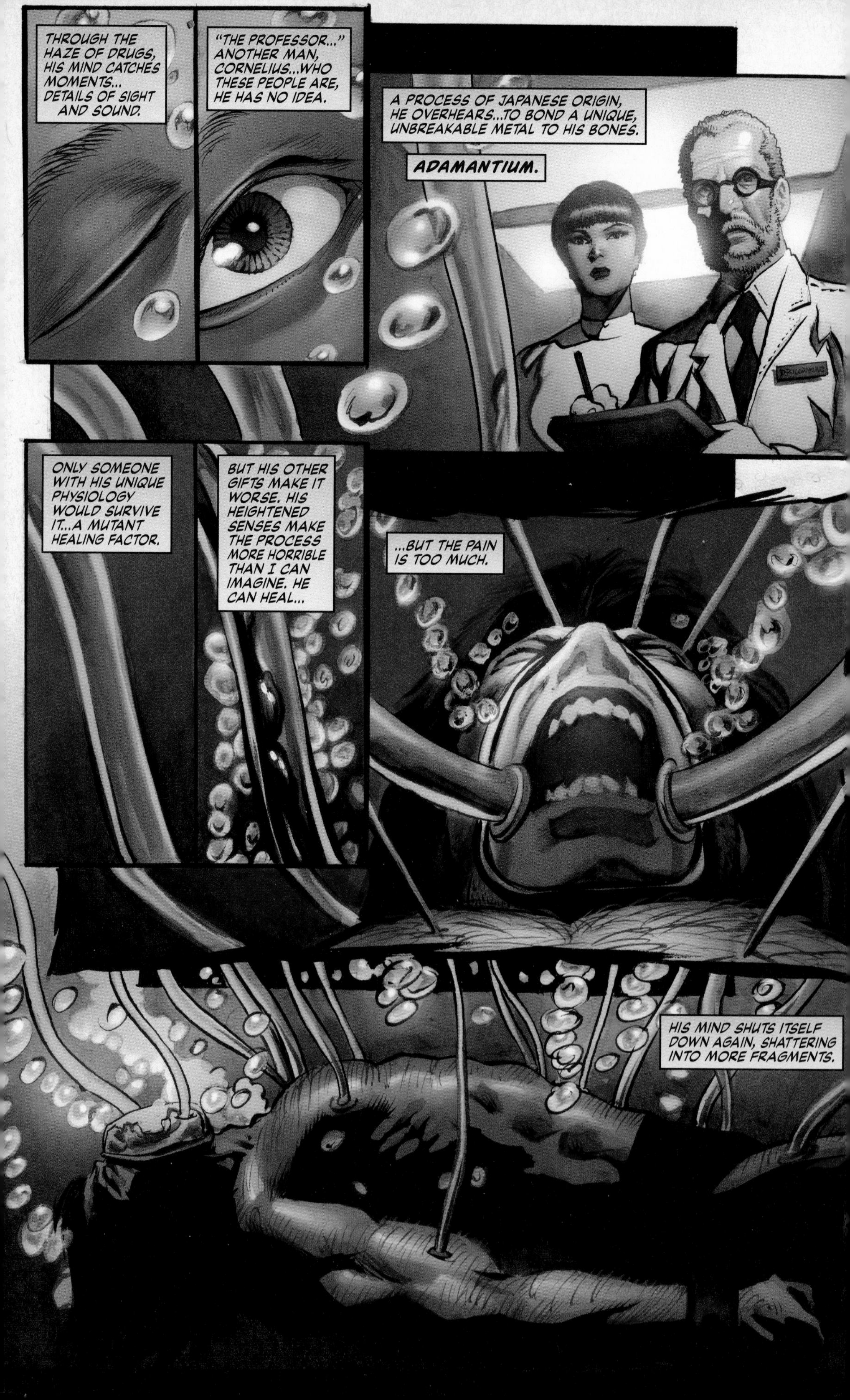
THROUGH THE HAZE OF DRUGS, HIS MIND CATCHES MOMENTS... DETAILS OF SIGHT AND SOUND.
"THE PROFESSOR..." ANOTHER MAN, CORNELIUS...WHO THESE PEOPLE ARE, HE HAS NO IDEA.
A PROCESS OF JAPANESE ORIGIN, HE OVERHEARS...TO BOND A UNIQUE, UNBREAKABLE METAL TO HIS BONES.
ADAMANTIUM.
ONLY SOMEONE WITH HIS UNIQUE PHYSIOLOGY WOULD SURVIVE IT...A MUTANT HEALING FACTOR.
BUT HIS OTHER GIFTS MAKE IT WORSE. HIS HEIGHTENED SENSES MAKE THE PROCESS MORE HORRIBLE THAN I CAN IMAGINE. HE CAN HEAL...
...BUT THE PAIN IS TOO MUCH.
HIS MIND SHUTS ITSELF DOWN AGAIN, SHATTERING INTO MORE FRAGMENTS.

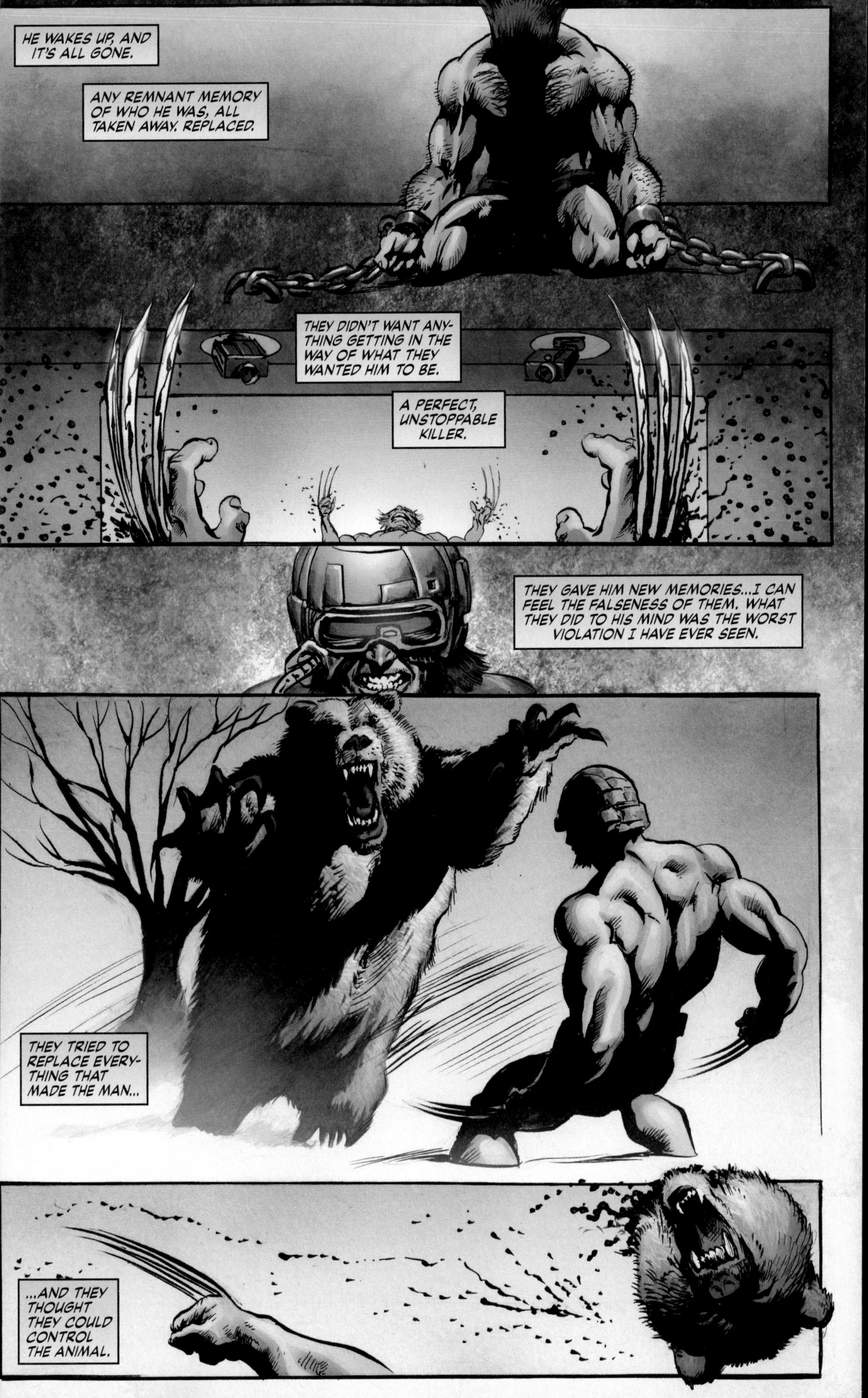
HE WAKES UP, AND IT'S ALL GONE.
ANY REMNANT MEMORY OF WHO HE WAS, ALL TAKEN AWAY. REPLACED.
THEY DIDN'T WANT ANY-THING GETTING IN THE WAY OF WHAT THEY WANTED HIM TO BE.
A PERFECT, UNSTOPPABLE KILLER.
THEY GAVE HIM NEW MEMORIES...I CAN FEEL THE FALSENESS OF THEM. WHAT THEY DID TO HIS MIND WAS THE WORST VIOLATION I HAVE EVER SEEN.
THEY TRIED TO REPLACE EVERY-THING THAT MADE THE MAN...
...AND THEY THOUGHT THEY COULD CONTROL THE ANIMAL.

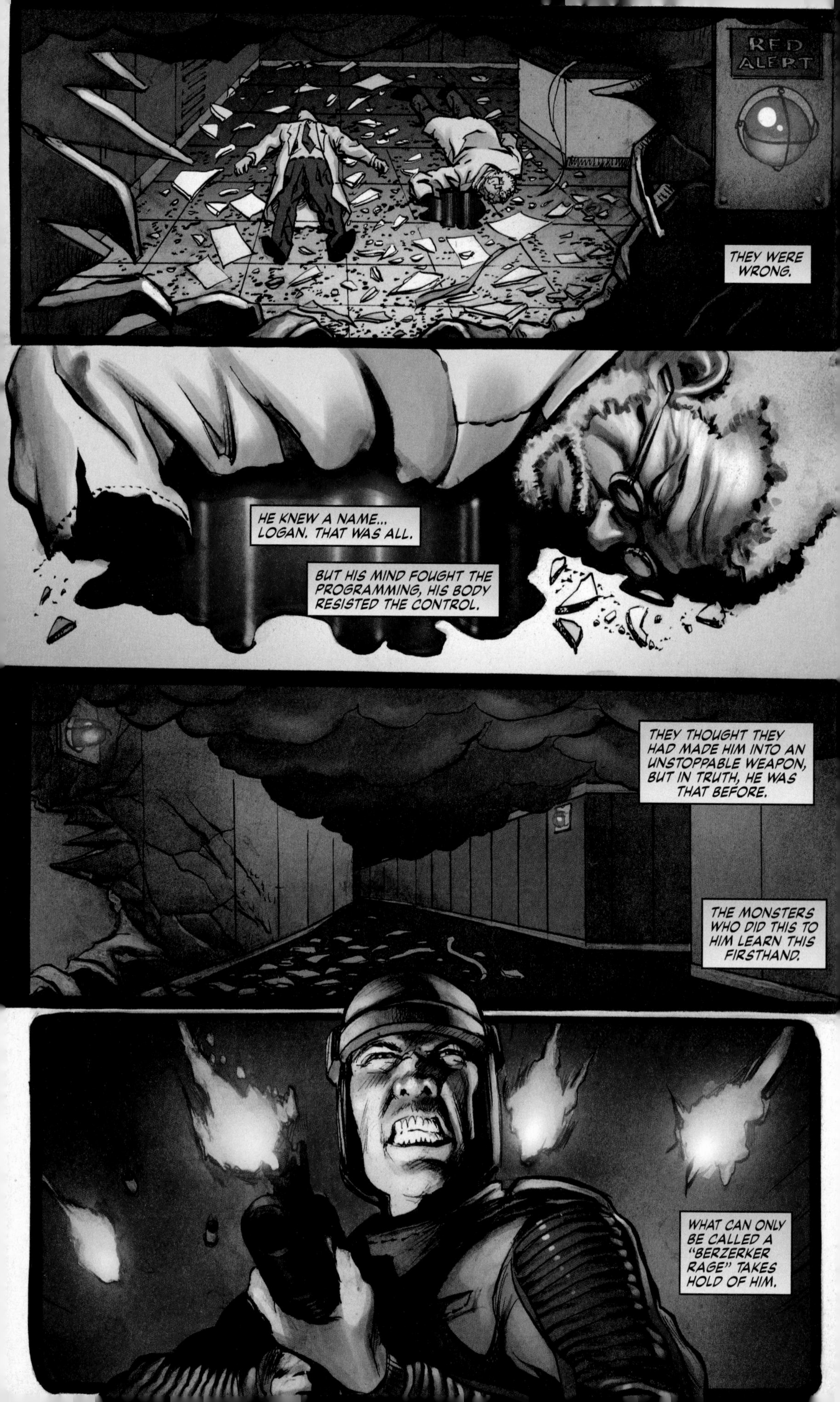

RED ALERT
THEY WERE WRONG.
HE KNEW A NAME... LOGAN. THAT WAS ALL.
BUT HIS MIND FOUGHT THE PROGRAMMING, HIS BODY RESISTED THE CONTROL.
THEY THOUGHT THEY HAD MADE HIM INTO AN UNSTOPPABLE WEAPON, BUT IN TRUTH, HE WAS THAT BEFORE.
THE MONSTERS WHO DID THIS TO HIM LEARN THIS FIRSTHAND.
WHAT CAN ONLY BE CALLED A "BERZERKER RAGE" TAKES HOLD OF HIM.

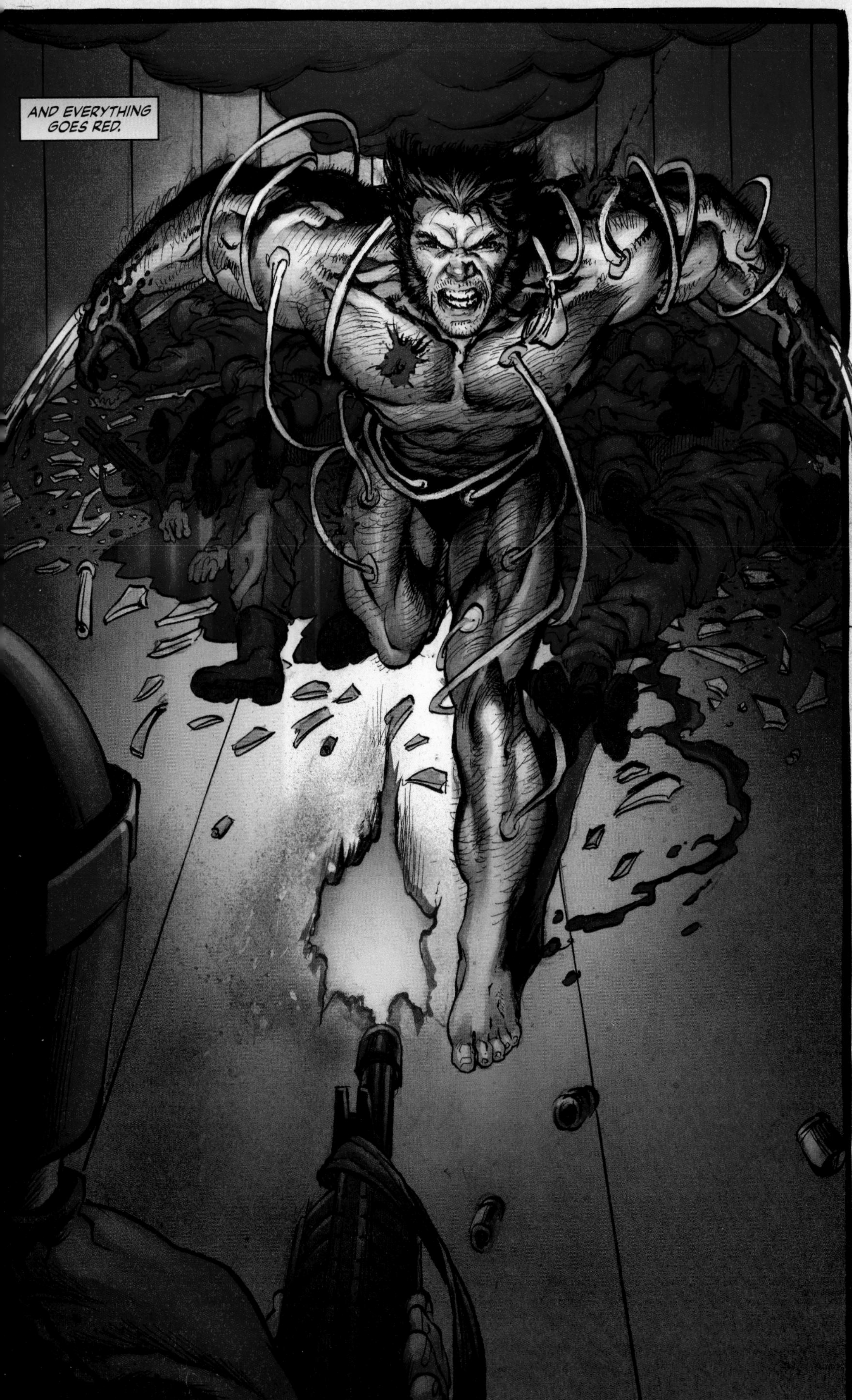
AND EVERYTHING GOES RED.

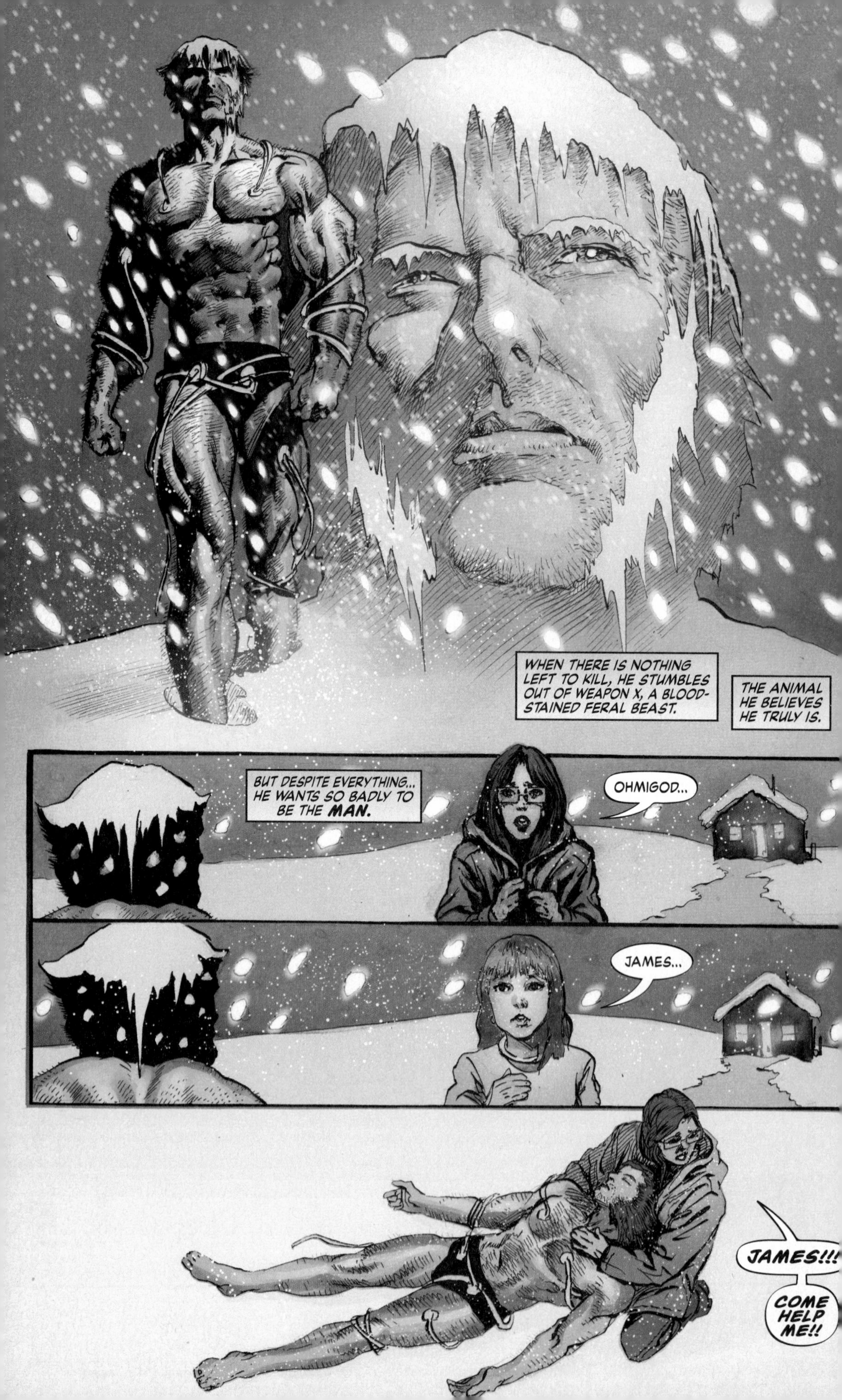

WHEN THERE IS NOTHING LEFT TO KILL, HE STUMBLES OUT OF WEAPON X, A BLOOD-STAINED FERAL BEAST.
THE ANIMAL HE BELIEVES HE TRULY IS.
BUT DESPITE EVERYTHING... HE WANTS SO BADLY TO BE THE MAN.
OHMIGOD...
JAMES...
JAMES!!!
COME HELP ME!!

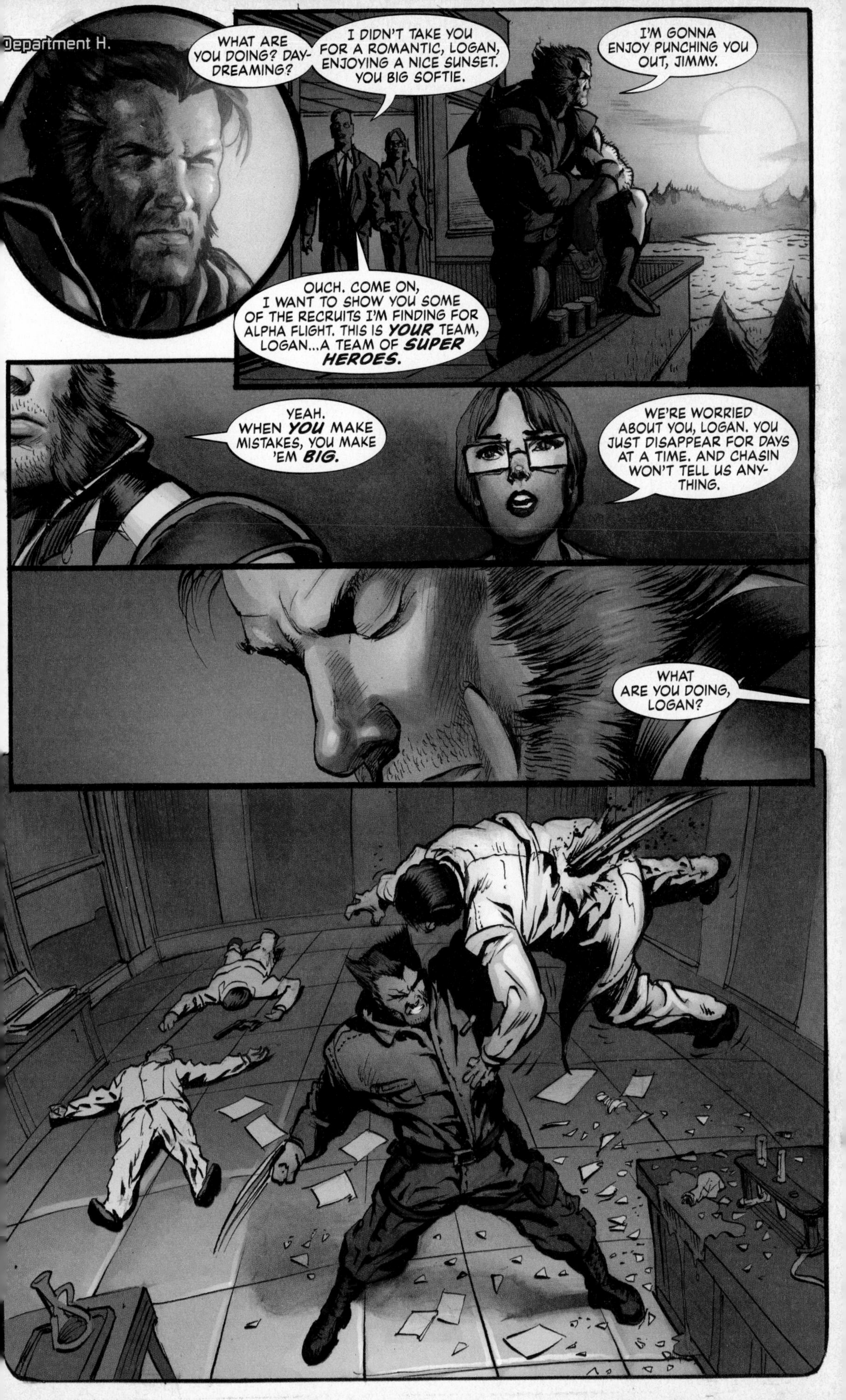
Department H.
WHAT ARE YOU DOING? DAY-DREAMING?
I DIDN'T TAKE YOU FOR A ROMANTIC, LOGAN, ENJOYING A NICE SUNSET. YOU BIG SOFTIE.
I'M GONNA ENJOY PUNCHING YOU OUT, JIMMY.
OUCH. COME ON, I WANT TO SHOW YOU SOME OF THE RECRUITS I'M FINDING FOR ALPHA FLIGHT. THIS IS YOUR TEAM, LOGAN...A TEAM OF SUPER HEROES.
YEAH. WHEN YOU MAKE MISTAKES, YOU MAKE 'EM BIG.
WE'RE WORRIED ABOUT YOU, LOGAN. YOU JUST DISAPPEAR FOR DAYS AT A TIME. AND CHASIN WON'T TELL US ANY-THING.
WHAT ARE YOU DOING, LOGAN?

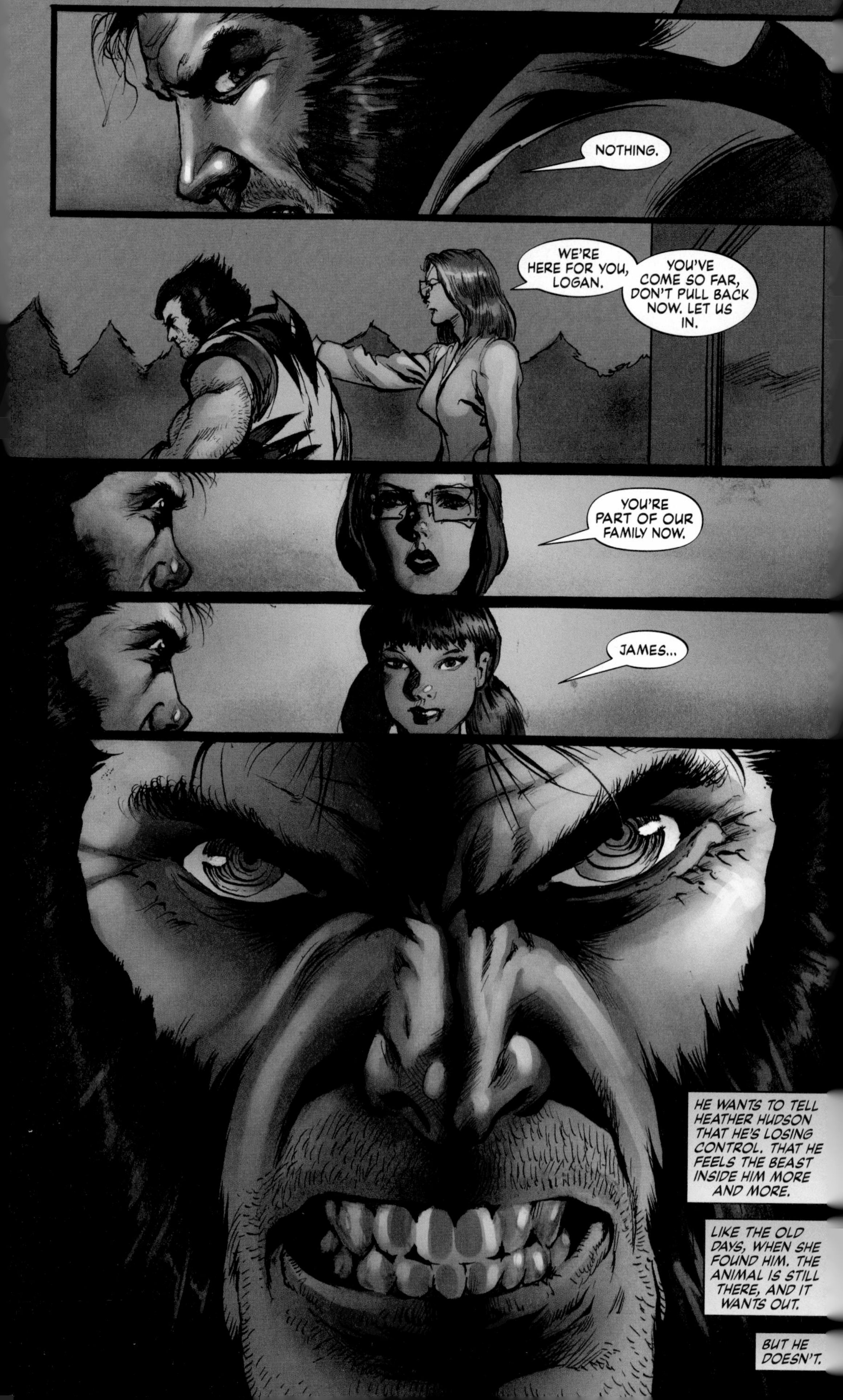
NOTHING.
WE'RE HERE FOR YOU, LOGAN.
YOU'VE COME SO FAR, DON'T PULL BACK NOW. LET US IN.
YOU'RE PART OF OUR FAMILY NOW.
JAMES...
HE WANTS TO TELL HEATHER HUDSON THAT HE'S LOSING CONTROL. THAT HE FEELS THE BEAST INSIDE HIM MORE AND MORE.
LIKE THE OLD DAYS, WHEN SHE FOUND HIM. THE ANIMAL IS STILL THERE, AND IT WANTS OUT.
BUT HE DOESN'T.

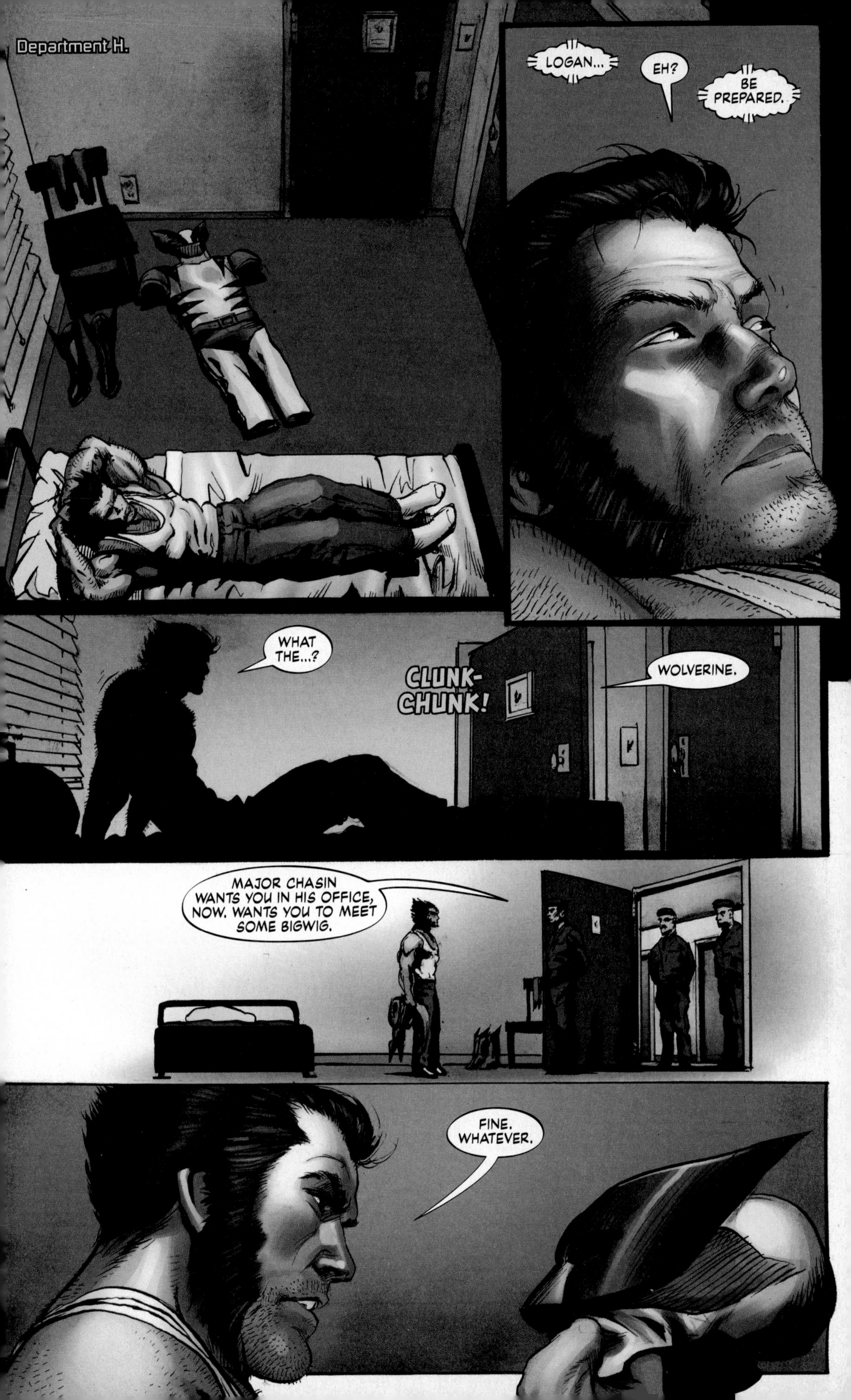
Department H.
LOGAN...
EH?
BE PREPARED.
WHAT THE...?
CLUNK-CHUNK!
WOLVERINE.
MAJOR CHASIN WANTS YOU IN HIS OFFICE, NOW. WANTS YOU TO MEET SOME BIGWIG.
FINE. WHATEVER.

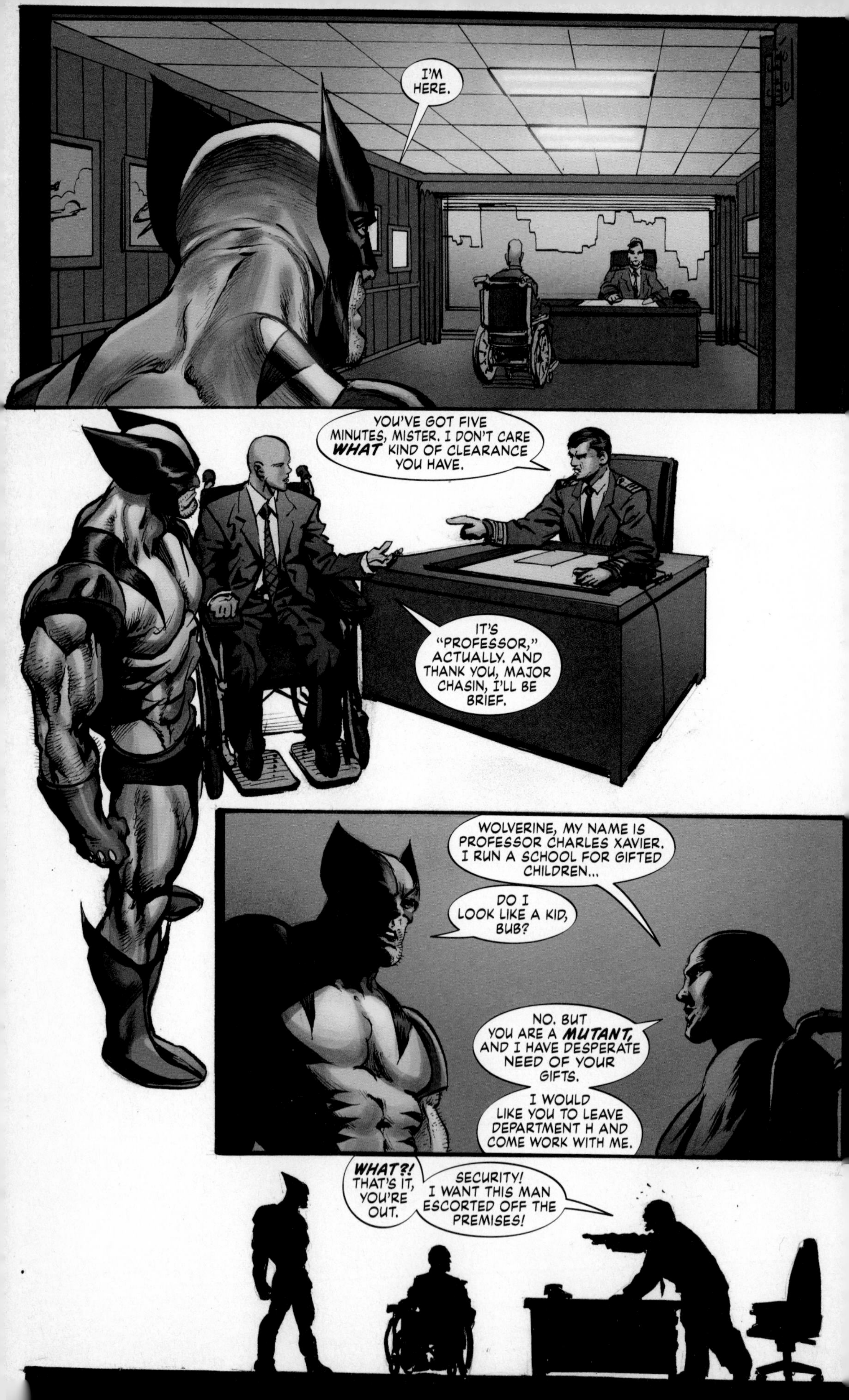
I'M HERE.
YOU'VE GOT FIVE MINUTES, MISTER. I DON'T CARE WHAT KIND OF CLEARANCE YOU HAVE.
IT'S "PROFESSOR," ACTUALLY. AND THANK YOU, MAJOR CHASIN, I'LL BE BRIEF.
WOLVERINE, MY NAME IS PROFESSOR CHARLES XAVIER. I RUN A SCHOOL FOR GIFTED CHILDREN...
DO I LOOK LIKE A KID, BUB?
NO. BUT YOU ARE A MUTANT, AND I HAVE DESPERATE NEED OF YOUR GIFTS.
I WOULD LIKE YOU TO LEAVE DEPARTMENT H AND COME WORK WITH ME.
WHAT?! THAT'S IT, YOU'RE OUT.
SECURITY! I WANT THIS MAN ESCORTED OFF THE PREMISES!

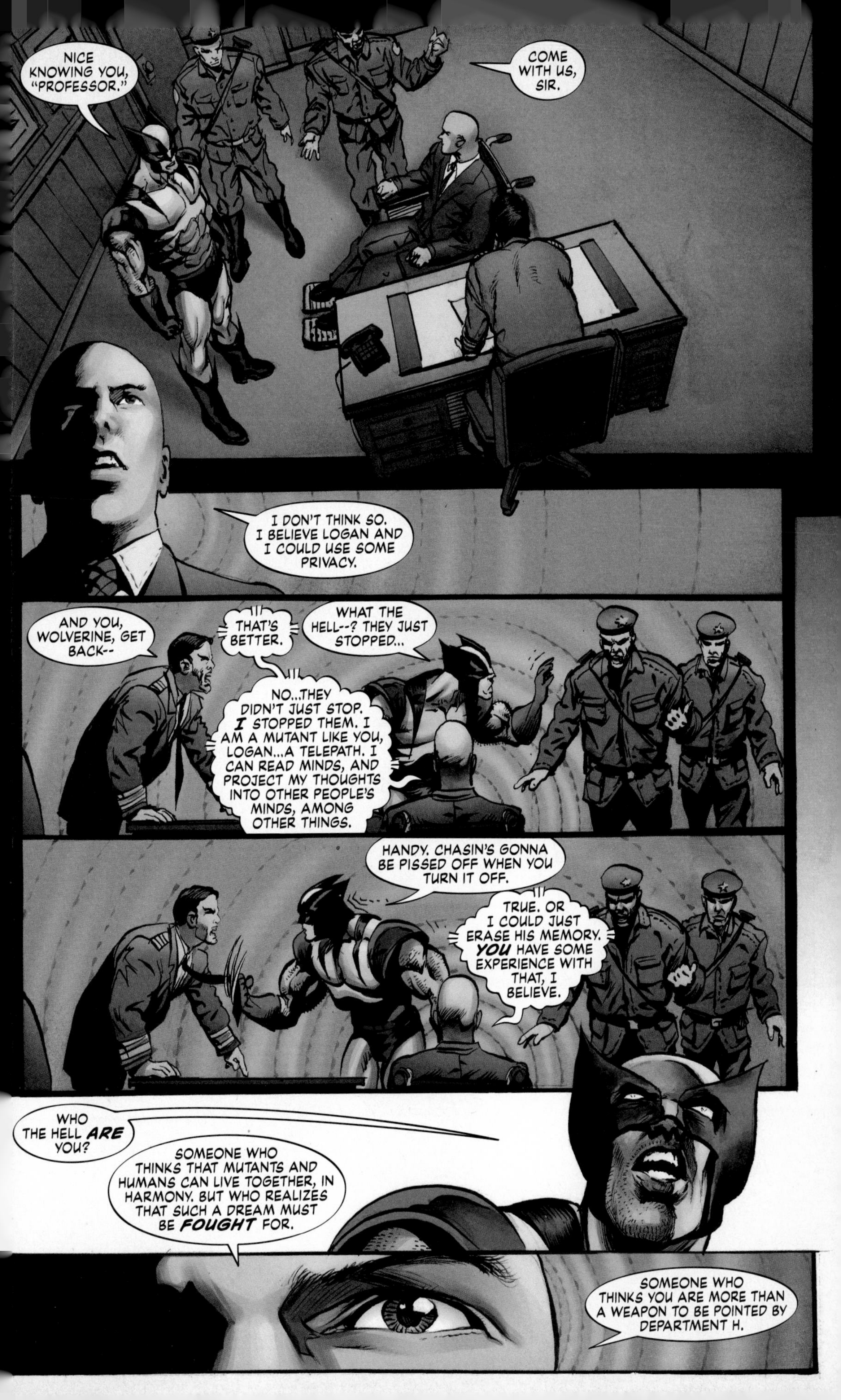
NICE KNOWING YOU, "PROFESSOR."
COME WITH US, SIR.
I DON'T THINK SO. I BELIEVE LOGAN AND I COULD USE SOME PRIVACY.
AND YOU, WOLVERINE, GET BACK--
THAT'S BETTER.
WHAT THE HELL--? THEY JUST STOPPED...
NO...THEY DIDN'T JUST STOP. *I* STOPPED THEM. I AM A MUTANT LIKE YOU, LOGAN...A TELEPATH. I CAN READ MINDS, AND PROJECT MY THOUGHTS INTO OTHER PEOPLE'S MINDS, AMONG OTHER THINGS.
HANDY. CHASIN'S GONNA BE PISSED OFF WHEN YOU TURN IT OFF.
TRUE. OR I COULD JUST ERASE HIS MEMORY. *YOU* HAVE SOME EXPERIENCE WITH THAT, I BELIEVE.
WHO THE HELL *ARE* YOU?
SOMEONE WHO THINKS THAT MUTANTS AND HUMANS CAN LIVE TOGETHER, IN HARMONY. BUT WHO REALIZES THAT SUCH A DREAM MUST BE *FOUGHT* FOR.
SOMEONE WHO THINKS YOU ARE MORE THAN A WEAPON TO BE POINTED BY DEPARTMENT H.

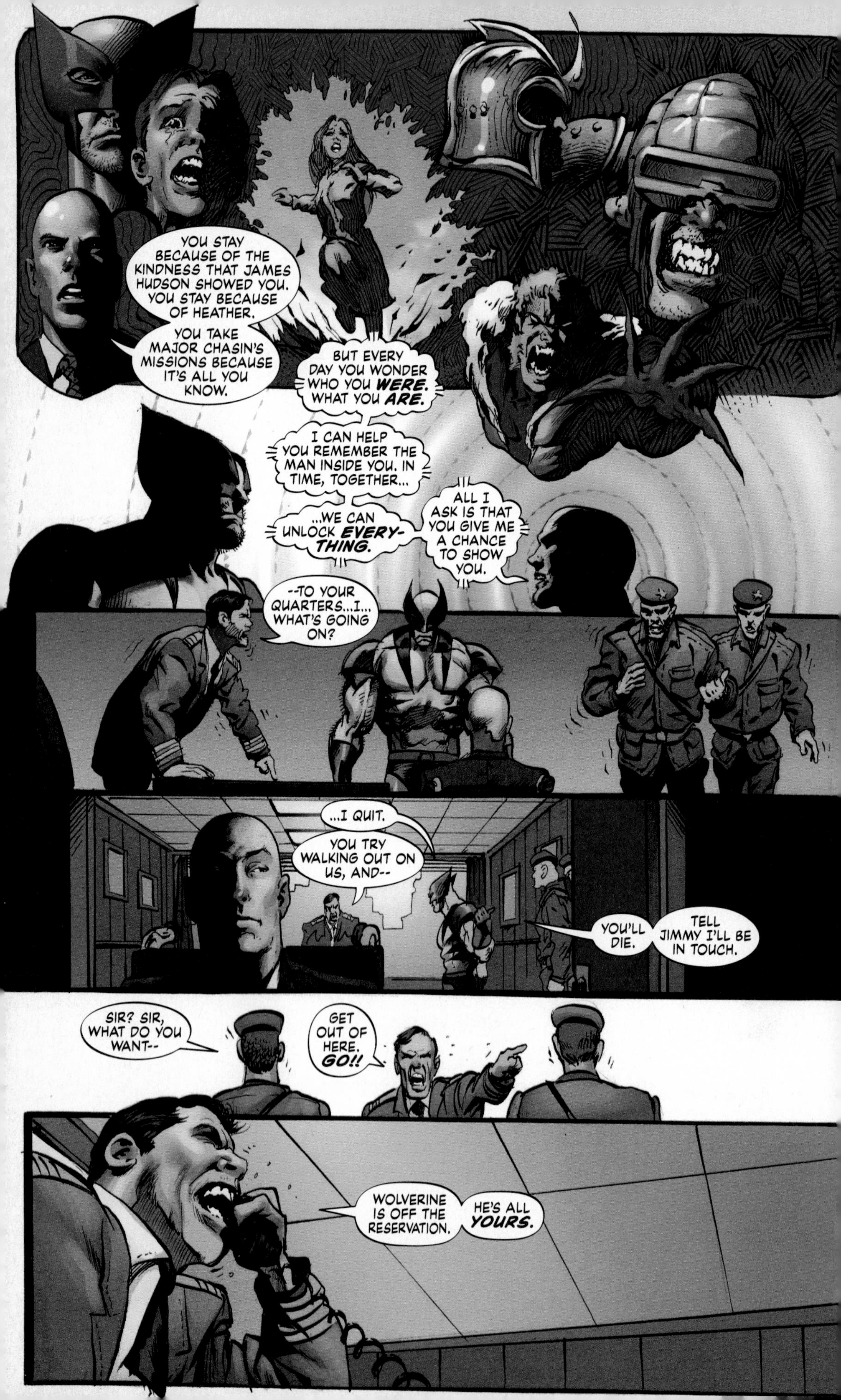
YOU STAY BECAUSE OF THE KINDNESS THAT JAMES HUDSON SHOWED YOU. YOU STAY BECAUSE OF HEATHER.
YOU TAKE MAJOR CHASIN'S MISSIONS BECAUSE IT'S ALL YOU KNOW.
BUT EVERY DAY YOU WONDER WHO YOU WERE. WHAT YOU ARE.
I CAN HELP YOU REMEMBER THE MAN INSIDE YOU. IN TIME, TOGETHER...
...WE CAN UNLOCK EVERYTHING.
ALL I ASK IS THAT YOU GIVE ME A CHANCE TO SHOW YOU.
--TO YOUR QUARTERS...I... WHAT'S GOING ON?
...I QUIT.
YOU TRY WALKING OUT ON US, AND--
YOU'LL DIE.
TELL JIMMY I'LL BE IN TOUCH.
SIR? SIR, WHAT DO YOU WANT--
GET OUT OF HERE. GO!!
WOLVERINE IS OFF THE RESERVATION.
HE'S ALL YOURS.

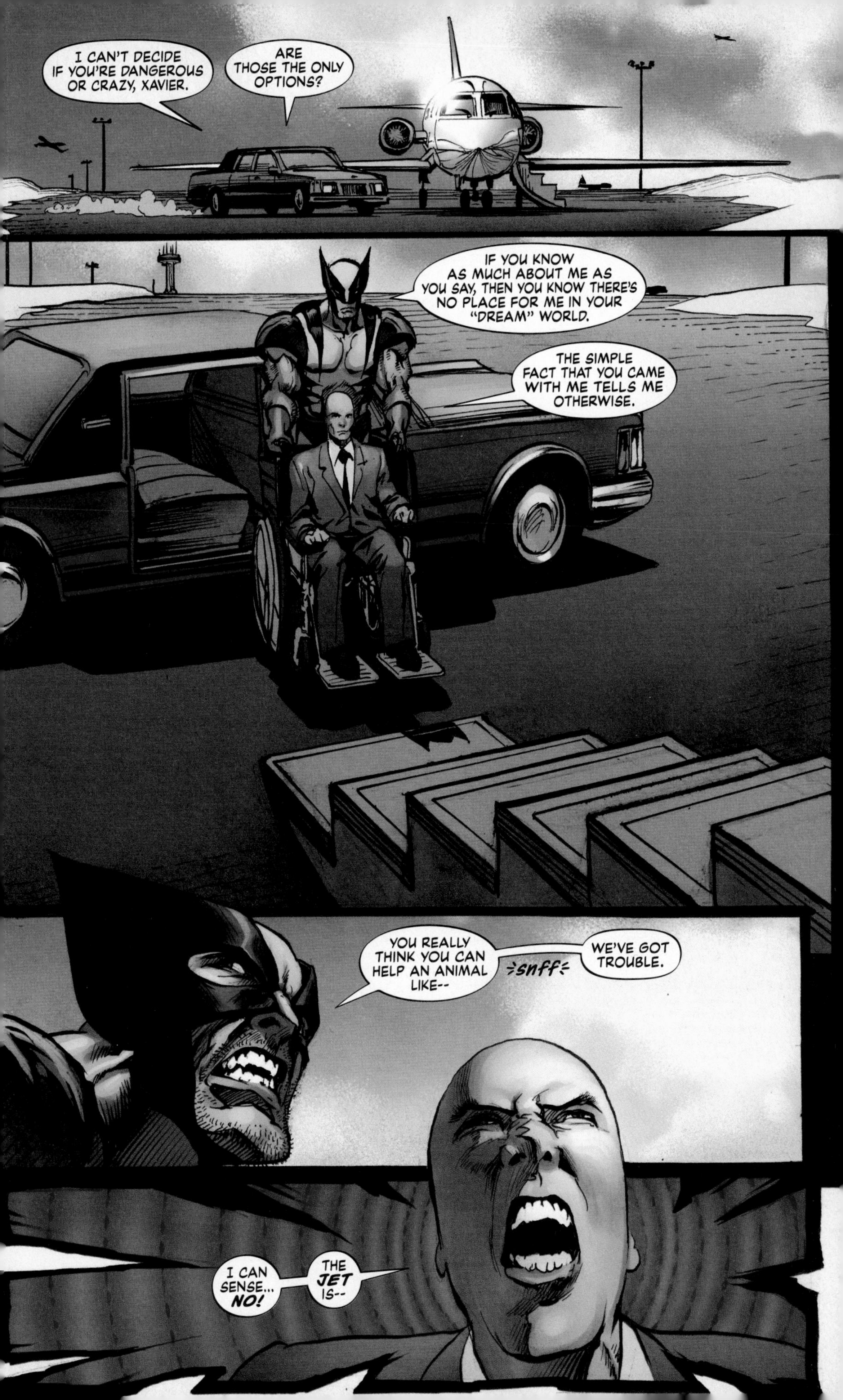
I CAN'T DECIDE IF YOU'RE DANGEROUS OR CRAZY, XAVIER.
ARE THOSE THE ONLY OPTIONS?
IF YOU KNOW AS MUCH ABOUT ME AS YOU SAY, THEN YOU KNOW THERE'S NO PLACE FOR ME IN YOUR "DREAM" WORLD.
THE SIMPLE FACT THAT YOU CAME WITH ME TELLS ME OTHERWISE.
YOU REALLY THINK YOU CAN HELP AN ANIMAL LIKE--
snff
WE'VE GOT TROUBLE.
I CAN SENSE... NO!
THE JET IS--

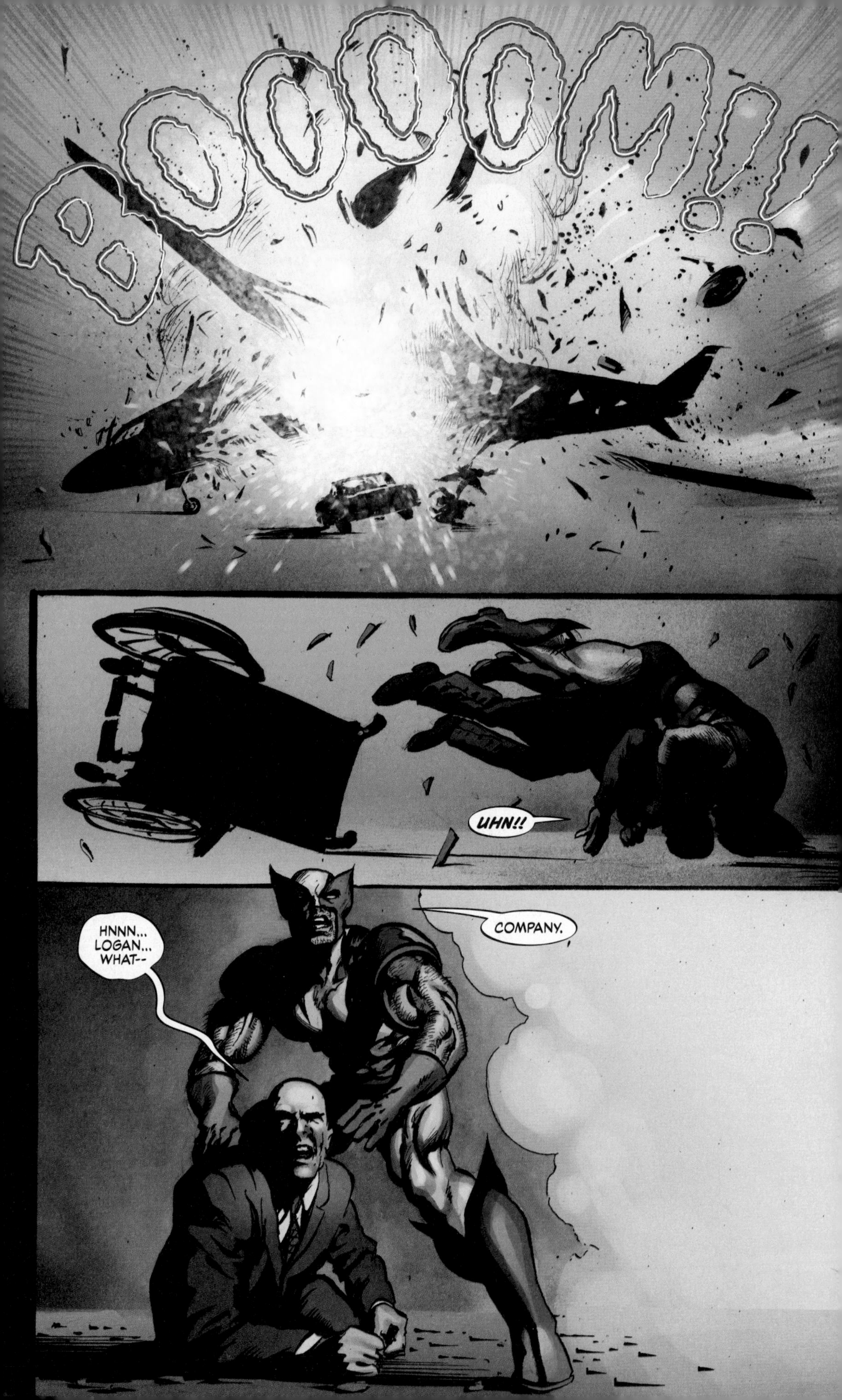
BOOOOOM!!
UHN!!
HNNN... LOGAN... WHAT--
COMPANY.

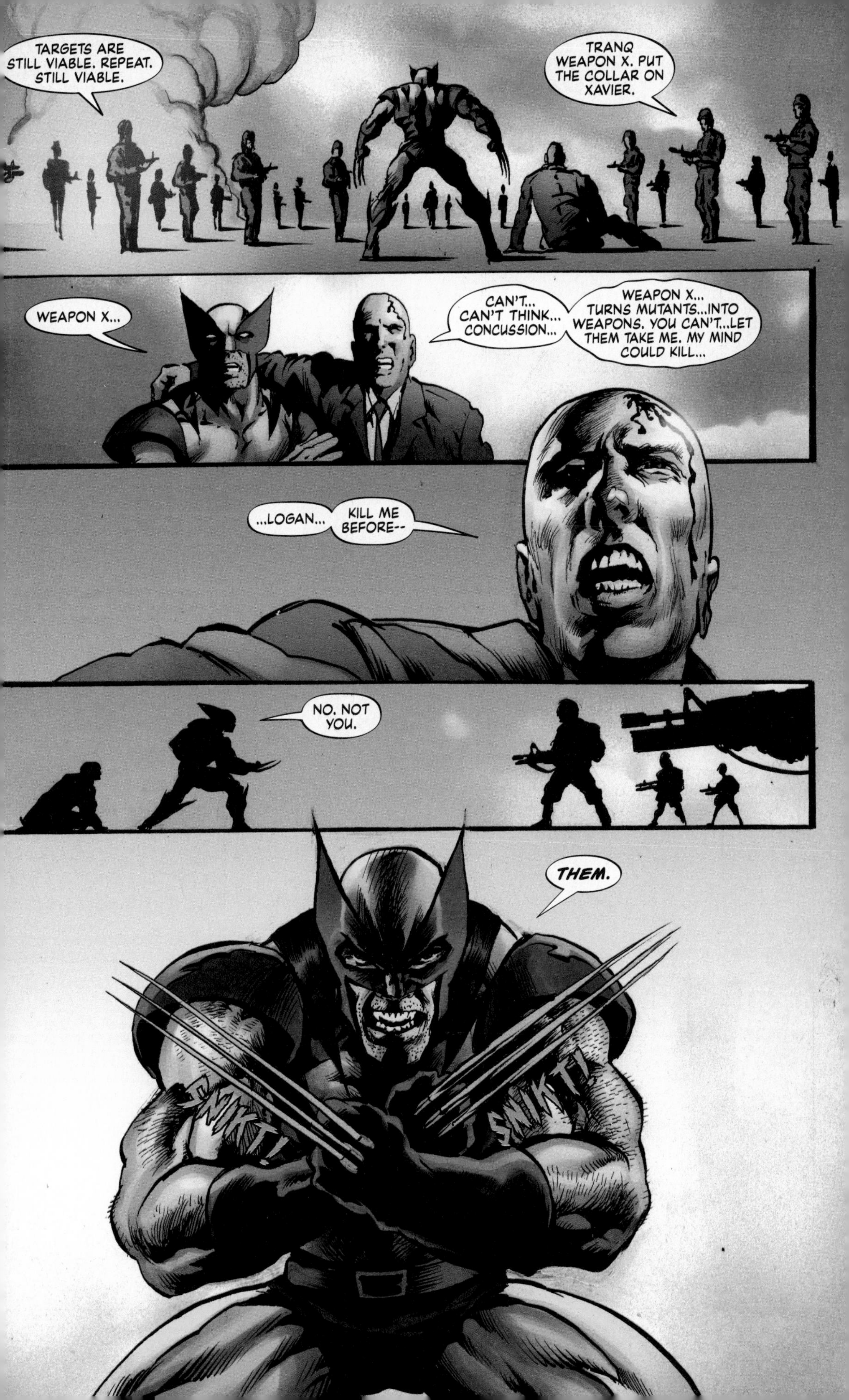
TARGETS ARE STILL VIABLE. REPEAT. STILL VIABLE.
TRANQ WEAPON X. PUT THE COLLAR ON XAVIER.
WEAPON X...
CAN'T... CAN'T THINK... CONCUSSION...
WEAPON X... TURNS MUTANTS...INTO WEAPONS. YOU CAN'T...LET THEM TAKE ME. MY MIND COULD KILL...
...LOGAN...
KILL ME BEFORE--
NO. NOT YOU.
THEM.
SNIKT!
SNIKT!

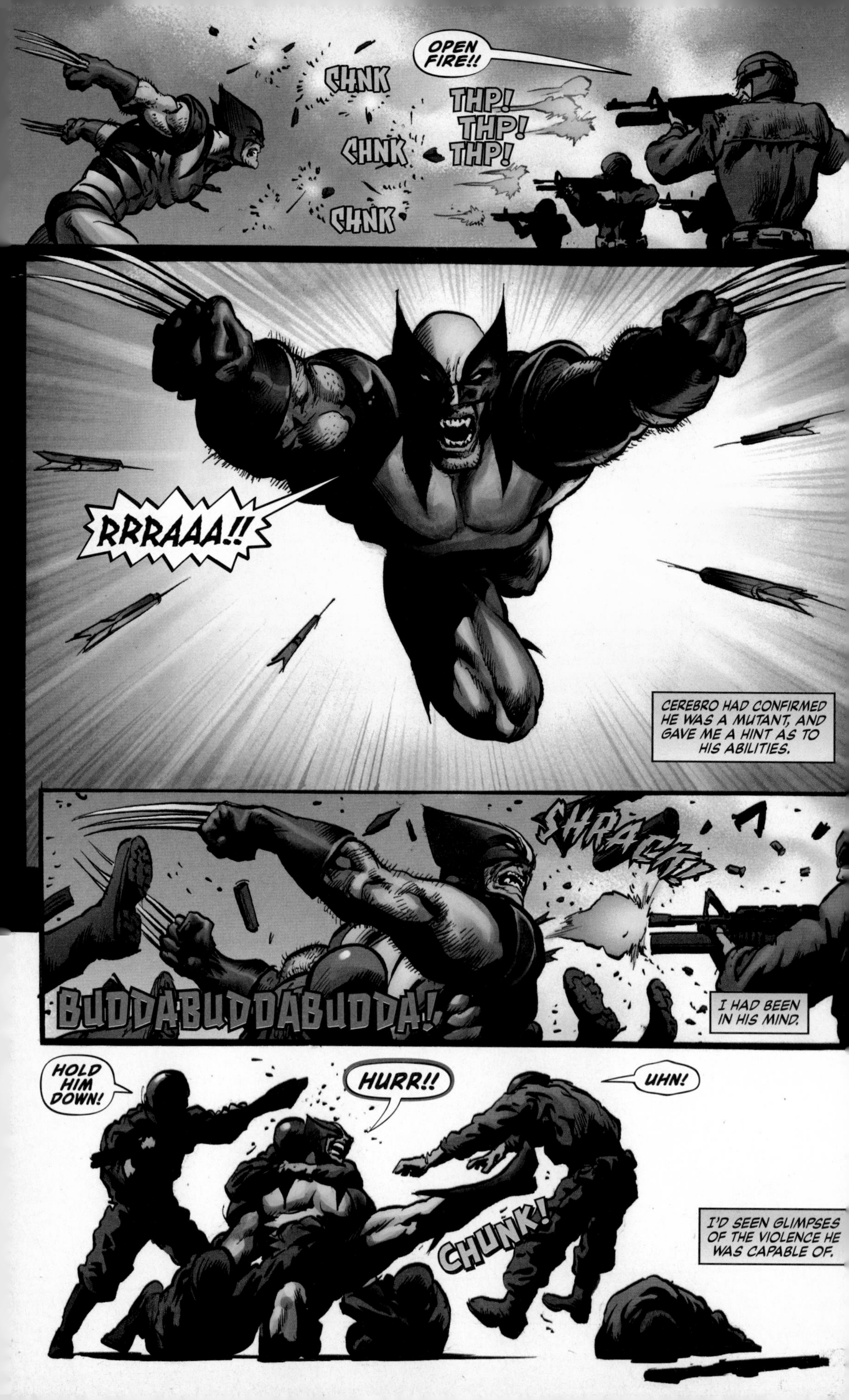
OPEN FIRE!!
CHNK
THP! THP! THP!
CHNK
CHNK
RRRAAA!!
CEREBRO HAD CONFIRMED HE WAS A MUTANT, AND GAVE ME A HINT AS TO HIS ABILITIES.
SHRACK!!
BUDDABUDDABUDDA!!
I HAD BEEN IN HIS MIND.
HOLD HIM DOWN!
HURR!!
UHN!
CHUNK!
I'D SEEN GLIMPSES OF THE VIOLENCE HE WAS CAPABLE OF.

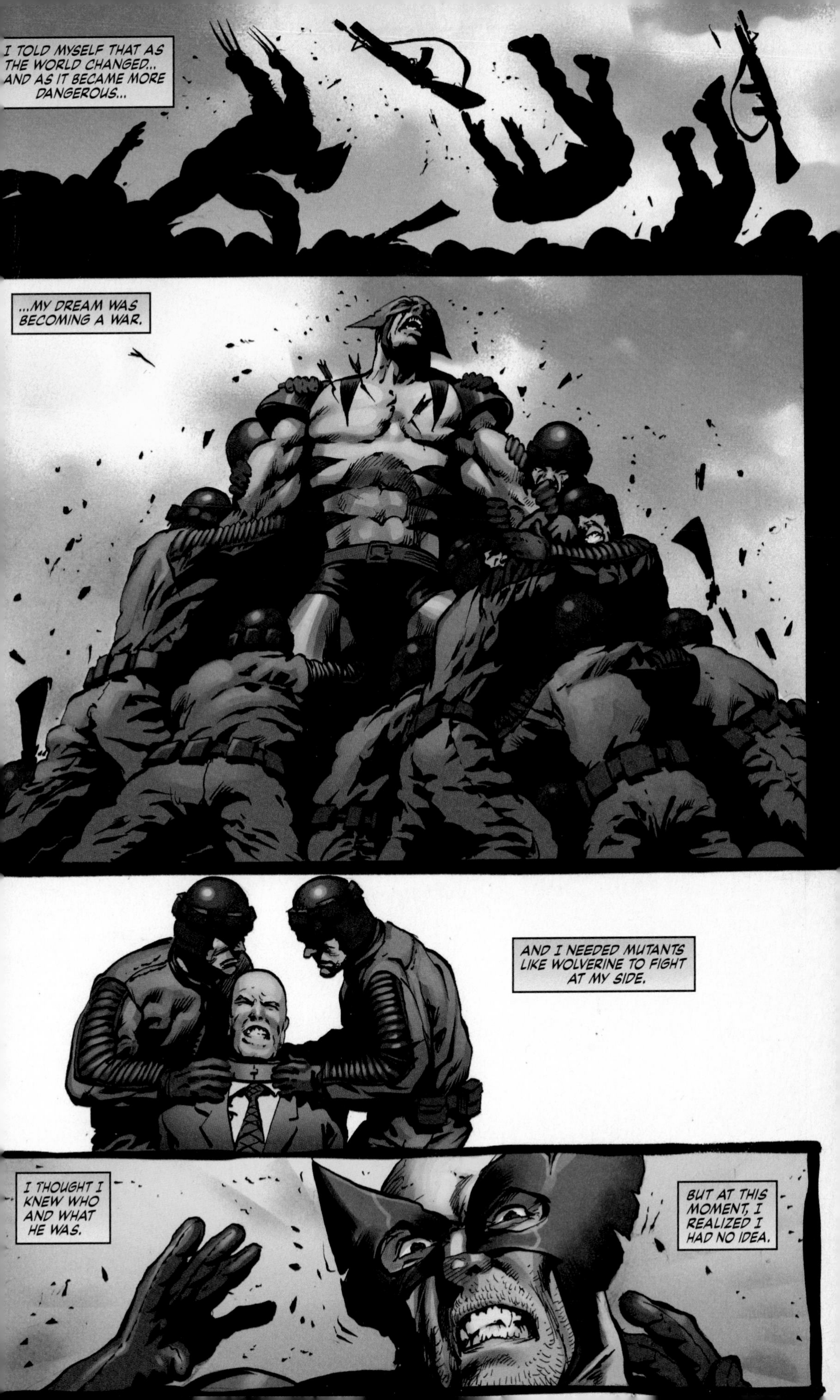

I TOLD MYSELF THAT AS THE WORLD CHANGED... AND AS IT BECAME MORE DANGEROUS...
...MY DREAM WAS BECOMING A WAR.
AND I NEEDED MUTANTS LIKE WOLVERINE TO FIGHT AT MY SIDE.
I THOUGHT I KNEW WHO AND WHAT HE WAS.
BUT AT THIS MOMENT, I REALIZED I HAD NO IDEA.

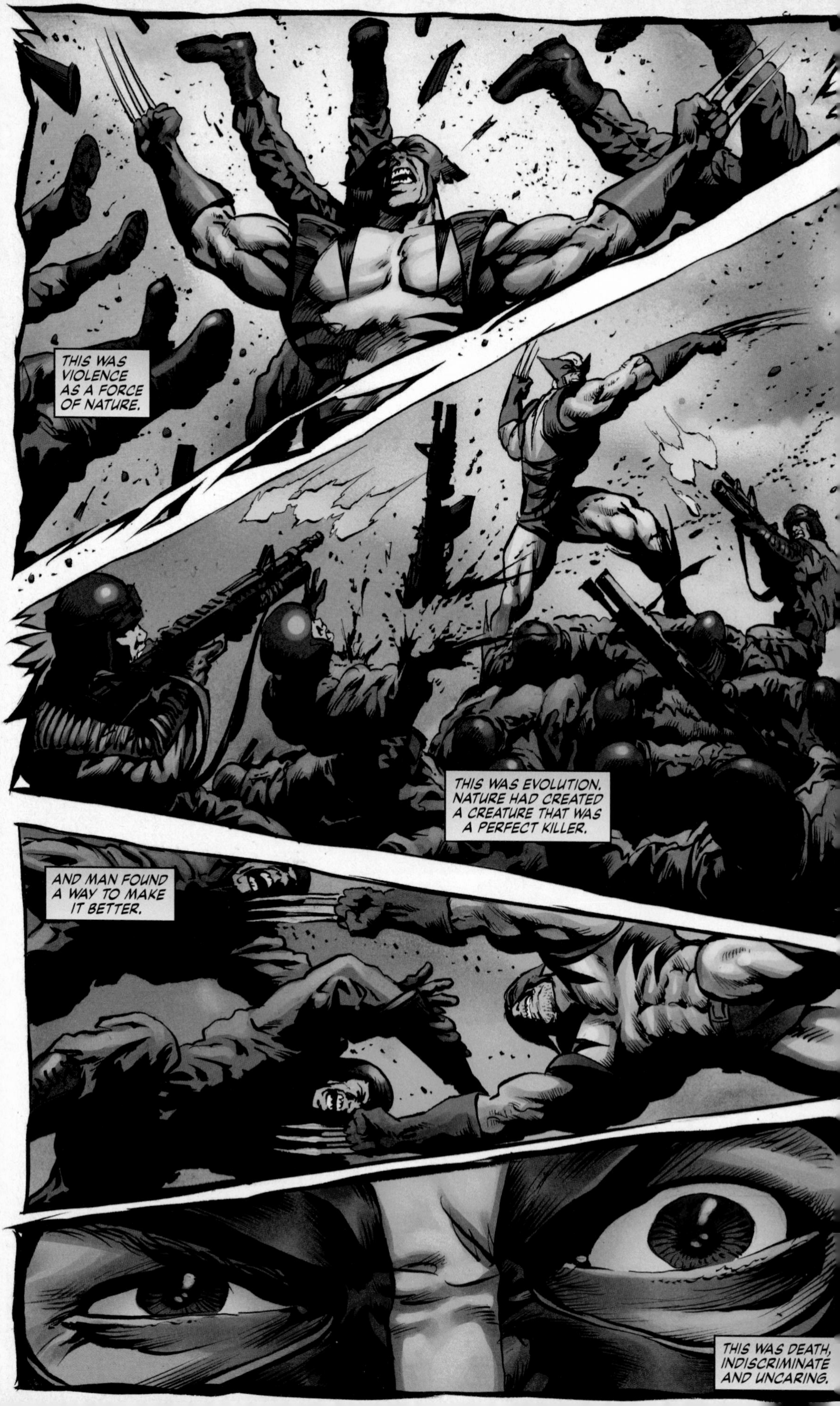
THIS WAS VIOLENCE AS A FORCE OF NATURE.
THIS WAS EVOLUTION. NATURE HAD CREATED A CREATURE THAT WAS A PERFECT KILLER.
AND MAN FOUND A WAY TO MAKE IT BETTER.
THIS WAS DEATH, INDISCRIMINATE AND UNCARING.

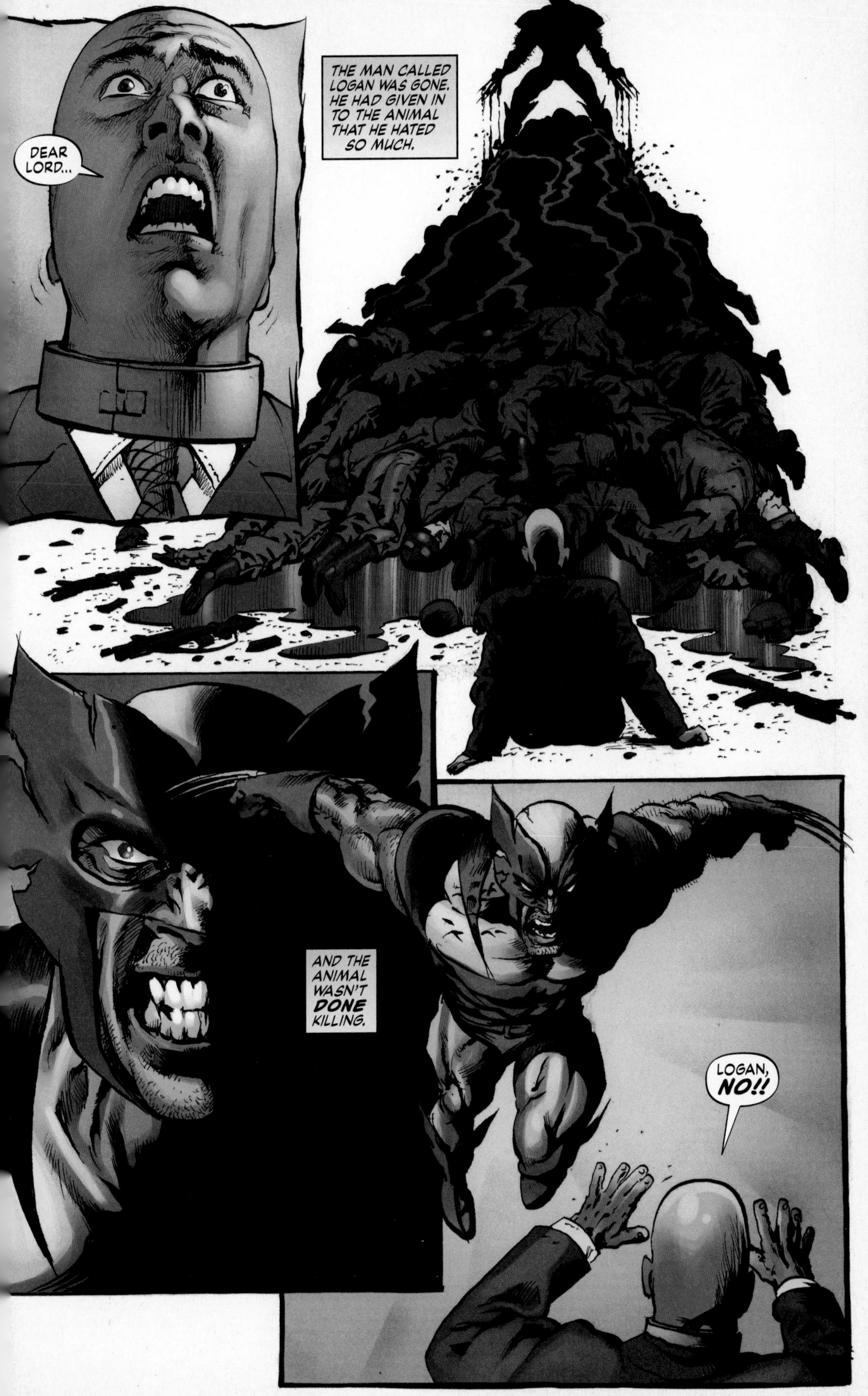
DEAR LORD...
THE MAN CALLED LOGAN WAS GONE. HE HAD GIVEN IN TO THE ANIMAL THAT HE HATED SO MUCH.
AND THE ANIMAL WASN'T **DONE** KILLING.
LOGAN, **NO!!**

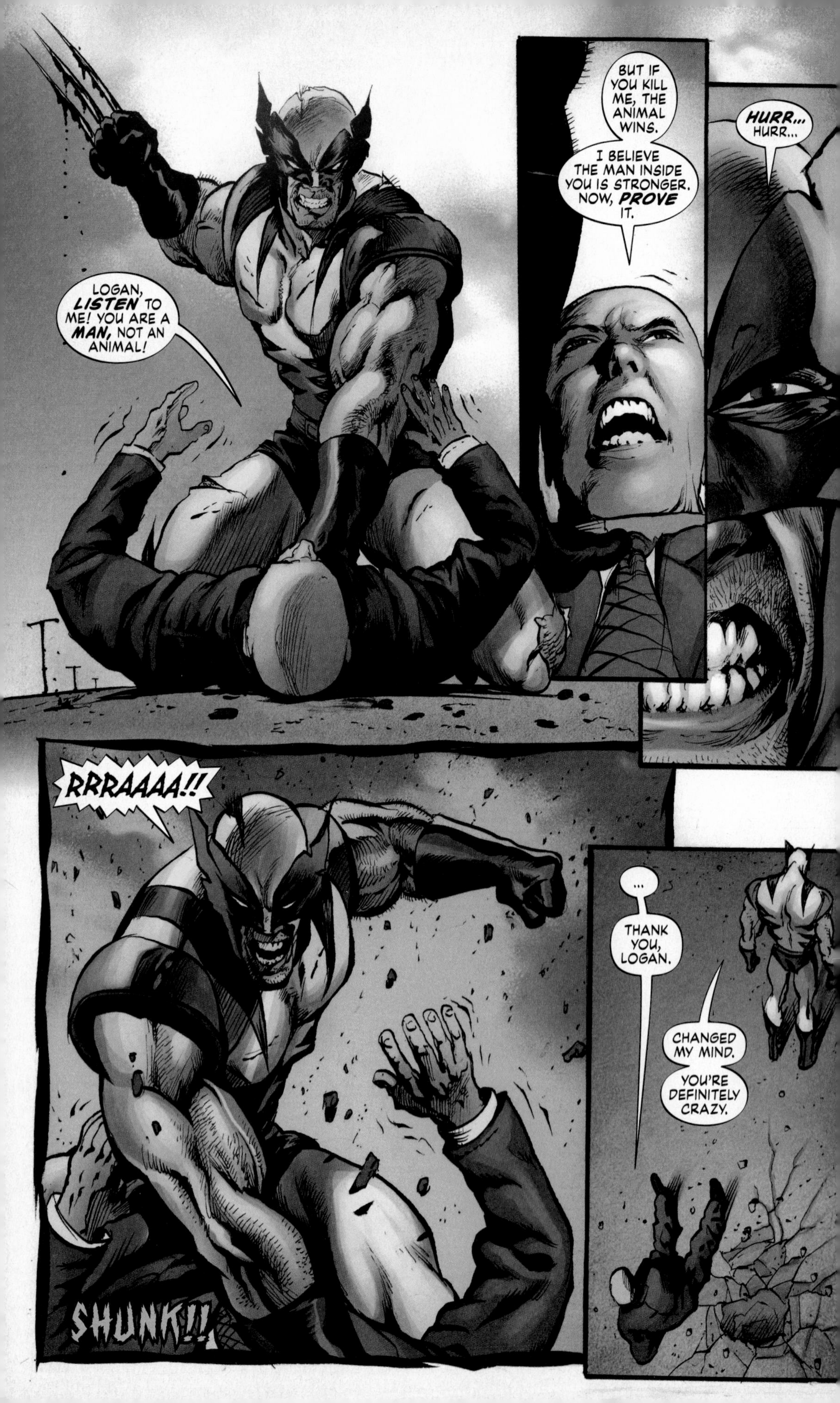
LOGAN, LISTEN TO ME! YOU ARE A MAN, NOT AN ANIMAL!
BUT IF YOU KILL ME, THE ANIMAL WINS.
I BELIEVE THE MAN INSIDE YOU IS STRONGER. NOW, PROVE IT.
HURR... HURR...
RRRAAAA!!
SHUNK!!
...
THANK YOU, LOGAN.
CHANGED MY MIND.
YOU'RE DEFINITELY CRAZY.

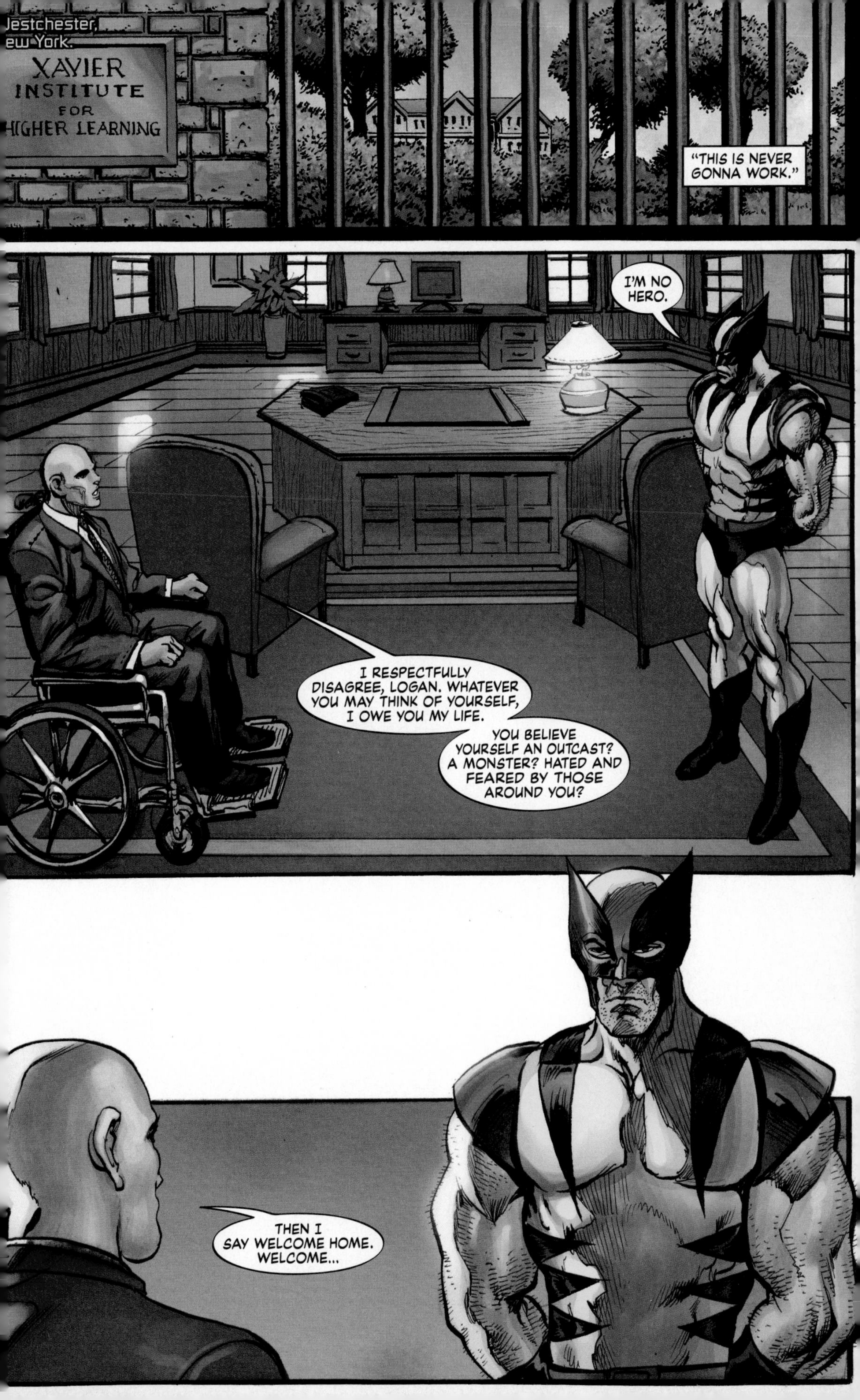

Jestchester,
ew York.
XAVIER INSTITUTE FOR HIGHER LEARNING
"THIS IS NEVER GONNA WORK."
I'M NO HERO.
I RESPECTFULLY DISAGREE, LOGAN. WHATEVER YOU MAY THINK OF YOURSELF, I OWE YOU MY LIFE.
YOU BELIEVE YOURSELF AN OUTCAST? A MONSTER? HATED AND FEARED BY THOSE AROUND YOU?
THEN I SAY WELCOME HOME. WELCOME...

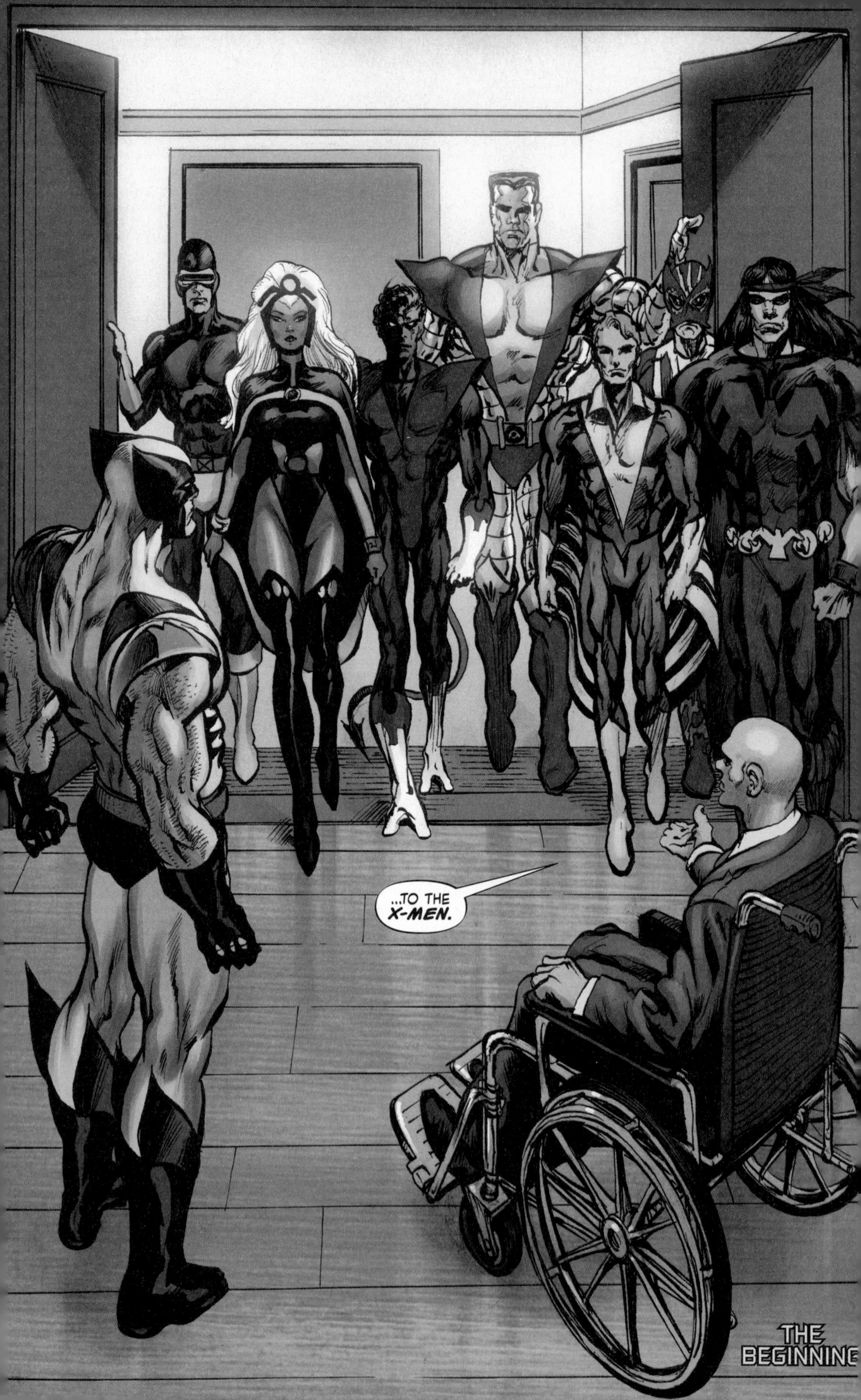
...TO THE X-MEN.
THE BEGINNING

X-MEN ORIGINS WOLVERINE

"BIRTH OF A WEAPON"

WRITTEN BY CHRIS YOST
DRAWN BY MARK TEXEIRA
COLORED BY JOHN RAUCH
LETTERED BY TODD KLEIN
COVER BY MARK TEXEIRA AND MORRY HOLLOWELL

PRODUCTION: JOE SABINO
ASSISTANT EDITOR: DANIEL KETCHUM
EDITOR: NICK LOWE
EDITOR IN CHIEF: JOE QUESADA
PUBLISHER: DAN BUCKLEY
EXECUTIVE PRODUCER: ALAN FINE

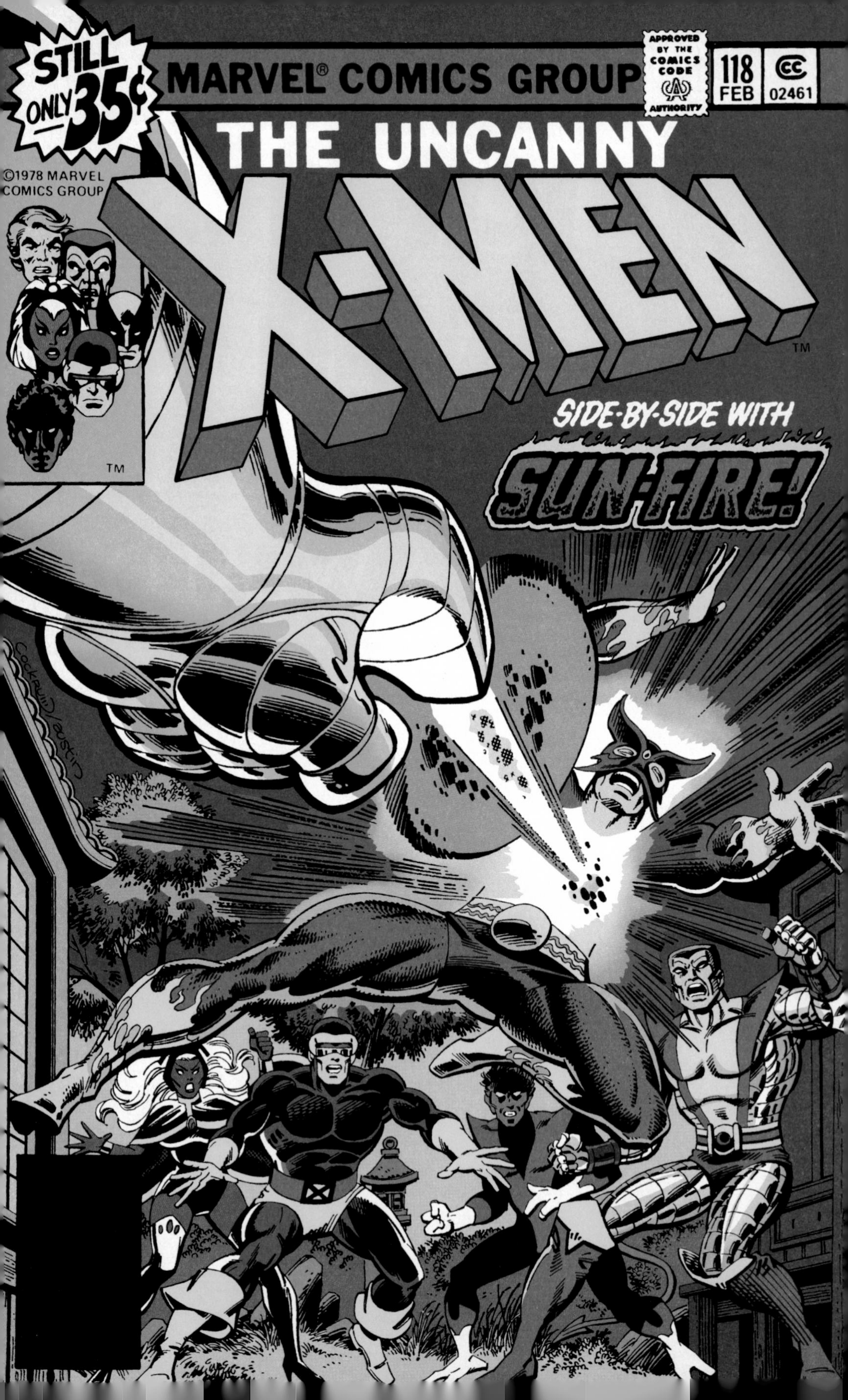
STILL ONLY 35¢
MARVEL® COMICS GROUP
APPROVED BY THE COMICS CODE AUTHORITY
118 FEB
CC 02461
THE UNCANNY
X-MEN
TM
©1978 MARVEL COMICS GROUP
TM
SIDE-BY-SIDE WITH
SUN-FIRE!

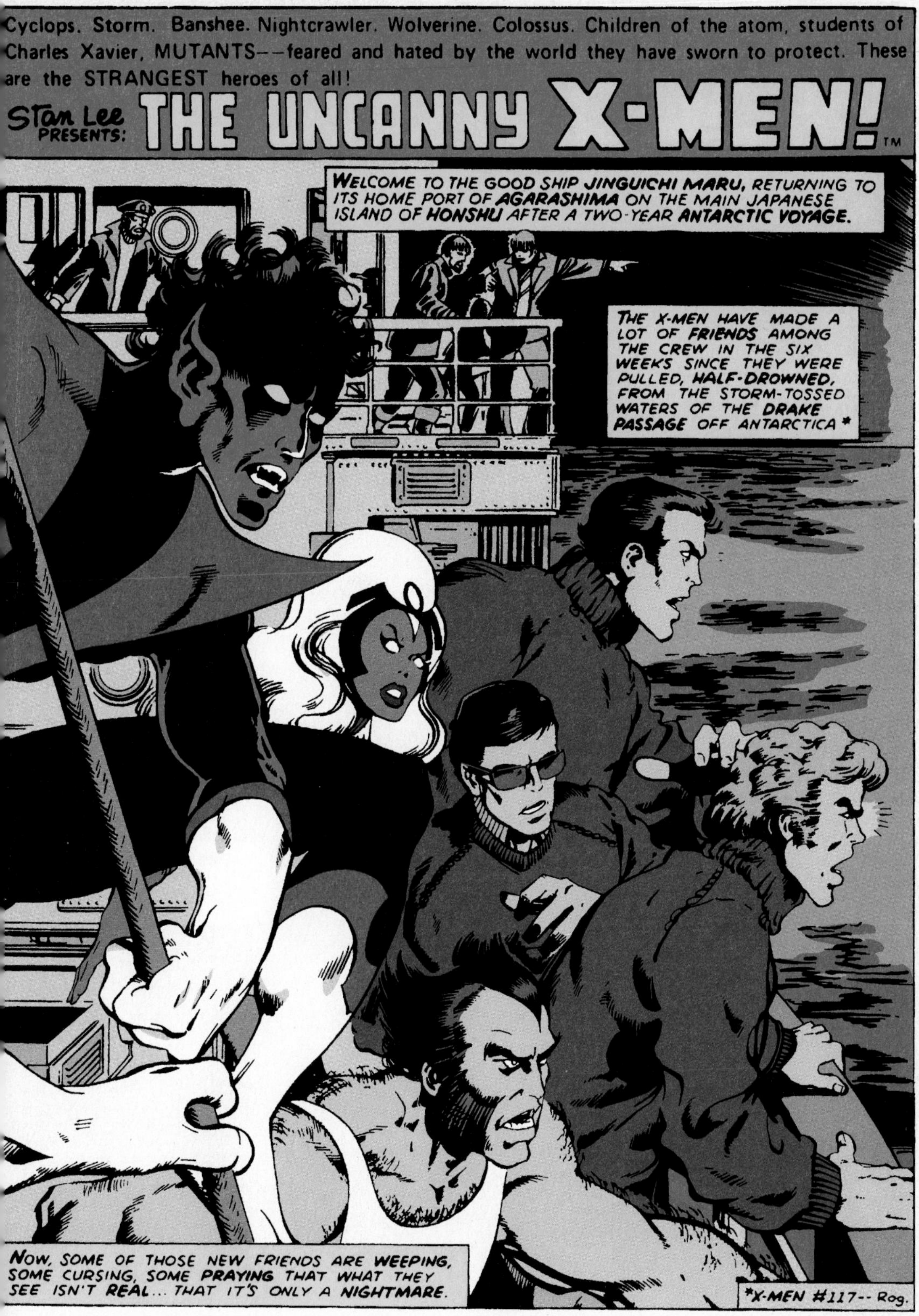
Cyclops. Storm. Banshee. Nightcrawler. Wolverine. Colossus. Children of the atom, students of Charles Xavier, MUTANTS--feared and hated by the world they have sworn to protect. These are the STRANGEST heroes of all!
Stan Lee PRESENTS: THE UNCANNY X-MEN! TM
WELCOME TO THE GOOD SHIP JINGUICHI MARU, RETURNING TO ITS HOME PORT OF AGARASHIMA ON THE MAIN JAPANESE ISLAND OF HONSHU AFTER A TWO-YEAR ANTARCTIC VOYAGE.
THE X-MEN HAVE MADE A LOT OF FRIENDS AMONG THE CREW IN THE SIX WEEKS SINCE THEY WERE PULLED, HALF-DROWNED, FROM THE STORM-TOSSED WATERS OF THE DRAKE PASSAGE OFF ANTARCTICA *
NOW, SOME OF THOSE NEW FRIENDS ARE WEEPING, SOME CURSING, SOME PRAYING THAT WHAT THEY SEE ISN'T REAL... THAT IT'S ONLY A NIGHTMARE.
*X-MEN #117-- Rog.

THE SUBMERGENCE
COMRADES... WE ARE TEN KILOMETERS FROM SHORE-- YET THAT FIRE IS AS HOT AS AN OPEN BLAST FURNACE.
ORORO-- IS THERE NOTHING WE CAN DO?!
I... NO, MY FRIEND. I DARE NOT EVEN TRY.
WHAT D'YE THINK CAUSED THIS?

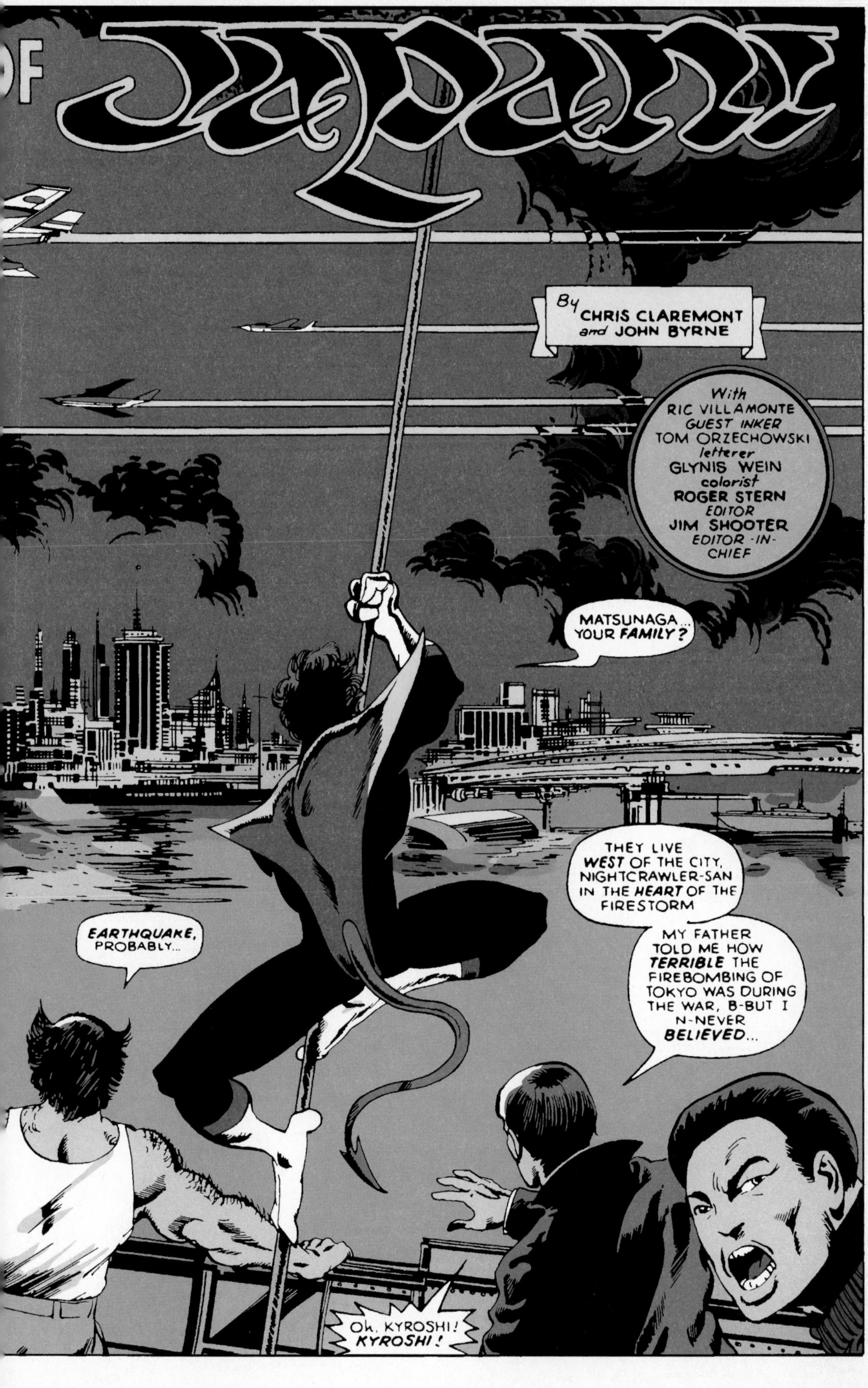

OF JAPAN
By CHRIS CLAREMONT and JOHN BYRNE
With RIC VILLAMONTE GUEST INKER TOM ORZECHOWSKI letterer GLYNIS WEIN colorist ROGER STERN EDITOR JIM SHOOTER EDITOR-IN-CHIEF
MATSUNAGA... YOUR FAMILY?
THEY LIVE WEST OF THE CITY, NIGHTCRAWLER-SAN IN THE HEART OF THE FIRESTORM
MY FATHER TOLD ME HOW TERRIBLE THE FIREBOMBING OF TOKYO WAS DURING THE WAR, B-BUT I N-NEVER BELIEVED...
EARTHQUAKE, PROBABLY...
Oh, KYROSHI! KYROSHI!

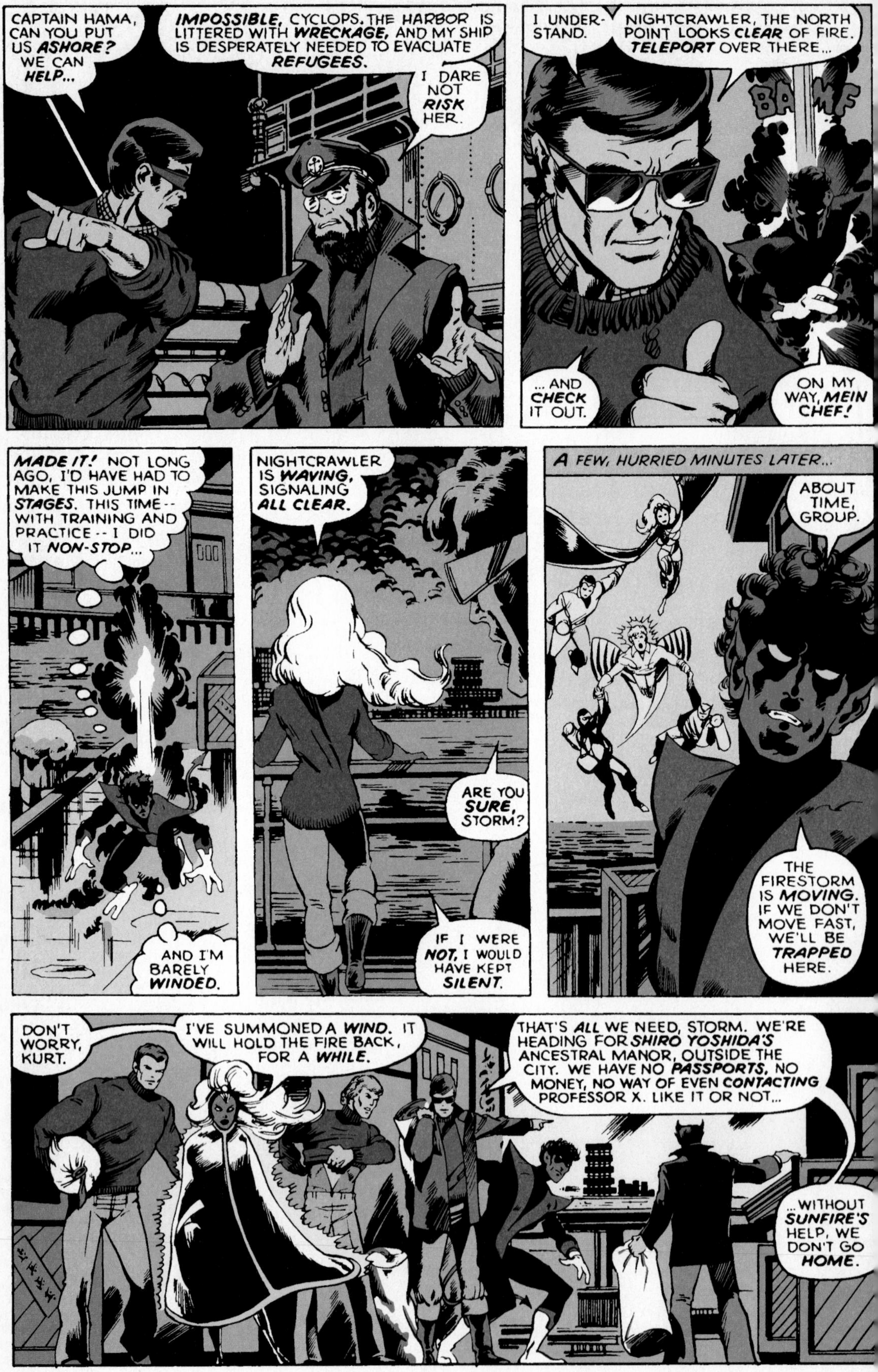

CAPTAIN HAMA, CAN YOU PUT US ASHORE? WE CAN HELP...
IMPOSSIBLE, CYCLOPS. THE HARBOR IS LITTERED WITH WRECKAGE, AND MY SHIP IS DESPERATELY NEEDED TO EVACUATE REFUGEES.
I DARE NOT RISK HER.
I UNDERSTAND.
NIGHTCRAWLER, THE NORTH POINT LOOKS CLEAR OF FIRE. TELEPORT OVER THERE...
BAMF
...AND CHECK IT OUT.
ON MY WAY, MEIN CHEF!
MADE IT! NOT LONG AGO, I'D HAVE HAD TO MAKE THIS JUMP IN STAGES. THIS TIME--WITH TRAINING AND PRACTICE--I DID IT NON-STOP...
AND I'M BARELY WINDED.
NIGHTCRAWLER IS WAVING, SIGNALING ALL CLEAR.
ARE YOU SURE, STORM?
IF I WERE NOT, I WOULD HAVE KEPT SILENT.
A FEW, HURRIED MINUTES LATER...
ABOUT TIME, GROUP.
THE FIRESTORM IS MOVING. IF WE DON'T MOVE FAST, WE'LL BE TRAPPED HERE.
DON'T WORRY, KURT.
I'VE SUMMONED A WIND. IT WILL HOLD THE FIRE BACK, FOR A WHILE.
THAT'S ALL WE NEED, STORM. WE'RE HEADING FOR SHIRO YOSHIDA'S ANCESTRAL MANOR, OUTSIDE THE CITY. WE HAVE NO PASSPORTS, NO MONEY, NO WAY OF EVEN CONTACTING PROFESSOR X. LIKE IT OR NOT...
...WITHOUT SUNFIRE'S HELP, WE DON'T GO HOME.

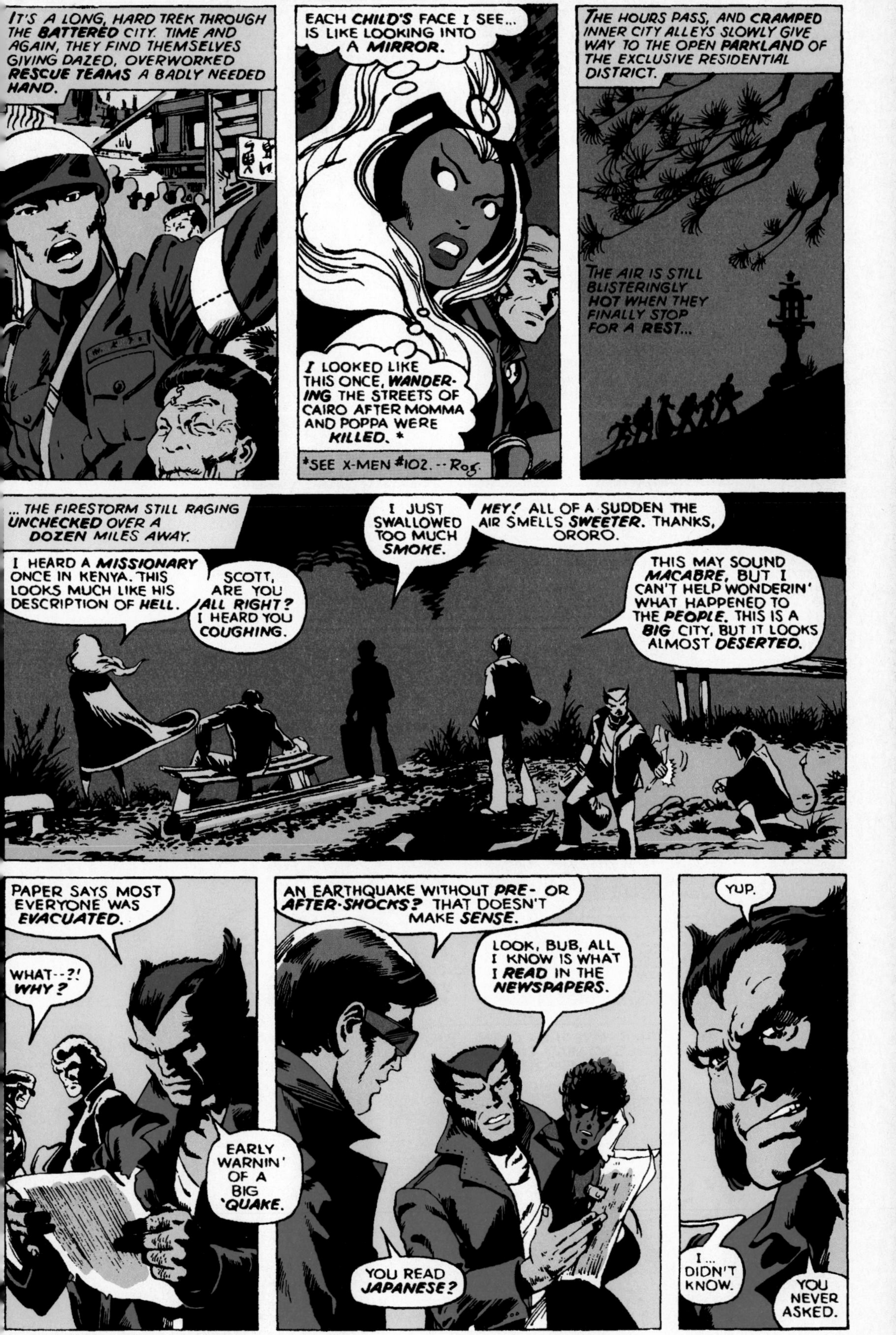
IT'S A LONG, HARD TREK THROUGH THE BATTERED CITY. TIME AND AGAIN, THEY FIND THEMSELVES GIVING DAZED, OVERWORKED RESCUE TEAMS A BADLY NEEDED HAND.
EACH CHILD'S FACE I SEE... IS LIKE LOOKING INTO A MIRROR.
I LOOKED LIKE THIS ONCE, WANDERING THE STREETS OF CAIRO AFTER MOMMA AND POPPA WERE KILLED. *
*SEE X-MEN #102. --Rog.
THE HOURS PASS, AND CRAMPED INNER CITY ALLEYS SLOWLY GIVE WAY TO THE OPEN PARKLAND OF THE EXCLUSIVE RESIDENTIAL DISTRICT.
THE AIR IS STILL BLISTERINGLY HOT WHEN THEY FINALLY STOP FOR A REST...
... THE FIRESTORM STILL RAGING UNCHECKED OVER A DOZEN MILES AWAY.
I HEARD A MISSIONARY ONCE IN KENYA. THIS LOOKS MUCH LIKE HIS DESCRIPTION OF HELL.
SCOTT, ARE YOU ALL RIGHT? I HEARD YOU COUGHING.
I JUST SWALLOWED TOO MUCH SMOKE.
HEY! ALL OF A SUDDEN THE AIR SMELLS SWEETER. THANKS, ORORO.
THIS MAY SOUND MACABRE, BUT I CAN'T HELP WONDERIN' WHAT HAPPENED TO THE PEOPLE. THIS IS A BIG CITY, BUT IT LOOKS ALMOST DESERTED.
PAPER SAYS MOST EVERYONE WAS EVACUATED.
WHAT--?! WHY?
EARLY WARNIN' OF A BIG 'QUAKE.
AN EARTHQUAKE WITHOUT PRE- OR AFTER-SHOCKS? THAT DOESN'T MAKE SENSE.
LOOK, BUB, ALL I KNOW IS WHAT I READ IN THE NEWSPAPERS.
YOU READ JAPANESE?
YUP.
I... DIDN'T KNOW.
YOU NEVER ASKED.

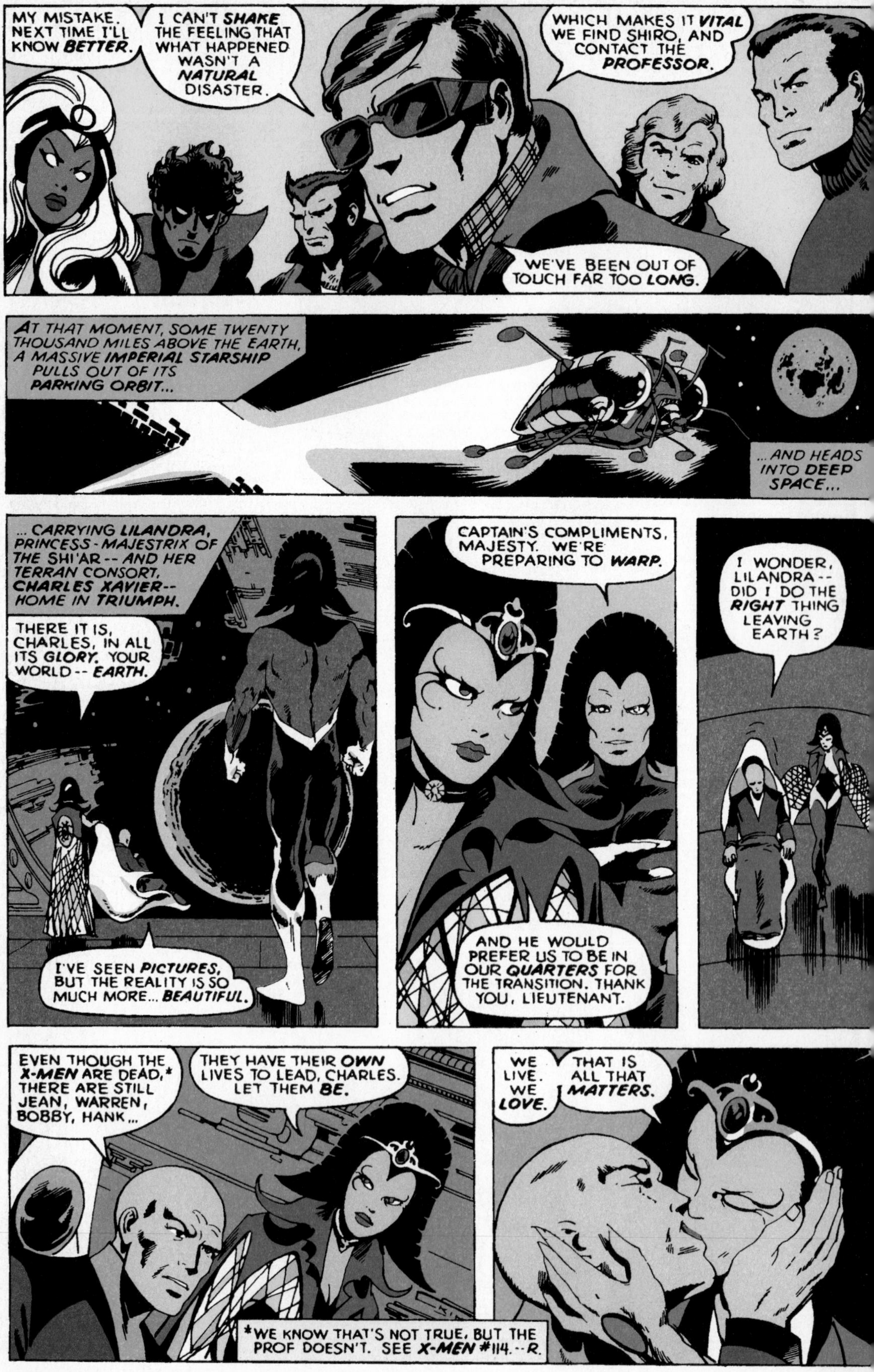

MY MISTAKE. NEXT TIME I'LL KNOW BETTER.
I CAN'T SHAKE THE FEELING THAT WHAT HAPPENED WASN'T A NATURAL DISASTER.
WHICH MAKES IT VITAL WE FIND SHIRO, AND CONTACT THE PROFESSOR.
WE'VE BEEN OUT OF TOUCH FAR TOO LONG.
AT THAT MOMENT, SOME TWENTY THOUSAND MILES ABOVE THE EARTH, A MASSIVE IMPERIAL STARSHIP PULLS OUT OF ITS PARKING ORBIT...
...AND HEADS INTO DEEP SPACE...
... CARRYING LILANDRA, PRINCESS-MAJESTRIX OF THE SHI'AR -- AND HER TERRAN CONSORT, CHARLES XAVIER -- HOME IN TRIUMPH.
THERE IT IS, CHARLES, IN ALL ITS GLORY. YOUR WORLD -- EARTH.
I'VE SEEN PICTURES, BUT THE REALITY IS SO MUCH MORE... BEAUTIFUL.
CAPTAIN'S COMPLIMENTS, MAJESTY. WE'RE PREPARING TO WARP.
AND HE WOULD PREFER US TO BE IN OUR QUARTERS FOR THE TRANSITION. THANK YOU, LIEUTENANT.
I WONDER, LILANDRA -- DID I DO THE RIGHT THING LEAVING EARTH?
EVEN THOUGH THE X-MEN ARE DEAD,* THERE ARE STILL JEAN, WARREN, BOBBY, HANK...
THEY HAVE THEIR OWN LIVES TO LEAD, CHARLES. LET THEM BE.
*WE KNOW THAT'S NOT TRUE, BUT THE PROF DOESN'T. SEE X-MEN #114. -- R.
WE LIVE. WE LOVE.
THAT IS ALL THAT MATTERS.

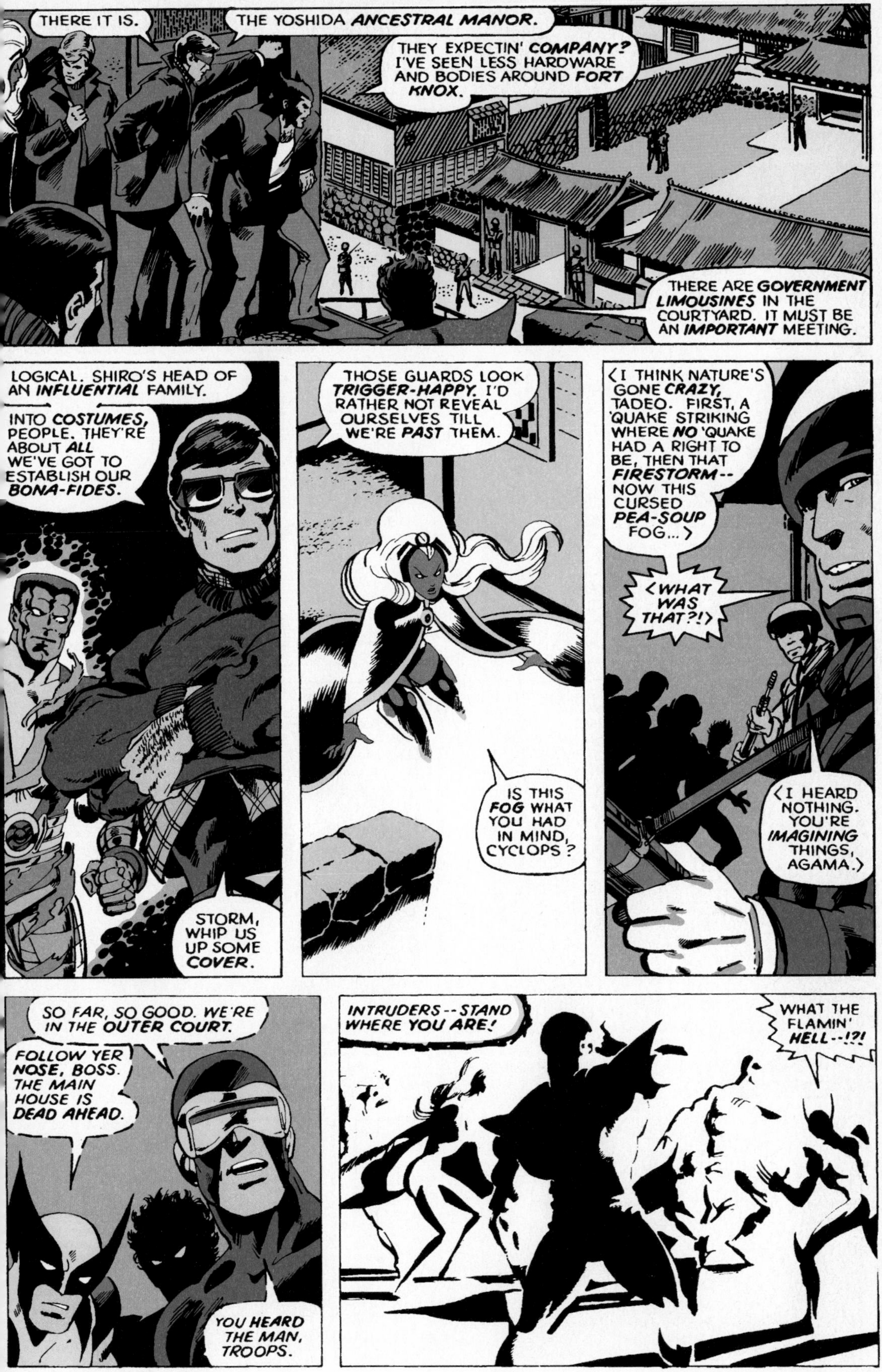
THERE IT IS.
THE YOSHIDA ANCESTRAL MANOR.
THEY EXPECTIN' COMPANY? I'VE SEEN LESS HARDWARE AND BODIES AROUND FORT KNOX.
THERE ARE GOVERNMENT LIMOUSINES IN THE COURTYARD. IT MUST BE AN IMPORTANT MEETING.
LOGICAL. SHIRO'S HEAD OF AN INFLUENTIAL FAMILY.
INTO COSTUMES, PEOPLE. THEY'RE ABOUT ALL WE'VE GOT TO ESTABLISH OUR BONA-FIDES.
STORM, WHIP US UP SOME COVER.
THOSE GUARDS LOOK TRIGGER-HAPPY. I'D RATHER NOT REVEAL OURSELVES TILL WE'RE PAST THEM.
IS THIS FOG WHAT YOU HAD IN MIND, CYCLOPS?
<I THINK NATURE'S GONE CRAZY, TADEO. FIRST, A 'QUAKE STRIKING WHERE NO 'QUAKE HAD A RIGHT TO BE, THEN THAT FIRESTORM-- NOW THIS CURSED PEA-SOUP FOG...>
<WHAT WAS THAT?!>
<I HEARD NOTHING. YOU'RE IMAGINING THINGS, AGAMA.>
SO FAR, SO GOOD. WE'RE IN THE OUTER COURT.
FOLLOW YER NOSE, BOSS. THE MAIN HOUSE IS DEAD AHEAD.
YOU HEARD THE MAN, TROOPS.
INTRUDERS--STAND WHERE YOU ARE!
WHAT THE FLAMIN' HELL--!?!

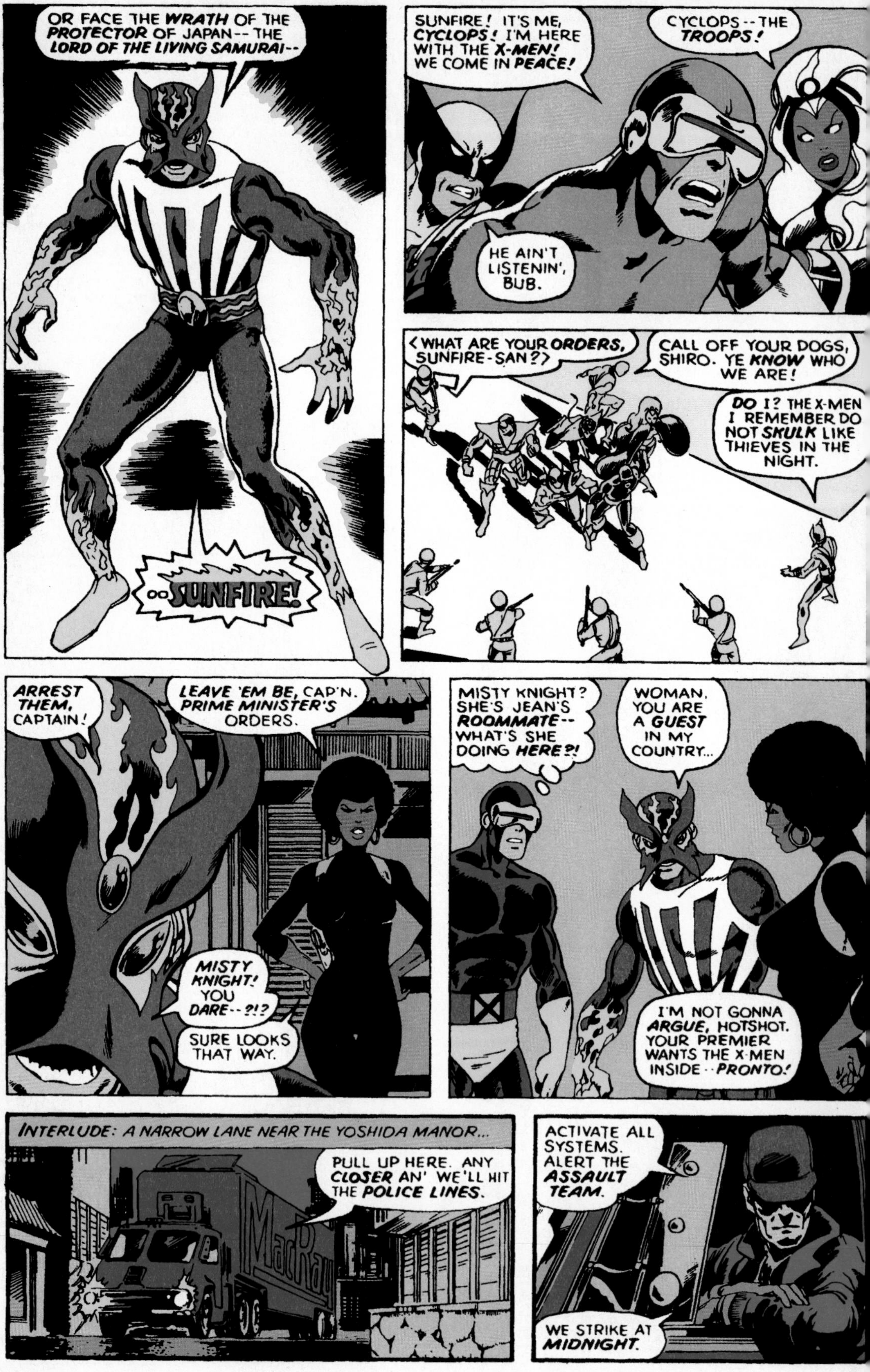

OR FACE THE WRATH OF THE PROTECTOR OF JAPAN-- THE LORD OF THE LIVING SAMURAI--
..SUNFIRE!
SUNFIRE! IT'S ME, CYCLOPS! I'M HERE WITH THE X-MEN! WE COME IN PEACE!
CYCLOPS--THE TROOPS!
HE AIN'T LISTENIN', BUB.
<WHAT ARE YOUR ORDERS, SUNFIRE-SAN?>
CALL OFF YOUR DOGS, SHIRO. YE KNOW WHO WE ARE!
DO I? THE X-MEN I REMEMBER DO NOT SKULK LIKE THIEVES IN THE NIGHT.
ARREST THEM, CAPTAIN!
LEAVE 'EM BE, CAP'N. PRIME MINISTER'S ORDERS.
MISTY KNIGHT! YOU DARE--?!?
SURE LOOKS THAT WAY.
MISTY KNIGHT? SHE'S JEAN'S ROOMMATE-- WHAT'S SHE DOING HERE?!
WOMAN, YOU ARE A GUEST IN MY COUNTRY...
I'M NOT GONNA ARGUE, HOTSHOT. YOUR PREMIER WANTS THE X-MEN INSIDE--PRONTO!
INTERLUDE: A NARROW LANE NEAR THE YOSHIDA MANOR...
PULL UP HERE. ANY CLOSER AN' WE'LL HIT THE POLICE LINES.
MacRay
ACTIVATE ALL SYSTEMS. ALERT THE ASSAULT TEAM.
WE STRIKE AT MIDNIGHT.

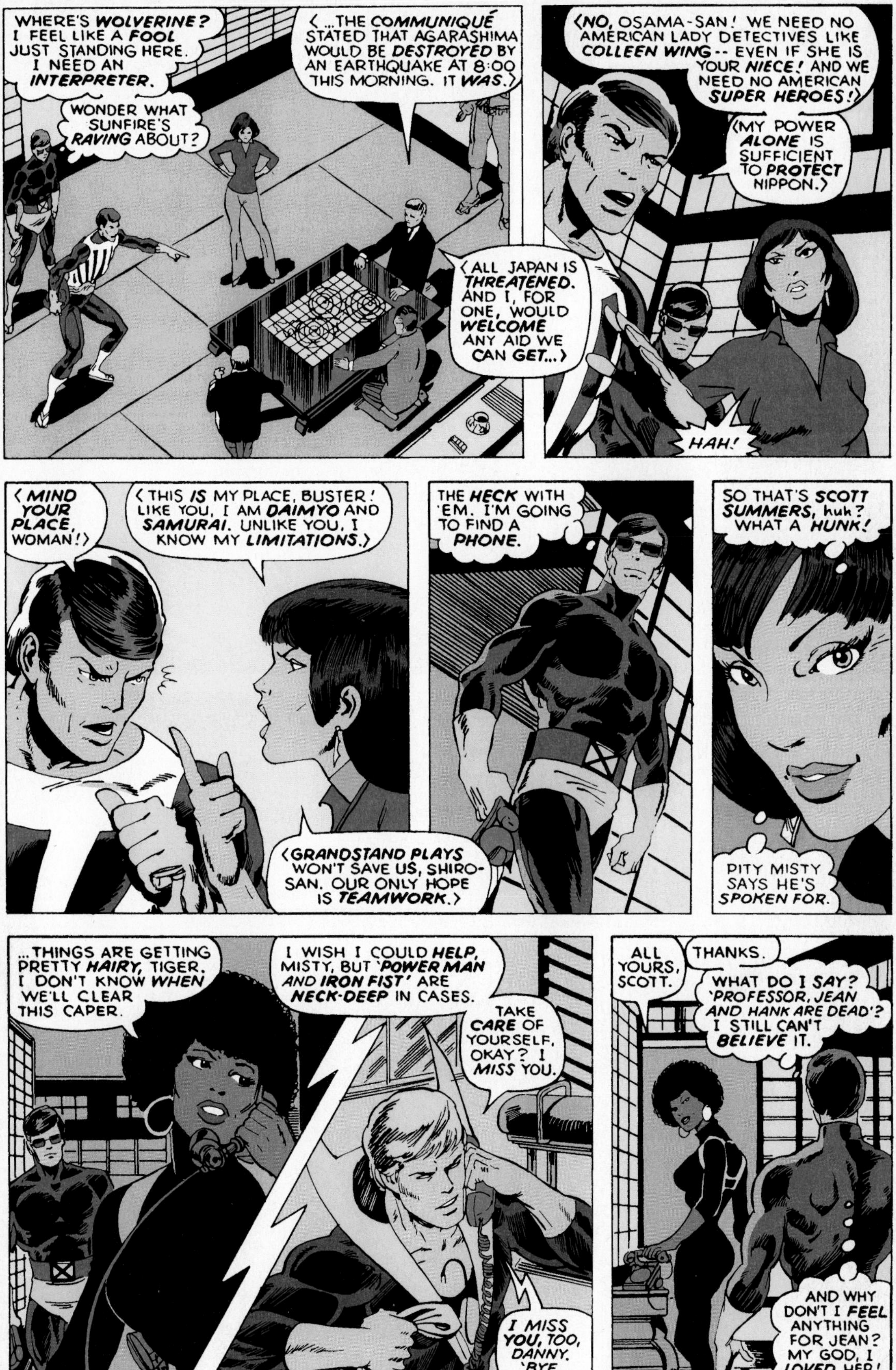

WHERE'S WOLVERINE? I FEEL LIKE A FOOL JUST STANDING HERE. I NEED AN INTERPRETER.
WONDER WHAT SUNFIRE'S RAVING ABOUT?
⟨...THE COMMUNIQUÉ STATED THAT AGARASHIMA WOULD BE DESTROYED BY AN EARTHQUAKE AT 8:00 THIS MORNING. IT WAS.⟩
⟨ALL JAPAN IS THREATENED. AND I, FOR ONE, WOULD WELCOME ANY AID WE CAN GET...⟩
⟨NO, OSAMA-SAN! WE NEED NO AMERICAN LADY DETECTIVES LIKE COLLEEN WING -- EVEN IF SHE IS YOUR NIECE! AND WE NEED NO AMERICAN SUPER HEROES!⟩
⟨MY POWER ALONE IS SUFFICIENT TO PROTECT NIPPON.⟩
HAH!
⟨MIND YOUR PLACE, WOMAN!⟩
⟨THIS IS MY PLACE, BUSTER! LIKE YOU, I AM DAIMYO AND SAMURAI. UNLIKE YOU, I KNOW MY LIMITATIONS.⟩
⟨GRANDSTAND PLAYS WON'T SAVE US, SHIRO-SAN. OUR ONLY HOPE IS TEAMWORK.⟩
THE HECK WITH 'EM. I'M GOING TO FIND A PHONE.
SO THAT'S SCOTT SUMMERS, huh? WHAT A HUNK!
PITY MISTY SAYS HE'S SPOKEN FOR.
...THINGS ARE GETTING PRETTY HAIRY, TIGER. I DON'T KNOW WHEN WE'LL CLEAR THIS CAPER.
I WISH I COULD HELP, MISTY, BUT 'POWER MAN AND IRON FIST' ARE NECK-DEEP IN CASES.
TAKE CARE OF YOURSELF, OKAY? I MISS YOU.
I MISS YOU, TOO, DANNY. 'BYE.
ALL YOURS, SCOTT.
THANKS.
WHAT DO I SAY? 'PROFESSOR, JEAN AND HANK ARE DEAD'? I STILL CAN'T BELIEVE IT.
AND WHY DON'T I FEEL ANYTHING FOR JEAN? MY GOD, I LOVED HER!

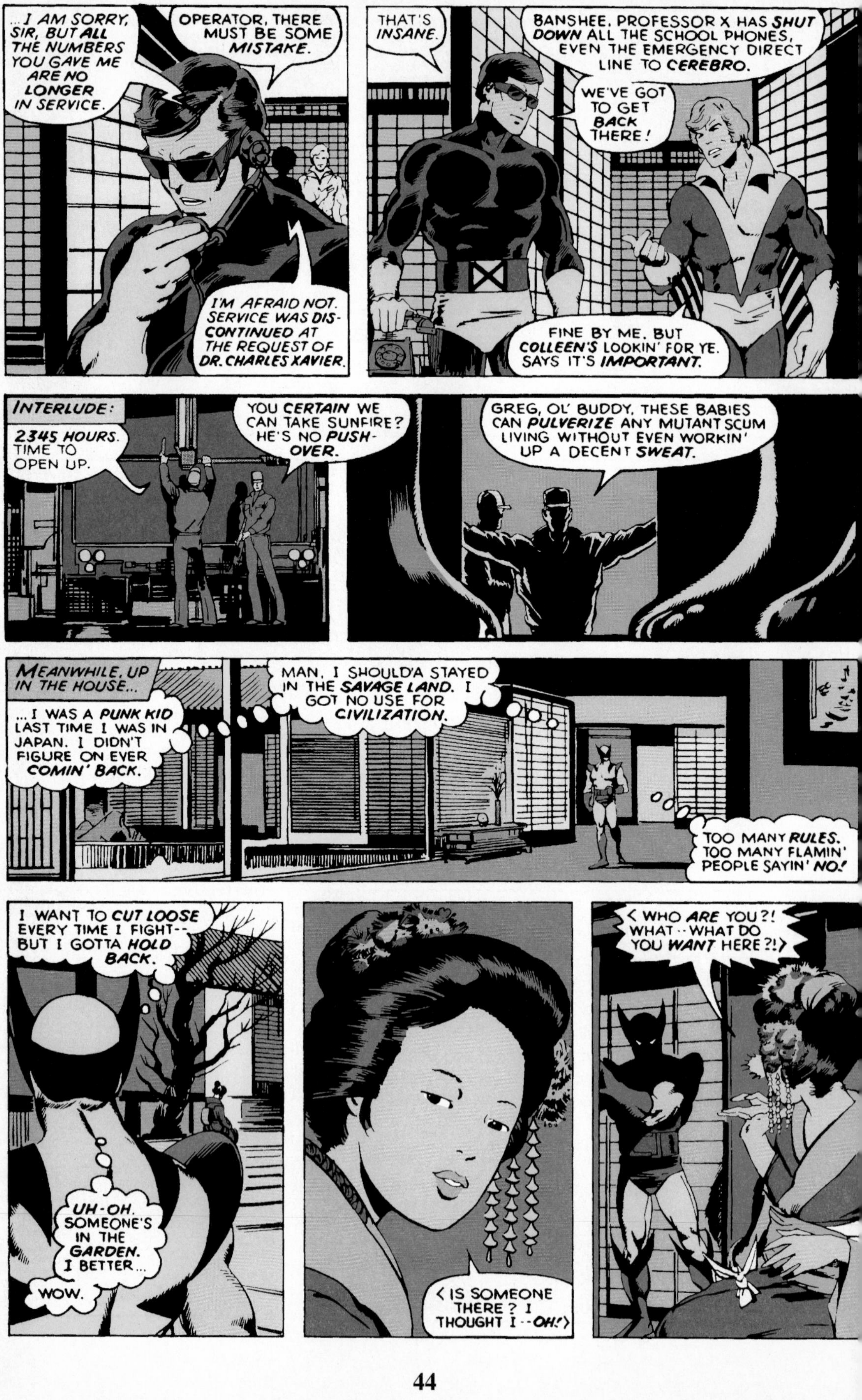
...I AM SORRY, SIR, BUT ALL THE NUMBERS YOU GAVE ME ARE NO LONGER IN SERVICE.
OPERATOR, THERE MUST BE SOME MISTAKE.
I'M AFRAID NOT. SERVICE WAS DISCONTINUED AT THE REQUEST OF DR. CHARLES XAVIER.
THAT'S INSANE.
BANSHEE, PROFESSOR X HAS SHUT DOWN ALL THE SCHOOL PHONES, EVEN THE EMERGENCY DIRECT LINE TO CEREBRO.
WE'VE GOT TO GET BACK THERE!
FINE BY ME, BUT COLLEEN'S LOOKIN' FOR YE. SAYS IT'S IMPORTANT.
INTERLUDE:
2345 HOURS. TIME TO OPEN UP.
YOU CERTAIN WE CAN TAKE SUNFIRE? HE'S NO PUSH-OVER.
GREG, OL' BUDDY, THESE BABIES CAN PULVERIZE ANY MUTANT SCUM LIVING WITHOUT EVEN WORKIN' UP A DECENT SWEAT.
MEANWHILE, UP IN THE HOUSE...
...I WAS A PUNK KID LAST TIME I WAS IN JAPAN. I DIDN'T FIGURE ON EVER COMIN' BACK.
MAN, I SHOULD'A STAYED IN THE SAVAGE LAND. I GOT NO USE FOR CIVILIZATION.
TOO MANY RULES. TOO MANY FLAMIN' PEOPLE SAYIN' NO!
I WANT TO CUT LOOSE EVERY TIME I FIGHT-- BUT I GOTTA HOLD BACK.
UH-OH. SOMEONE'S IN THE GARDEN. I BETTER...
WOW.
<IS SOMEONE THERE? I THOUGHT I--OH!>
<WHO ARE YOU?! WHAT--WHAT DO YOU WANT HERE?!>

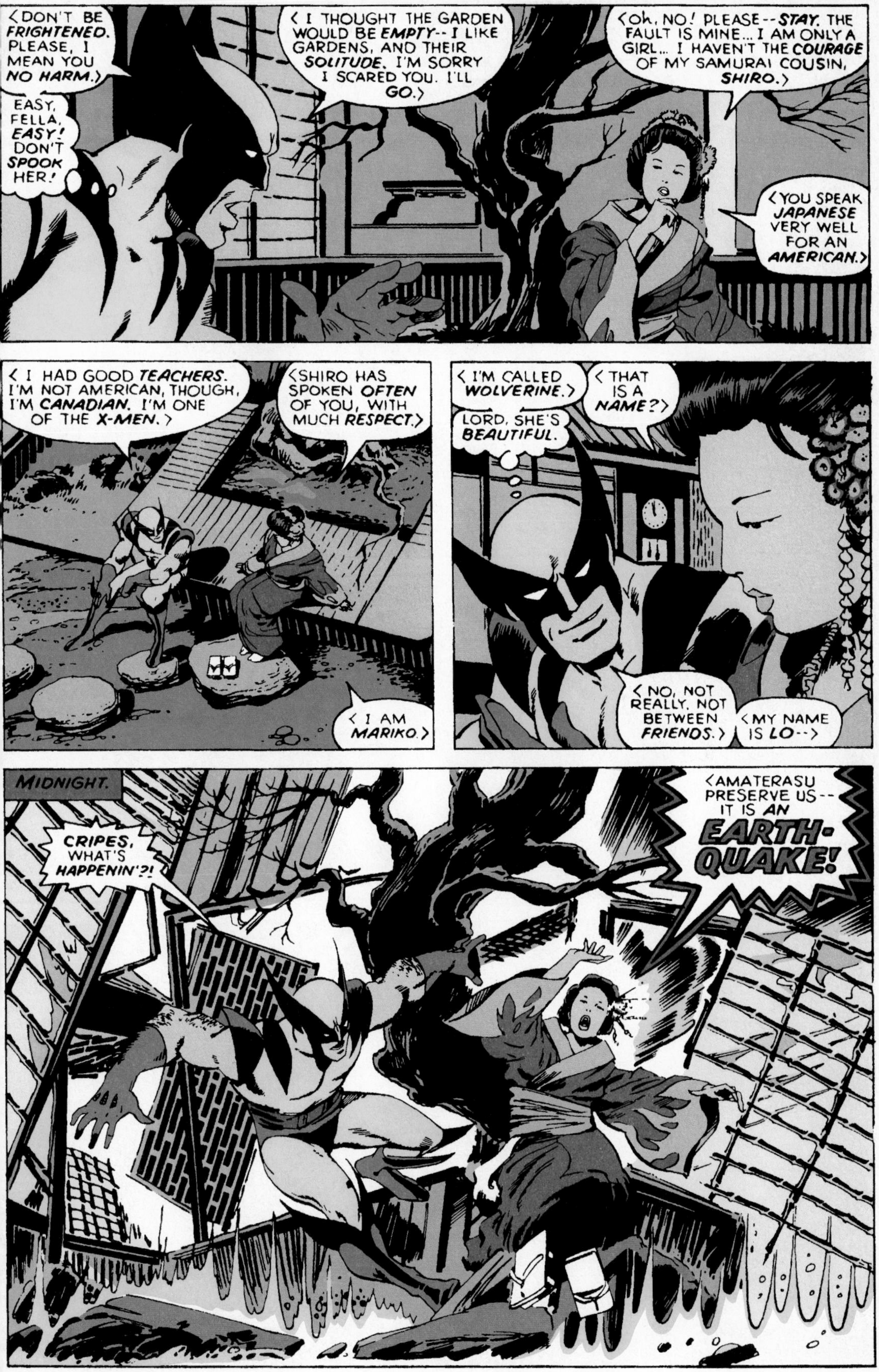
‹DON'T BE FRIGHTENED. PLEASE, I MEAN YOU NO HARM.›
EASY, FELLA, EASY! DON'T SPOOK HER!
‹I THOUGHT THE GARDEN WOULD BE EMPTY-- I LIKE GARDENS, AND THEIR SOLITUDE. I'M SORRY I SCARED YOU. I'LL GO.›
‹Oh, NO! PLEASE-- STAY. THE FAULT IS MINE... I AM ONLY A GIRL... I HAVEN'T THE COURAGE OF MY SAMURAI COUSIN, SHIRO.›
‹YOU SPEAK JAPANESE VERY WELL FOR AN AMERICAN.›
‹I HAD GOOD TEACHERS. I'M NOT AMERICAN, THOUGH, I'M CANADIAN. I'M ONE OF THE X-MEN.›
‹SHIRO HAS SPOKEN OFTEN OF YOU, WITH MUCH RESPECT.›
‹I AM MARIKO.›
‹I'M CALLED WOLVERINE.›
‹THAT IS A NAME?›
LORD, SHE'S BEAUTIFUL.
‹NO, NOT REALLY. NOT BETWEEN FRIENDS.›
‹MY NAME IS LO--›
MIDNIGHT.
CRIPES, WHAT'S HAPPENIN'?!
‹AMATERASU PRESERVE US-- IT IS AN EARTH-QUAKE!

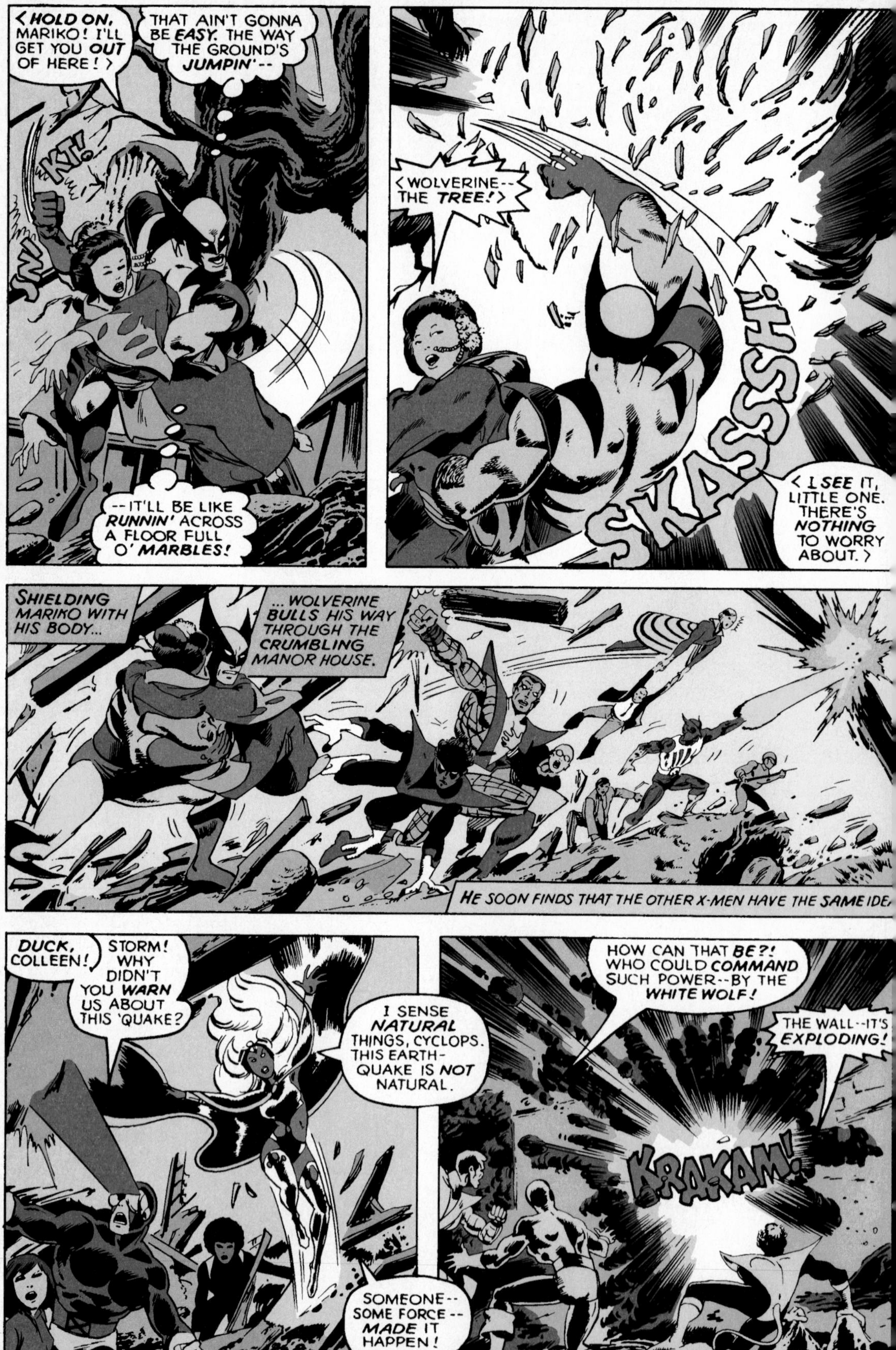
< HOLD ON, MARIKO! I'LL GET YOU OUT OF HERE! >
THAT AIN'T GONNA BE EASY. THE WAY THE GROUND'S JUMPIN'--
SNIKT!
--IT'LL BE LIKE RUNNIN' ACROSS A FLOOR FULL O' MARBLES!
< WOLVERINE-- THE TREE! >
SKASSSH!
< I SEE IT, LITTLE ONE. THERE'S NOTHING TO WORRY ABOUT. >
SHIELDING MARIKO WITH HIS BODY...
...WOLVERINE BULLS HIS WAY THROUGH THE CRUMBLING MANOR HOUSE.
HE SOON FINDS THAT THE OTHER X-MEN HAVE THE SAME IDE
DUCK, COLLEEN!
STORM! WHY DIDN'T YOU WARN US ABOUT THIS 'QUAKE?
I SENSE NATURAL THINGS, CYCLOPS. THIS EARTH-QUAKE IS NOT NATURAL.
SOMEONE-- SOME FORCE-- MADE IT HAPPEN!
HOW CAN THAT BE?! WHO COULD COMMAND SUCH POWER--BY THE WHITE WOLF!
THE WALL--IT'S EXPLODING!
KRAKAM!

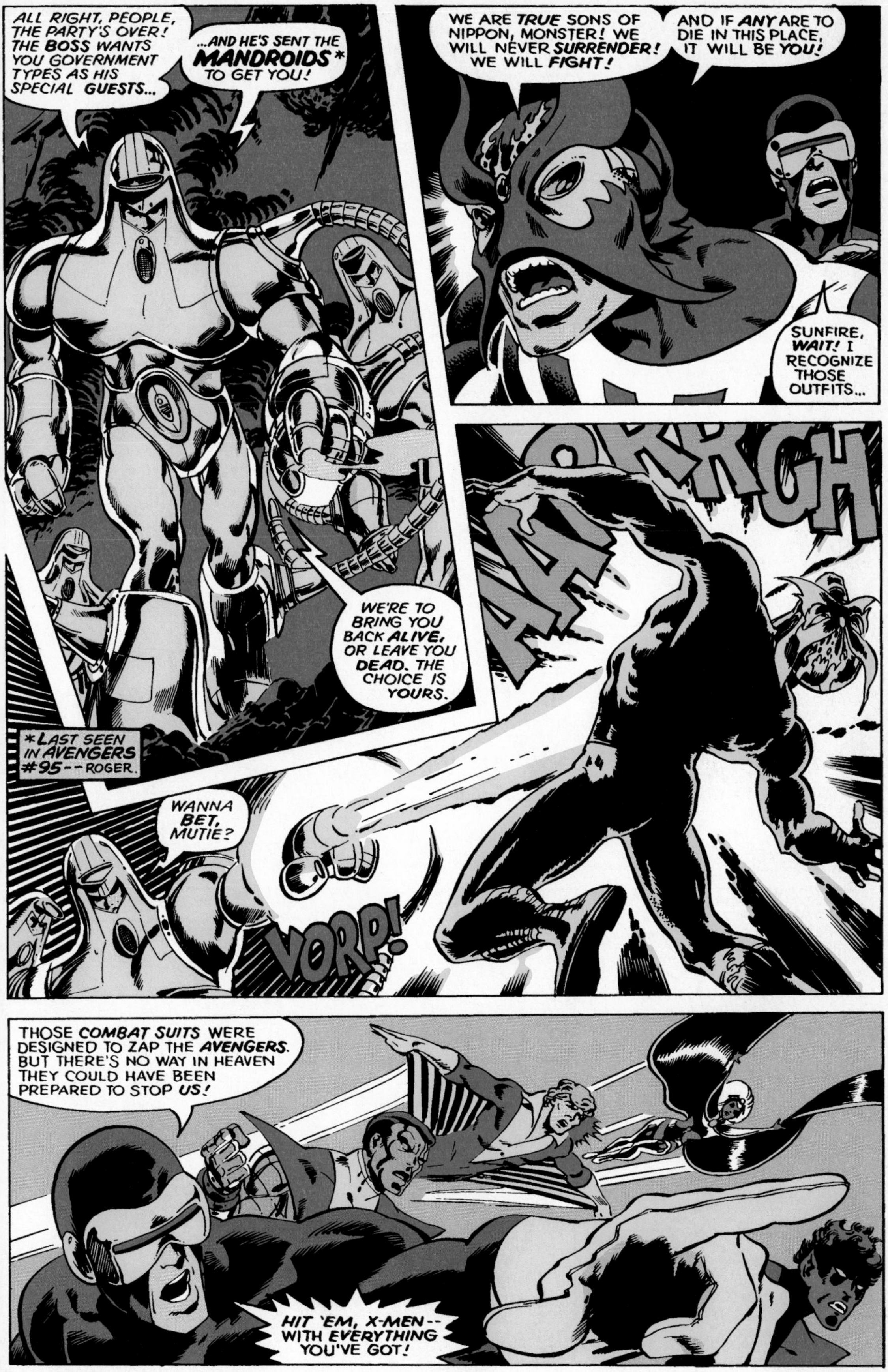
ALL RIGHT, PEOPLE, THE PARTY'S OVER! THE BOSS WANTS YOU GOVERNMENT TYPES AS HIS SPECIAL GUESTS...
...AND HE'S SENT THE MANDROIDS* TO GET YOU!
WE'RE TO BRING YOU BACK ALIVE, OR LEAVE YOU DEAD. THE CHOICE IS YOURS.
*LAST SEEN IN AVENGERS #95--ROGER.
WE ARE TRUE SONS OF NIPPON, MONSTER! WE WILL NEVER SURRENDER! WE WILL FIGHT!
AND IF ANY ARE TO DIE IN THIS PLACE, IT WILL BE YOU!
SUNFIRE, WAIT! I RECOGNIZE THOSE OUTFITS...
AAARRRGH
WANNA BET, MUTIE?
VORP!
THOSE COMBAT SUITS WERE DESIGNED TO ZAP THE AVENGERS. BUT THERE'S NO WAY IN HEAVEN THEY COULD HAVE BEEN PREPARED TO STOP US!
HIT 'EM, X-MEN-- WITH EVERYTHING YOU'VE GOT!

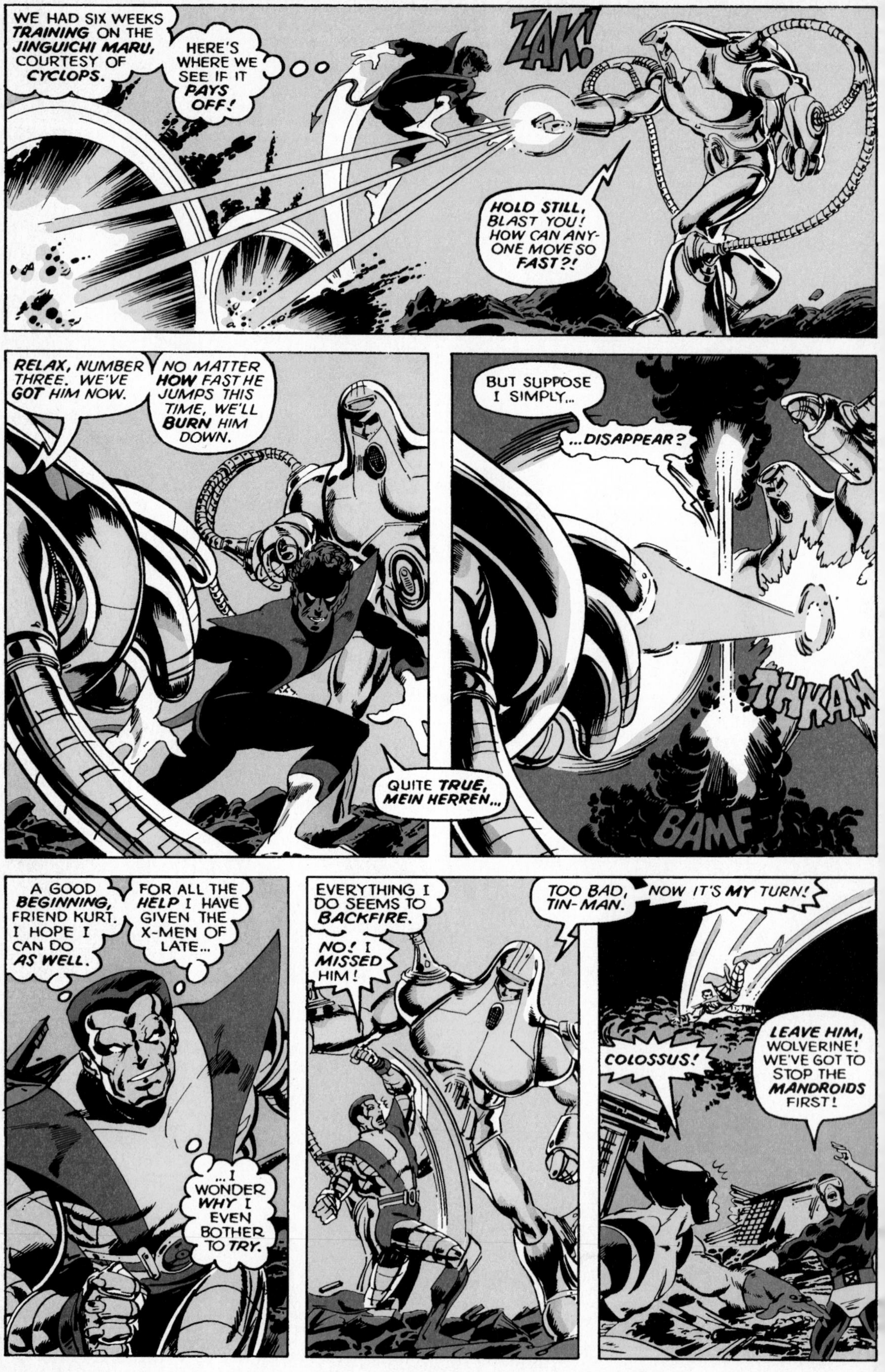
WE HAD SIX WEEKS TRAINING ON THE JINGUICHI MARU, COURTESY OF CYCLOPS.
HERE'S WHERE WE SEE IF IT PAYS OFF!
ZAK!
HOLD STILL, BLAST YOU! HOW CAN ANYONE MOVE SO FAST?!
RELAX, NUMBER THREE. WE'VE GOT HIM NOW.
NO MATTER HOW FAST HE JUMPS THIS TIME, WE'LL BURN HIM DOWN.
QUITE TRUE, MEIN HERREN...
BUT SUPPOSE I SIMPLY...
...DISAPPEAR?
THKAM
BAMF
A GOOD BEGINNING, FRIEND KURT. I HOPE I CAN DO AS WELL.
FOR ALL THE HELP I HAVE GIVEN THE X-MEN OF LATE...
...I WONDER WHY I EVEN BOTHER TO TRY.
EVERYTHING I DO SEEMS TO BACKFIRE.
NO! I MISSED HIM!
TOO BAD, TIN-MAN.
NOW IT'S MY TURN!
COLOSSUS!
LEAVE HIM, WOLVERINE! WE'VE GOT TO STOP THE MANDROIDS FIRST!

SNIKT!!

BOSS, THAT'LL BE A *PLEASURE!*

... BUT IT DON'T RATE *DIDDLEY* AGAINST *ADAMANTIUM CLAWS!*

BUB, THAT *REVERSE POLARITY* MAGNETIC ZAP MAY HAVE WORKED AGAINST MY *STEEL BUDDY*--

ONE DOWN, *TWO* TO GO. WE'VE GOT THEM *OFF-BALANCE*-- WE'VE GOT TO *KEEP* THEM THAT WAY.

IF I *PULSE* MY OPTIC BEAMS...

... SETTING UP A *SPECIFIC* VIBRATION PATTERN IN THE MANDROID *ARMOR*--!

BANSHEE--*GO!!*

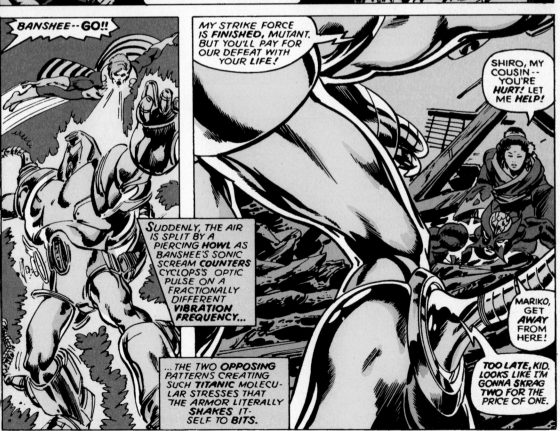

MY STRIKE FORCE IS *FINISHED,* MUTANT. BUT YOU'LL PAY FOR OUR DEFEAT WITH YOUR *LIFE!*

SHIRO, MY COUSIN-- YOU'RE *HURT!* LET ME *HELP!*

SUDDENLY, THE AIR IS SPLIT BY A PIERCING *HOWL* AS BANSHEE'S SONIC SCREAM *COUNTERS* CYCLOPS'S OPTIC PULSE ON A FRACTIONALLY DIFFERENT *VIBRATION FREQUENCY*...

... THE TWO *OPPOSING* PATTERNS CREATING SUCH *TITANIC* MOLECULAR STRESSES THAT THE ARMOR LITERALLY *SHAKES* ITSELF TO BITS.

MARIKO, GET *AWAY* FROM HERE!

TOO LATE, KID. LOOKS LIKE I'M GONNA *SKRAG* TWO FOR THE PRICE OF ONE.

49

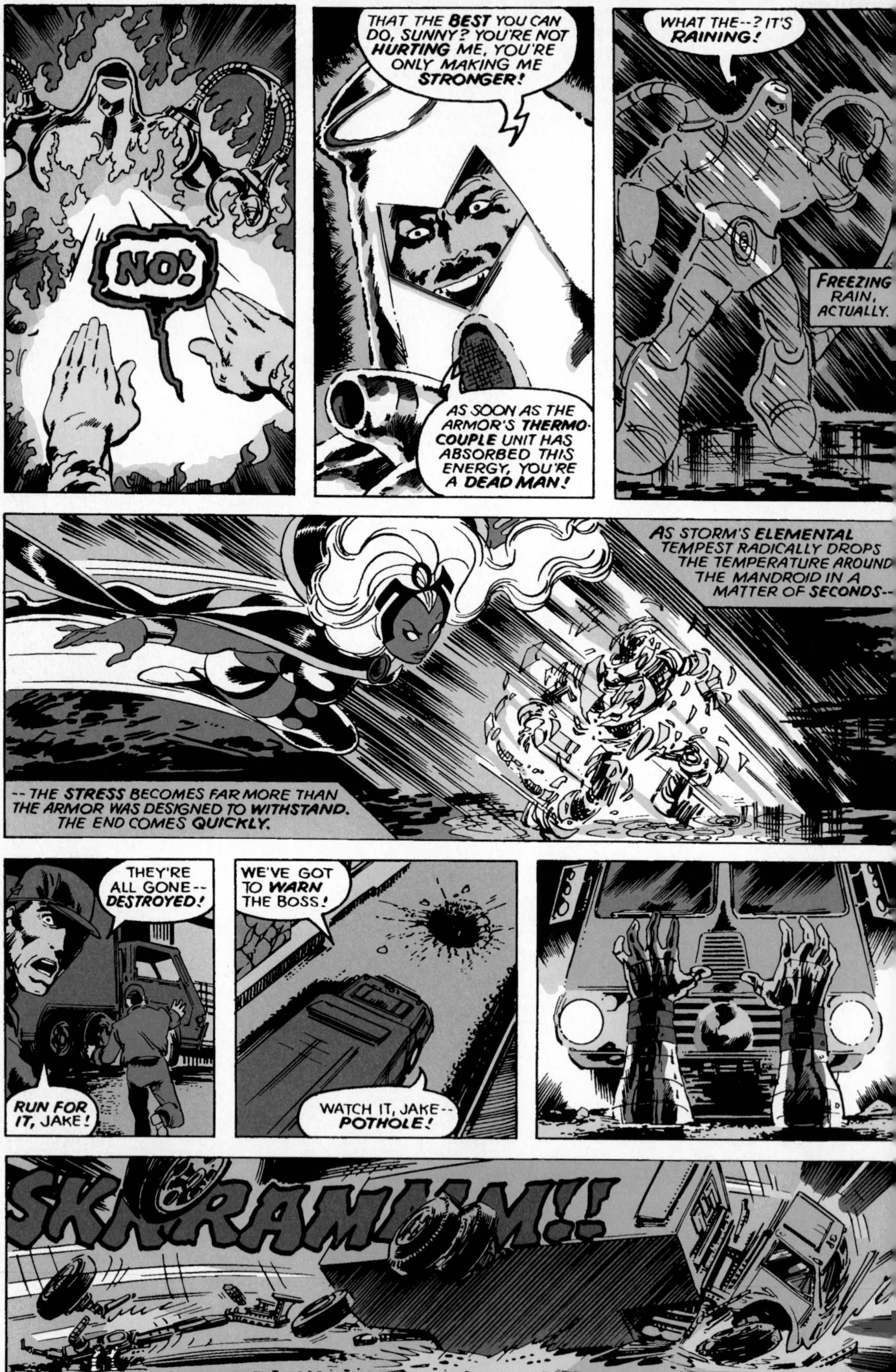
NO!
THAT THE BEST YOU CAN DO, SUNNY? YOU'RE NOT HURTING ME, YOU'RE ONLY MAKING ME STRONGER!
AS SOON AS THE ARMOR'S THERMO-COUPLE UNIT HAS ABSORBED THIS ENERGY, YOU'RE A DEAD MAN!
WHAT THE--? IT'S RAINING!
FREEZING RAIN, ACTUALLY.
AS STORM'S ELEMENTAL TEMPEST RADICALLY DROPS THE TEMPERATURE AROUND THE MANDROID IN A MATTER OF SECONDS--
--THE STRESS BECOMES FAR MORE THAN THE ARMOR WAS DESIGNED TO WITHSTAND. THE END COMES QUICKLY.
THEY'RE ALL GONE-- DESTROYED!
RUN FOR IT, JAKE!
WE'VE GOT TO WARN THE BOSS!
WATCH IT, JAKE-- POTHOLE!
SKRAMMMM!!

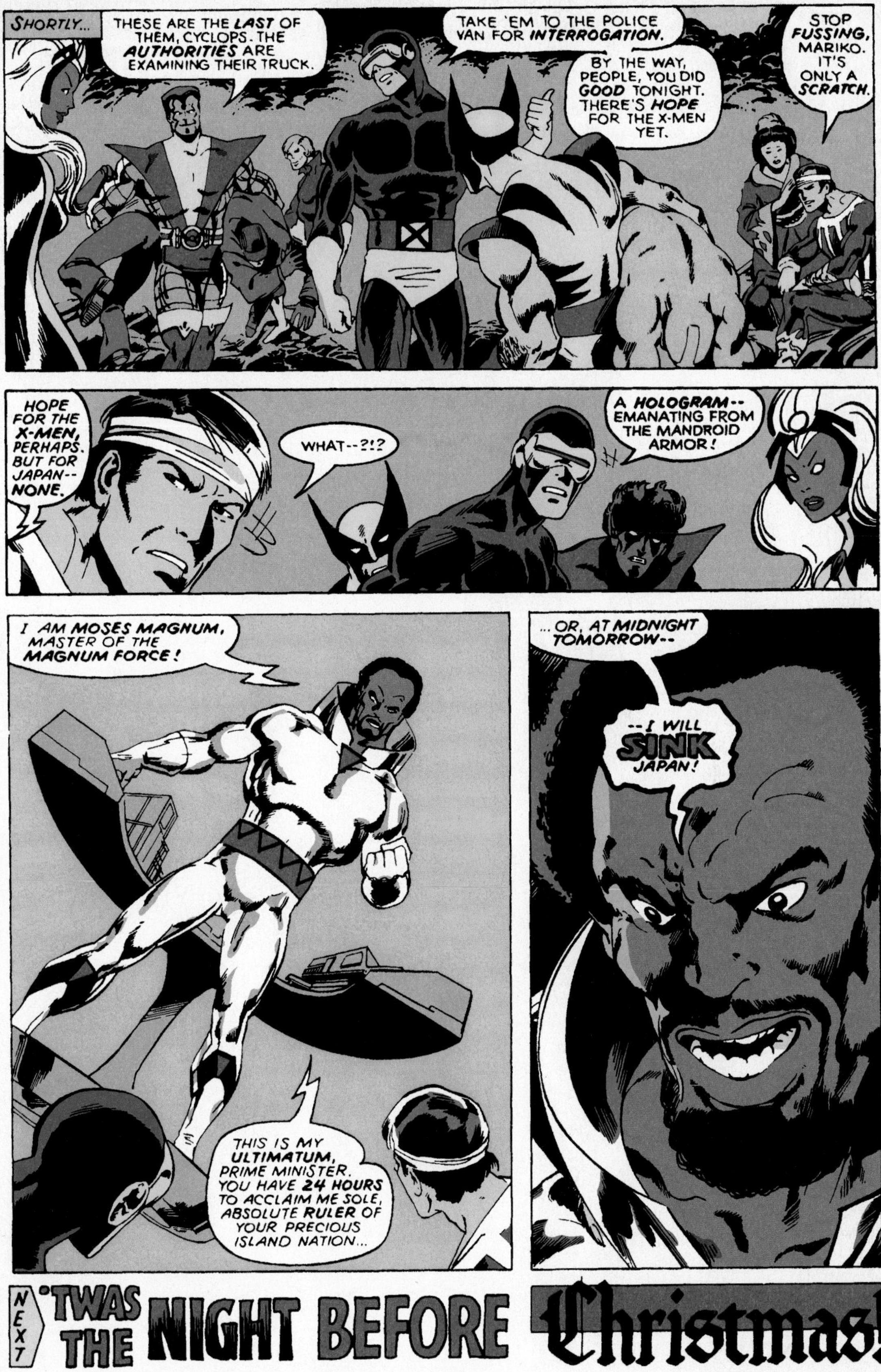
SHORTLY...
THESE ARE THE LAST OF THEM, CYCLOPS. THE AUTHORITIES ARE EXAMINING THEIR TRUCK.
TAKE 'EM TO THE POLICE VAN FOR INTERROGATION.
BY THE WAY, PEOPLE, YOU DID GOOD TONIGHT. THERE'S HOPE FOR THE X-MEN YET.
STOP FUSSING, MARIKO. IT'S ONLY A SCRATCH.
HOPE FOR THE X-MEN, PERHAPS. BUT FOR JAPAN-- NONE.
WHAT--?!?
A HOLOGRAM-- EMANATING FROM THE MANDROID ARMOR!
I AM MOSES MAGNUM, MASTER OF THE MAGNUM FORCE!
THIS IS MY ULTIMATUM, PRIME MINISTER. YOU HAVE 24 HOURS TO ACCLAIM ME SOLE, ABSOLUTE RULER OF YOUR PRECIOUS ISLAND NATION...
...OR, AT MIDNIGHT TOMORROW--
--I WILL SINK JAPAN!
NEXT
'TWAS THE NIGHT BEFORE Christmas!

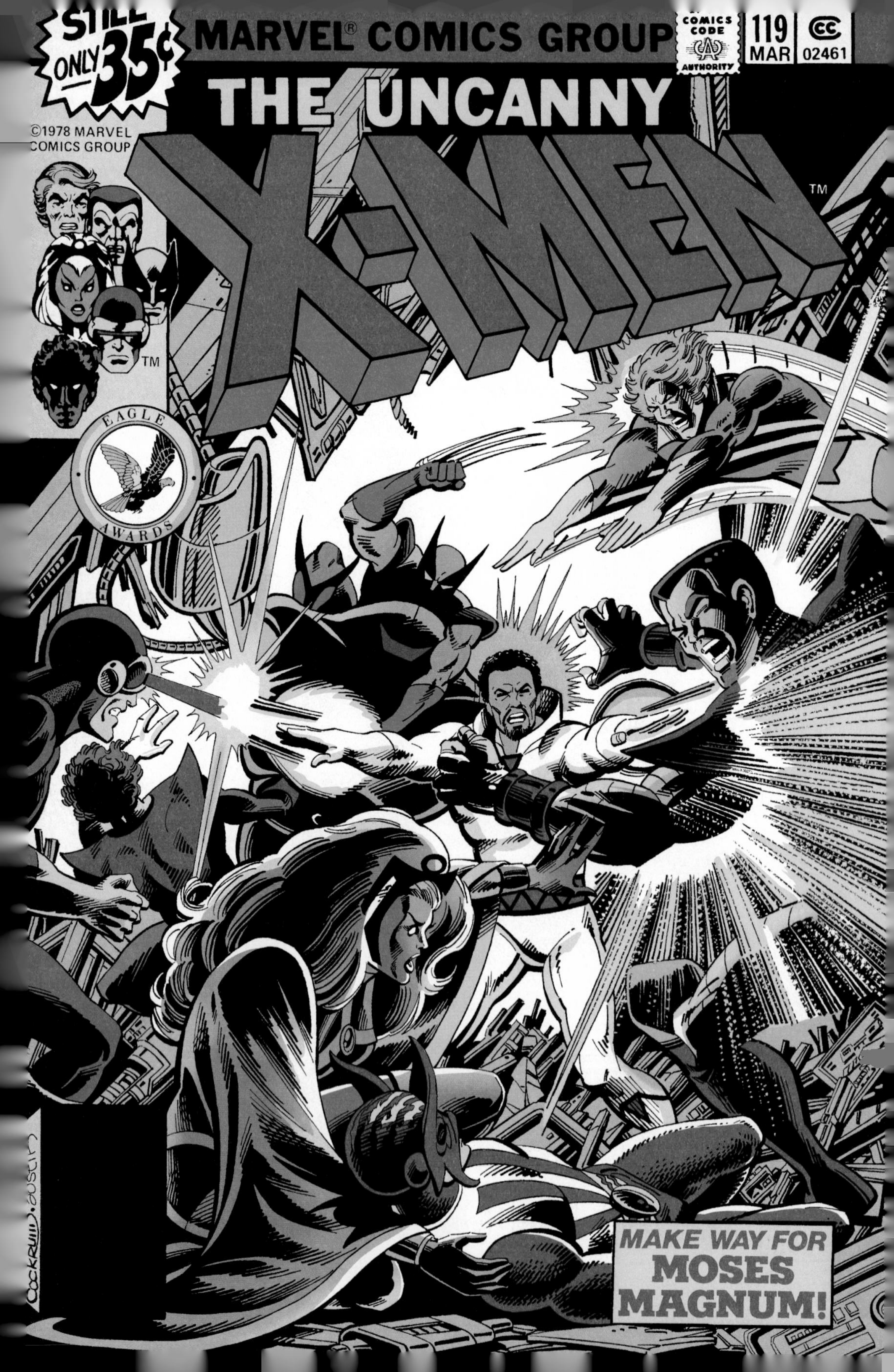
STILL ONLY 35¢
MARVEL® COMICS GROUP
COMICS CODE AUTHORITY
119 MAR
CC 02461
THE UNCANNY
X-MEN™
©1978 MARVEL COMICS GROUP
EAGLE AWARDS
MAKE WAY FOR MOSES MAGNUM!

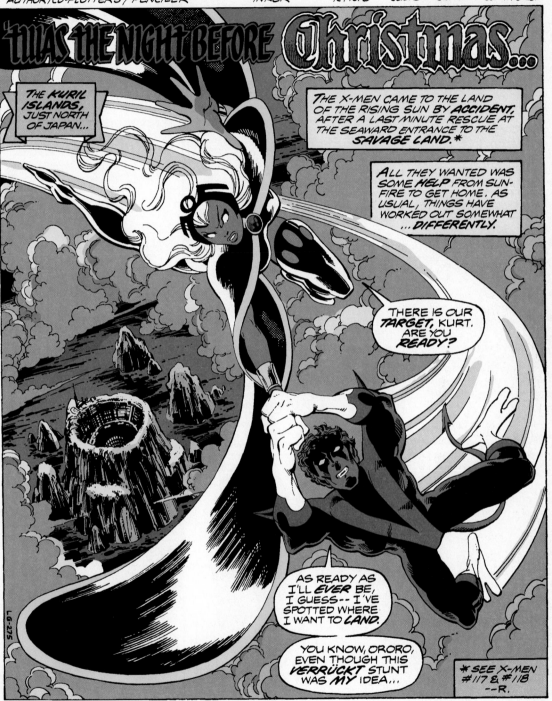

STAN LEE PRESENTS: THE UNCANNY X-MEN! ™

CHRIS CLAREMONT | JOHN BYRNE | TERRY AUSTIN | COSTANZA | G.WEIN | R.STERN | J.SHOOTER
AUTHOR/CO-PLOTTERS / PENCILER | INKER | letters | colors | editor | ed.-in-chief

"'TWAS THE NIGHT BEFORE Christmas...

THE KURIL ISLANDS, JUST NORTH OF JAPAN...

THE X-MEN CAME TO THE LAND OF THE RISING SUN BY ACCIDENT, AFTER A LAST MINUTE RESCUE AT THE SEAWARD ENTRANCE TO THE SAVAGE LAND.*

ALL THEY WANTED WAS SOME HELP FROM SUN-FIRE TO GET HOME. AS USUAL, THINGS HAVE WORKED OUT SOMEWHAT ...DIFFERENTLY.

THERE IS OUR TARGET, KURT. ARE YOU READY?

AS READY AS I'LL EVER BE, I GUESS-- I'VE SPOTTED WHERE I WANT TO LAND.

YOU KNOW, ORORO, EVEN THOUGH THIS VERRÜCKT STUNT WAS MY IDEA...

* SEE X-MEN #117 & #118 --R.

53

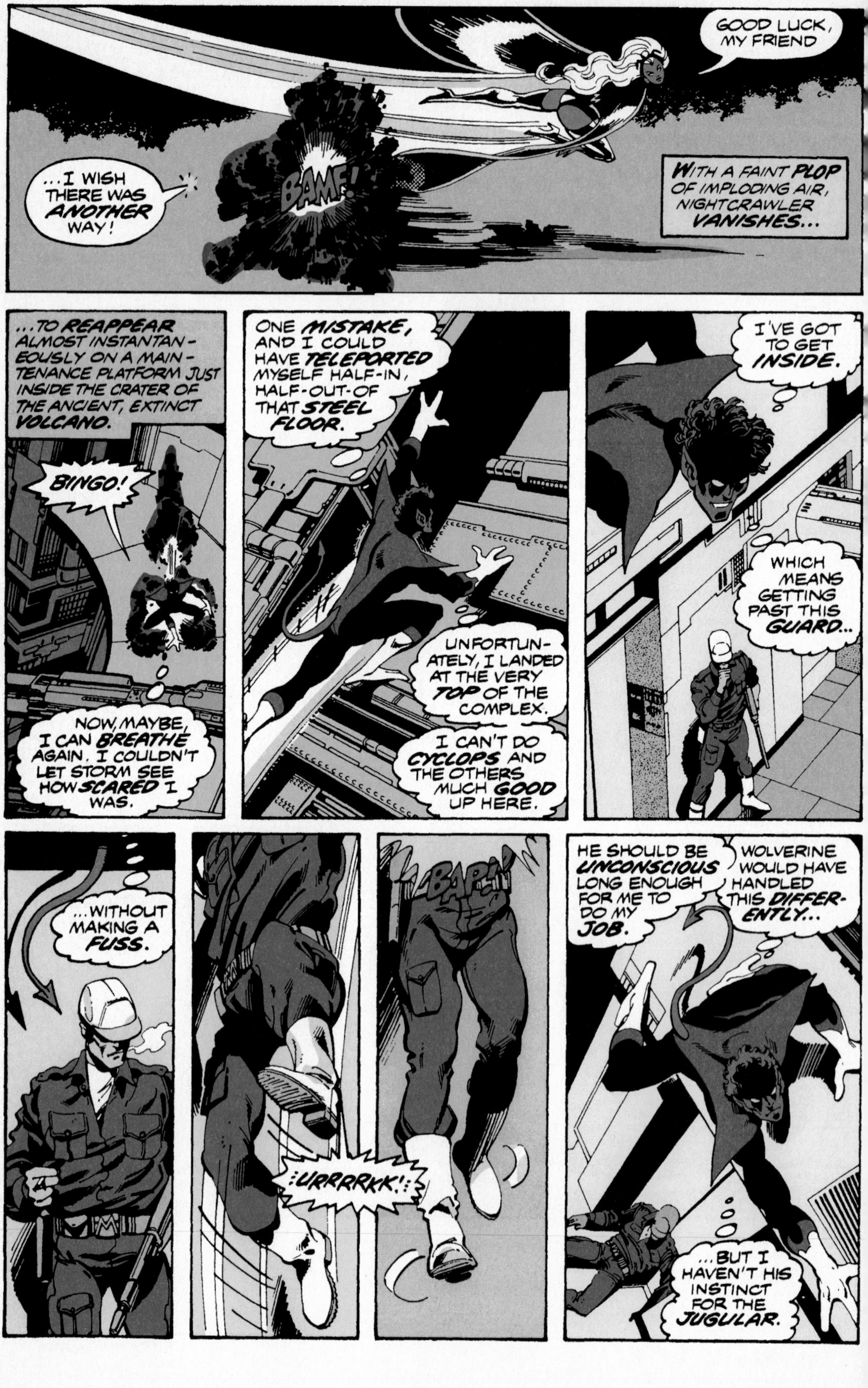
GOOD LUCK, MY FRIEND
...I WISH THERE WAS ANOTHER WAY!
BAMF!
WITH A FAINT PLOP OF IMPLODING AIR, NIGHTCRAWLER VANISHES...
...TO REAPPEAR ALMOST INSTANTANEOUSLY ON A MAINTENANCE PLATFORM JUST INSIDE THE CRATER OF THE ANCIENT, EXTINCT VOLCANO.
BINGO!
NOW, MAYBE, I CAN BREATHE AGAIN. I COULDN'T LET STORM SEE HOW SCARED I WAS.
ONE MISTAKE, AND I COULD HAVE TELEPORTED MYSELF HALF-IN, HALF-OUT-OF THAT STEEL FLOOR.
UNFORTUNATELY, I LANDED AT THE VERY TOP OF THE COMPLEX.
I CAN'T DO CYCLOPS AND THE OTHERS MUCH GOOD UP HERE.
I'VE GOT TO GET INSIDE.
WHICH MEANS GETTING PAST THIS GUARD...
...WITHOUT MAKING A FUSS.
URRRRKK!
BAP!
HE SHOULD BE UNCONSCIOUS LONG ENOUGH FOR ME TO DO MY JOB.
WOLVERINE WOULD HAVE HANDLED THIS DIFFERENTLY...
...BUT I HAVEN'T HIS INSTINCT FOR THE JUGULAR.

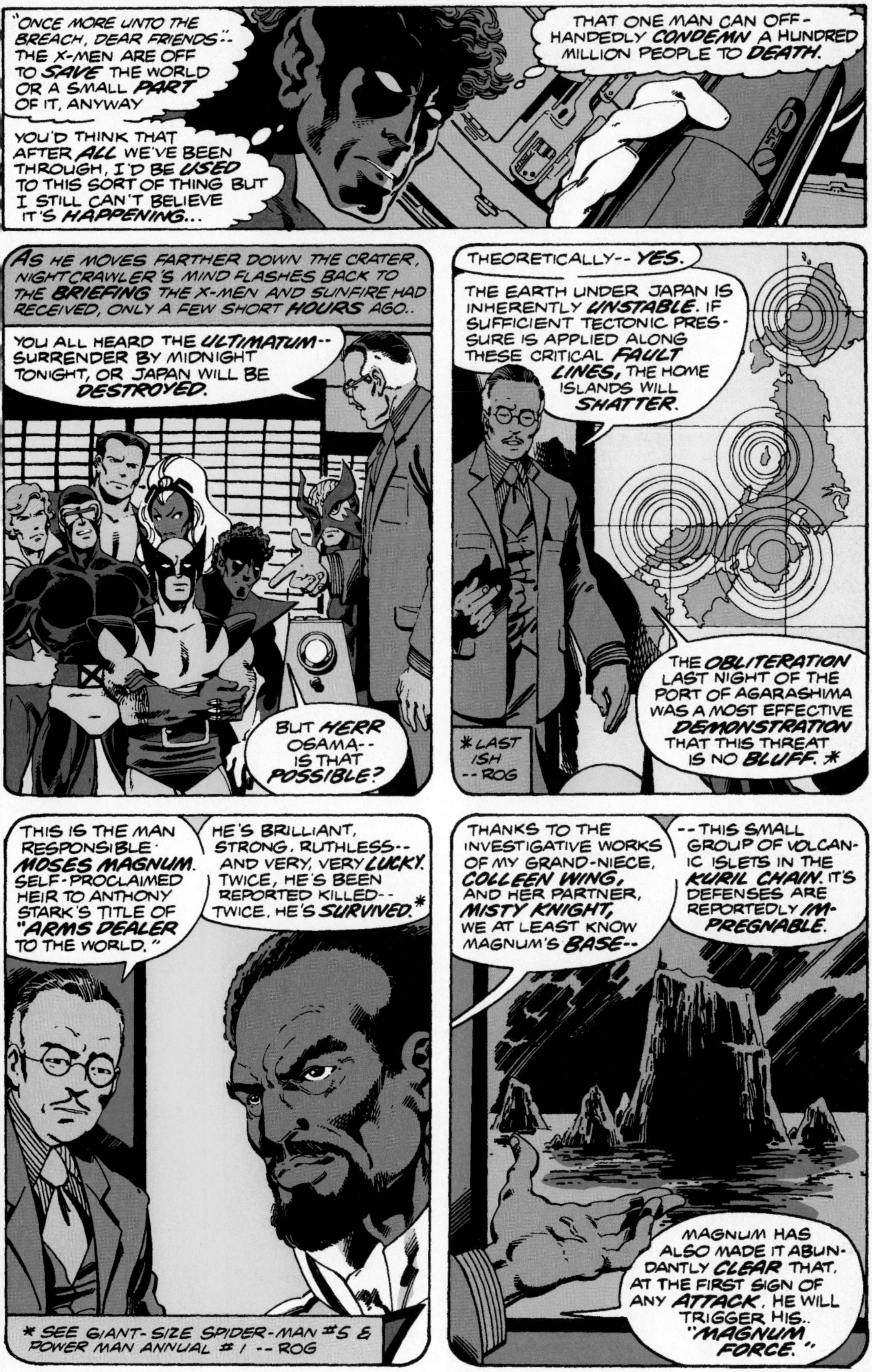
"ONCE MORE UNTO THE BREACH, DEAR FRIENDS"-- THE X-MEN ARE OFF TO SAVE THE WORLD OR A SMALL PART OF IT, ANYWAY
YOU'D THINK THAT AFTER ALL WE'VE BEEN THROUGH, I'D BE USED TO THIS SORT OF THING BUT I STILL CAN'T BELIEVE IT'S HAPPENING...
THAT ONE MAN CAN OFF-HANDEDLY CONDEMN A HUNDRED MILLION PEOPLE TO DEATH.
AS HE MOVES FARTHER DOWN THE CRATER, NIGHTCRAWLER'S MIND FLASHES BACK TO THE BRIEFING THE X-MEN AND SUNFIRE HAD RECEIVED, ONLY A FEW SHORT HOURS AGO..
YOU ALL HEARD THE ULTIMATUM-- SURRENDER BY MIDNIGHT TONIGHT, OR JAPAN WILL BE DESTROYED.
BUT HERR OSAMA-- IS THAT POSSIBLE?
THEORETICALLY-- YES.
THE EARTH UNDER JAPAN IS INHERENTLY UNSTABLE. IF SUFFICIENT TECTONIC PRES-SURE IS APPLIED ALONG THESE CRITICAL FAULT LINES, THE HOME ISLANDS WILL SHATTER.
THE OBLITERATION LAST NIGHT OF THE PORT OF AGARASHIMA WAS A MOST EFFECTIVE DEMONSTRATION THAT THIS THREAT IS NO BLUFF. *
* LAST ISH -- ROG
THIS IS THE MAN RESPONSIBLE. MOSES MAGNUM. SELF-PROCLAIMED HEIR TO ANTHONY STARK'S TITLE OF "ARMS DEALER TO THE WORLD."
HE'S BRILLIANT, STRONG, RUTHLESS-- AND VERY, VERY LUCKY. TWICE, HE'S BEEN REPORTED KILLED-- TWICE, HE'S SURVIVED.*
* SEE GIANT-SIZE SPIDER-MAN #5 & POWER MAN ANNUAL #1 -- ROG
THANKS TO THE INVESTIGATIVE WORKS OF MY GRAND-NIECE, COLLEEN WING, AND HER PARTNER, MISTY KNIGHT, WE AT LEAST KNOW MAGNUM'S BASE--
-- THIS SMALL GROUP OF VOLCAN-IC ISLETS IN THE KURIL CHAIN. IT'S DEFENSES ARE REPORTEDLY IM-PREGNABLE.
MAGNUM HAS ALSO MADE IT ABUN-DANTLY CLEAR THAT, AT THE FIRST SIGN OF ANY ATTACK, HE WILL TRIGGER HIS.. "MAGNUM FORCE."

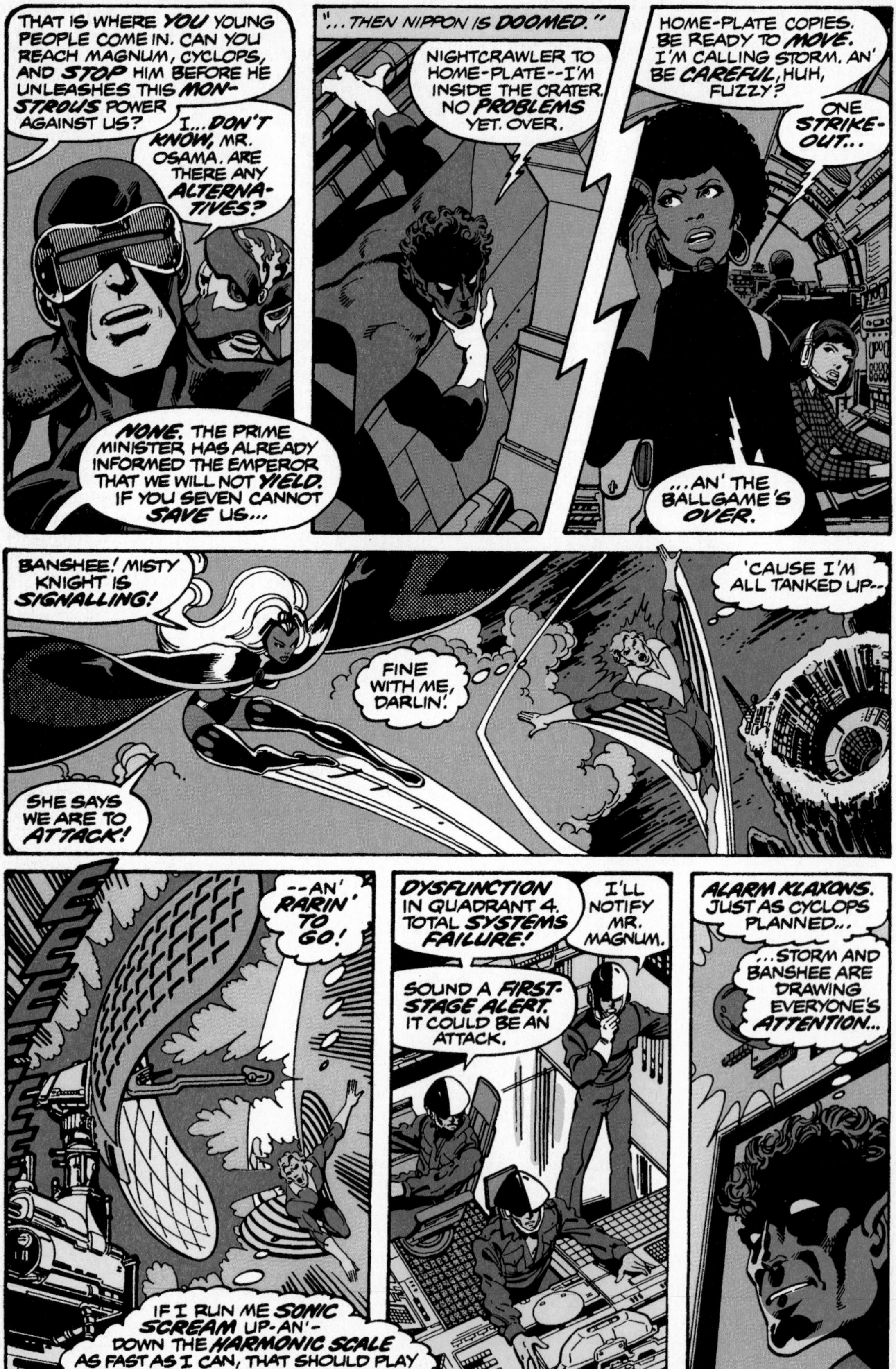
THAT IS WHERE YOU YOUNG PEOPLE COME IN. CAN YOU REACH MAGNUM, CYCLOPS, AND STOP HIM BEFORE HE UNLEASHES THIS MONSTROUS POWER AGAINST US?
I... DON'T KNOW, MR. OSAMA. ARE THERE ANY ALTERNATIVES?
NONE. THE PRIME MINISTER HAS ALREADY INFORMED THE EMPEROR THAT WE WILL NOT YIELD. IF YOU SEVEN CANNOT SAVE US...
"...THEN NIPPON IS DOOMED."
NIGHTCRAWLER TO HOME-PLATE--I'M INSIDE THE CRATER. NO PROBLEMS YET. OVER.
HOME-PLATE COPIES. BE READY TO MOVE. I'M CALLING STORM. AN' BE CAREFUL, HUH, FUZZY?
ONE STRIKE-OUT...
...AN' THE BALLGAME'S OVER.
BANSHEE! MISTY KNIGHT IS SIGNALLING!
SHE SAYS WE ARE TO ATTACK!
FINE WITH ME, DARLIN'.
'CAUSE I'M ALL TANKED UP--
--AN' RARIN' TO GO!
IF I RUN ME SONIC SCREAM UP-AN'-DOWN THE HARMONIC SCALE AS FAST AS I CAN, THAT SHOULD PLAY MERRY HOB WITH MAGNUM'S SCANNERS.
DYSFUNCTION IN QUADRANT 4. TOTAL SYSTEMS FAILURE!
I'LL NOTIFY MR. MAGNUM.
SOUND A FIRST-STAGE ALERT. IT COULD BE AN ATTACK.
ALARM KLAXONS. JUST AS CYCLOPS PLANNED...
...STORM AND BANSHEE ARE DRAWING EVERYONE'S ATTENTION...

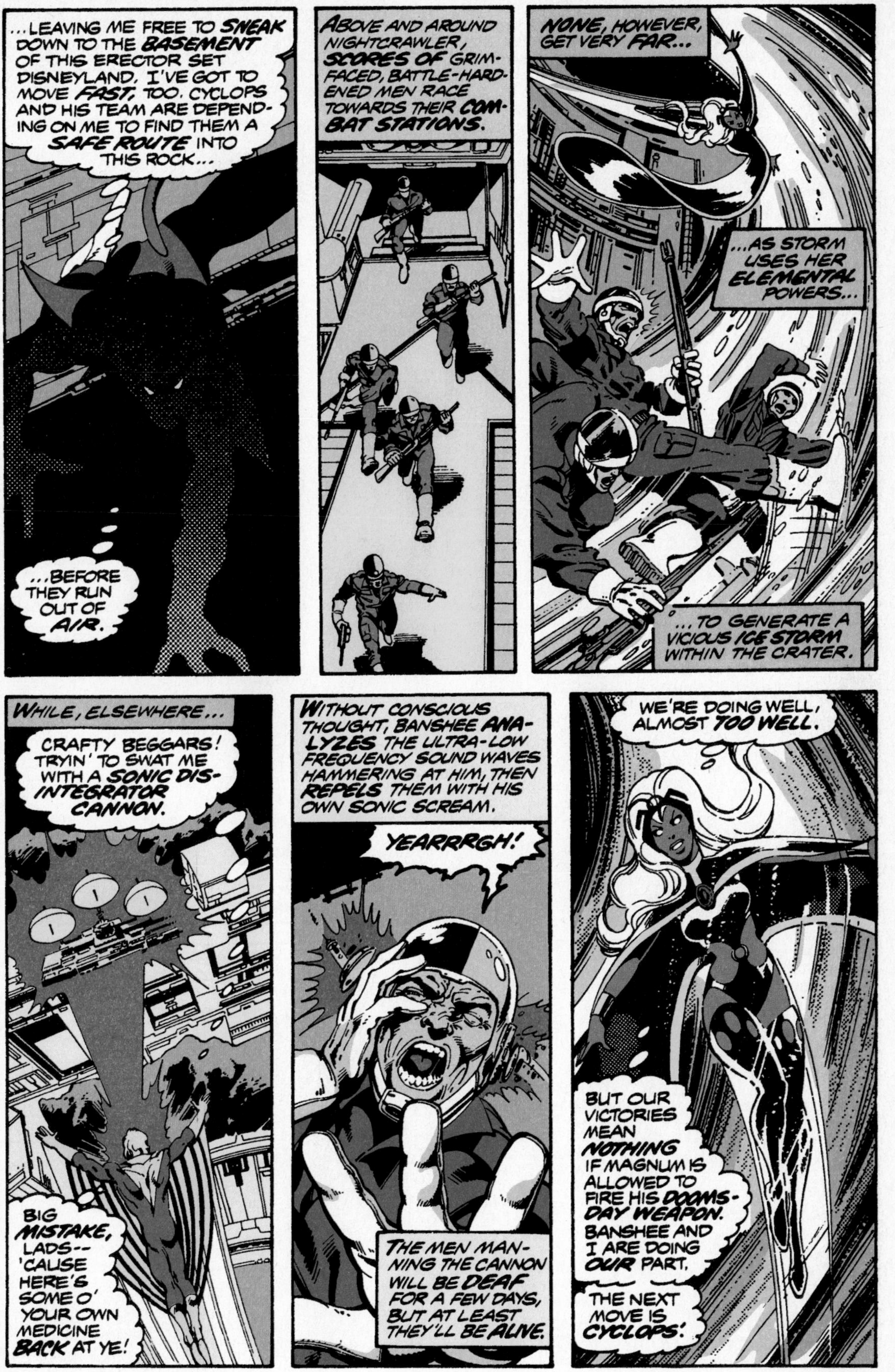

...LEAVING ME FREE TO SNEAK DOWN TO THE BASEMENT OF THIS ERECTOR SET DISNEYLAND. I'VE GOT TO MOVE FAST, TOO. CYCLOPS AND HIS TEAM ARE DEPENDING ON ME TO FIND THEM A SAFE ROUTE INTO THIS ROCK...
...BEFORE THEY RUN OUT OF AIR.
ABOVE AND AROUND NIGHTCRAWLER, SCORES OF GRIM-FACED, BATTLE-HARDENED MEN RACE TOWARDS THEIR COMBAT STATIONS.
NONE, HOWEVER, GET VERY FAR...
...AS STORM USES HER ELEMENTAL POWERS...
...TO GENERATE A VICIOUS ICE STORM WITHIN THE CRATER.
WHILE, ELSEWHERE...
CRAFTY BEGGARS! TRYIN' TO SWAT ME WITH A SONIC DISINTEGRATOR CANNON.
BIG MISTAKE, LADS-- 'CAUSE HERE'S SOME O' YOUR OWN MEDICINE BACK AT YE!
WITHOUT CONSCIOUS THOUGHT, BANSHEE ANALYZES THE ULTRA-LOW FREQUENCY SOUND WAVES HAMMERING AT HIM, THEN REPELS THEM WITH HIS OWN SONIC SCREAM.
YEARRRGH!
THE MEN MANNING THE CANNON WILL BE DEAF FOR A FEW DAYS, BUT AT LEAST THEY'LL BE ALIVE.
WE'RE DOING WELL, ALMOST TOO WELL.
BUT OUR VICTORIES MEAN NOTHING IF MAGNUM IS ALLOWED TO FIRE HIS DOOMSDAY WEAPON. BANSHEE AND I ARE DOING OUR PART.
THE NEXT MOVE IS CYCLOPS'.

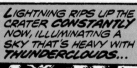

LIGHTNING RIPS UP THE CRATER *CONSTANTLY* NOW, ILLUMINATING A SKY THAT'S HEAVY WITH *THUNDERCLOUDS...*

...AS STORM'S POWERS BEGIN TO *EFFECT* WEATHER PATTERNS AROUND THE ISLAND...

...THE *DISRUPTION* SPREADING QUICKLY, LIKE *RIPPLES* ACROSS A POND.

AT THE SAME TIME, JUST OFF-SHORE AND ABOUT A HUNDRED FEET BELOW THE SEA BED...

...THE REST OF THE X-MEN--AND SUN-FIRE--ARE MAKING THEIR WAY TOWARDS MAGNUM'S BASE IN A STYLE UNIQUELY THEIR OWN.

HOW'S YOUR *POWER* HOLDING UP, SUN-FIRE?

I HAVE *SUFFICIENT.* BUT I WOULD PREFER USING IT IN A MORE *DIRECT* ATTACK, STEALING UP ON MAGNUM WITH THIS *TUNNEL...*

...I FEEL MORE LIKE A *THIEF* IN THE NIGHT THAN A *SAMURAI.*

ARE YOU ALL RIGHT, WOLVERINE? THE *HEAT--!*

I'VE STOOD *WORSE.*

IT'S THE *ONLY* WAY OF REACHING THE HEART OF MAGNUM'S COMPLEX *UNDETECTED.*

STILL NO *SIGNAL* FROM NIGHTCRAWLER. WITHOUT HIS RADIO BEAM TO GIVE US A PRECISE TARGET, WE'RE *STUCK.*

TUNNELING *BLIND,* WE COULD PUNCH THROUGH TO THE OCEAN INSTEAD OF MAGNUM'S BASE. WHERE *ARE* YOU, MISTER?! WE'RE RUNNING OUT OF TIME--AND *AIR!*

THIS CHAMBER LOOKS *PERFECT--* BUT IT TOOK *LONGER* THAN I THOUGHT TO FIND IT.

I'D BETTER ACTIVATE THE *HOMER.* CYCLOPS MUST BE GETTING *WORRIED.*

WAS IST--?!? THAT *SOUND--!?!*

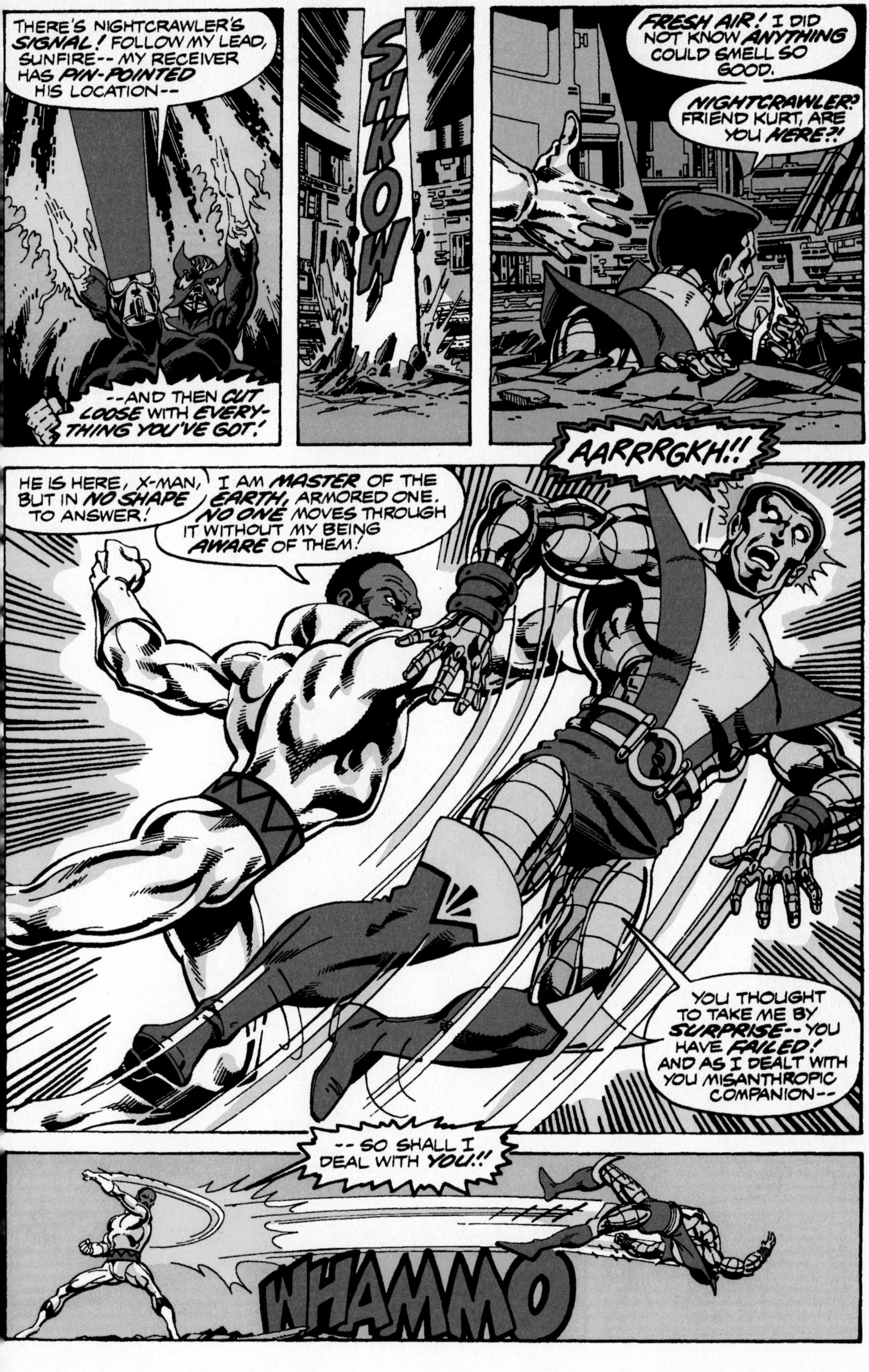

THERE'S NIGHTCRAWLER'S SIGNAL! FOLLOW MY LEAD, SUNFIRE-- MY RECEIVER HAS PIN-POINTED HIS LOCATION--
--AND THEN CUT LOOSE WITH EVERY-THING YOU'VE GOT!
SHKOW
FRESH AIR! I DID NOT KNOW ANYTHING COULD SMELL SO GOOD.
NIGHTCRAWLER? FRIEND KURT, ARE YOU HERE?!
AARRRGKH!!
HE IS HERE, X-MAN, BUT IN NO SHAPE TO ANSWER!
I AM MASTER OF THE EARTH, ARMORED ONE. NO ONE MOVES THROUGH IT WITHOUT MY BEING AWARE OF THEM!
YOU THOUGHT TO TAKE ME BY SURPRISE-- YOU HAVE FAILED! AND AS I DEALT WITH YOU MISANTHROPIC COMPANION--
-- SO SHALL I DEAL WITH YOU!!
WHAMMO

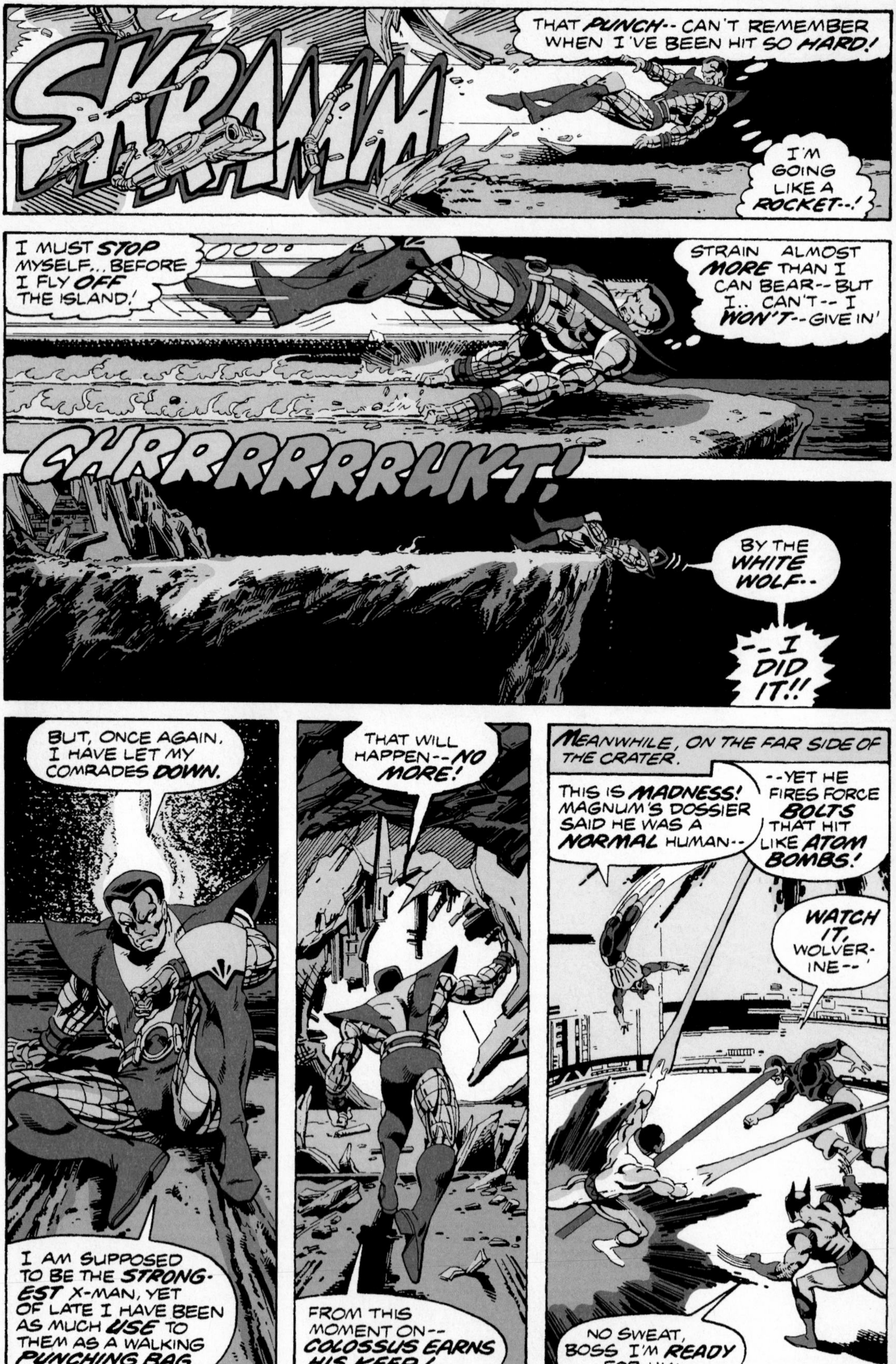
SKRAMM
THAT PUNCH-- CAN'T REMEMBER WHEN I'VE BEEN HIT SO HARD!
I'M GOING LIKE A ROCKET--!
I MUST STOP MYSELF... BEFORE I FLY OFF THE ISLAND!
STRAIN ALMOST MORE THAN I CAN BEAR-- BUT I.. CAN'T-- I WON'T-- GIVE IN!
CHRRRRRRUKT!
BY THE WHITE WOLF--
--I DID IT!!
BUT, ONCE AGAIN, I HAVE LET MY COMRADES DOWN.
I AM SUPPOSED TO BE THE STRONG-EST X-MAN, YET OF LATE I HAVE BEEN AS MUCH USE TO THEM AS A WALKING PUNCHING BAG.
THAT WILL HAPPEN--NO MORE!
FROM THIS MOMENT ON-- COLOSSUS EARNS HIS KEEP!
MEANWHILE, ON THE FAR SIDE OF THE CRATER.
THIS IS MADNESS! MAGNUM'S DOSSIER SAID HE WAS A NORMAL HUMAN--
--YET HE FIRES FORCE BOLTS THAT HIT LIKE ATOM BOMBS!
WATCH IT, WOLVER-INE--!
NO SWEAT, BOSS I'M READY FOR HIM

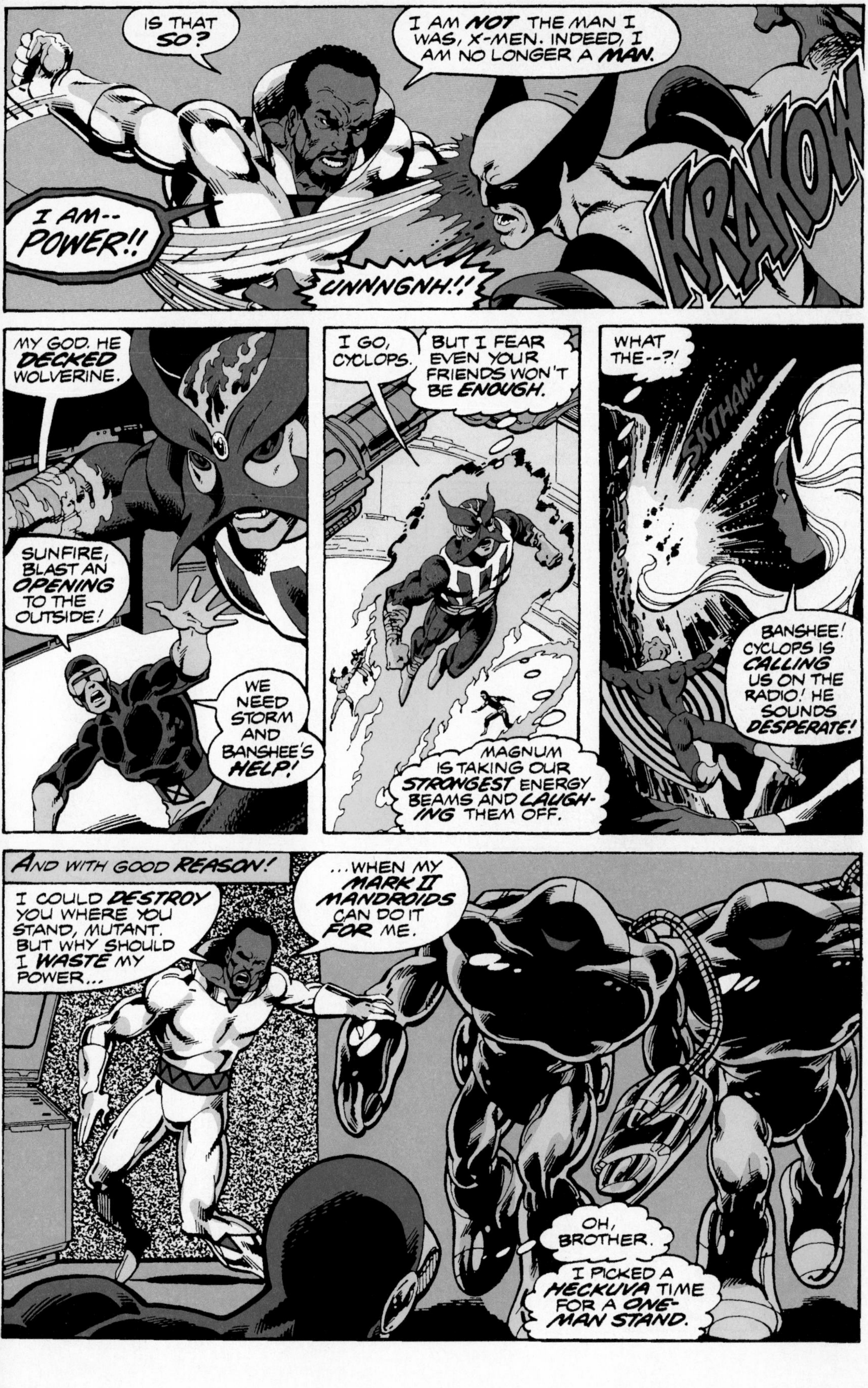
IS THAT SO?
I AM NOT THE MAN I WAS, X-MEN. INDEED, I AM NO LONGER A MAN.
I AM-- POWER!!
KRAKOW
UNNNGNH!!
MY GOD. HE DECKED WOLVERINE.
SUNFIRE, BLAST AN OPENING TO THE OUTSIDE!
WE NEED STORM AND BANSHEE'S HELP!
I GO, CYCLOPS.
BUT I FEAR EVEN YOUR FRIENDS WON'T BE ENOUGH.
MAGNUM IS TAKING OUR STRONGEST ENERGY BEAMS AND LAUGHING THEM OFF.
WHAT THE--?!
SKTHAM!
BANSHEE! CYCLOPS IS CALLING US ON THE RADIO! HE SOUNDS DESPERATE!
AND WITH GOOD REASON!
I COULD DESTROY YOU WHERE YOU STAND, MUTANT. BUT WHY SHOULD I WASTE MY POWER...
...WHEN MY MARK II MANDROIDS CAN DO IT FOR ME.
OH, BROTHER.
I PICKED A HECKUVA TIME FOR A ONE-MAN STAND.

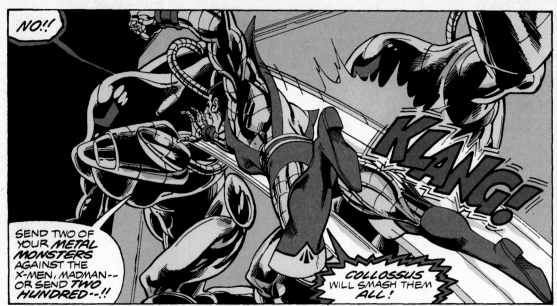

NO!!

KLANG!

SEND TWO OF YOUR *METAL MONSTERS* AGAINST THE X-MEN, MADMAN-- OR SEND *TWO HUNDRED*--!!

COLLOSSUS WILL SMASH THEM *ALL*!

THE BATTLE'S *SHORT-AND-SWEET* AS COLOSSUS, MOVING WITH A SPEED THAT'S *BELIED* BY HIS MASSIVE ARMORED FORM...

...*TRASHES* THE MAN-DROIDS FROM ONE END OF THE CHAMBER TO THE OTHER, *TAKING* THEIR PUNCHES, DODGING THEIR *LASERS*...

...TOSSING THE *VANADIUM STEEL* COMBAT SUITS AROUND LIKE THEY WERE *RAG DOLLS.*

UNTIL....

YOU'VE WON A *BATTLE,* MUTANTS --BUT YOU'LL *LOSE* THE WAR!

I *SWORE* THAT, IF ATTACKED, I WOULD *DESTROY JAPAN!*

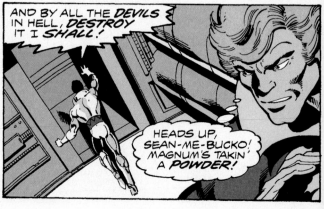

AND BY ALL THE *DEVILS* IN HELL, *DESTROY* IT I *SHALL!*

HEADS UP, SEAN-ME-BUCKO! MAGNUM'S TAKIN' A *POWDER!*

TOO SLOW, CURSE THE LUCK! HE GOT AWAY!

I MUST BE GETTIN' OLD.

BUT ONCE I BLAST THESE DOORS, I'LL-- NO GOOD! SOMETHIN'S DEFLECTIN' ME SONIC SCREAM. WHAT NOW?! WE CAN'T STAND HERE AND LET MAGNUM SINK JAPAN.

WAIT A MINUTE! MR. OSAMA SAID THAT HIS SCIENTISTS FIGURED THE AGARASHIMA 'QUAKE WAS TRIGGERED BY AN INTENSE BEAM OF ENERGY.

AN', ON THE RADIO, I HEARD SUNFIRE SCREAMIN' ABOUT MAGNUM FIRIN' ENERGY BLASTS.

IT'S A LONG SHOT, BUT I'VE GOT TO PLAY IT. IF THE 'MAGNUM FORCE' IS SOME KIND OF ENERGY BEAM...

...THEN I'M THE ONLY X-MAN WHO HAS A PRAYER O' STOPPIN' IT!

CYCLOPS-- GET EVERYONE OFF THIS ROCK! AN' FOR PITY'S SAKE-- HURRY!

I WARNED THEM, BUT THOSE SENILE OLD FOOLS IN TOKYO WOULDN'T LISTEN. NOW THEY'LL LEARN ONCE AND FOR ALL...

...THAT MOSES MAGNUM IS NOT TO BE TRIFLED WITH!

AS HE RUNS, HE CAN FEEL THE POWER BURNING WITHIN HIM, STRUGGLING TO BE FREE...

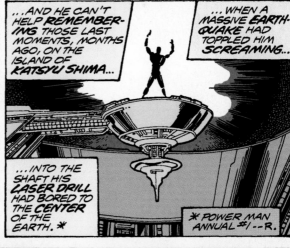

...AND HE CAN'T HELP REMEMBERING THOSE LAST MOMENTS, MONTHS AGO, ON THE ISLAND OF KATSYU SHIMA...

...WHEN A MASSIVE EARTHQUAKE HAD TOPPLED HIM SCREAMING...

...INTO THE SHAFT HIS LASER DRILL HAD BORED TO THE CENTER OF THE EARTH. *

* POWER MAN ANNUAL #1 --R.

HE SHOULD HAVE DIED. BUT, AS HE FELL, THE LASER BEAM, THE EXOTIC WEAPONRY OF HIS COMBAT SUIT, THE ELEMENTAL FORCE OF THE 'QUAKE ITSELF...

...HAD ALL COMBINED WITHIN HIM IN SOME MAD, ARCANE FASHION TO GIVE HIM THE POWER PRIMAL-- THE ABILITY TO FOCUS AN INFINITE AMOUNT OF ENERGY ANYWHERE ON EARTH, IN ANY MANNER HE CHOSE...

IN THIS CASE, TO CREATE AN EARTHQUAKE.

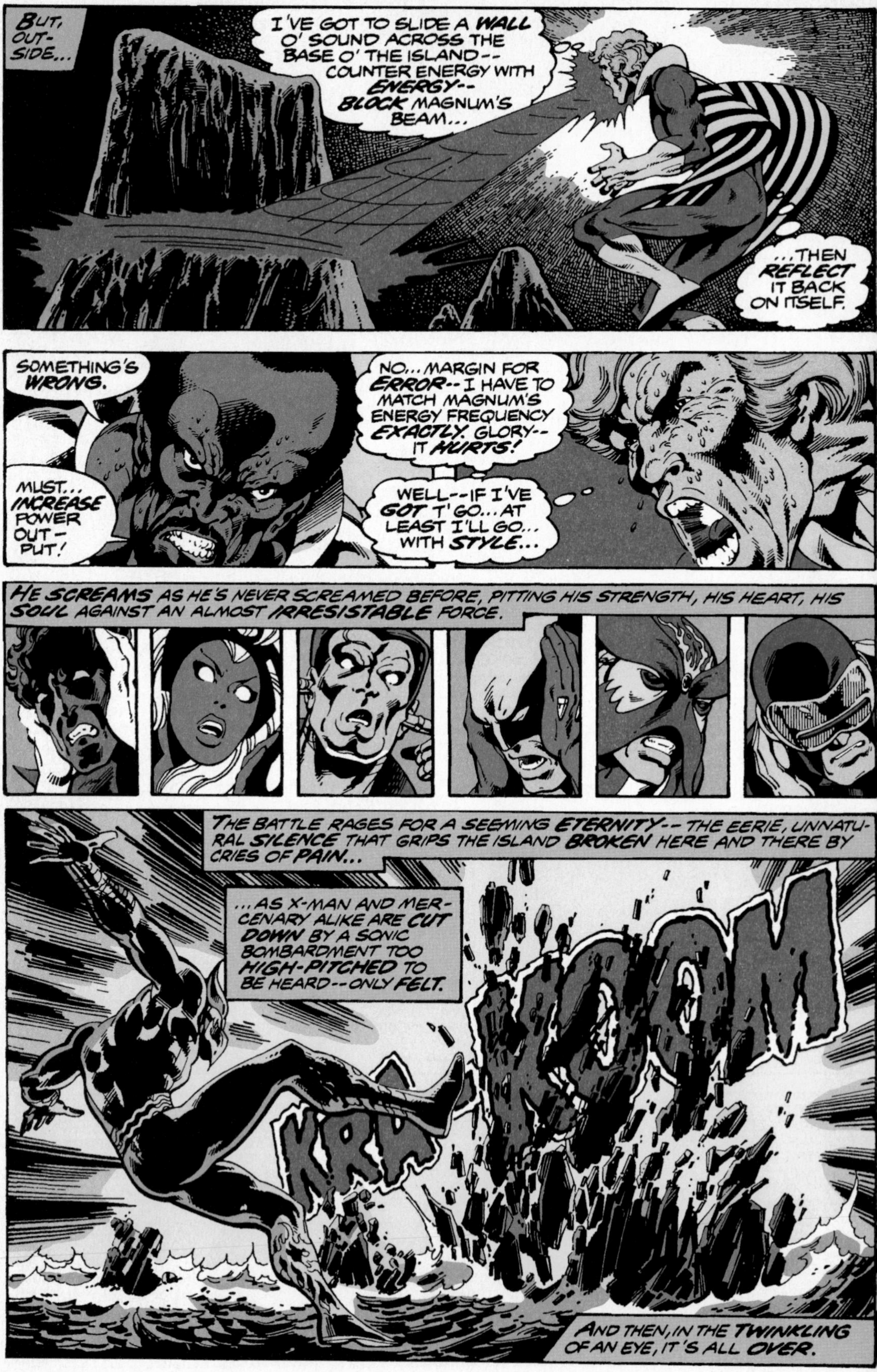

BUT, OUT-SIDE...
I'VE GOT TO SLIDE A WALL O' SOUND ACROSS THE BASE O' THE ISLAND-- COUNTER ENERGY WITH ENERGY-- BLOCK MAGNUM'S BEAM...
...THEN REFLECT IT BACK ON ITSELF.
SOMETHING'S WRONG.
MUST... INCREASE POWER OUT-PUT!
NO... MARGIN FOR ERROR-- I HAVE TO MATCH MAGNUM'S ENERGY FREQUENCY EXACTLY. GLORY-- IT HURTS!
WELL--IF I'VE GOT T'GO... AT LEAST I'LL GO... WITH STYLE...
HE SCREAMS AS HE'S NEVER SCREAMED BEFORE, PITTING HIS STRENGTH, HIS HEART, HIS SOUL AGAINST AN ALMOST IRRESISTABLE FORCE.
THE BATTLE RAGES FOR A SEEMING ETERNITY-- THE EERIE, UNNATURAL SILENCE THAT GRIPS THE ISLAND BROKEN HERE AND THERE BY CRIES OF PAIN...
...AS X-MAN AND MERCENARY ALIKE ARE CUT DOWN BY A SONIC BOMBARDMENT TOO HIGH-PITCHED TO BE HEARD--ONLY FELT.
KRA-VOOM
AND THEN, IN THE TWINKLING OF AN EYE, IT'S ALL OVER.

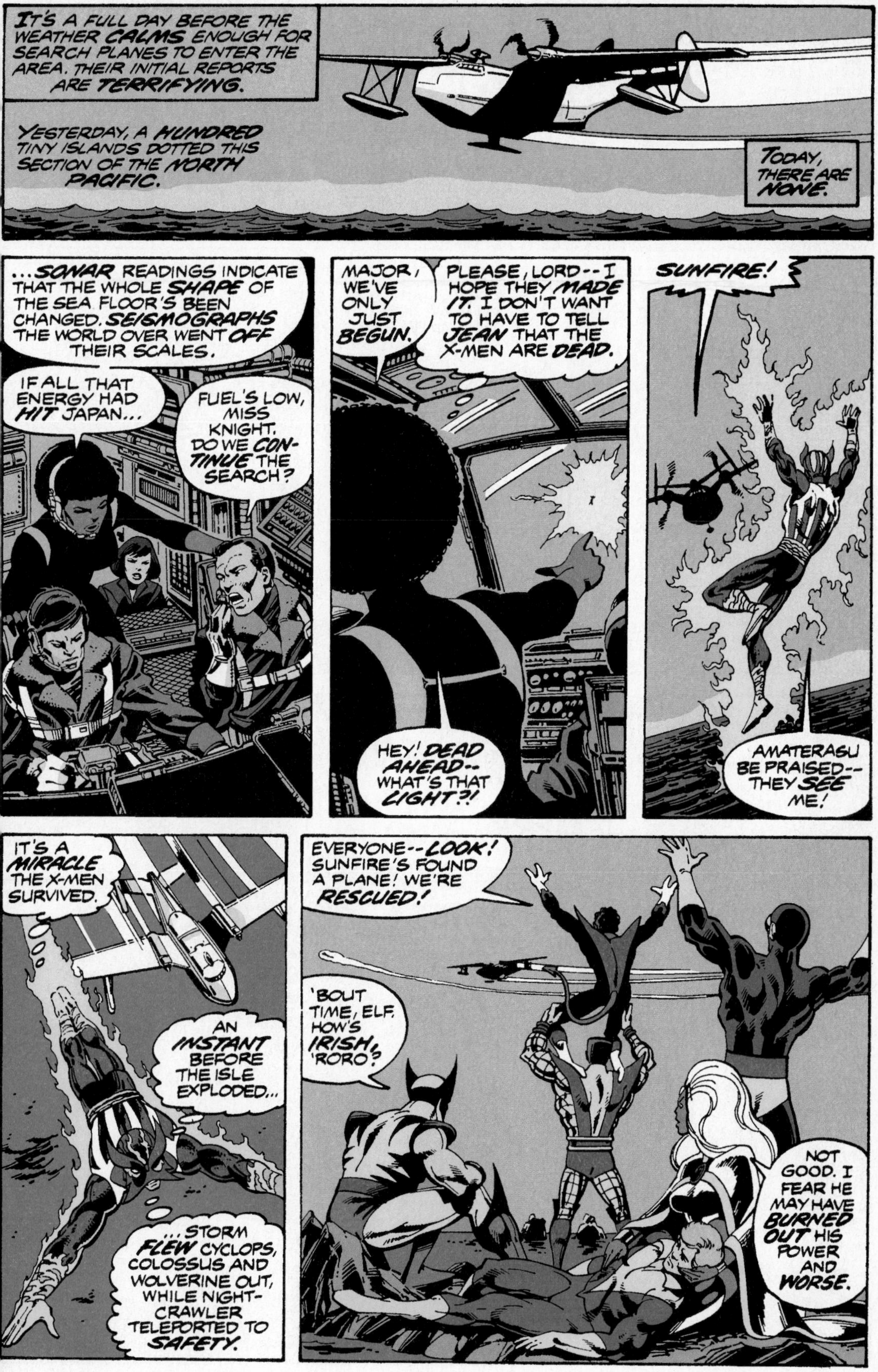
IT'S A FULL DAY BEFORE THE WEATHER CALMS ENOUGH FOR SEARCH PLANES TO ENTER THE AREA. THEIR INITIAL REPORTS ARE TERRIFYING.
YESTERDAY, A HUNDRED TINY ISLANDS DOTTED THIS SECTION OF THE NORTH PACIFIC.
TODAY, THERE ARE NONE.
...SONAR READINGS INDICATE THAT THE WHOLE SHAPE OF THE SEA FLOOR'S BEEN CHANGED. SEISMOGRAPHS THE WORLD OVER WENT OFF THEIR SCALES.
IF ALL THAT ENERGY HAD HIT JAPAN...
FUEL'S LOW, MISS KNIGHT. DO WE CONTINUE THE SEARCH?
MAJOR, WE'VE ONLY JUST BEGUN.
PLEASE, LORD--I HOPE THEY MADE IT. I DON'T WANT TO HAVE TO TELL JEAN THAT THE X-MEN ARE DEAD.
HEY! DEAD AHEAD--WHAT'S THAT LIGHT?!
SUNFIRE!
AMATERASU BE PRAISED--THEY SEE ME!
IT'S A MIRACLE THE X-MEN SURVIVED.
AN INSTANT BEFORE THE ISLE EXPLODED...
...STORM FLEW CYCLOPS, COLOSSUS AND WOLVERINE OUT, WHILE NIGHT-CRAWLER TELEPORTED TO SAFETY.
EVERYONE--LOOK! SUNFIRE'S FOUND A PLANE! WE'RE RESCUED!
'BOUT TIME, ELF. HOW'S IRISH, 'RORO?
NOT GOOD. I FEAR HE MAY HAVE BURNED OUT HIS POWER AND WORSE.

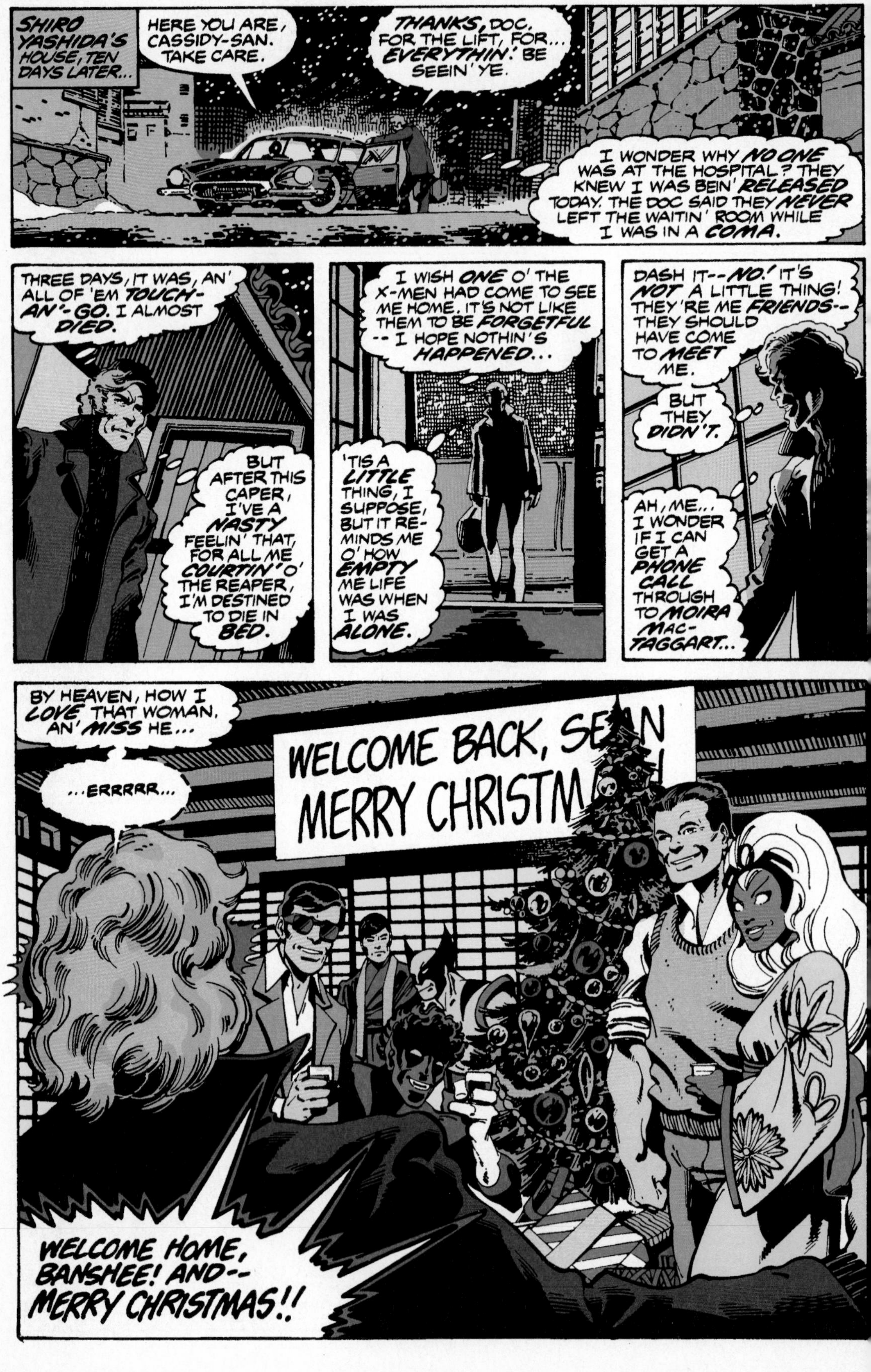
SHIRO YASHIDA'S HOUSE, TEN DAYS LATER...
HERE YOU ARE, CASSIDY-SAN. TAKE CARE.
THANKS, DOC. FOR THE LIFT, FOR... EVERYTHIN'. BE SEEIN' YE.
I WONDER WHY NO ONE WAS AT THE HOSPITAL? THEY KNEW I WAS BEIN' RELEASED TODAY. THE DOC SAID THEY NEVER LEFT THE WAITIN' ROOM WHILE I WAS IN A COMA.
THREE DAYS, IT WAS, AN' ALL OF 'EM TOUCH-AN'-GO. I ALMOST DIED.
BUT AFTER THIS CAPER, I'VE A NASTY FEELIN' THAT, FOR ALL ME COURTIN' O' THE REAPER, I'M DESTINED TO DIE IN BED.
I WISH ONE O' THE X-MEN HAD COME TO SEE ME HOME. IT'S NOT LIKE THEM TO BE FORGETFUL -- I HOPE NOTHIN'S HAPPENED...
'TIS A LITTLE THING, I SUPPOSE, BUT IT REMINDS ME O' HOW EMPTY ME LIFE WAS WHEN I WAS ALONE.
DASH IT--NO! IT'S NOT A LITTLE THING! THEY'RE ME FRIENDS--THEY SHOULD HAVE COME TO MEET ME.
BUT THEY DIDN'T.
AH, ME... I WONDER IF I CAN GET A PHONE CALL THROUGH TO MOIRA MACTAGGART...
BY HEAVEN, HOW I LOVE THAT WOMAN, AN' MISS HE...
...ERRRRR...
WELCOME BACK, SE N
MERRY CHRISTM
WELCOME HOME, BANSHEE! AND--MERRY CHRISTMAS!!

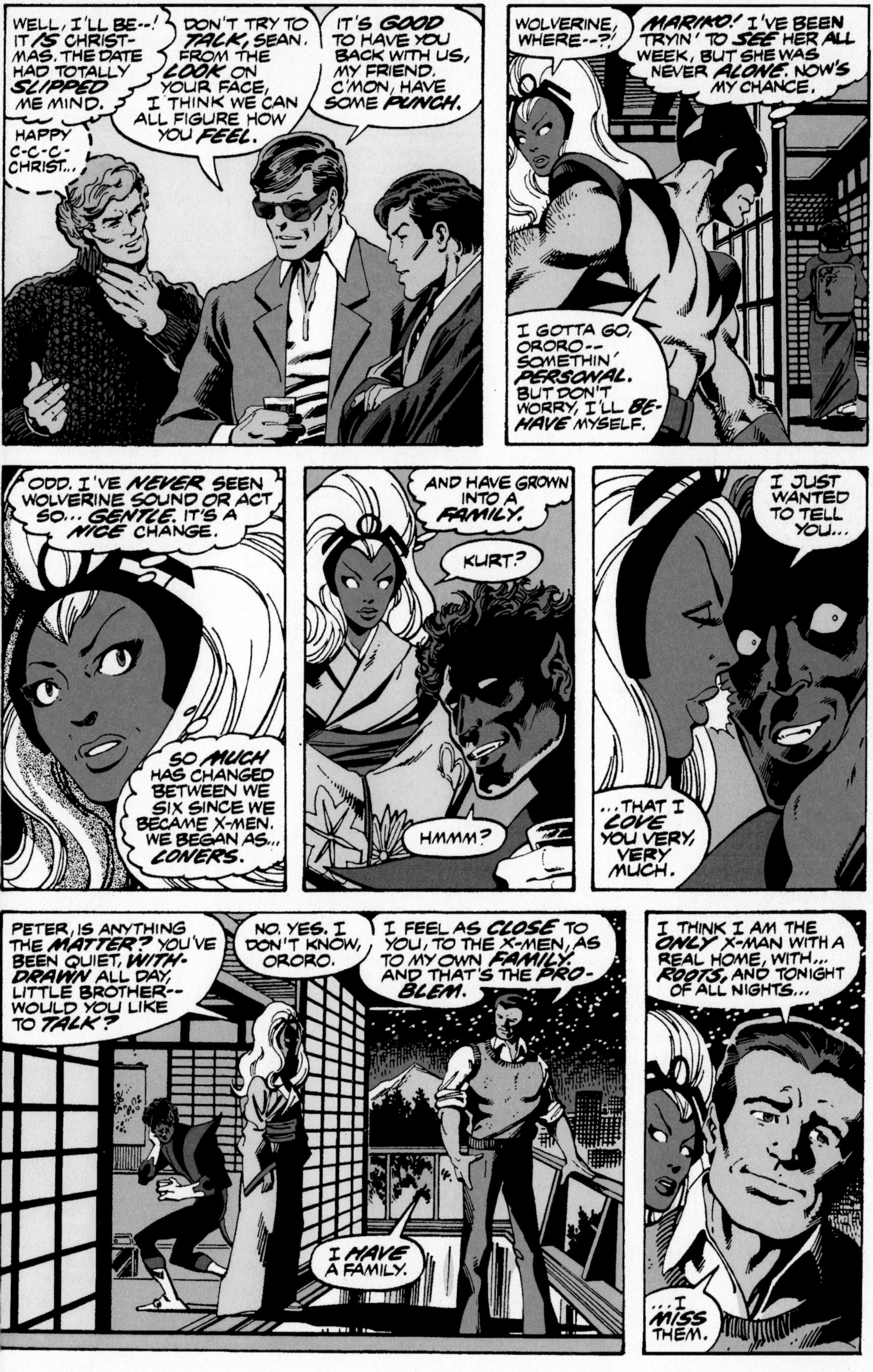
WELL, I'LL BE--! IT IS CHRISTMAS. THE DATE HAD TOTALLY SLIPPED ME MIND.
HAPPY C-C-C-CHRIST...
DON'T TRY TO TALK, SEAN. FROM THE LOOK ON YOUR FACE, I THINK WE CAN ALL FIGURE HOW YOU FEEL.
IT'S GOOD TO HAVE YOU BACK WITH US, MY FRIEND. C'MON, HAVE SOME PUNCH.
WOLVERINE, WHERE--?!
MARIKO! I'VE BEEN TRYIN' TO SEE HER ALL WEEK, BUT SHE WAS NEVER ALONE. NOW'S MY CHANCE.
I GOTTA GO, ORORO-- SOMETHIN' PERSONAL. BUT DON'T WORRY, I'LL BEHAVE MYSELF.
ODD. I'VE NEVER SEEN WOLVERINE SOUND OR ACT SO... GENTLE. IT'S A NICE CHANGE.
SO MUCH HAS CHANGED BETWEEN WE SIX SINCE WE BECAME X-MEN. WE BEGAN AS... LONERS.
AND HAVE GROWN INTO A FAMILY.
KURT?
HMMM?
I JUST WANTED TO TELL YOU...
...THAT I LOVE YOU VERY, VERY MUCH.
PETER, IS ANYTHING THE MATTER? YOU'VE BEEN QUIET, WITHDRAWN ALL DAY, LITTLE BROTHER-- WOULD YOU LIKE TO TALK?
NO. YES. I DON'T KNOW, ORORO.
I FEEL AS CLOSE TO YOU, TO THE X-MEN, AS TO MY OWN FAMILY. AND THAT'S THE PROBLEM.
I HAVE A FAMILY.
I THINK I AM THE ONLY X-MAN WITH A REAL HOME, WITH... ROOTS, AND TONIGHT OF ALL NIGHTS...
...I MISS THEM.

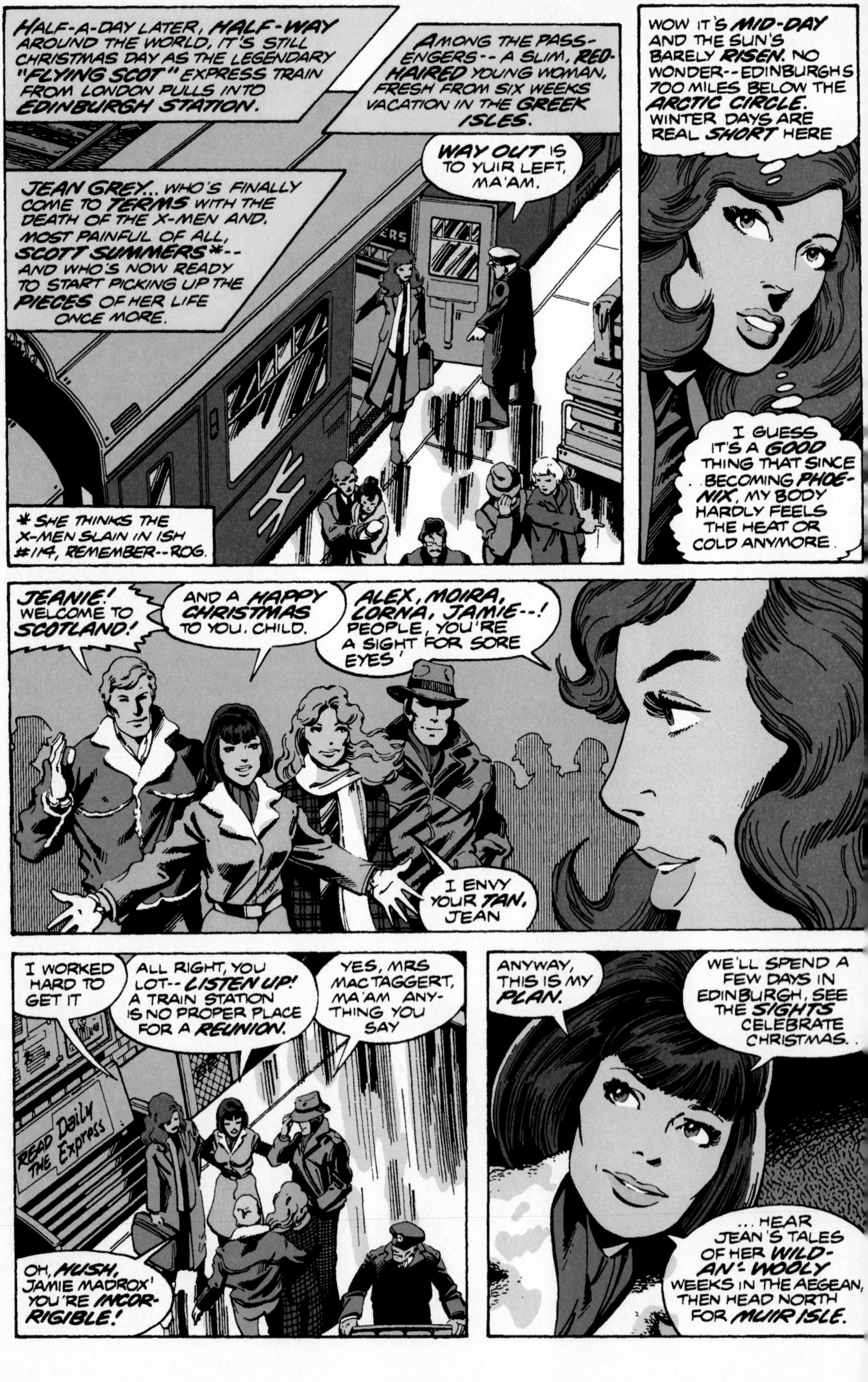
HALF-A-DAY LATER, HALF-WAY AROUND THE WORLD, IT'S STILL CHRISTMAS DAY AS THE LEGENDARY "FLYING SCOT" EXPRESS TRAIN FROM LONDON PULLS INTO EDINBURGH STATION.
AMONG THE PASSENGERS-- A SLIM, RED-HAIRED YOUNG WOMAN, FRESH FROM SIX WEEKS VACATION IN THE GREEK ISLES.
JEAN GREY... WHO'S FINALLY COME TO TERMS WITH THE DEATH OF THE X-MEN AND, MOST PAINFUL OF ALL, SCOTT SUMMERS*-- AND WHO'S NOW READY TO START PICKING UP THE PIECES OF HER LIFE ONCE MORE.
WAY OUT IS TO YUIR LEFT, MA'AM.
* SHE THINKS THE X-MEN SLAIN IN ISH #114, REMEMBER--ROG.
WOW IT'S MID-DAY AND THE SUN'S BARELY RISEN. NO WONDER--EDINBURGH'S 700 MILES BELOW THE ARCTIC CIRCLE. WINTER DAYS ARE REAL SHORT HERE
I GUESS IT'S A GOOD THING THAT SINCE BECOMING PHOENIX, MY BODY HARDLY FEELS THE HEAT OR COLD ANYMORE.
JEANIE! WELCOME TO SCOTLAND!
AND A HAPPY CHRISTMAS TO YOU, CHILD.
ALEX, MOIRA, LORNA, JAMIE--! PEOPLE, YOU'RE A SIGHT FOR SORE EYES!
I ENVY YOUR TAN, JEAN
I WORKED HARD TO GET IT
ALL RIGHT, YOU LOT--LISTEN UP! A TRAIN STATION IS NO PROPER PLACE FOR A REUNION.
YES, MRS MACTAGGERT, MA'AM ANYTHING YOU SAY
READ THE Daily Express
OH, HUSH, JAMIE MADROX! YOU'RE INCORRIGIBLE!
ANYWAY, THIS IS MY PLAN.
WE'LL SPEND A FEW DAYS IN EDINBURGH, SEE THE SIGHTS CELEBRATE CHRISTMAS.
...HEAR JEAN'S TALES OF HER WILD-AN'-WOOLY WEEKS IN THE AEGEAN, THEN HEAD NORTH FOR MUIR ISLE.

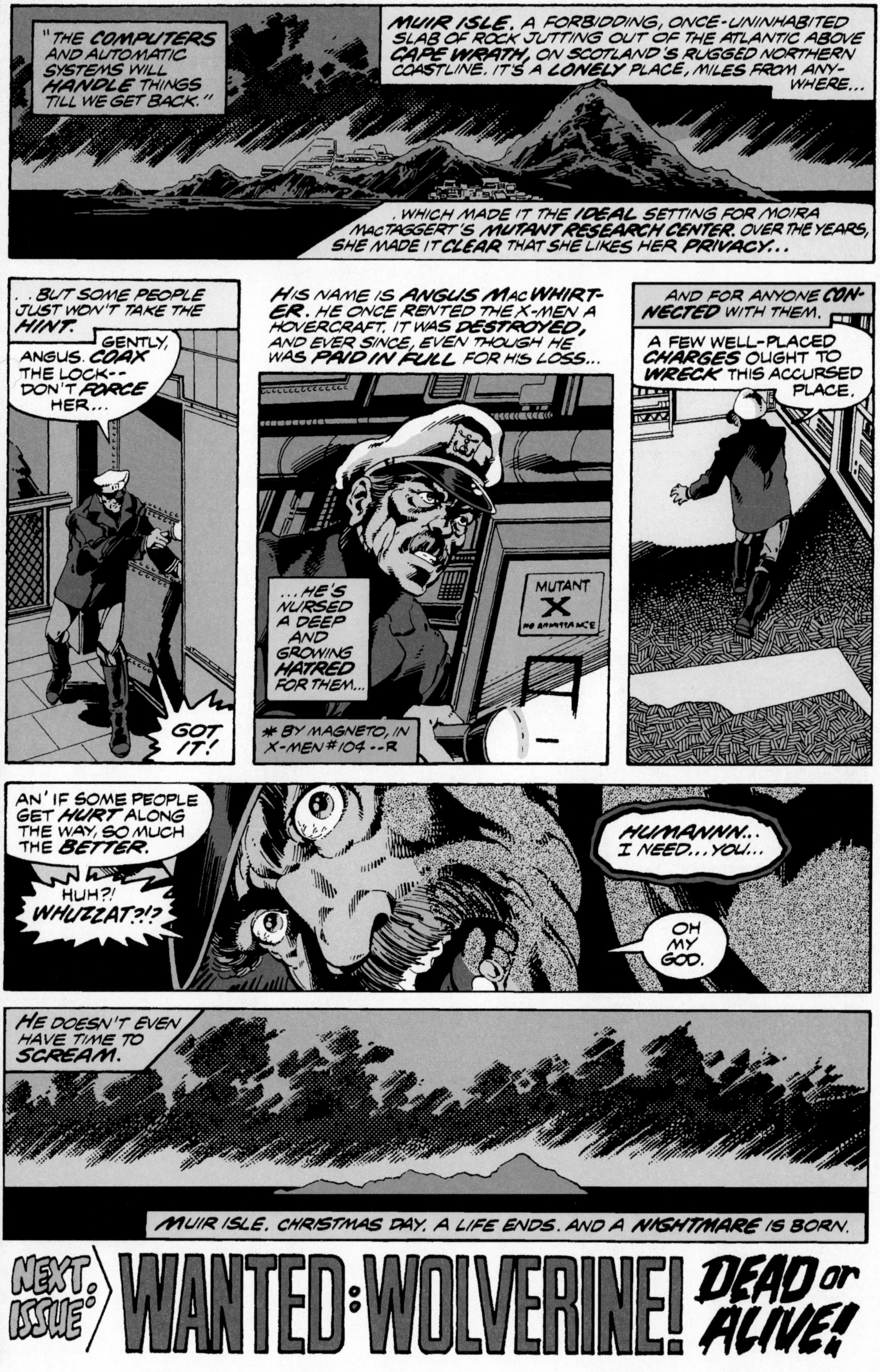
"THE COMPUTERS AND AUTOMATIC SYSTEMS WILL HANDLE THINGS TILL WE GET BACK."
MUIR ISLE. A FORBIDDING, ONCE-UNINHABITED SLAB OF ROCK JUTTING OUT OF THE ATLANTIC ABOVE CAPE WRATH, ON SCOTLAND'S RUGGED NORTHERN COASTLINE. IT'S A LONELY PLACE, MILES FROM ANYWHERE...
...WHICH MADE IT THE IDEAL SETTING FOR MOIRA MACTAGGERT'S MUTANT RESEARCH CENTER. OVER THE YEARS, SHE MADE IT CLEAR THAT SHE LIKES HER PRIVACY...
...BUT SOME PEOPLE JUST WON'T TAKE THE HINT.
GENTLY, ANGUS. COAX THE LOCK--DON'T FORCE HER...
GOT IT!
HIS NAME IS ANGUS MACWHIRTER. HE ONCE RENTED THE X-MEN A HOVERCRAFT. IT WAS DESTROYED, AND EVER SINCE, EVEN THOUGH HE WAS PAID IN FULL FOR HIS LOSS...
...HE'S NURSED A DEEP AND GROWING HATRED FOR THEM...
MUTANT
X
NO ADMITTANCE
* BY MAGNETO, IN X-MEN #104 --R
AND FOR ANYONE CONNECTED WITH THEM.
A FEW WELL-PLACED CHARGES OUGHT TO WRECK THIS ACCURSED PLACE.
AN' IF SOME PEOPLE GET HURT ALONG THE WAY, SO MUCH THE BETTER.
HUH?! WHUZZAT?!?
HUMANNN... I NEED... YOU...
OH MY GOD.
HE DOESN'T EVEN HAVE TIME TO SCREAM.
MUIR ISLE. CHRISTMAS DAY. A LIFE ENDS. AND A NIGHTMARE IS BORN.
NEXT ISSUE:
WANTED: WOLVERINE! DEAD OR ALIVE!

The team begins their journey back to America in this excerpt from *X-Men #120*...

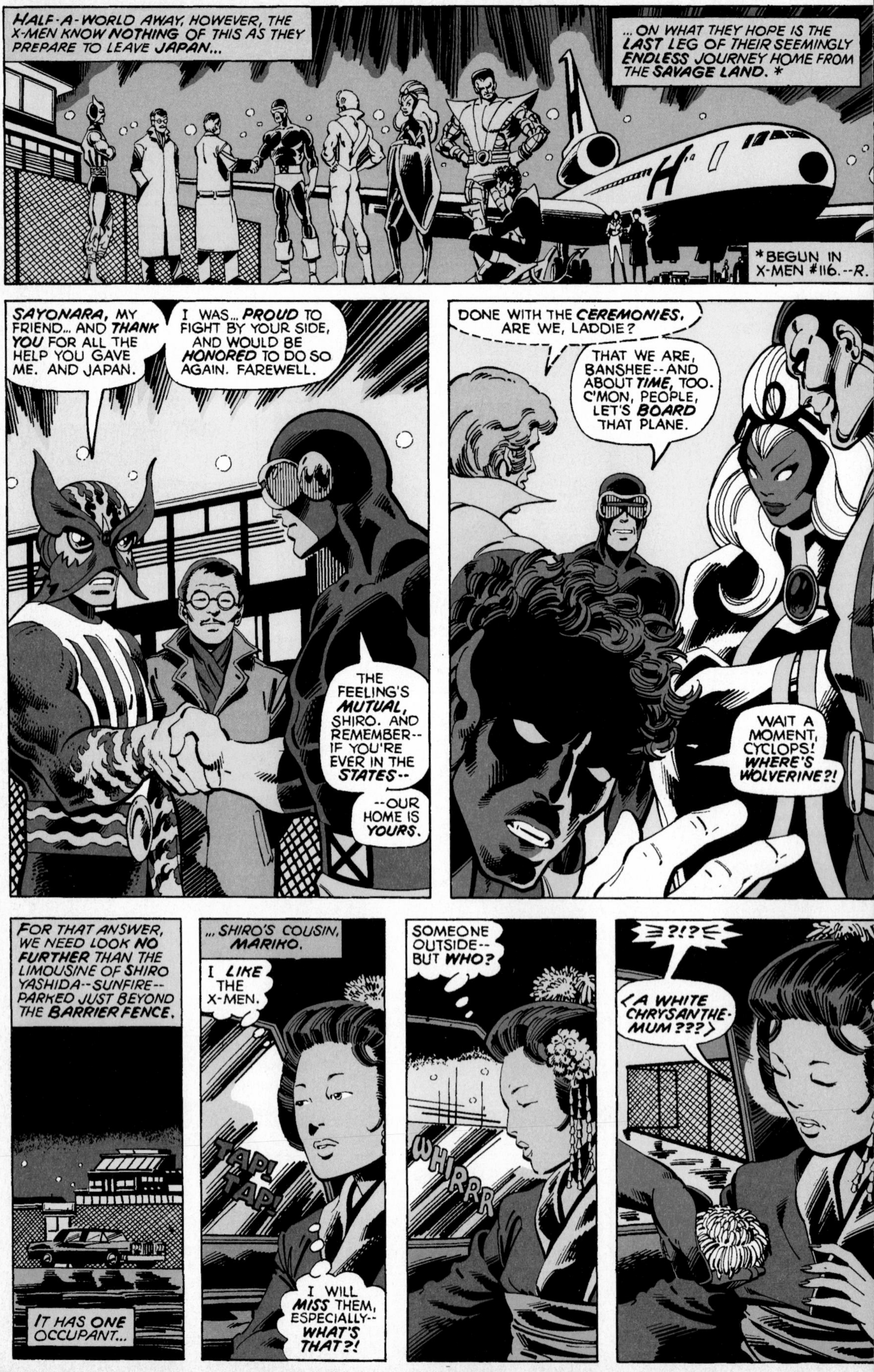
HALF-A-WORLD AWAY, HOWEVER, THE X-MEN KNOW NOTHING OF THIS AS THEY PREPARE TO LEAVE JAPAN...
...ON WHAT THEY HOPE IS THE LAST LEG OF THEIR SEEMINGLY ENDLESS JOURNEY HOME FROM THE SAVAGE LAND. *
*BEGUN IN X-MEN #116. --R.
SAYONARA, MY FRIEND... AND THANK YOU FOR ALL THE HELP YOU GAVE ME. AND JAPAN.
I WAS... PROUD TO FIGHT BY YOUR SIDE, AND WOULD BE HONORED TO DO SO AGAIN. FAREWELL.
THE FEELING'S MUTUAL, SHIRO. AND REMEMBER-- IF YOU'RE EVER IN THE STATES--
--OUR HOME IS YOURS.
DONE WITH THE CEREMONIES, ARE WE, LADDIE?
THAT WE ARE, BANSHEE--AND ABOUT TIME, TOO. C'MON, PEOPLE, LET'S BOARD THAT PLANE.
WAIT A MOMENT, CYCLOPS! WHERE'S WOLVERINE?!
FOR THAT ANSWER, WE NEED LOOK NO FURTHER THAN THE LIMOUSINE OF SHIRO YASHIDA--SUNFIRE--PARKED JUST BEYOND THE BARRIER FENCE.
IT HAS ONE OCCUPANT...
...SHIRO'S COUSIN, MARIKO.
I LIKE THE X-MEN.
TAP! TAP!
I WILL MISS THEM, ESPECIALLY-- WHAT'S THAT?!
SOMEONE OUTSIDE-- BUT WHO?
WHIRRR
?!?
<A WHITE CHRYSANTHEMUM???>

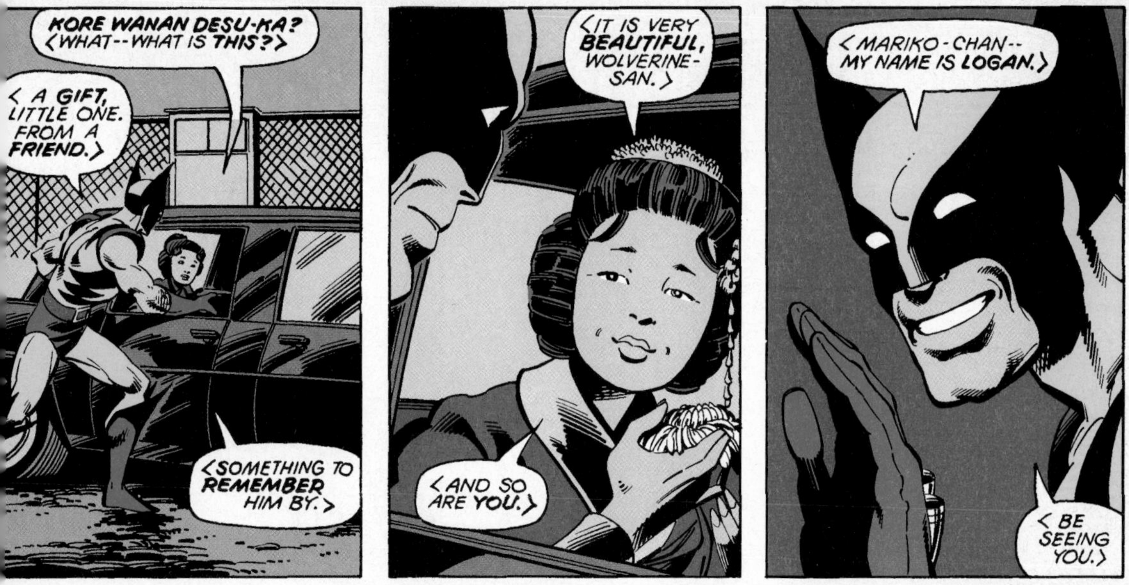
KORE WANAN DESU-KA? ⟨WHAT--WHAT IS THIS?⟩
⟨A GIFT, LITTLE ONE. FROM A FRIEND.⟩
⟨SOMETHING TO REMEMBER HIM BY.⟩
⟨IT IS VERY BEAUTIFUL, WOLVERINE-SAN.⟩
⟨AND SO ARE YOU.⟩
⟨MARIKO-CHAN-- MY NAME IS LOGAN.⟩
⟨BE SEEING YOU.⟩

...unfortunately for the X-Men, nothing is ever as easy as it seems. Follow the mighty mutants' adventures as they circle the globe on their long journey home in *Marvel Masterworks: The Uncanny X-Men Vol. 3!*

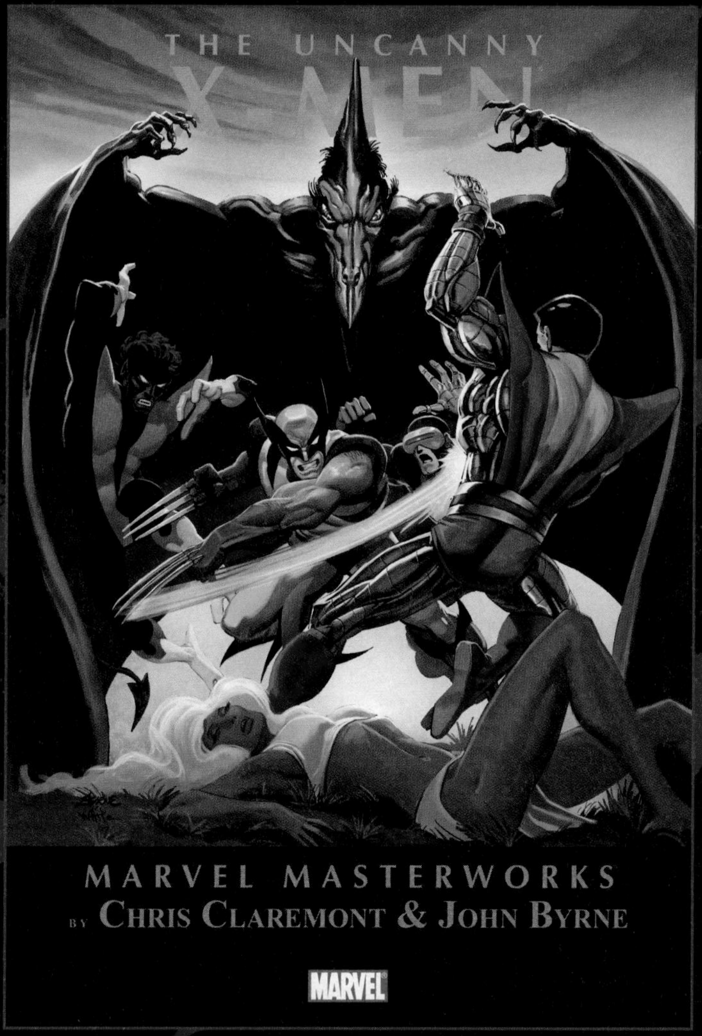
THE UNCANNY
X-MEN
MARVEL MASTERWORKS
BY CHRIS CLAREMONT & JOHN BYRNE
MARVEL

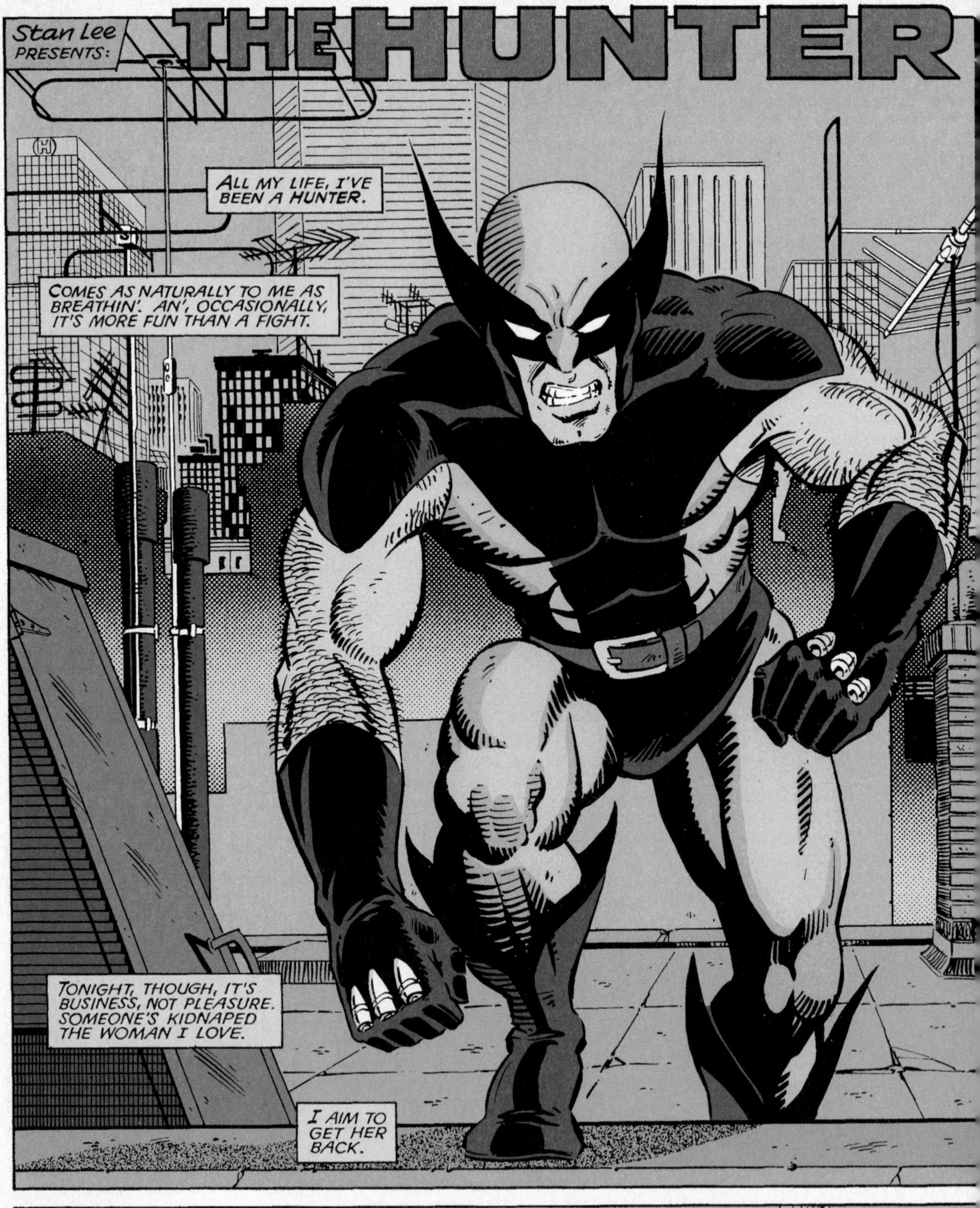
Stan Lee PRESENTS:
THE HUNTER
ALL MY LIFE, I'VE BEEN A HUNTER.
COMES AS NATURALLY TO ME AS BREATHIN'. AN', OCCASIONALLY, IT'S MORE FUN THAN A FIGHT.
TONIGHT, THOUGH, IT'S BUSINESS, NOT PLEASURE. SOMEONE'S KIDNAPED THE WOMAN I LOVE.
I AIM TO GET HER BACK.

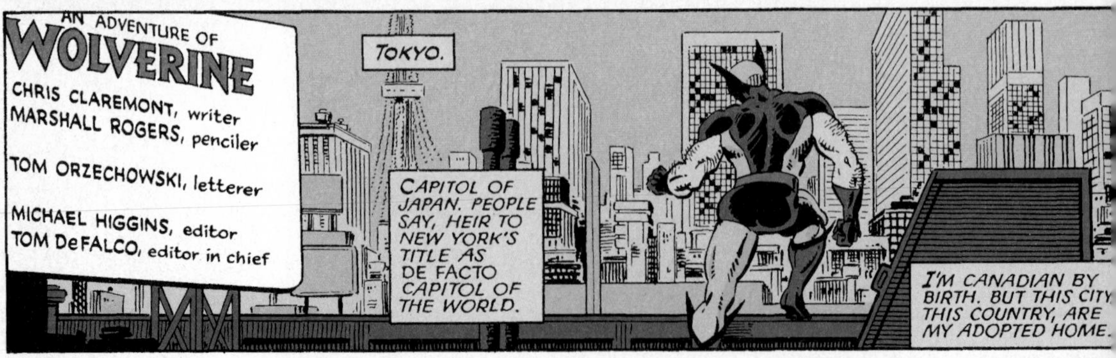
AN ADVENTURE OF WOLVERINE
CHRIS CLAREMONT, writer
MARSHALL ROGERS, penciler
TOM ORZECHOWSKI, letterer
MICHAEL HIGGINS, editor
TOM DeFALCO, editor in chief
TOKYO.
CAPITOL OF JAPAN. PEOPLE SAY, HEIR TO NEW YORK'S TITLE AS DE FACTO CAPITOL OF THE WORLD.
I'M CANADIAN BY BIRTH. BUT THIS CITY, THIS COUNTRY, ARE MY ADOPTED HOME.

NOTE SAID BRING THE RANSOM HERE, TO THIS LOWLIFE DISTRICT. I'D BE MET, PRESUMABLY BY THOSE TWO JOY-BOYS AN' A SMALL ARMY O' PALS.

DO AS I'M TOLD, NOBODY GETS HURT.

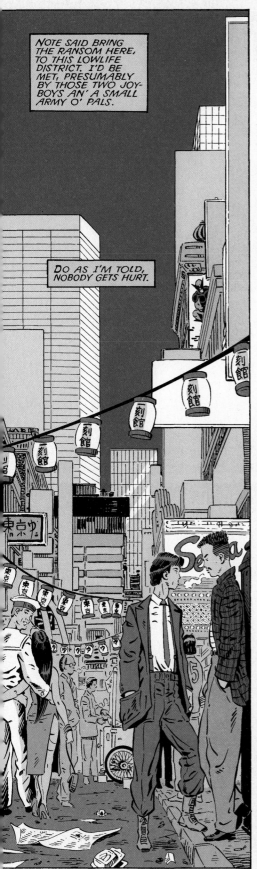

FAT FLAMIN' CHANCE, ON BOTH COUNTS.

YOU STEAL MY LADY...

...I'M NOT THE ONE WHO PAYS.

I DON'T NEED THEM TO FIND HER.

I'M A MUTANT. MORE THAN HUMAN. A BONAFIDE HERO, TOO, THAT'S WHY THE FANCY OUTFIT. PART OF MY POWER IS EXCEPTIONALLY ACUTE PHYSICAL SENSES, KEENER THAN ANY ANIMAL'S.

MEANS I CAN FOLLOW ANY TRAIL, NO MATTER HOW OLD, OR HOW FAINT.

AIN'T ALWAYS EASY, 'SPECIALLY IN A TOWN AS BIG AN' CROWDED AS THIS.

BUT, EVENTUALLY, I GET THE JOB DONE.

AN ESTATE, ON THE FRINGES OF THE CITY. I KNOW THE PLACE, AN' THE OWNER-- MAINLINE TYCOON WITH MORE THAN A FEW CONNECTIONS TO THE YAKUZA, THE JAPANESE UNDERWORLD.

MAN'S A HISTORY BUFF, SO HE BUILT HIMSELF A CASTLE. REPRODUCTION OF AN ANCIENT FORTRESS SUPPOSED TO HAVE STOOD ON THIS SITE.

IMPRESSIVE.

PROTECTED, TOO.

I'M UPWIND, BREEZE BLOWIN' ACROSS THE BATTLEMENTS TOWARDS ME.

COUPLE O' BREATHS, I KNOW THE ODDS.

MOAT'S NO PROBLEM.

NEITHER IS THE WALL.

PERFECT LOCATION. NO GUARDS IN SIGHT, THIS STRETCH OF WALL SHROUDED BY SHADOW. TOO GOOD TO BE TRUE.

BUT ANYBODY BREECHIN' THE WALL WILL BREAK THE LASER SECURITY LINK--

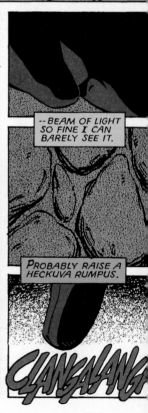

--BEAM OF LIGHT SO FINE I CAN BARELY SEE IT.

PROBABLY RAISE A HECKUVA RUMPUS.

CLANGALANG

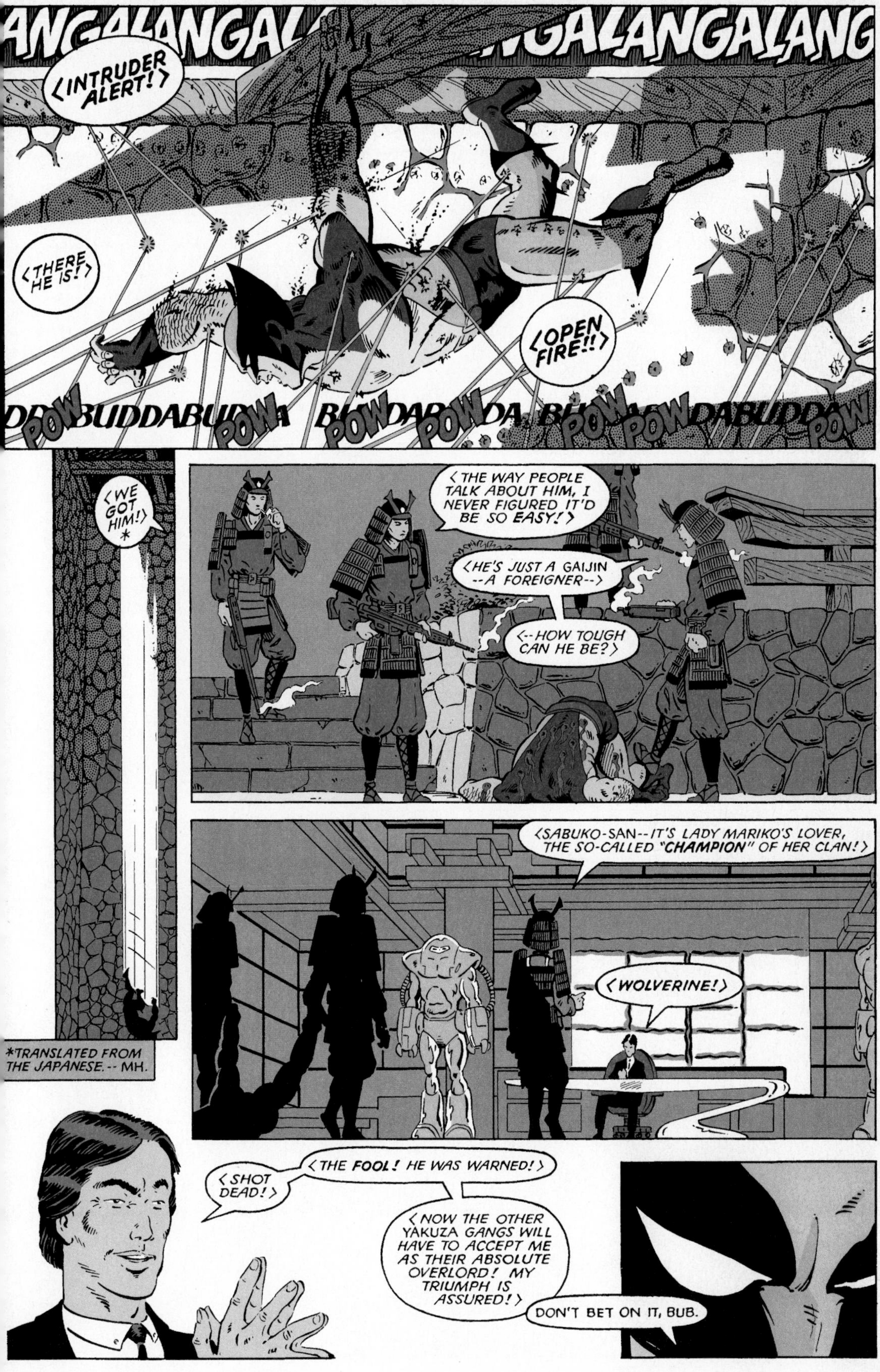
ANGALANGALANGALANGALANGALANG
<INTRUDER ALERT!>
<THERE HE IS!>
<OPEN FIRE!!>
POW BUDDABUDDA POW BUDDA POW BUDDA POW BUDDA POW BUDDABUDDA POW
<WE GOT HIM!> *
<THE WAY PEOPLE TALK ABOUT HIM, I NEVER FIGURED IT'D BE SO EASY!>
<HE'S JUST A GAIJIN --A FOREIGNER-->
<--HOW TOUGH CAN HE BE?>
<SABUKO-SAN--IT'S LADY MARIKO'S LOVER, THE SO-CALLED "CHAMPION" OF HER CLAN!>
<WOLVERINE!>
*TRANSLATED FROM THE JAPANESE.-- MH.
<SHOT DEAD!>
<THE FOOL! HE WAS WARNED!>
<NOW THE OTHER YAKUZA GANGS WILL HAVE TO ACCEPT ME AS THEIR ABSOLUTE OVERLORD! MY TRIUMPH IS ASSURED!>
DON'T BET ON IT, BUB.

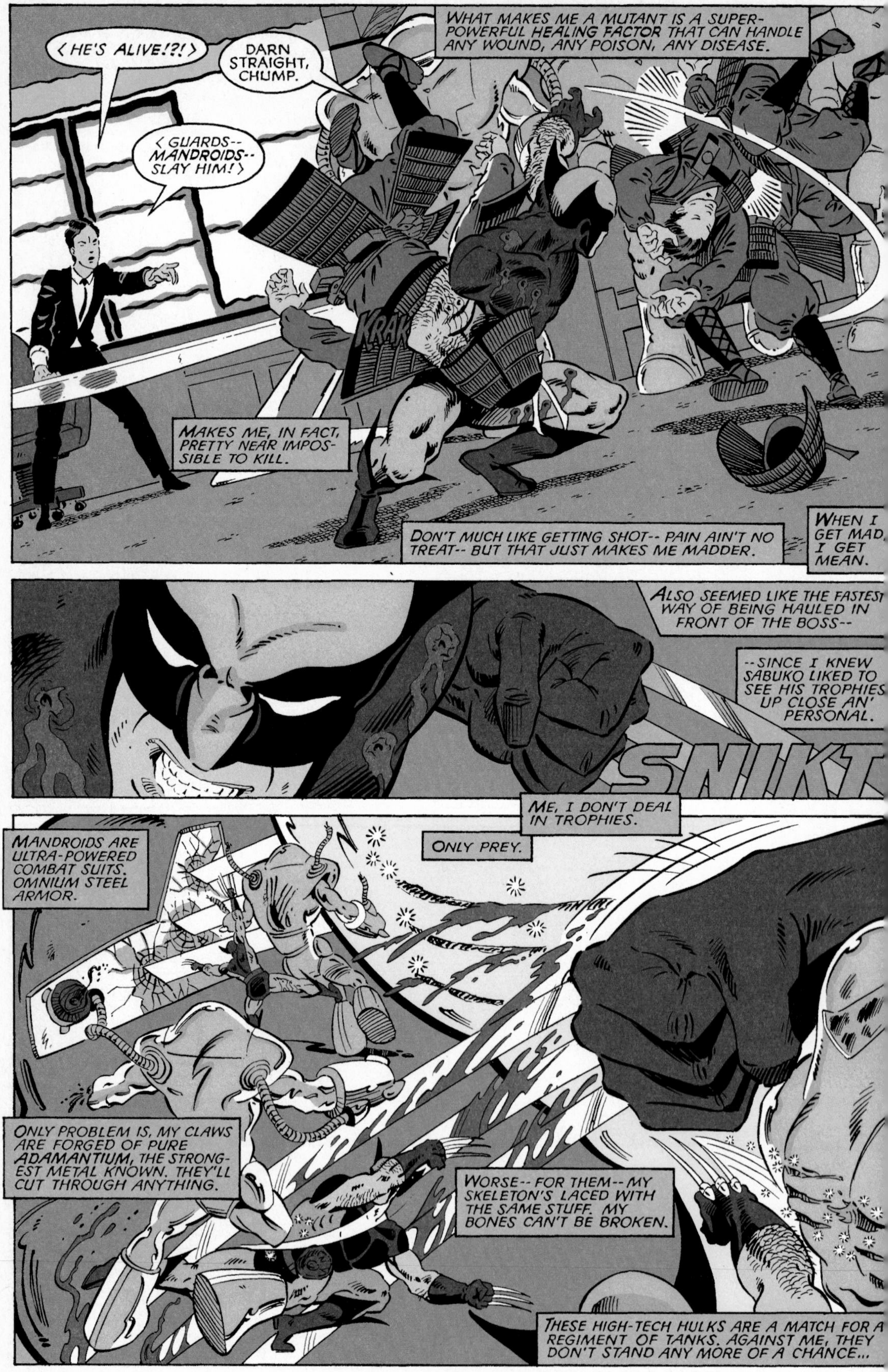
WHAT MAKES ME A MUTANT IS A SUPER-POWERFUL HEALING FACTOR THAT CAN HANDLE ANY WOUND, ANY POISON, ANY DISEASE.
< HE'S ALIVE!?! >
DARN STRAIGHT, CHUMP.
< GUARDS-- MANDROIDS-- SLAY HIM! >
KRAK
MAKES ME, IN FACT, PRETTY NEAR IMPOSSIBLE TO KILL.
DON'T MUCH LIKE GETTING SHOT-- PAIN AIN'T NO TREAT-- BUT THAT JUST MAKES ME MADDER.
WHEN I GET MAD, I GET MEAN.
ALSO SEEMED LIKE THE FASTEST WAY OF BEING HAULED IN FRONT OF THE BOSS--
--SINCE I KNEW SABUKO LIKED TO SEE HIS TROPHIES UP CLOSE AN' PERSONAL.
SNIKT
ME, I DON'T DEAL IN TROPHIES.
ONLY PREY.
MANDROIDS ARE ULTRA-POWERED COMBAT SUITS. OMNIUM STEEL ARMOR.
ONLY PROBLEM IS, MY CLAWS ARE FORGED OF PURE ADAMANTIUM, THE STRONGEST METAL KNOWN. THEY'LL CUT THROUGH ANYTHING.
WORSE-- FOR THEM-- MY SKELETON'S LACED WITH THE SAME STUFF. MY BONES CAN'T BE BROKEN.
THESE HIGH-TECH HULKS ARE A MATCH FOR A REGIMENT OF TANKS. AGAINST ME, THEY DON'T STAND ANY MORE OF A CHANCE...

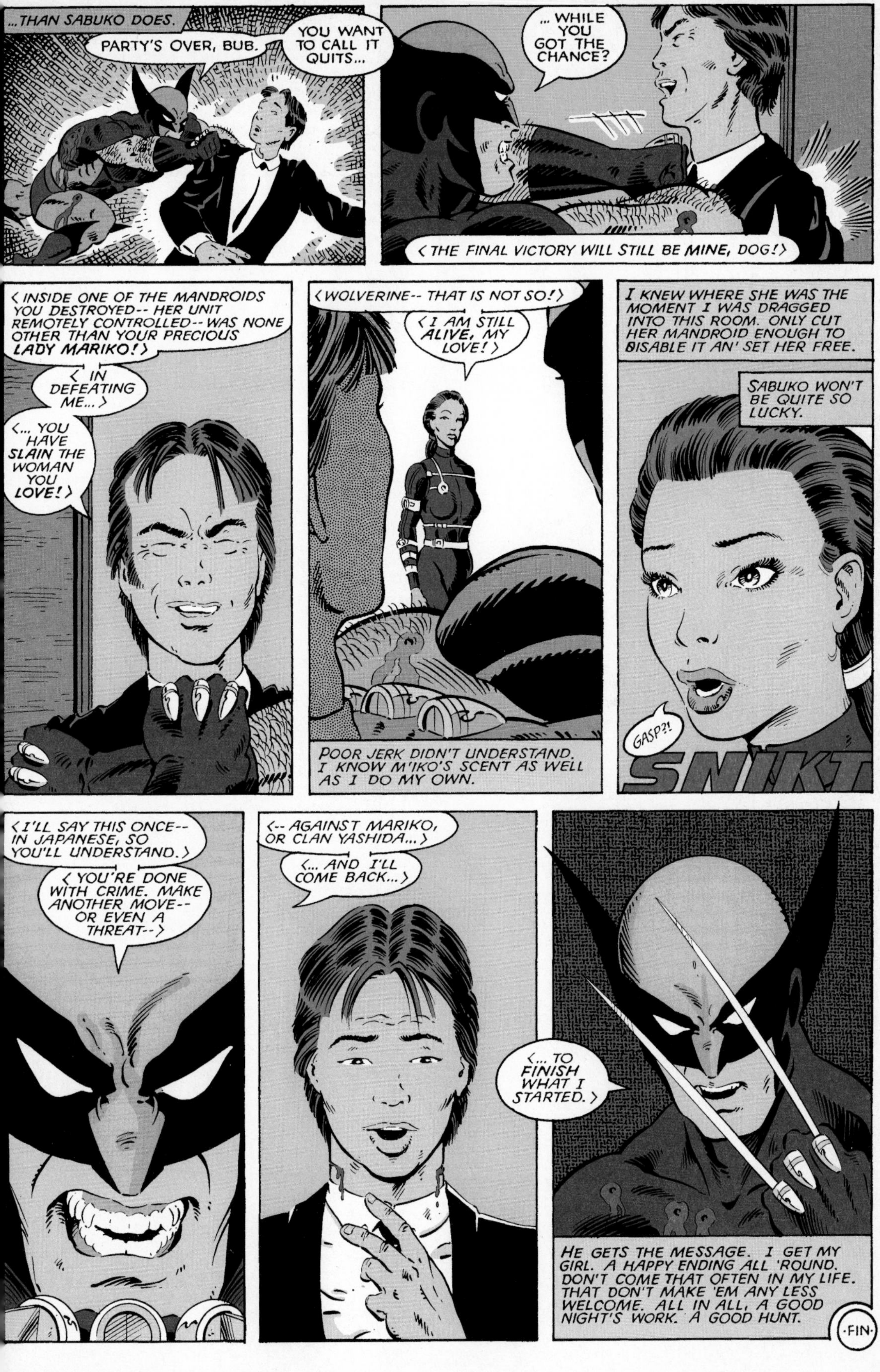
...THAN SABUKO DOES.
PARTY'S OVER, BUB.
YOU WANT TO CALL IT QUITS...
... WHILE YOU GOT THE CHANCE?
<THE FINAL VICTORY WILL STILL BE MINE, DOG!>
<INSIDE ONE OF THE MANDROIDS YOU DESTROYED-- HER UNIT REMOTELY CONTROLLED-- WAS NONE OTHER THAN YOUR PRECIOUS LADY MARIKO!>
<IN DEFEATING ME...>
<... YOU HAVE SLAIN THE WOMAN YOU LOVE!>
<WOLVERINE-- THAT IS NOT SO!>
<I AM STILL ALIVE, MY LOVE!>
POOR JERK DIDN'T UNDERSTAND. I KNOW M'IKO'S SCENT AS WELL AS I DO MY OWN.
I KNEW WHERE SHE WAS THE MOMENT I WAS DRAGGED INTO THIS ROOM. ONLY CUT HER MANDROID ENOUGH TO DISABLE IT AN' SET HER FREE.
SABUKO WON'T BE QUITE SO LUCKY.
GASP?!
SNIKT
<I'LL SAY THIS ONCE-- IN JAPANESE, SO YOU'LL UNDERSTAND.>
<YOU'RE DONE WITH CRIME. MAKE ANOTHER MOVE-- OR EVEN A THREAT-->
<-- AGAINST MARIKO, OR CLAN YASHIDA...>
<... AND I'LL COME BACK...>
<... TO FINISH WHAT I STARTED.>
HE GETS THE MESSAGE. I GET MY GIRL. A HAPPY ENDING ALL 'ROUND. DON'T COME THAT OFTEN IN MY LIFE. THAT DON'T MAKE 'EM ANY LESS WELCOME. ALL IN ALL, A GOOD NIGHT'S WORK. A GOOD HUNT.
·FIN·

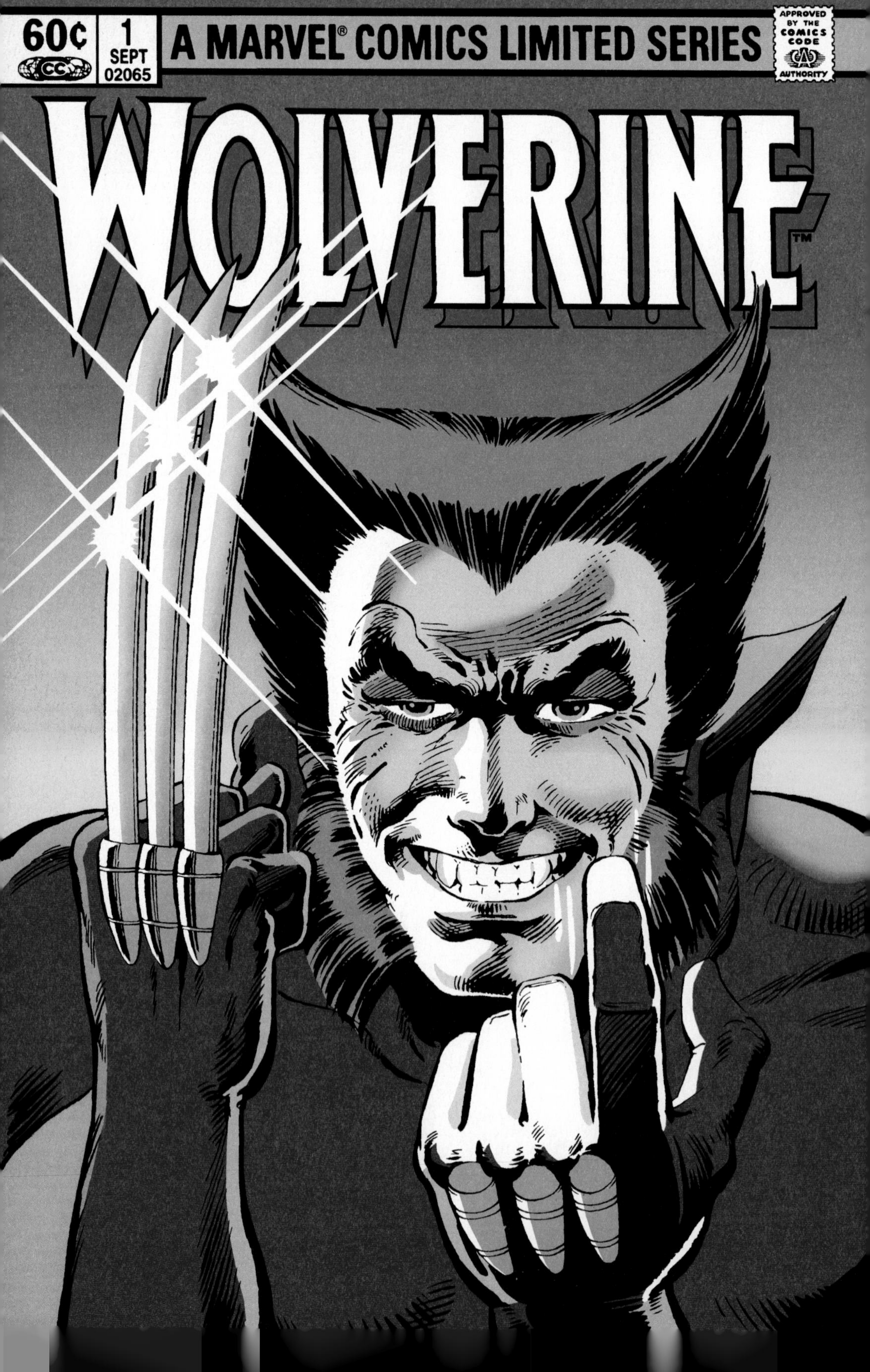

60¢
CC
1
SEPT
02065
A MARVEL® COMICS LIMITED SERIES
APPROVED BY THE COMICS CODE AUTHORITY
WOLVERINE™

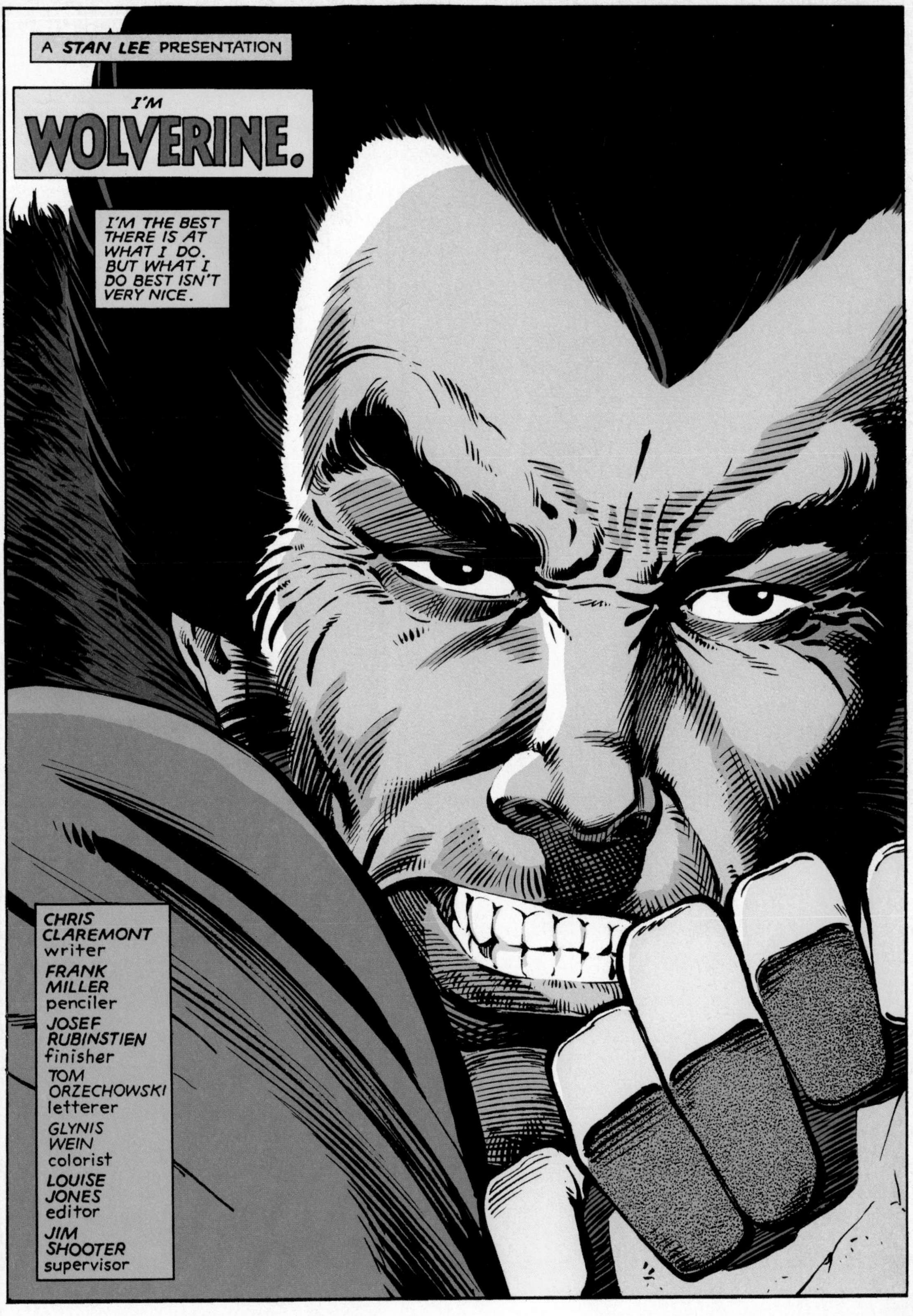

A STAN LEE PRESENTATION
I'M WOLVERINE.
I'M THE BEST THERE IS AT WHAT I DO. BUT WHAT I DO BEST ISN'T VERY NICE.
CHRIS CLAREMONT writer
FRANK MILLER penciler
JOSEF RUBINSTIEN finisher
TOM ORZECHOWSKI letterer
GLYNIS WEIN colorist
LOUISE JONES editor
JIM SHOOTER supervisor

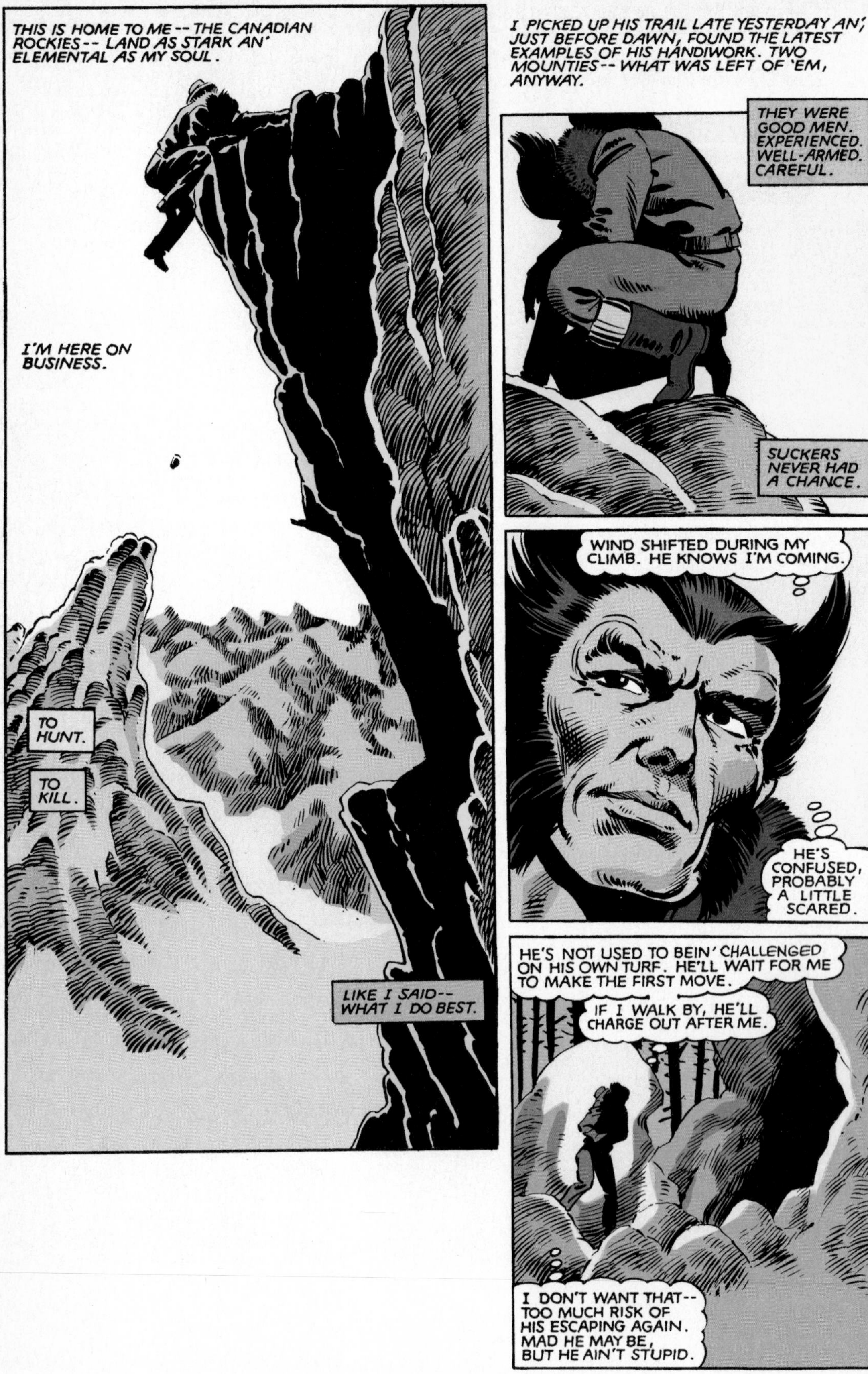

THIS IS HOME TO ME -- THE CANADIAN ROCKIES -- LAND AS STARK AN' ELEMENTAL AS MY SOUL.
I'M HERE ON BUSINESS.
TO HUNT.
TO KILL.
LIKE I SAID-- WHAT I DO BEST.
I PICKED UP HIS TRAIL LATE YESTERDAY AN', JUST BEFORE DAWN, FOUND THE LATEST EXAMPLES OF HIS HANDIWORK. TWO MOUNTIES -- WHAT WAS LEFT OF 'EM, ANYWAY.
THEY WERE GOOD MEN. EXPERIENCED. WELL-ARMED. CAREFUL.
SUCKERS NEVER HAD A CHANCE.
WIND SHIFTED DURING MY CLIMB. HE KNOWS I'M COMING.
HE'S CONFUSED, PROBABLY A LITTLE SCARED.
HE'S NOT USED TO BEIN' CHALLENGED ON HIS OWN TURF. HE'LL WAIT FOR ME TO MAKE THE FIRST MOVE.
IF I WALK BY, HE'LL CHARGE OUT AFTER ME.
I DON'T WANT THAT-- TOO MUCH RISK OF HIS ESCAPING AGAIN. MAD HE MAY BE, BUT HE AIN'T STUPID.

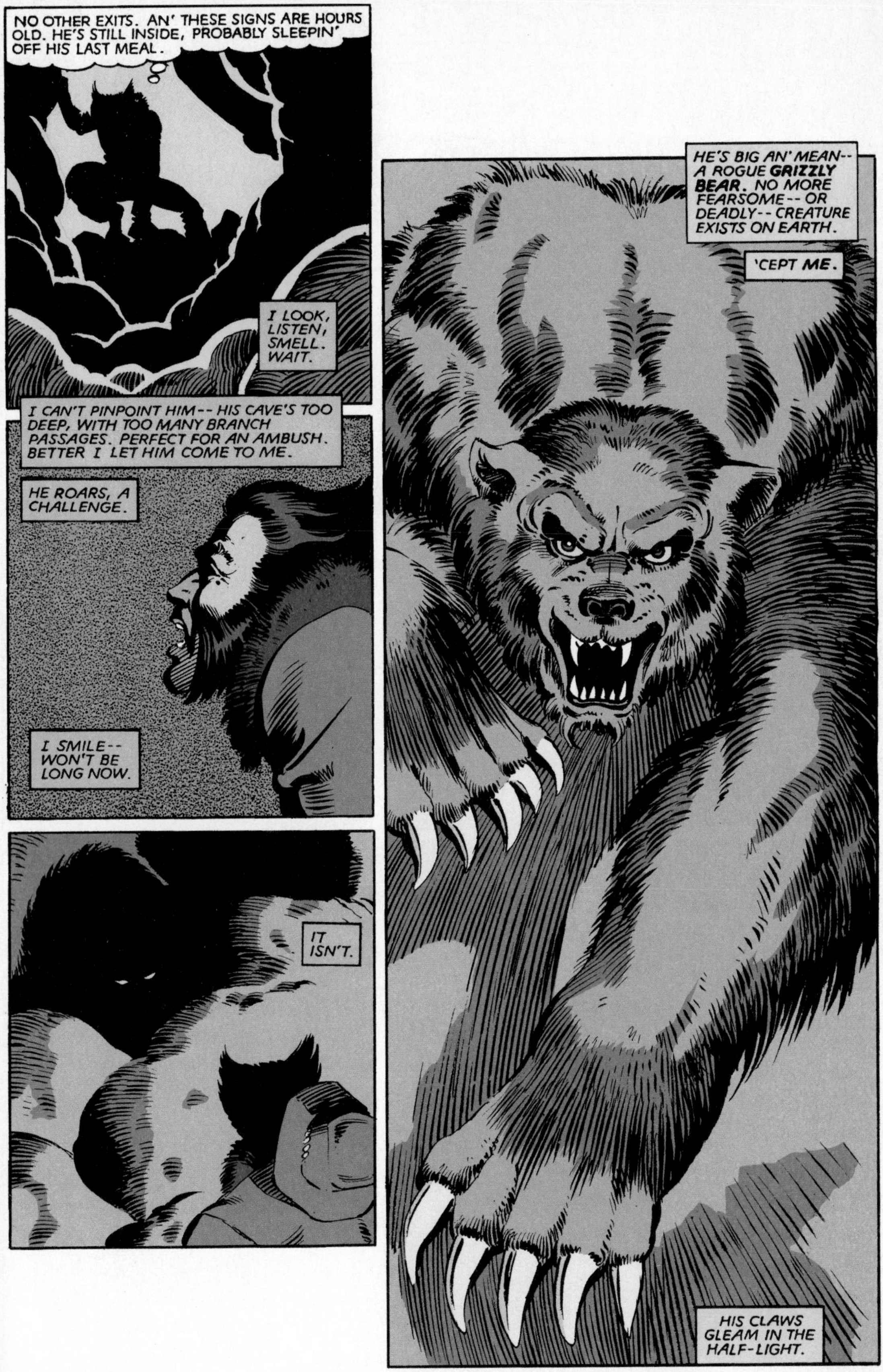
NO OTHER EXITS. AN' THESE SIGNS ARE HOURS OLD. HE'S STILL INSIDE, PROBABLY SLEEPIN' OFF HIS LAST MEAL.
I LOOK, LISTEN, SMELL. WAIT.
I CAN'T PINPOINT HIM-- HIS CAVE'S TOO DEEP, WITH TOO MANY BRANCH PASSAGES. PERFECT FOR AN AMBUSH. BETTER I LET HIM COME TO ME.
HE ROARS, A CHALLENGE.
I SMILE-- WON'T BE LONG NOW.
IT ISN'T.
HE'S BIG AN' MEAN-- A ROGUE GRIZZLY BEAR. NO MORE FEARSOME-- OR DEADLY-- CREATURE EXISTS ON EARTH.
'CEPT ME.
HIS CLAWS GLEAM IN THE HALF-LIGHT.

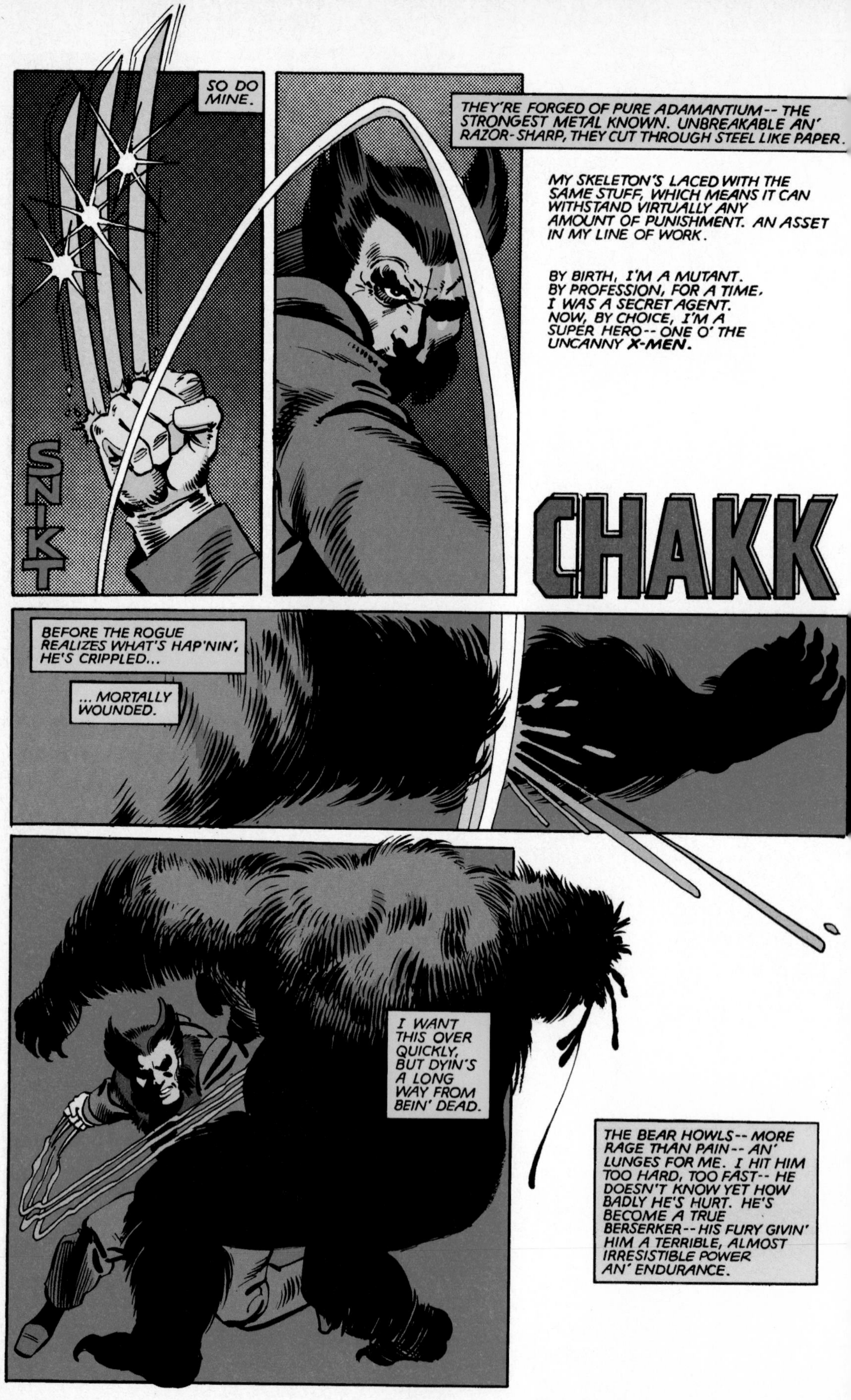
SO DO MINE.
SNIKT
THEY'RE FORGED OF PURE ADAMANTIUM-- THE STRONGEST METAL KNOWN. UNBREAKABLE AN' RAZOR-SHARP, THEY CUT THROUGH STEEL LIKE PAPER.
MY SKELETON'S LACED WITH THE SAME STUFF, WHICH MEANS IT CAN WITHSTAND VIRTUALLY ANY AMOUNT OF PUNISHMENT. AN ASSET IN MY LINE OF WORK.
BY BIRTH, I'M A MUTANT. BY PROFESSION, FOR A TIME, I WAS A SECRET AGENT. NOW, BY CHOICE, I'M A SUPER HERO-- ONE O' THE UNCANNY X-MEN.
CHAKK
BEFORE THE ROGUE REALIZES WHAT'S HAP'NIN', HE'S CRIPPLED...
...MORTALLY WOUNDED.
I WANT THIS OVER QUICKLY, BUT DYIN'S A LONG WAY FROM BEIN' DEAD.
THE BEAR HOWLS-- MORE RAGE THAN PAIN-- AN' LUNGES FOR ME. I HIT HIM TOO HARD, TOO FAST-- HE DOESN'T KNOW YET HOW BADLY HE'S HURT. HE'S BECOME A TRUE BERSERKER-- HIS FURY GIVIN' HIM A TERRIBLE, ALMOST IRRESISTIBLE POWER AN' ENDURANCE.

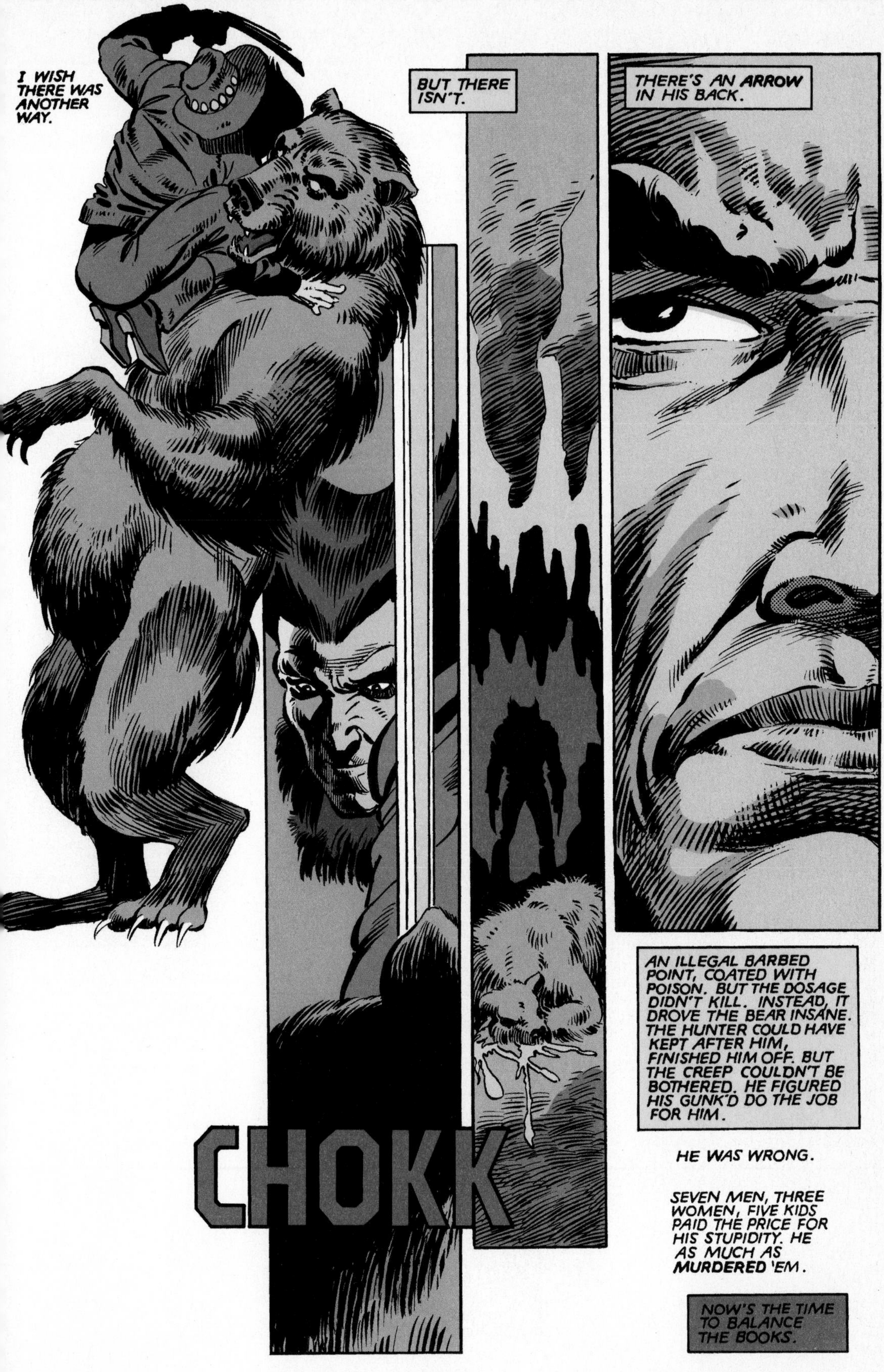
I WISH THERE WAS ANOTHER WAY.
BUT THERE ISN'T.
THERE'S AN ARROW IN HIS BACK.
AN ILLEGAL BARBED POINT, COATED WITH POISON. BUT THE DOSAGE DIDN'T KILL. INSTEAD, IT DROVE THE BEAR INSANE. THE HUNTER COULD HAVE KEPT AFTER HIM, FINISHED HIM OFF. BUT THE CREEP COULDN'T BE BOTHERED. HE FIGURED HIS GUNK'D DO THE JOB FOR HIM.
CHOKK
HE WAS WRONG.
SEVEN MEN, THREE WOMEN, FIVE KIDS PAID THE PRICE FOR HIS STUPIDITY. HE AS MUCH AS MURDERED 'EM.
NOW'S THE TIME TO BALANCE THE BOOKS.

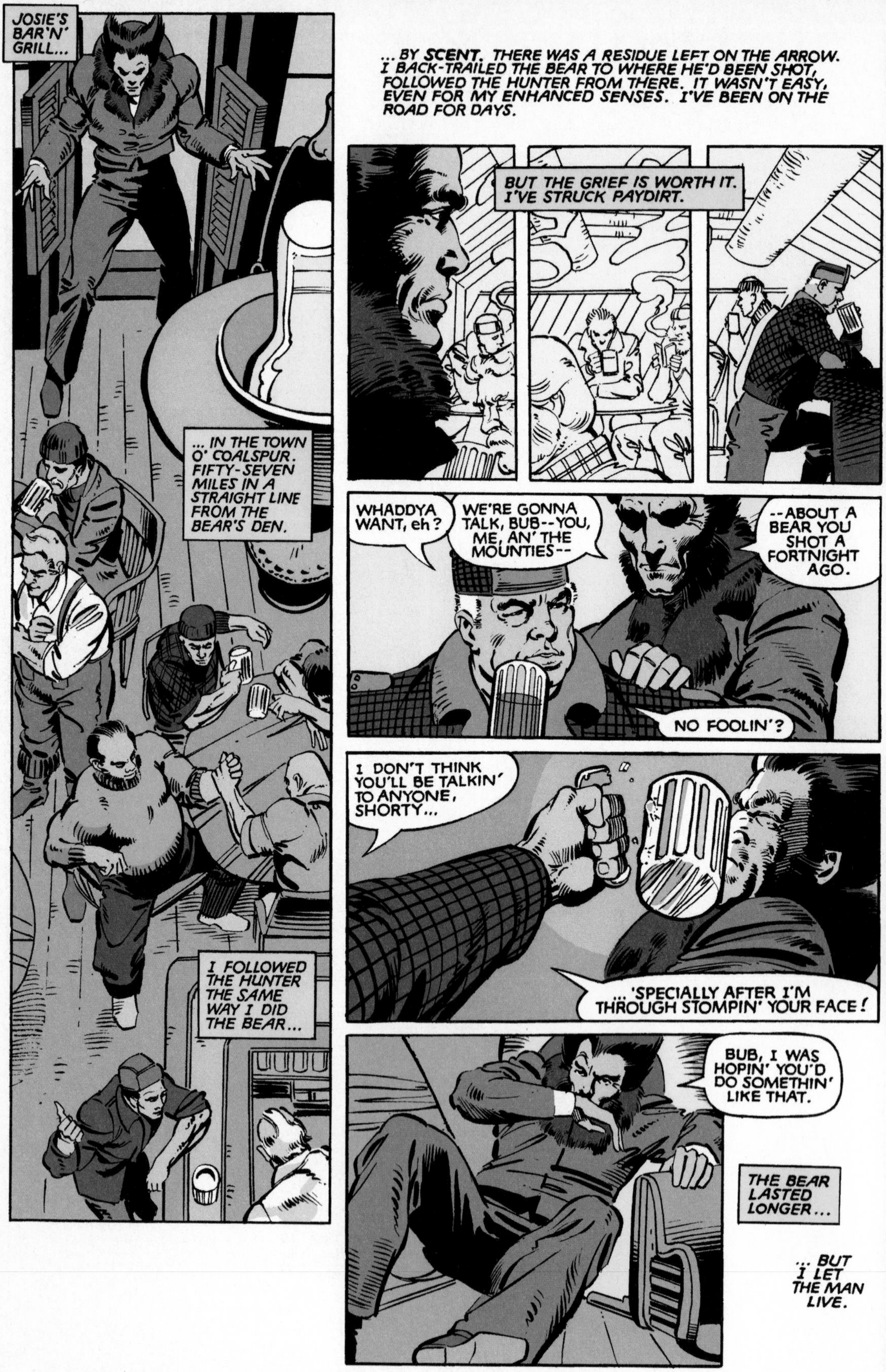
JOSIE'S BAR'N' GRILL...
... IN THE TOWN O' COALSPUR. FIFTY-SEVEN MILES IN A STRAIGHT LINE FROM THE BEAR'S DEN.
I FOLLOWED THE HUNTER THE SAME WAY I DID THE BEAR...
... BY SCENT. THERE WAS A RESIDUE LEFT ON THE ARROW. I BACK-TRAILED THE BEAR TO WHERE HE'D BEEN SHOT, FOLLOWED THE HUNTER FROM THERE. IT WASN'T EASY, EVEN FOR MY ENHANCED SENSES. I'VE BEEN ON THE ROAD FOR DAYS.
BUT THE GRIEF IS WORTH IT. I'VE STRUCK PAYDIRT.
WHADDYA WANT, eh?
WE'RE GONNA TALK, BUB--YOU, ME, AN' THE MOUNTIES--
--ABOUT A BEAR YOU SHOT A FORTNIGHT AGO.
NO FOOLIN'?
I DON'T THINK YOU'LL BE TALKIN' TO ANYONE, SHORTY...
...'SPECIALLY AFTER I'M THROUGH STOMPIN' YOUR FACE!
BUB, I WAS HOPIN' YOU'D DO SOMETHIN' LIKE THAT.
THE BEAR LASTED LONGER...
... BUT I LET THE MAN LIVE.

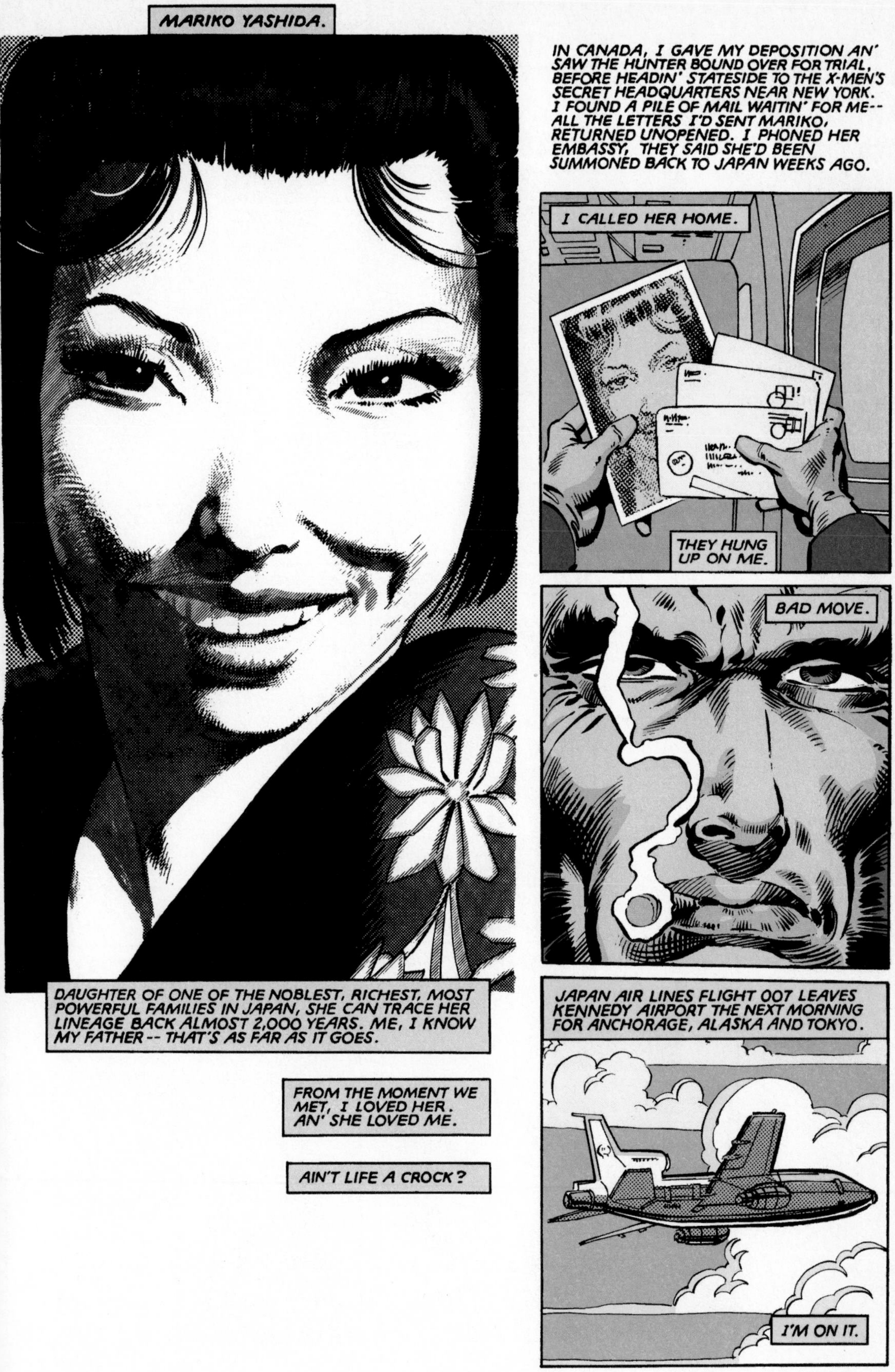
MARIKO YASHIDA.
DAUGHTER OF ONE OF THE NOBLEST, RICHEST, MOST POWERFUL FAMILIES IN JAPAN, SHE CAN TRACE HER LINEAGE BACK ALMOST 2,000 YEARS. ME, I KNOW MY FATHER -- THAT'S AS FAR AS IT GOES.
FROM THE MOMENT WE MET, I LOVED HER. AN' SHE LOVED ME.
AIN'T LIFE A CROCK?
IN CANADA, I GAVE MY DEPOSITION AN' SAW THE HUNTER BOUND OVER FOR TRIAL, BEFORE HEADIN' STATESIDE TO THE X-MEN'S SECRET HEADQUARTERS NEAR NEW YORK. I FOUND A PILE OF MAIL WAITIN' FOR ME-- ALL THE LETTERS I'D SENT MARIKO, RETURNED UNOPENED. I PHONED HER EMBASSY, THEY SAID SHE'D BEEN SUMMONED BACK TO JAPAN WEEKS AGO.
I CALLED HER HOME.
THEY HUNG UP ON ME.
BAD MOVE.
JAPAN AIR LINES FLIGHT 007 LEAVES KENNEDY AIRPORT THE NEXT MORNING FOR ANCHORAGE, ALASKA AND TOKYO.
I'M ON IT.

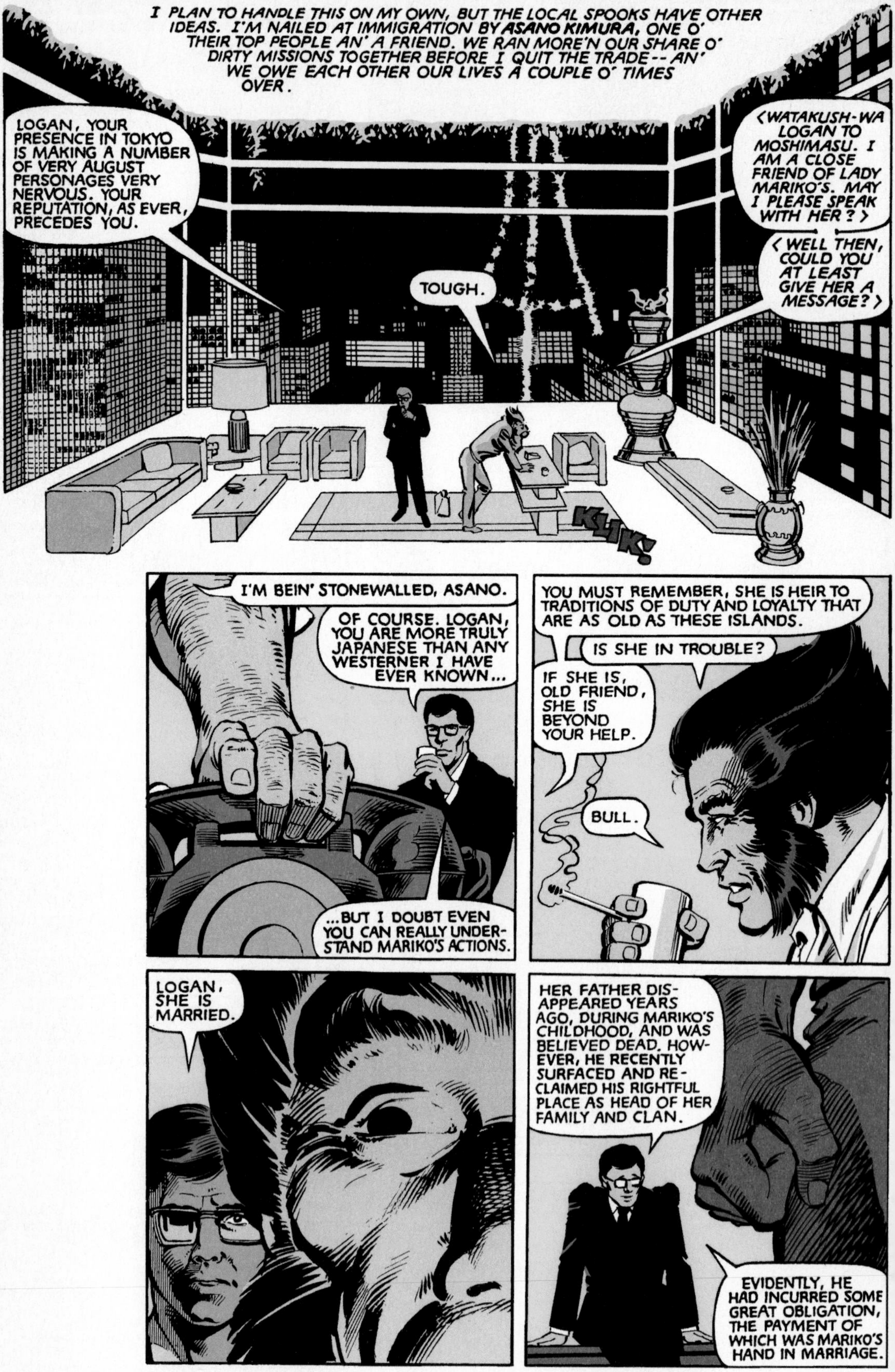
I PLAN TO HANDLE THIS ON MY OWN, BUT THE LOCAL SPOOKS HAVE OTHER IDEAS. I'M NAILED AT IMMIGRATION BY ASANO KIMURA, ONE O' THEIR TOP PEOPLE AN' A FRIEND. WE RAN MORE'N OUR SHARE O' DIRTY MISSIONS TOGETHER BEFORE I QUIT THE TRADE -- AN' WE OWE EACH OTHER OUR LIVES A COUPLE O' TIMES OVER.
LOGAN, YOUR PRESENCE IN TOKYO IS MAKING A NUMBER OF VERY AUGUST PERSONAGES VERY NERVOUS. YOUR REPUTATION, AS EVER, PRECEDES YOU.
<WATAKUSH-WA LOGAN TO MOSHIMASU. I AM A CLOSE FRIEND OF LADY MARIKO'S. MAY I PLEASE SPEAK WITH HER?>
TOUGH.
<WELL THEN, COULD YOU AT LEAST GIVE HER A MESSAGE?>
KLIK!
I'M BEIN' STONEWALLED, ASANO.
OF COURSE. LOGAN, YOU ARE MORE TRULY JAPANESE THAN ANY WESTERNER I HAVE EVER KNOWN...
...BUT I DOUBT EVEN YOU CAN REALLY UNDERSTAND MARIKO'S ACTIONS.
YOU MUST REMEMBER, SHE IS HEIR TO TRADITIONS OF DUTY AND LOYALTY THAT ARE AS OLD AS THESE ISLANDS.
IS SHE IN TROUBLE?
IF SHE IS, OLD FRIEND, SHE IS BEYOND YOUR HELP.
BULL.
LOGAN, SHE IS MARRIED.
HER FATHER DISAPPEARED YEARS AGO, DURING MARIKO'S CHILDHOOD, AND WAS BELIEVED DEAD. HOWEVER, HE RECENTLY SURFACED AND RECLAIMED HIS RIGHTFUL PLACE AS HEAD OF HER FAMILY AND CLAN.
EVIDENTLY, HE HAD INCURRED SOME GREAT OBLIGATION, THE PAYMENT OF WHICH WAS MARIKO'S HAND IN MARRIAGE.

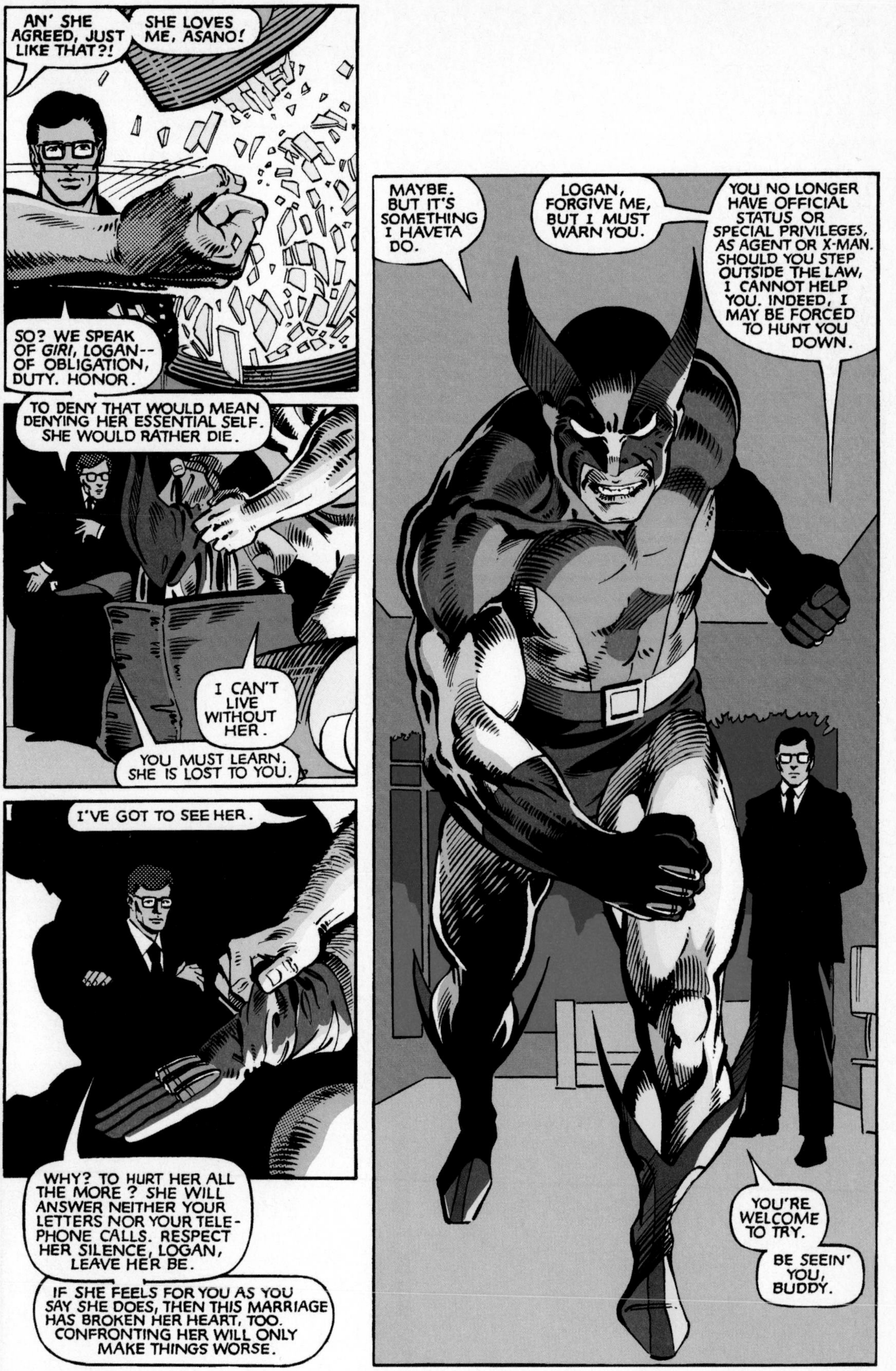
AN' SHE AGREED, JUST LIKE THAT?!
SHE LOVES ME, ASANO!
SO? WE SPEAK OF GIRI, LOGAN-- OF OBLIGATION, DUTY. HONOR.
TO DENY THAT WOULD MEAN DENYING HER ESSENTIAL SELF. SHE WOULD RATHER DIE.
I CAN'T LIVE WITHOUT HER.
YOU MUST LEARN. SHE IS LOST TO YOU.
I'VE GOT TO SEE HER.
WHY? TO HURT HER ALL THE MORE? SHE WILL ANSWER NEITHER YOUR LETTERS NOR YOUR TELE-PHONE CALLS. RESPECT HER SILENCE, LOGAN, LEAVE HER BE.
IF SHE FEELS FOR YOU AS YOU SAY SHE DOES, THEN THIS MARRIAGE HAS BROKEN HER HEART, TOO. CONFRONTING HER WILL ONLY MAKE THINGS WORSE.
MAYBE. BUT IT'S SOMETHING I HAVETA DO.
LOGAN, FORGIVE ME, BUT I MUST WARN YOU.
YOU NO LONGER HAVE OFFICIAL STATUS OR SPECIAL PRIVILEGES, AS AGENT OR X-MAN. SHOULD YOU STEP OUTSIDE THE LAW, I CANNOT HELP YOU. INDEED, I MAY BE FORCED TO HUNT YOU DOWN.
YOU'RE WELCOME TO TRY.
BE SEEIN' YOU, BUDDY.

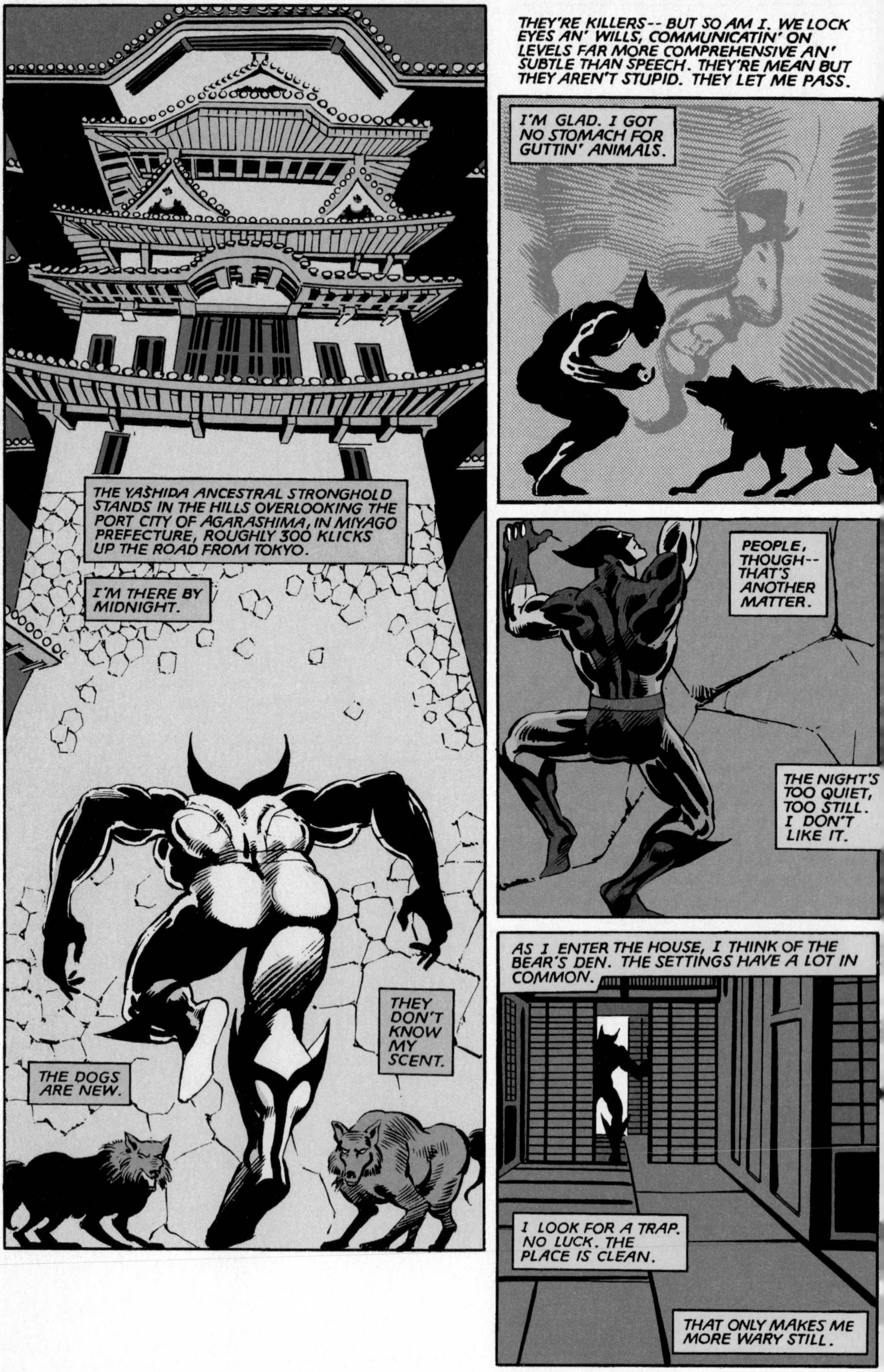
THE YASHIDA ANCESTRAL STRONGHOLD STANDS IN THE HILLS OVERLOOKING THE PORT CITY OF AGARASHIMA, IN MIYAGO PREFECTURE, ROUGHLY 300 KLICKS UP THE ROAD FROM TOKYO.
I'M THERE BY MIDNIGHT.
THE DOGS ARE NEW.
THEY DON'T KNOW MY SCENT.
THEY'RE KILLERS-- BUT SO AM I. WE LOCK EYES AN' WILLS, COMMUNICATIN' ON LEVELS FAR MORE COMPREHENSIVE AN' SUBTLE THAN SPEECH. THEY'RE MEAN BUT THEY AREN'T STUPID. THEY LET ME PASS.
I'M GLAD. I GOT NO STOMACH FOR GUTTIN' ANIMALS.
PEOPLE, THOUGH-- THAT'S ANOTHER MATTER.
THE NIGHT'S TOO QUIET, TOO STILL. I DON'T LIKE IT.
AS I ENTER THE HOUSE, I THINK OF THE BEAR'S DEN. THE SETTINGS HAVE A LOT IN COMMON.
I LOOK FOR A TRAP. NO LUCK. THE PLACE IS CLEAN.
THAT ONLY MAKES ME MORE WARY STILL.

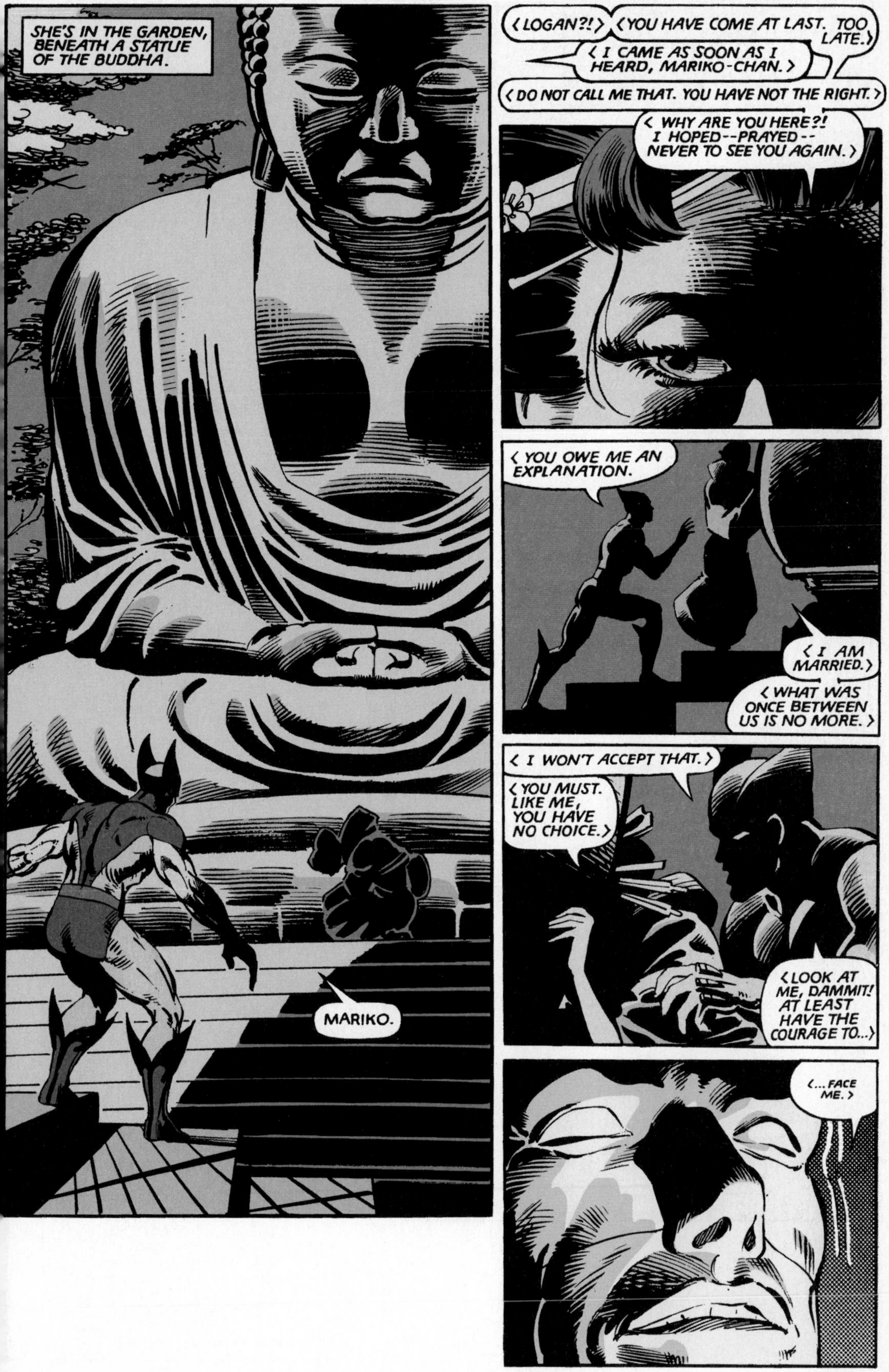
SHE'S IN THE GARDEN, BENEATH A STATUE OF THE BUDDHA.
MARIKO.
‹ LOGAN?! ›
‹ YOU HAVE COME AT LAST. TOO LATE. ›
‹ I CAME AS SOON AS I HEARD, MARIKO-CHAN. ›
‹ DO NOT CALL ME THAT. YOU HAVE NOT THE RIGHT. ›
‹ WHY ARE YOU HERE?! I HOPED--PRAYED-- NEVER TO SEE YOU AGAIN. ›
‹ YOU OWE ME AN EXPLANATION.
‹ I AM MARRIED. ›
‹ WHAT WAS ONCE BETWEEN US IS NO MORE. ›
‹ I WON'T ACCEPT THAT. ›
‹ YOU MUST. LIKE ME, YOU HAVE NO CHOICE. ›
‹ LOOK AT ME, DAMMIT! AT LEAST HAVE THE COURAGE TO... ›
‹ ... FACE ME. ›

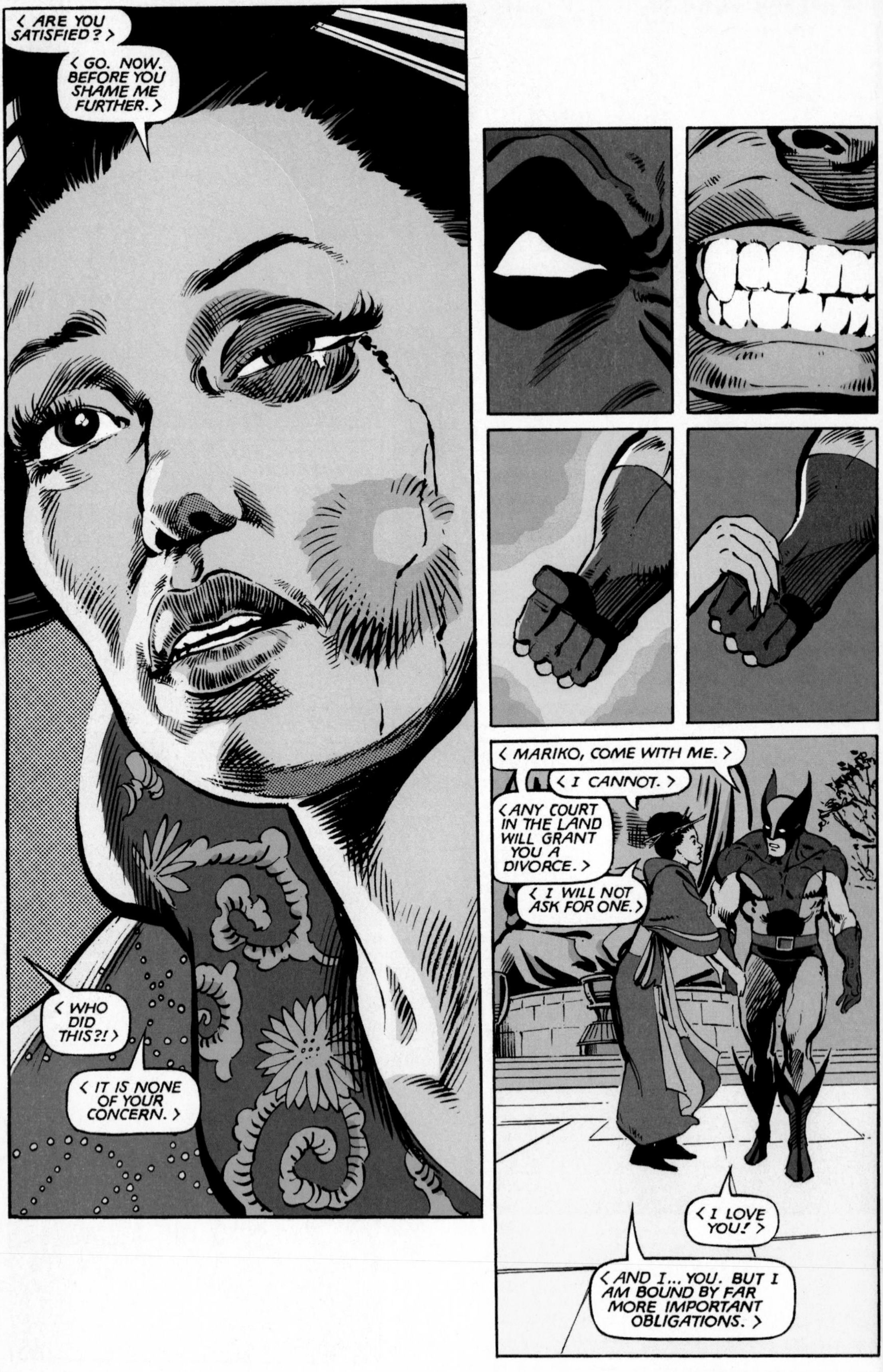
< ARE YOU SATISFIED? >
< GO. NOW. BEFORE YOU SHAME ME FURTHER. >
< WHO DID THIS?! >
< IT IS NONE OF YOUR CONCERN. >
< MARIKO, COME WITH ME. >
< I CANNOT. >
< ANY COURT IN THE LAND WILL GRANT YOU A DIVORCE. >
< I WILL NOT ASK FOR ONE. >
< I LOVE YOU! >
< AND I... YOU. BUT I AM BOUND BY FAR MORE IMPORTANT OBLIGATIONS. >

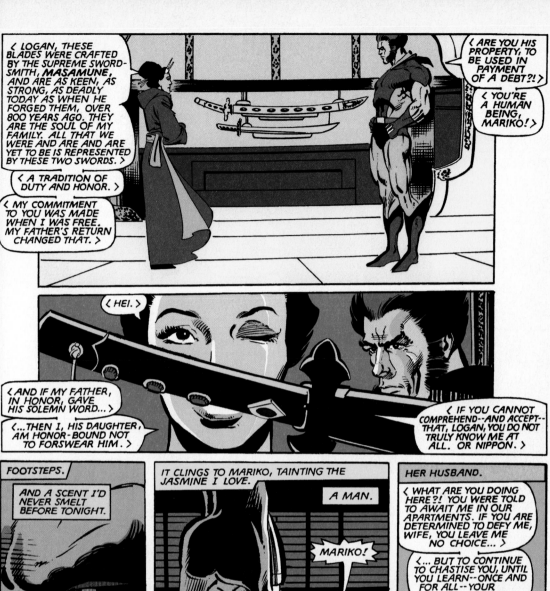

< LOGAN, THESE BLADES WERE CRAFTED BY THE SUPREME SWORD-SMITH, MASAMUNE, AND ARE AS KEEN, AS STRONG, AS DEADLY TODAY AS WHEN HE FORGED THEM, OVER 800 YEARS AGO. THEY ARE THE SOUL OF MY FAMILY. ALL THAT WE WERE AND ARE AND ARE YET TO BE IS REPRESENTED BY THESE TWO SWORDS. >

< A TRADITION OF DUTY AND HONOR. >

< MY COMMITMENT TO YOU WAS MADE WHEN I WAS FREE. MY FATHER'S RETURN CHANGED THAT. >

< ARE YOU HIS PROPERTY, TO BE USED IN PAYMENT OF A DEBT?! >

< YOU'RE A HUMAN BEING, MARIKO! >

< HEI. >

< AND IF MY FATHER, IN HONOR, GAVE HIS SOLEMN WORD... >

< ...THEN I, HIS DAUGHTER, AM HONOR-BOUND NOT TO FORSWEAR HIM. >

< IF YOU CANNOT COMPREHEND--AND ACCEPT--THAT, LOGAN, YOU DO NOT TRULY KNOW ME AT ALL. OR NIPPON. >

FOOTSTEPS.

AND A SCENT I'D NEVER SMELT BEFORE TONIGHT.

YET ONE I RECOGNIZE INSTANTLY.

IT CLINGS TO MARIKO, TAINTING THE JASMINE I LOVE.

A MAN.

MARIKO!

HER HUSBAND.

< WHAT ARE YOU DOING HERE?! YOU WERE TOLD TO AWAIT ME IN OUR APARTMENTS. IF YOU ARE DETERMINED TO DEFY ME, WIFE, YOU LEAVE ME NO CHOICE... >

< ...BUT TO CONTINUE TO CHASTISE YOU, UNTIL YOU LEARN--ONCE AND FOR ALL--YOUR PROPER PLACE. >

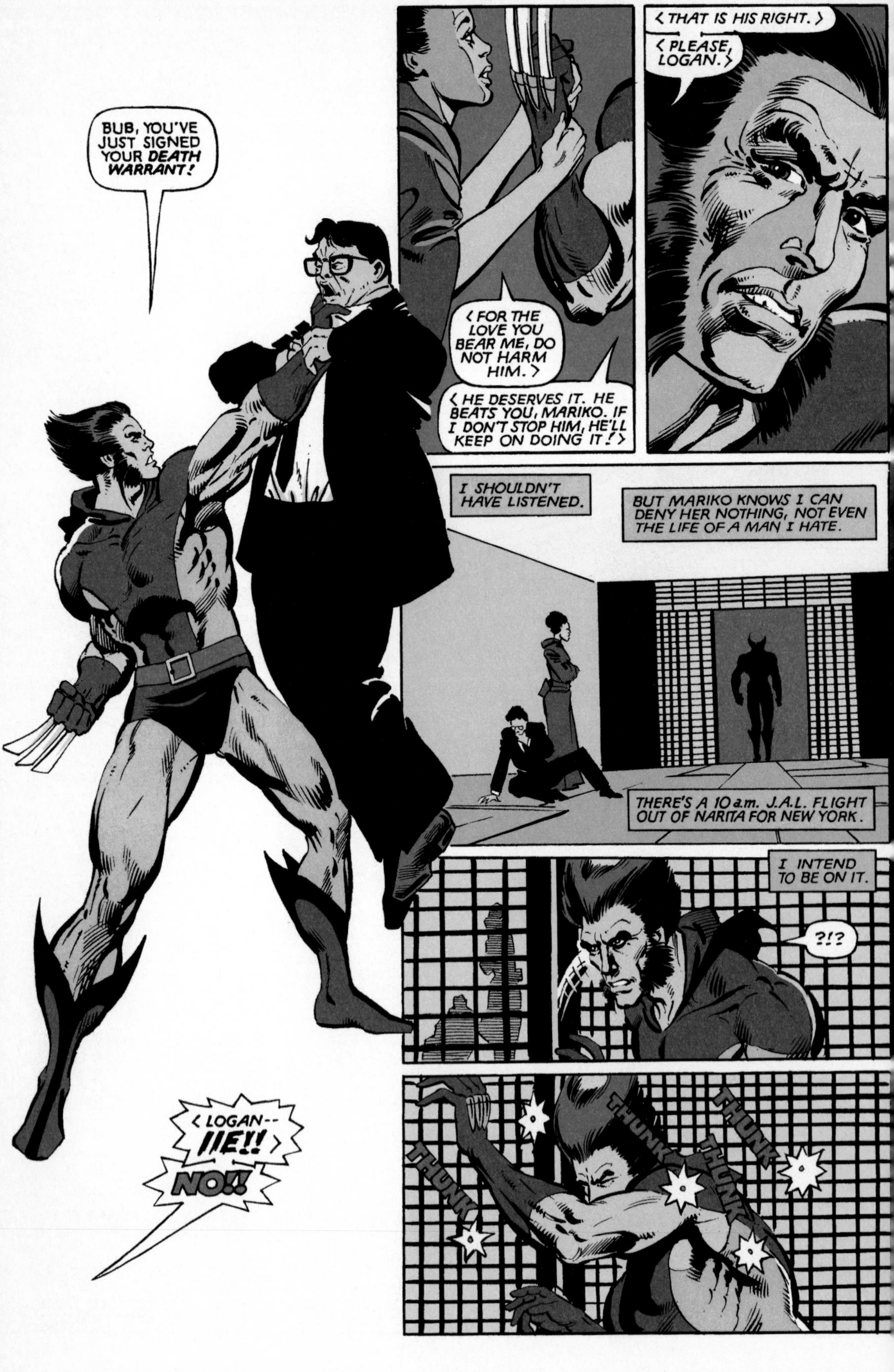
BUB, YOU'VE JUST SIGNED YOUR DEATH WARRANT!
< LOGAN-- IIE!! >
NO!!
< FOR THE LOVE YOU BEAR ME, DO NOT HARM HIM. >
< HE DESERVES IT. HE BEATS YOU, MARIKO. IF I DON'T STOP HIM, HE'LL KEEP ON DOING IT! >
< THAT IS HIS RIGHT. >
< PLEASE, LOGAN. >
I SHOULDN'T HAVE LISTENED.
BUT MARIKO KNOWS I CAN DENY HER NOTHING, NOT EVEN THE LIFE OF A MAN I HATE.
THERE'S A 10 a.m. J.A.L. FLIGHT OUT OF NARITA FOR NEW YORK.
I INTEND TO BE ON IT.
?!?
THUNK
THUNK
THUNK
THUNK

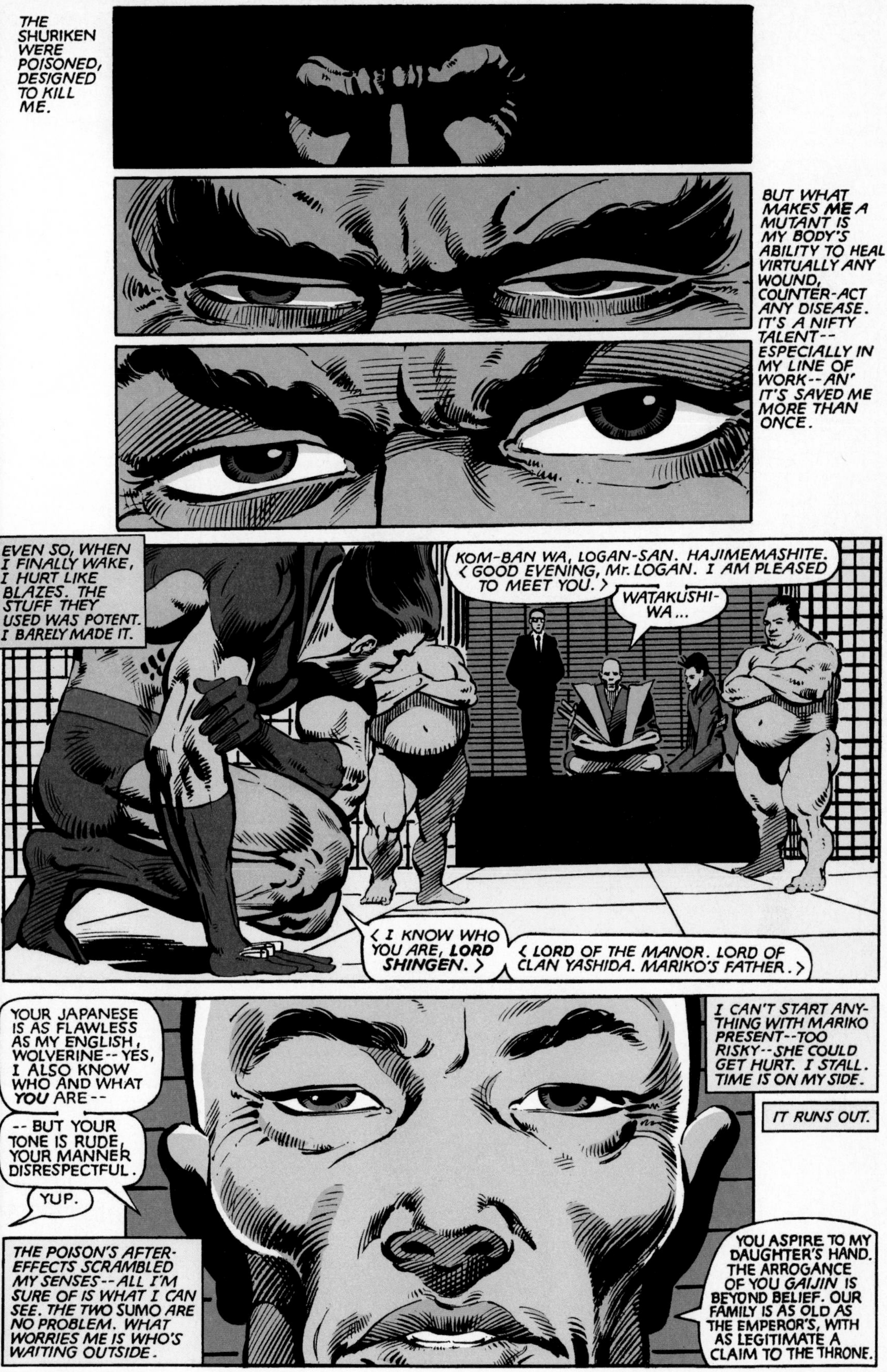

THE SHURIKEN WERE POISONED, DESIGNED TO KILL ME.
BUT WHAT MAKES ME A MUTANT IS MY BODY'S ABILITY TO HEAL VIRTUALLY ANY WOUND, COUNTER-ACT ANY DISEASE. IT'S A NIFTY TALENT-- ESPECIALLY IN MY LINE OF WORK-- AN' IT'S SAVED ME MORE THAN ONCE.
EVEN SO, WHEN I FINALLY WAKE, I HURT LIKE BLAZES. THE STUFF THEY USED WAS POTENT. I BARELY MADE IT.
KOM-BAN WA, LOGAN-SAN. HAJIMEMASHITE. < GOOD EVENING, Mr. LOGAN. I AM PLEASED TO MEET YOU. >
WATAKUSHI-WA...
< I KNOW WHO YOU ARE, LORD SHINGEN. >
< LORD OF THE MANOR. LORD OF CLAN YASHIDA. MARIKO'S FATHER. >
YOUR JAPANESE IS AS FLAWLESS AS MY ENGLISH, WOLVERINE-- YES, I ALSO KNOW WHO AND WHAT YOU ARE--
-- BUT YOUR TONE IS RUDE, YOUR MANNER DISRESPECTFUL.
YUP.
I CAN'T START ANYTHING WITH MARIKO PRESENT--TOO RISKY--SHE COULD GET HURT. I STALL. TIME IS ON MY SIDE.
IT RUNS OUT.
THE POISON'S AFTER-EFFECTS SCRAMBLED MY SENSES-- ALL I'M SURE OF IS WHAT I CAN SEE. THE TWO SUMO ARE NO PROBLEM. WHAT WORRIES ME IS WHO'S WAITING OUTSIDE.
YOU ASPIRE TO MY DAUGHTER'S HAND. THE ARROGANCE OF YOU GAIJIN IS BEYOND BELIEF. OUR FAMILY IS AS OLD AS THE EMPEROR'S, WITH AS LEGITIMATE A CLAIM TO THE THRONE.

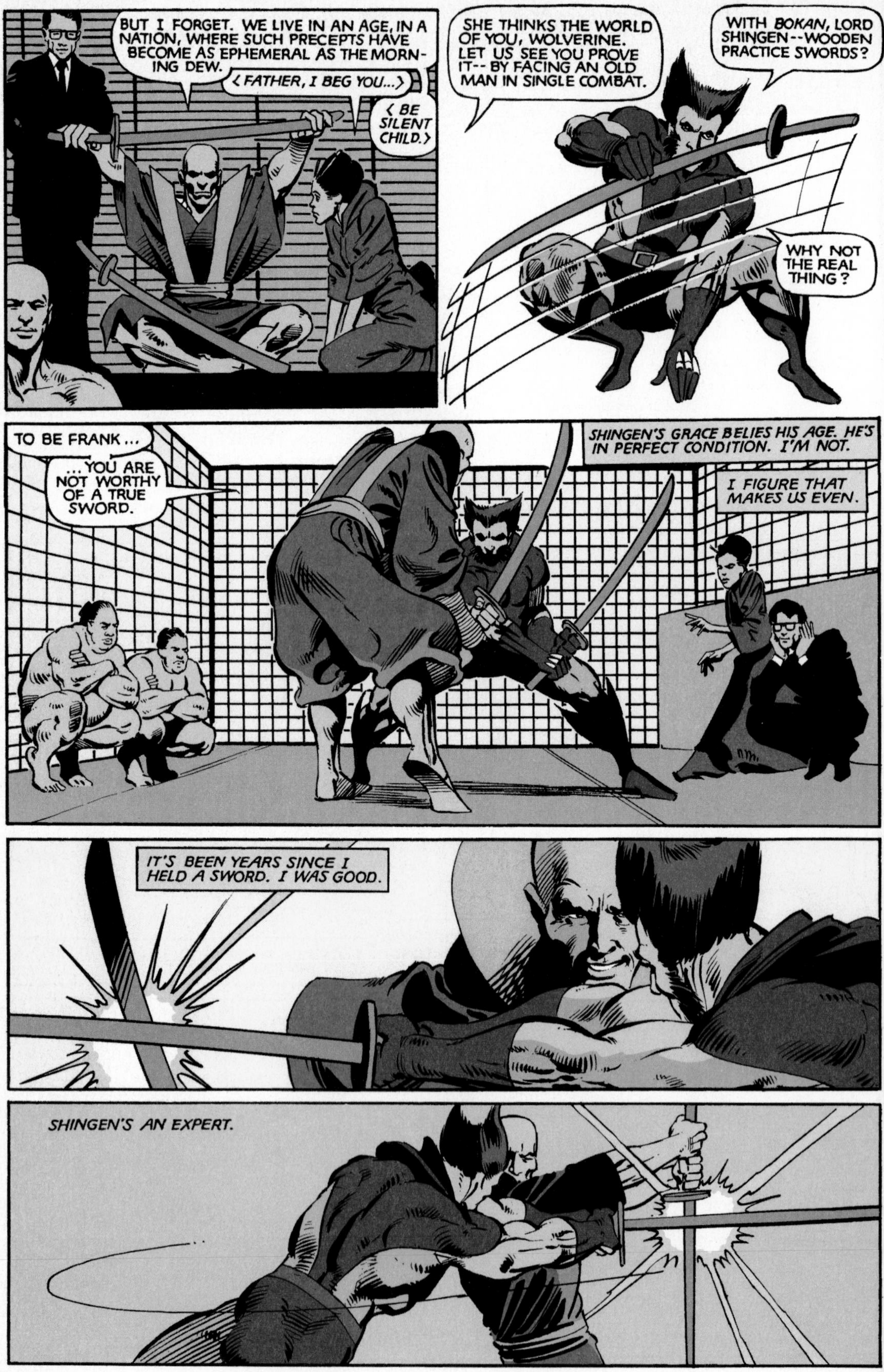
BUT I FORGET. WE LIVE IN AN AGE, IN A NATION, WHERE SUCH PRECEPTS HAVE BECOME AS EPHEMERAL AS THE MORNING DEW.
‹FATHER, I BEG YOU...›
‹BE SILENT CHILD.›
SHE THINKS THE WORLD OF YOU, WOLVERINE. LET US SEE YOU PROVE IT-- BY FACING AN OLD MAN IN SINGLE COMBAT.
WITH BOKAN, LORD SHINGEN--WOODEN PRACTICE SWORDS?
WHY NOT THE REAL THING?
TO BE FRANK...
...YOU ARE NOT WORTHY OF A TRUE SWORD.
SHINGEN'S GRACE BELIES HIS AGE. HE'S IN PERFECT CONDITION. I'M NOT.
I FIGURE THAT MAKES US EVEN.
IT'S BEEN YEARS SINCE I HELD A SWORD. I WAS GOOD.
SHINGEN'S AN EXPERT.

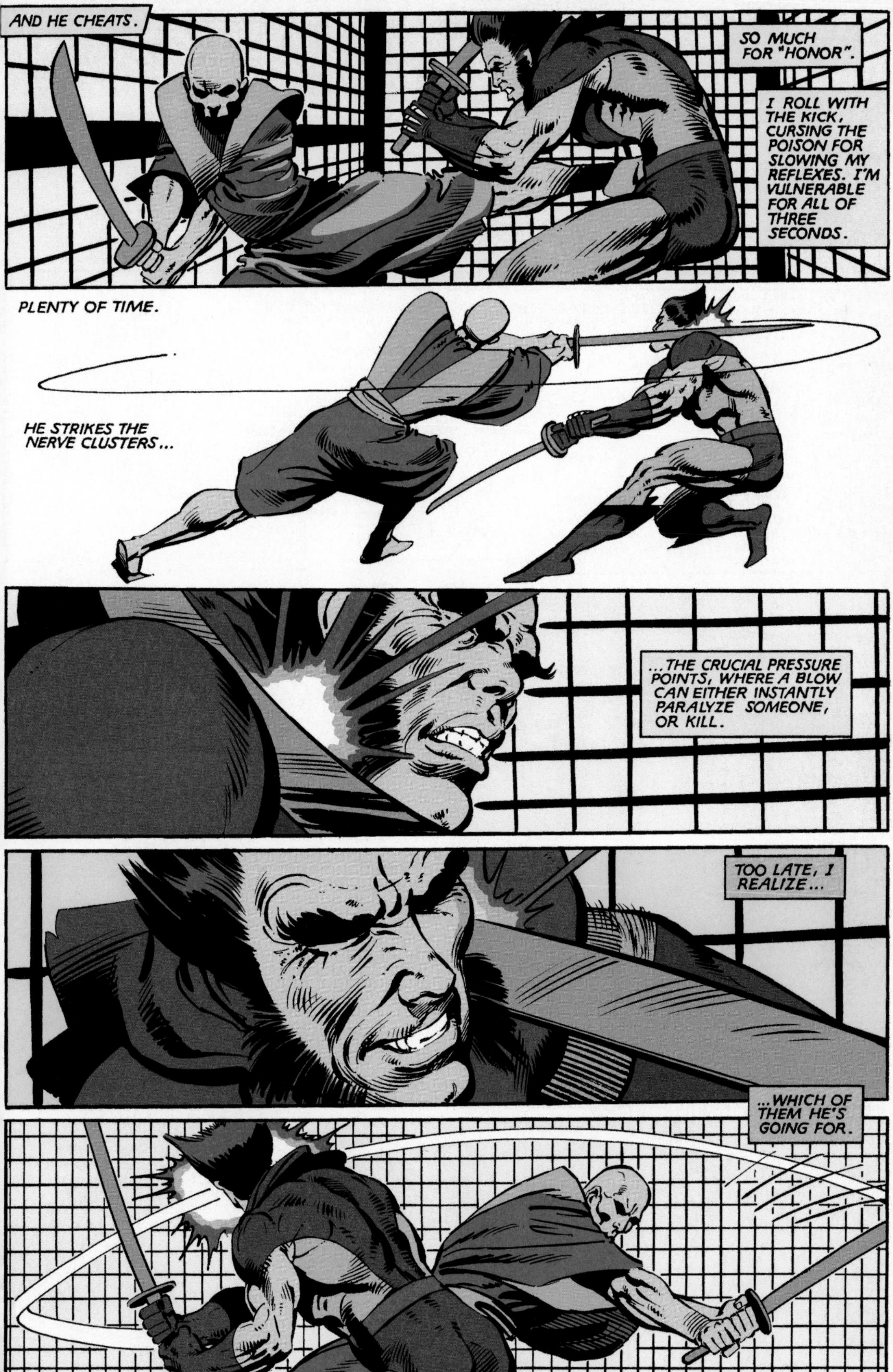
AND HE CHEATS.
SO MUCH FOR "HONOR".
I ROLL WITH THE KICK, CURSING THE POISON FOR SLOWING MY REFLEXES. I'M VULNERABLE FOR ALL OF THREE SECONDS.
PLENTY OF TIME.
HE STRIKES THE NERVE CLUSTERS...
...THE CRUCIAL PRESSURE POINTS, WHERE A BLOW CAN EITHER INSTANTLY PARALYZE SOMEONE, OR KILL.
TOO LATE, I REALIZE...
...WHICH OF THEM HE'S GOING FOR.

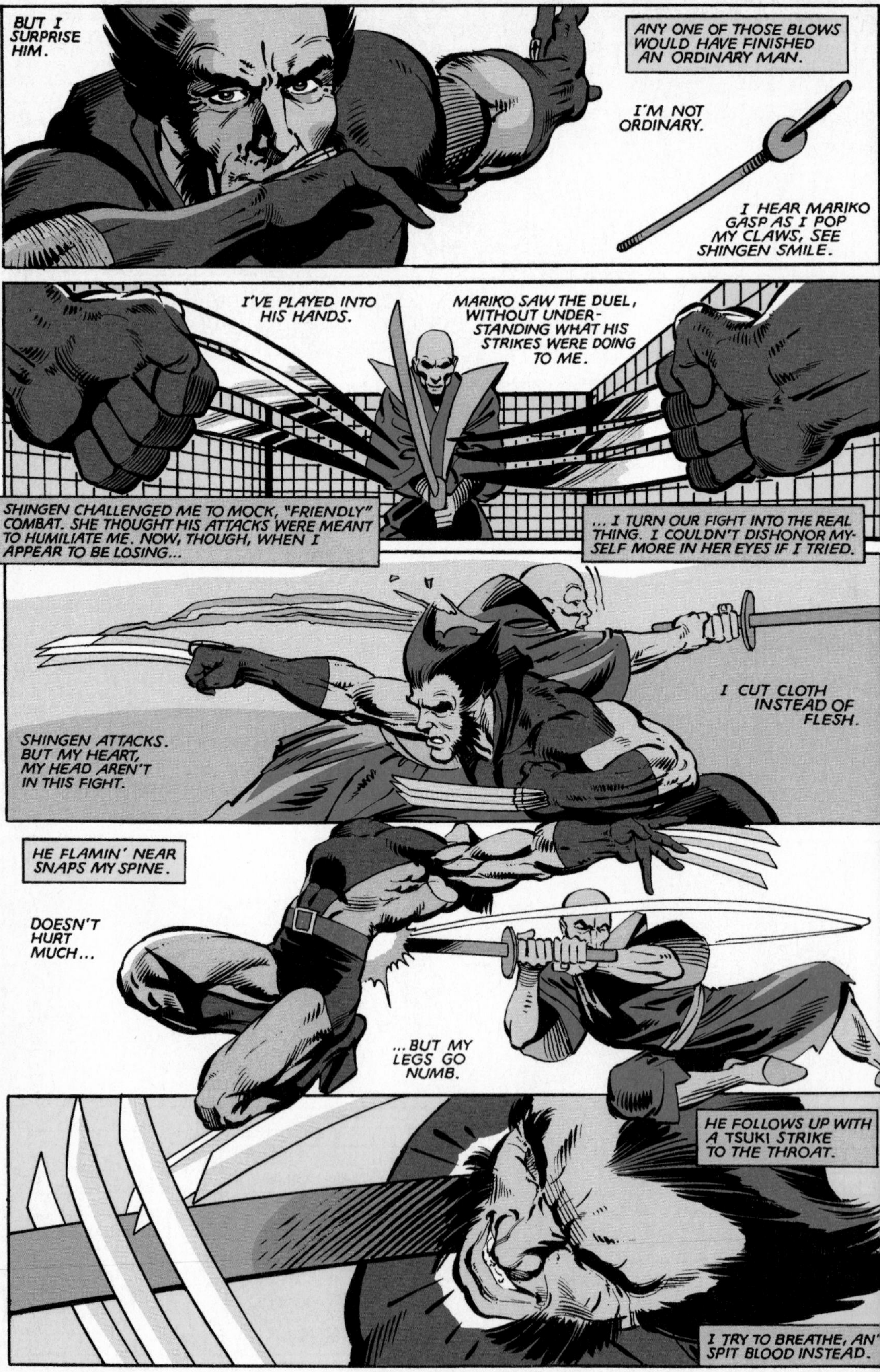
BUT I SURPRISE HIM.
ANY ONE OF THOSE BLOWS WOULD HAVE FINISHED AN ORDINARY MAN.
I'M NOT ORDINARY.
I HEAR MARIKO GASP AS I POP MY CLAWS, SEE SHINGEN SMILE.
I'VE PLAYED INTO HIS HANDS.
MARIKO SAW THE DUEL, WITHOUT UNDER-STANDING WHAT HIS STRIKES WERE DOING TO ME.
SHINGEN CHALLENGED ME TO MOCK, "FRIENDLY" COMBAT. SHE THOUGHT HIS ATTACKS WERE MEANT TO HUMILIATE ME. NOW, THOUGH, WHEN I APPEAR TO BE LOSING...
... I TURN OUR FIGHT INTO THE REAL THING. I COULDN'T DISHONOR MY-SELF MORE IN HER EYES IF I TRIED.
SHINGEN ATTACKS. BUT MY HEART, MY HEAD AREN'T IN THIS FIGHT.
I CUT CLOTH INSTEAD OF FLESH.
HE FLAMIN' NEAR SNAPS MY SPINE.
DOESN'T HURT MUCH...
...BUT MY LEGS GO NUMB.
HE FOLLOWS UP WITH A TSUKI STRIKE TO THE THROAT.
I TRY TO BREATHE, AN' SPIT BLOOD INSTEAD.

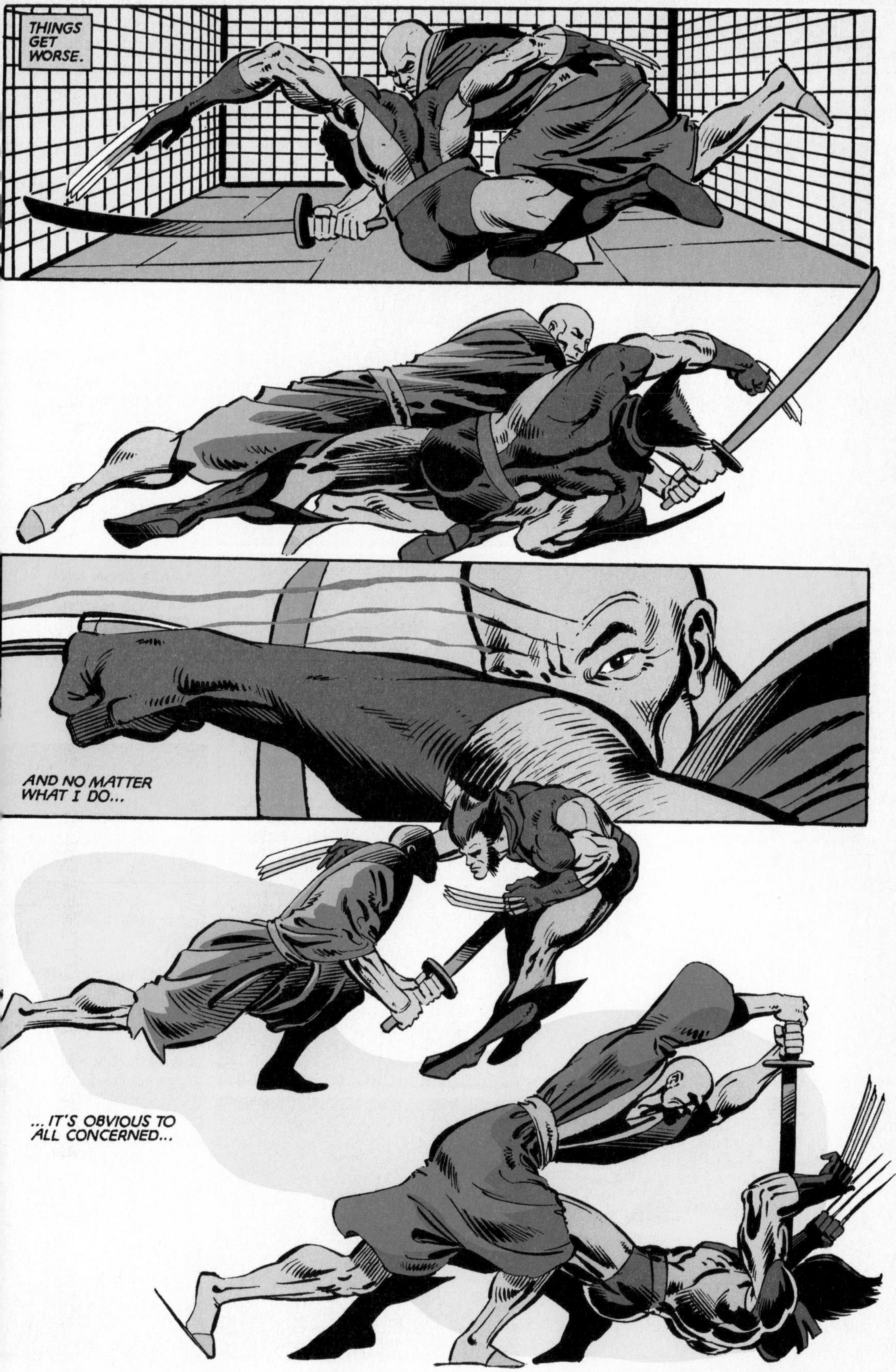
THINGS GET WORSE.
AND NO MATTER WHAT I DO...
...IT'S OBVIOUS TO ALL CONCERNED...

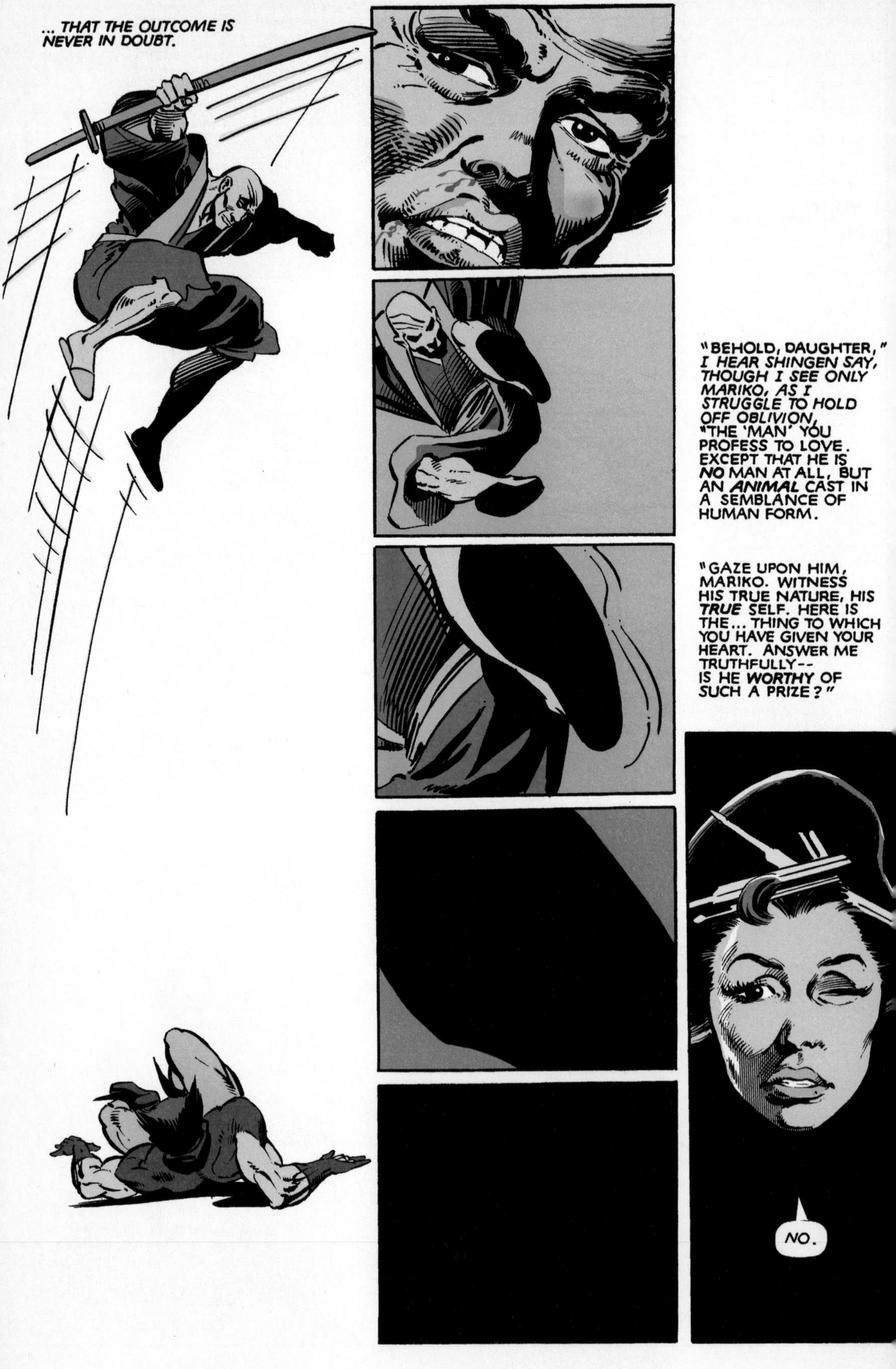

... THAT THE OUTCOME IS NEVER IN DOUBT.
"BEHOLD, DAUGHTER," I HEAR SHINGEN SAY, THOUGH I SEE ONLY MARIKO, AS I STRUGGLE TO HOLD OFF OBLIVION, "THE 'MAN' YOU PROFESS TO LOVE. EXCEPT THAT HE IS NO MAN AT ALL, BUT AN ANIMAL CAST IN A SEMBLANCE OF HUMAN FORM.
"GAZE UPON HIM, MARIKO. WITNESS HIS TRUE NATURE, HIS TRUE SELF. HERE IS THE... THING TO WHICH YOU HAVE GIVEN YOUR HEART. ANSWER ME TRUTHFULLY-- IS HE WORTHY OF SUCH A PRIZE?"
NO.

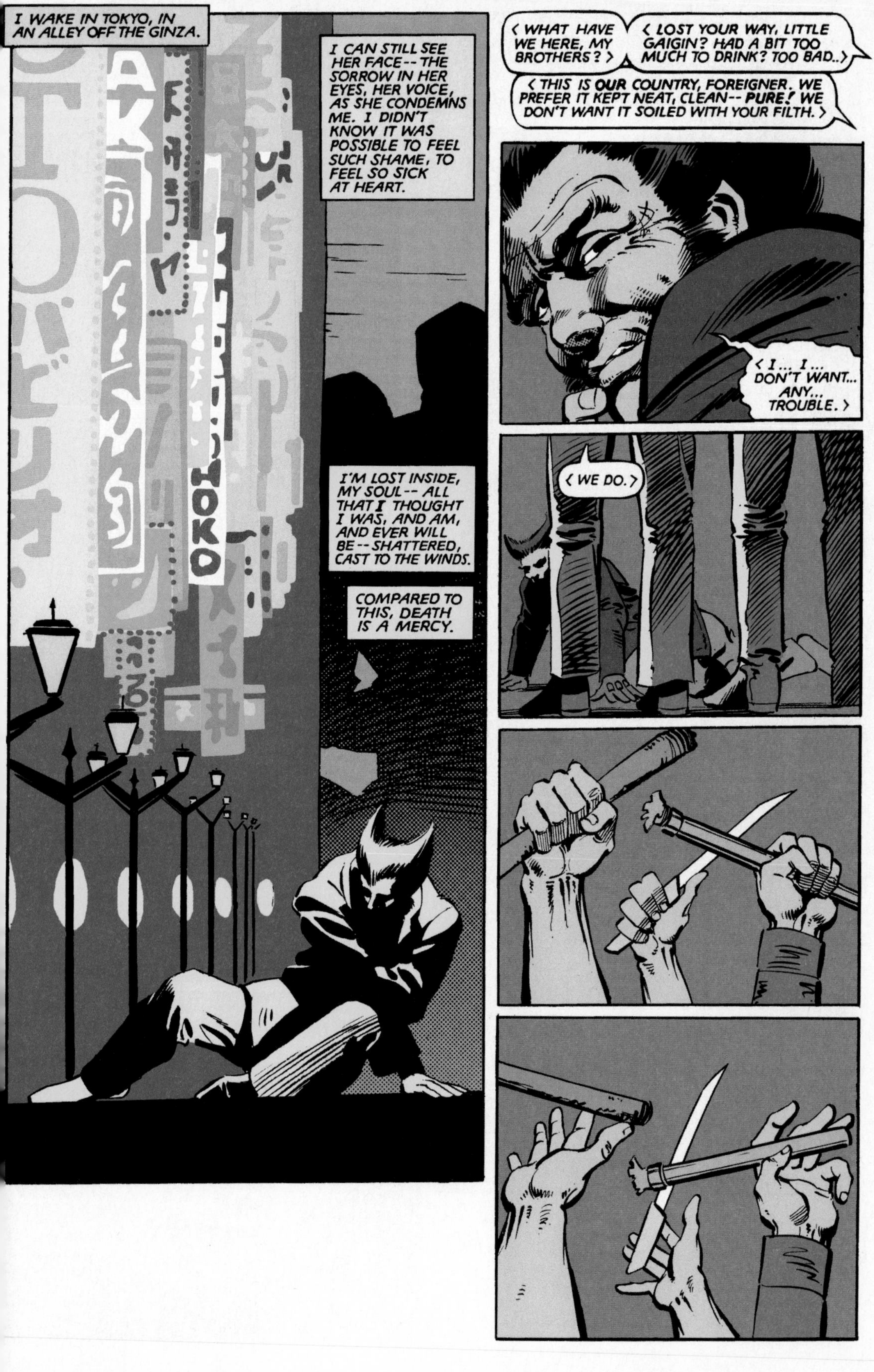

I WAKE IN TOKYO, IN AN ALLEY OFF THE GINZA.
I CAN STILL SEE HER FACE-- THE SORROW IN HER EYES, HER VOICE, AS SHE CONDEMNS ME. I DIDN'T KNOW IT WAS POSSIBLE TO FEEL SUCH SHAME, TO FEEL SO SICK AT HEART.
I'M LOST INSIDE, MY SOUL-- ALL THAT I THOUGHT I WAS, AND AM, AND EVER WILL BE-- SHATTERED, CAST TO THE WINDS.
COMPARED TO THIS, DEATH IS A MERCY.
‹ WHAT HAVE WE HERE, MY BROTHERS? ›
‹ LOST YOUR WAY, LITTLE GAIGIN? HAD A BIT TOO MUCH TO DRINK? TOO BAD.. ›
‹ THIS IS OUR COUNTRY, FOREIGNER. WE PREFER IT KEPT NEAT, CLEAN-- PURE! WE DON'T WANT IT SOILED WITH YOUR FILTH. ›
‹ I... I... DON'T WANT... ANY... TROUBLE. ›
‹ WE DO. ›

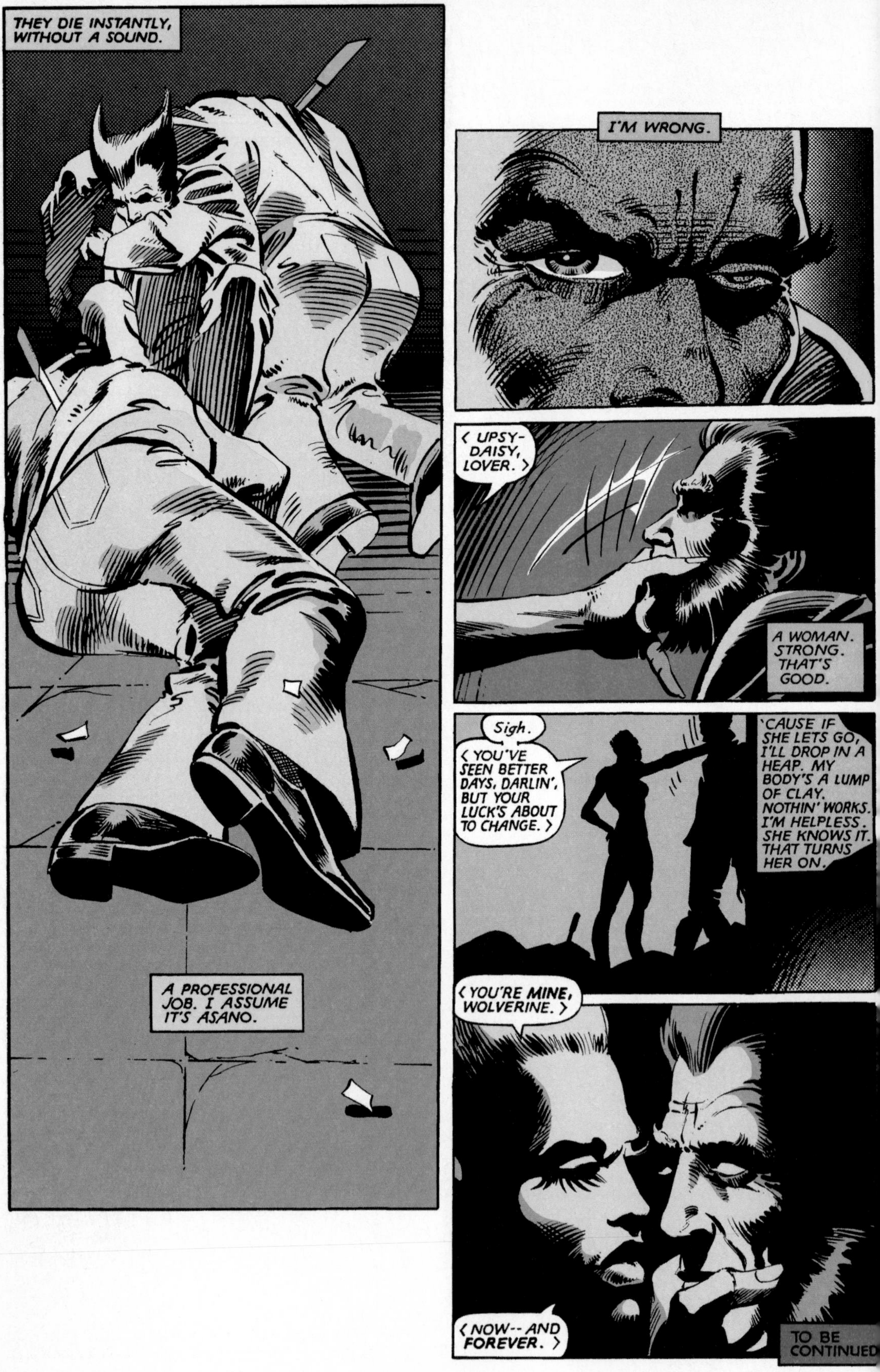
THEY DIE INSTANTLY, WITHOUT A SOUND.
A PROFESSIONAL JOB. I ASSUME IT'S ASANO.
I'M WRONG.
‹ UPSY-DAISY, LOVER. ›
A WOMAN. STRONG. THAT'S GOOD.
Sigh.
‹ YOU'VE SEEN BETTER DAYS, DARLIN', BUT YOUR LUCK'S ABOUT TO CHANGE. ›
'CAUSE IF SHE LETS GO, I'LL DROP IN A HEAP. MY BODY'S A LUMP OF CLAY. NOTHIN' WORKS. I'M HELPLESS. SHE KNOWS IT. THAT TURNS HER ON.
‹ YOU'RE MINE, WOLVERINE. ›
‹ NOW-- AND FOREVER. ›
TO BE CONTINUED

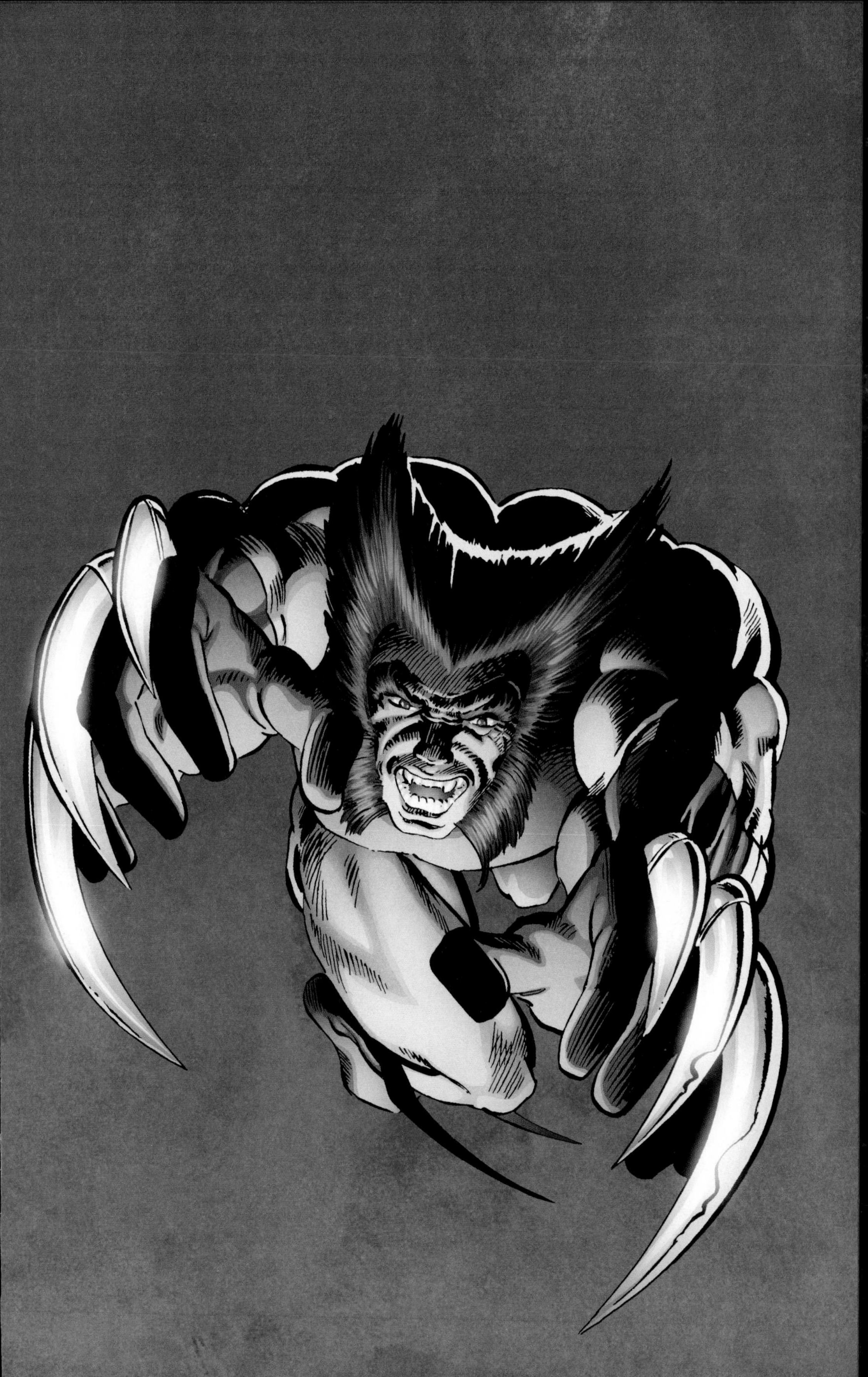

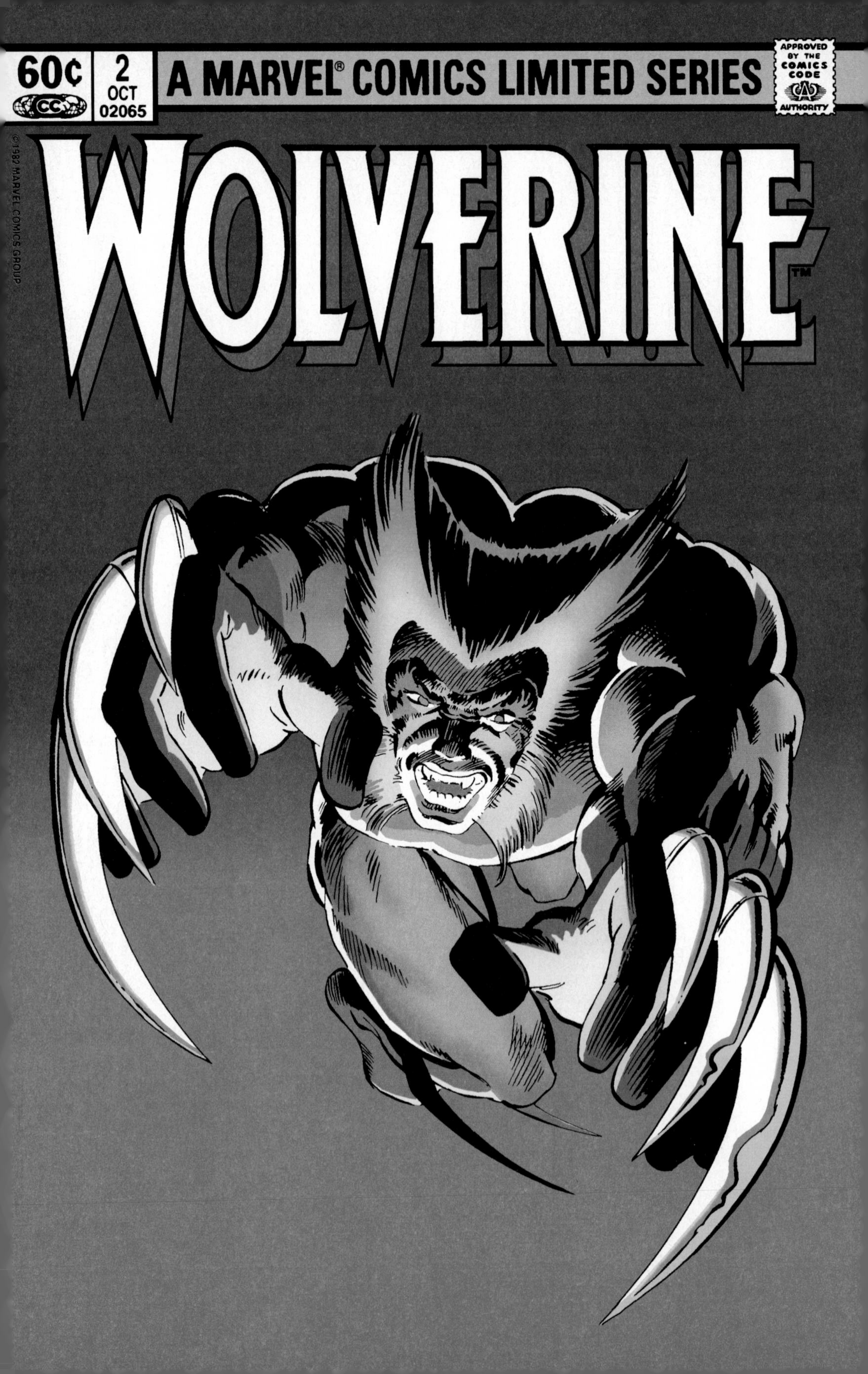
60¢
2
OCT
02065
A MARVEL® COMICS LIMITED SERIES
APPROVED BY THE COMICS CODE AUTHORITY
© 1982 MARVEL COMICS GROUP
WOLVERINE™

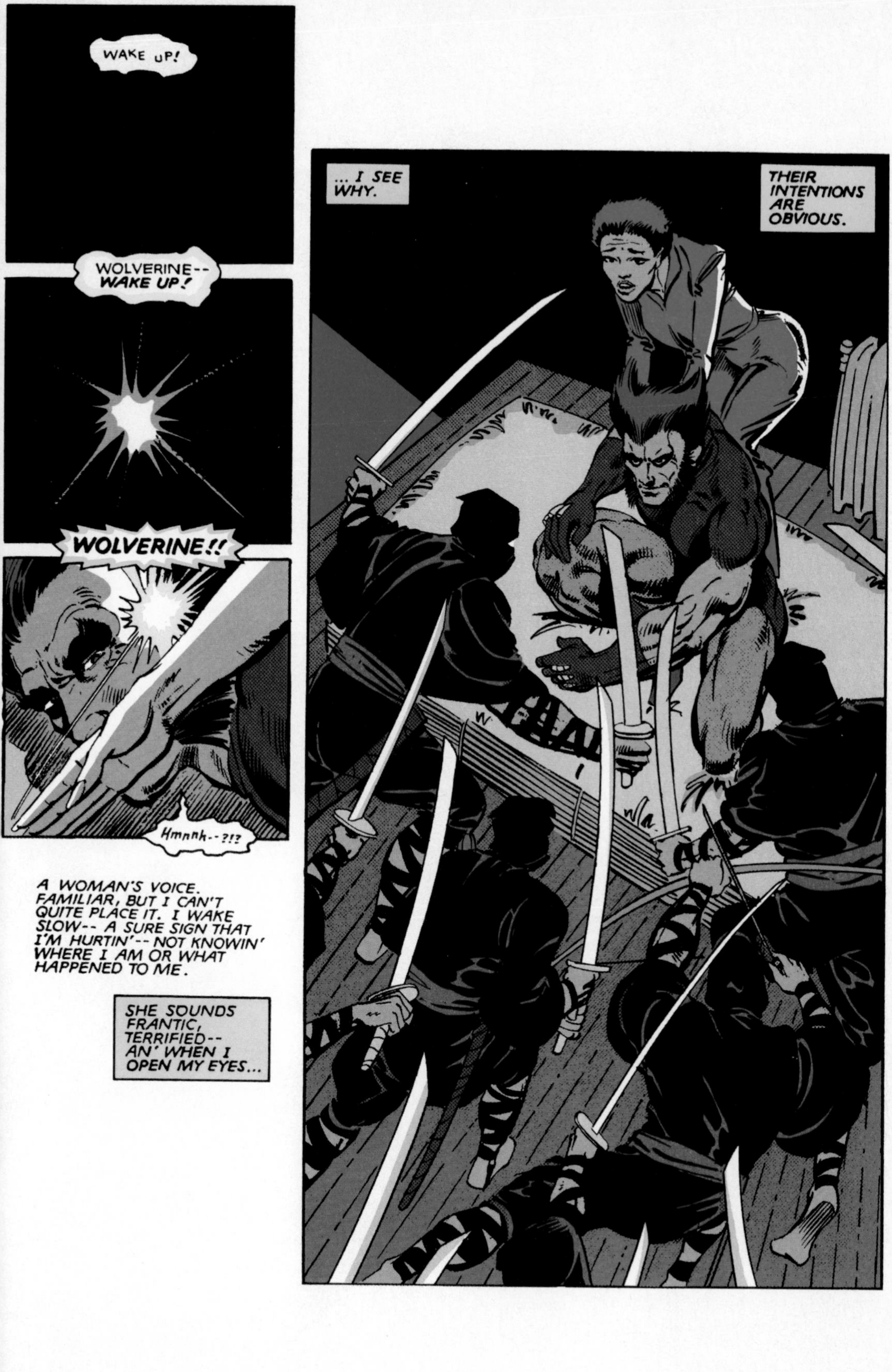
WAKE UP!
WOLVERINE-- WAKE UP!
WOLVERINE!!
Hmnnh--?!?
A WOMAN'S VOICE. FAMILIAR, BUT I CAN'T QUITE PLACE IT. I WAKE SLOW-- A SURE SIGN THAT I'M HURTIN'-- NOT KNOWIN' WHERE I AM OR WHAT HAPPENED TO ME.
SHE SOUNDS FRANTIC, TERRIFIED-- AN' WHEN I OPEN MY EYES...
...I SEE WHY.
THEIR INTENTIONS ARE OBVIOUS.

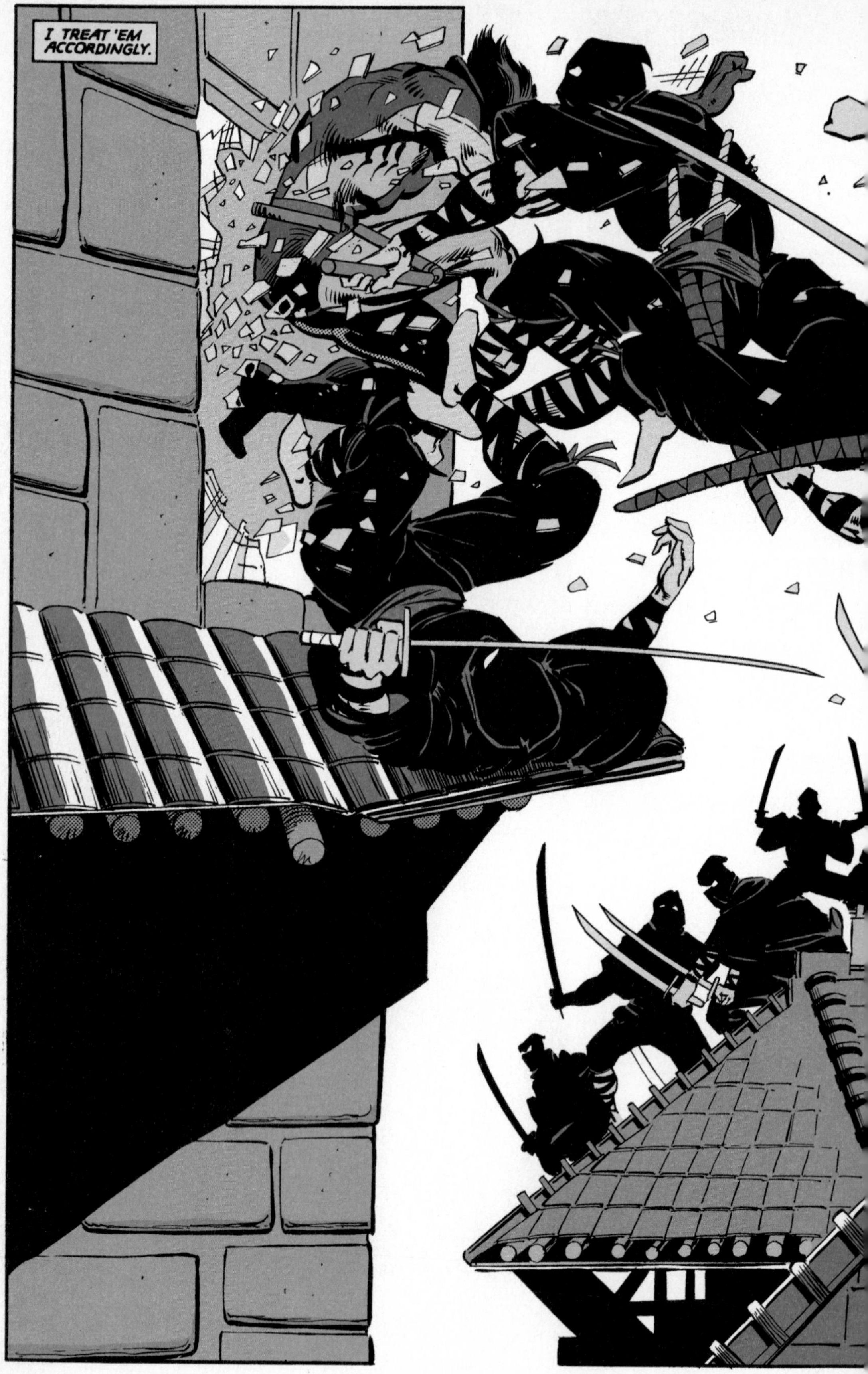
I TREAT 'EM ACCORDINGLY.

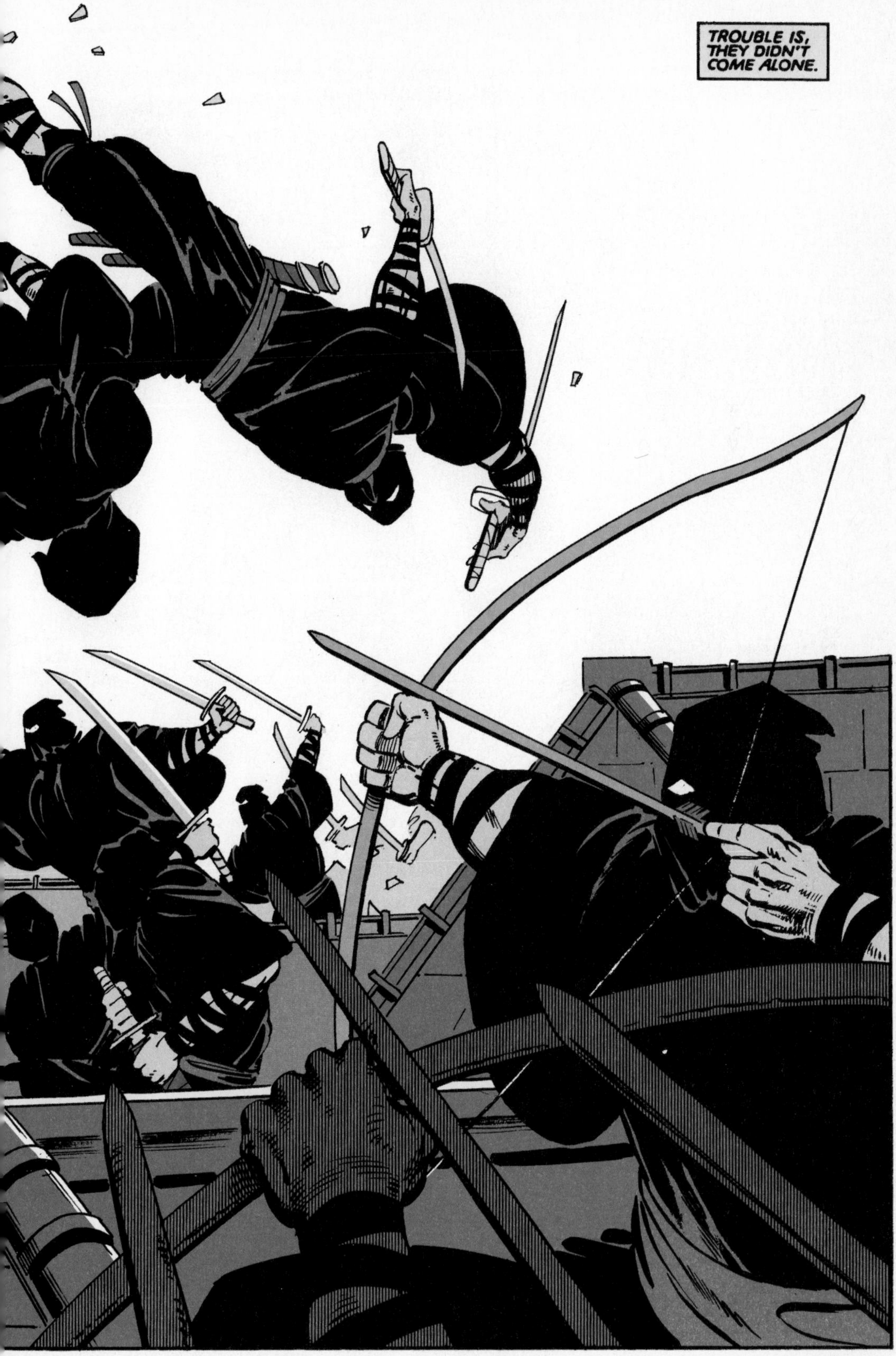
TROUBLE IS, THEY DIDN'T COME ALONE.

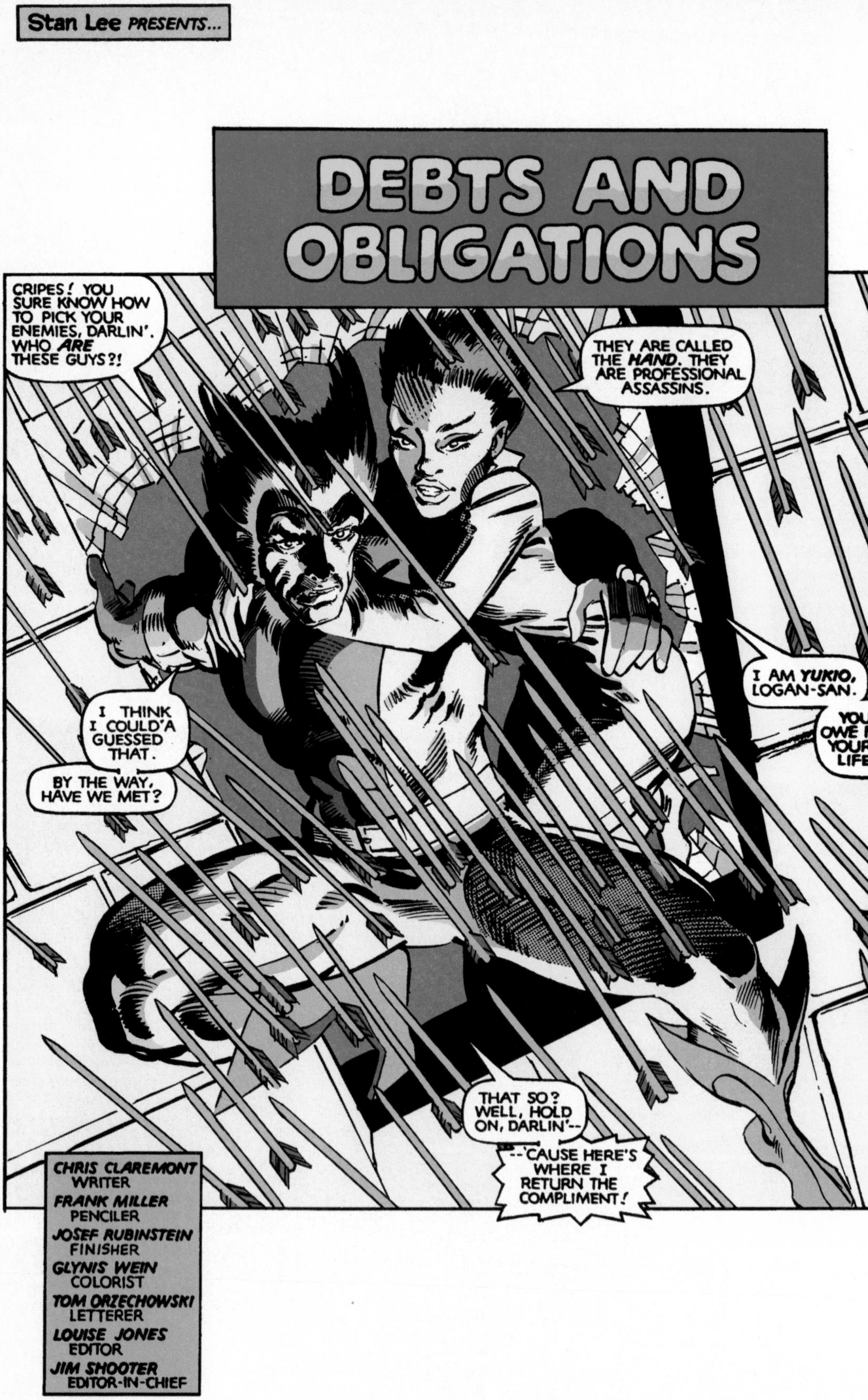
Stan Lee PRESENTS...
DEBTS AND OBLIGATIONS
CRIPES! YOU SURE KNOW HOW TO PICK YOUR ENEMIES, DARLIN'. WHO ARE THESE GUYS?!
THEY ARE CALLED THE HAND. THEY ARE PROFESSIONAL ASSASSINS.
I THINK I COULD'A GUESSED THAT.
BY THE WAY, HAVE WE MET?
I AM YUKIO, LOGAN-SAN.
YOU OWE ME YOUR LIFE.
THAT SO? WELL, HOLD ON, DARLIN'--
--'CAUSE HERE'S WHERE I RETURN THE COMPLIMENT!
CHRIS CLAREMONT WRITER
FRANK MILLER PENCILER
JOSEF RUBINSTEIN FINISHER
GLYNIS WEIN COLORIST
TOM ORZECHOWSKI LETTERER
LOUISE JONES EDITOR
JIM SHOOTER EDITOR-IN-CHIEF

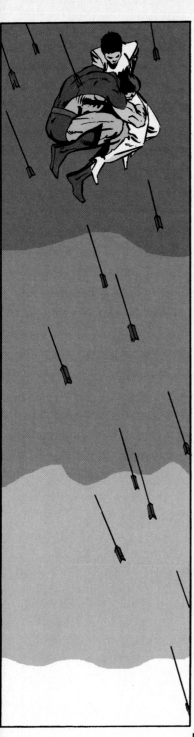

AS I MOVE-- AS ADRENALIN PUMPS THROUGH MY SYSTEM-- MY SKULL FINALLY KICKS INTO GEAR. THE CITY IS TOKYO. I'D COME HERE LOOKIN' FOR THE WOMAN I'D LOVED-- *MARIKO YASHIDA*-- AN' FOUND HER MARRIED TO ANOTHER MAN. FOR MY TROUBLES, I WAS BEATEN NEAR TO DEATH BY HER FATHER, *SHINGEN.*

HE MEANT TO KILL ME, BUT HE HADN'T RECKONED WITH MY BODY'S MUTANT ABILITY TO HEAL ITSELF. THANKS TO THAT, I CAN SURVIVE PRETTY MUCH ANY INJURY.

I ALSO HAVE ENHANCED PHYSICAL SENSES. I'M FAST, STRONG, MEAN -- HELL ON WHEELS.

BUT SOME PEOPLE ARE NEVER SATISFIED. THEY LOVE TO TINKER, TO "IM-PROVE" ON NATURE. IN MY CASE, THESE BRIGHT BOYS DECIDED TO LACE MY SKELETON WITH ADAMANTIUM...

...MAKIN' MY BONES VIRTUALLY UNBREAKABLE. PUNCHIN' ME IS LIKE HITTIN' SOLID STEEL.

LIKE-WISE, THE OTHER WAY 'ROUND.

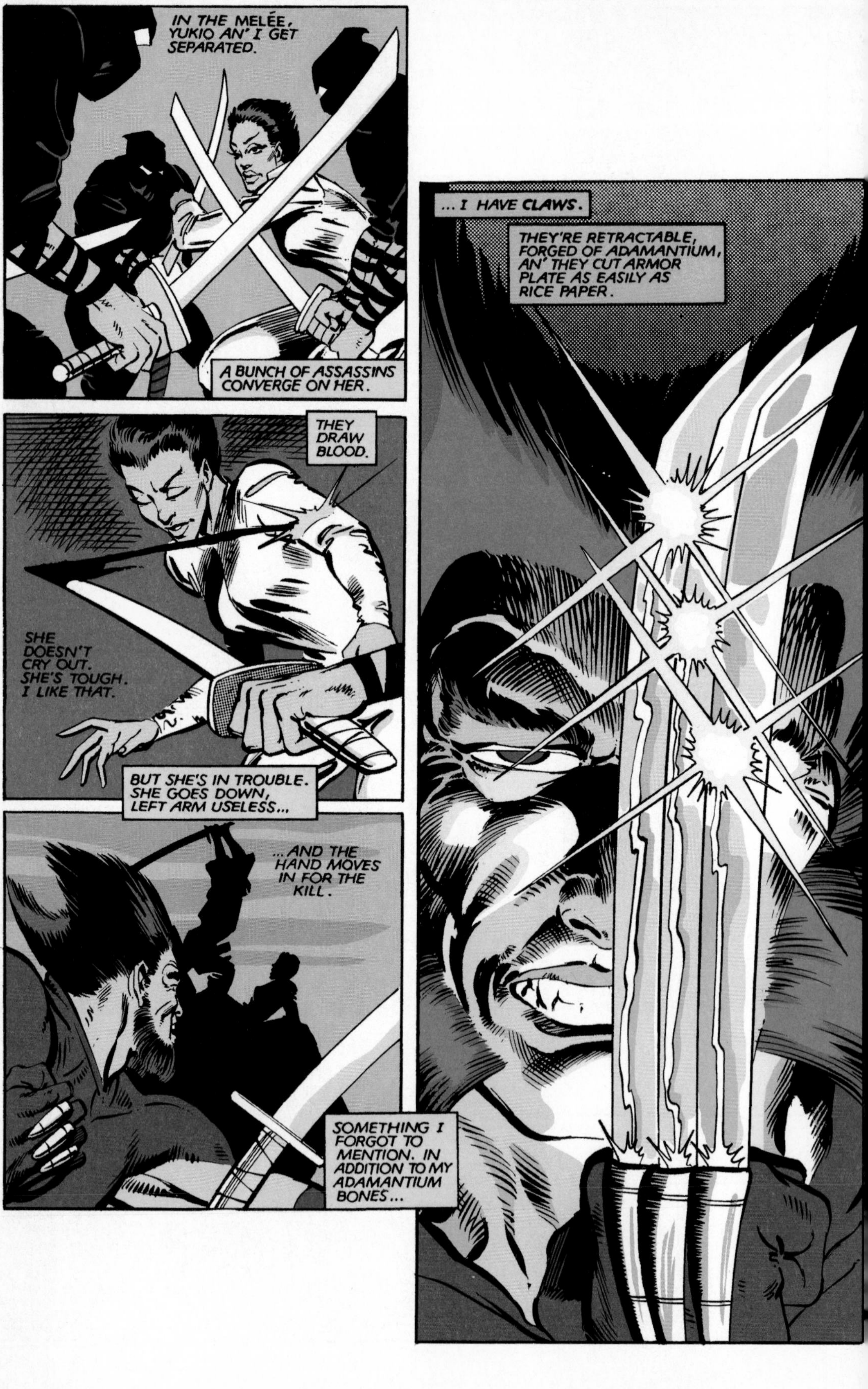
IN THE MELÉE, YUKIO AN' I GET SEPARATED.
A BUNCH OF ASSASSINS CONVERGE ON HER.
THEY DRAW BLOOD.
SHE DOESN'T CRY OUT. SHE'S TOUGH. I LIKE THAT.
BUT SHE'S IN TROUBLE. SHE GOES DOWN, LEFT ARM USELESS...
...AND THE HAND MOVES IN FOR THE KILL.
SOMETHING I FORGOT TO MENTION. IN ADDITION TO MY ADAMANTIUM BONES...
...I HAVE CLAWS.
THEY'RE RETRACTABLE, FORGED OF ADAMANTIUM, AN' THEY CUT ARMOR PLATE AS EASILY AS RICE PAPER.

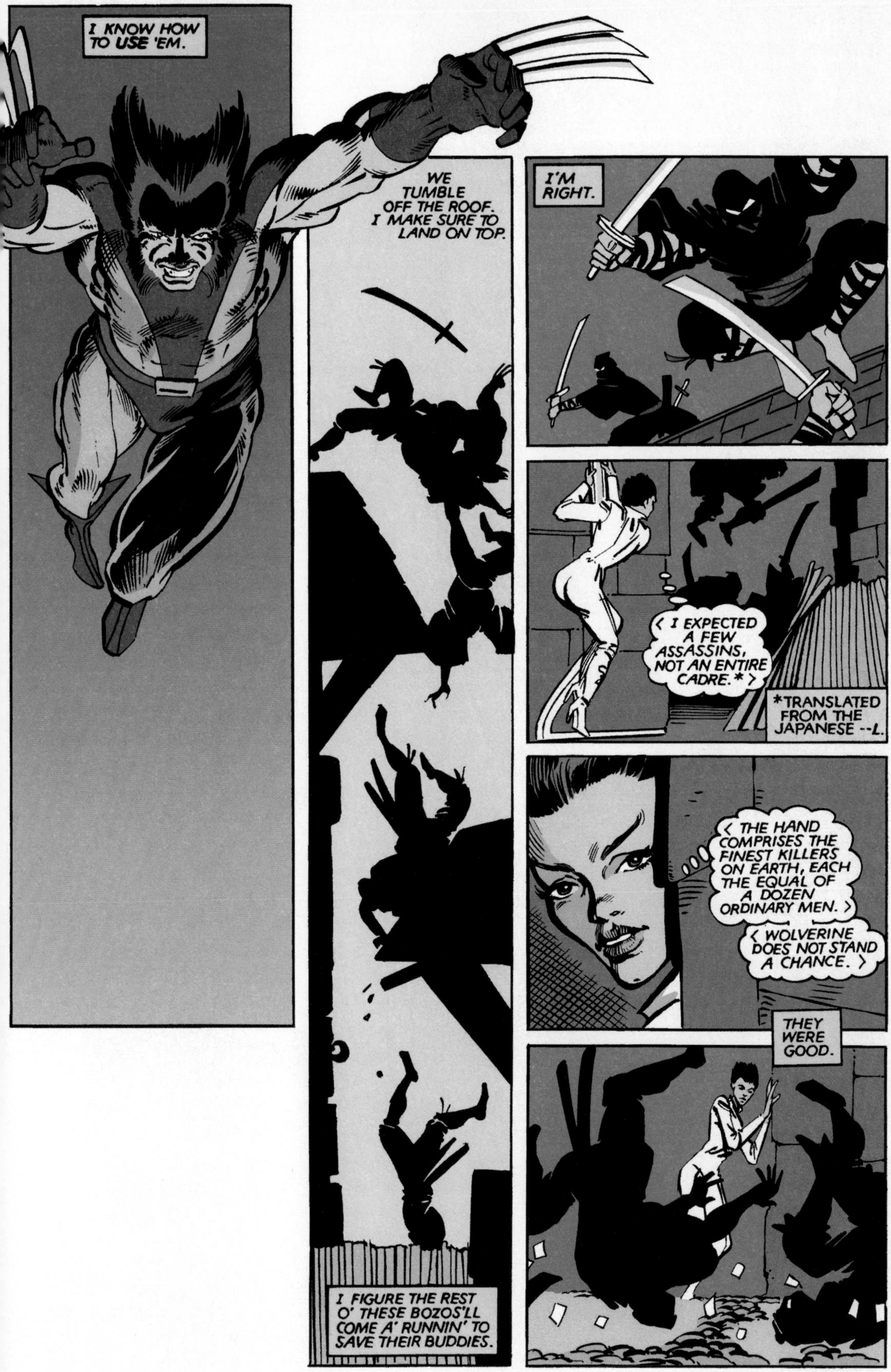
I KNOW HOW TO USE 'EM.
WE TUMBLE OFF THE ROOF. I MAKE SURE TO LAND ON TOP.
I FIGURE THE REST O' THESE BOZOS'LL COME A' RUNNIN' TO SAVE THEIR BUDDIES.
I'M RIGHT.
< I EXPECTED A FEW ASSASSINS, NOT AN ENTIRE CADRE.* >
*TRANSLATED FROM THE JAPANESE --L.
< THE HAND COMPRISES THE FINEST KILLERS ON EARTH, EACH THE EQUAL OF A DOZEN ORDINARY MEN. >
< WOLVERINE DOES NOT STAND A CHANCE. >
THEY WERE GOOD.

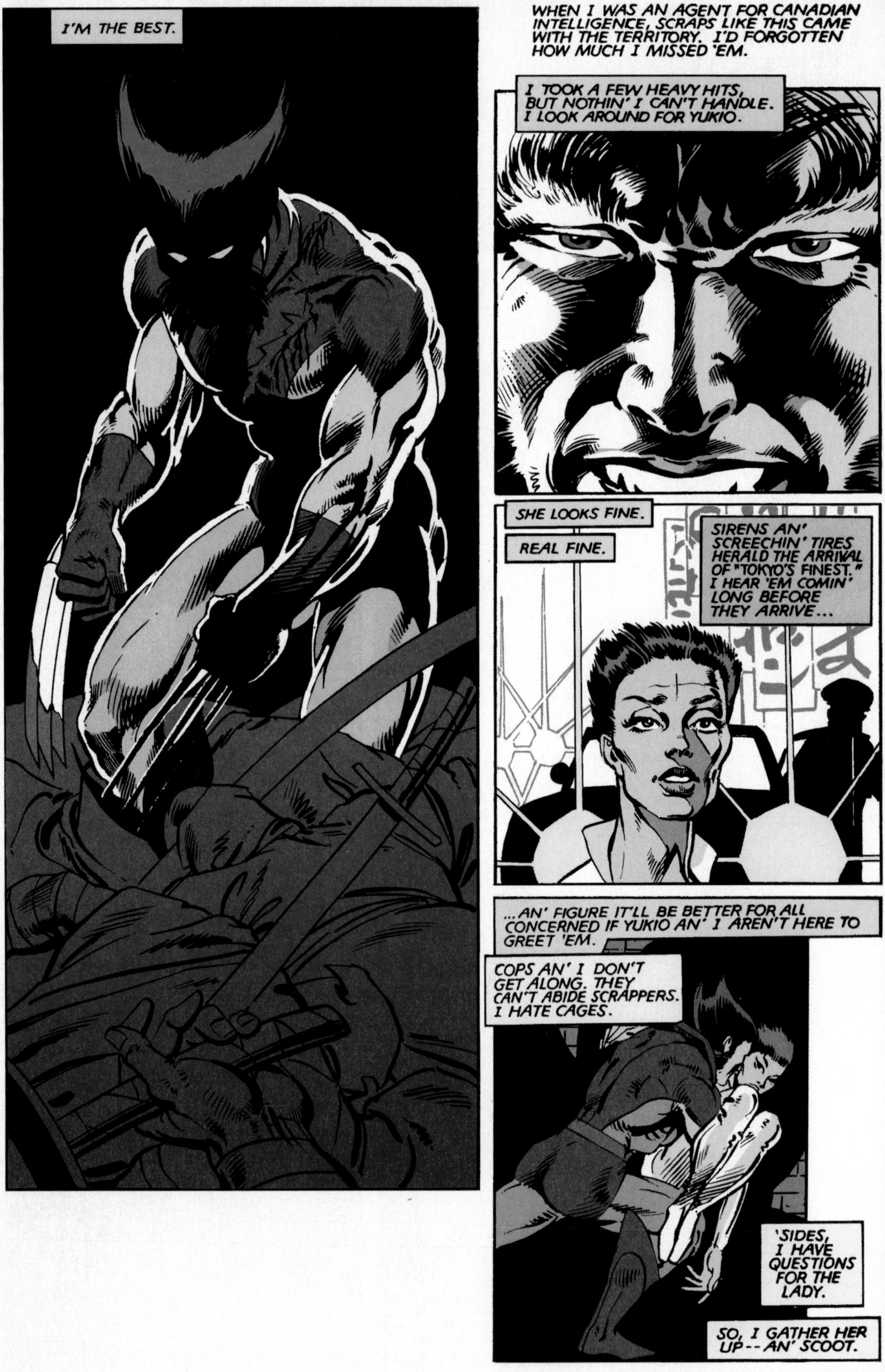

I'M THE BEST.
WHEN I WAS AN AGENT FOR CANADIAN INTELLIGENCE, SCRAPS LIKE THIS CAME WITH THE TERRITORY. I'D FORGOTTEN HOW MUCH I MISSED 'EM.
I TOOK A FEW HEAVY HITS, BUT NOTHIN' I CAN'T HANDLE. I LOOK AROUND FOR YUKIO.
SHE LOOKS FINE.
REAL FINE.
SIRENS AN' SCREECHIN' TIRES HERALD THE ARRIVAL OF "TOKYO'S FINEST." I HEAR 'EM COMIN' LONG BEFORE THEY ARRIVE...
...AN' FIGURE IT'LL BE BETTER FOR ALL CONCERNED IF YUKIO AN' I AREN'T HERE TO GREET 'EM.
COPS AN' I DON'T GET ALONG. THEY CAN'T ABIDE SCRAPPERS. I HATE CAGES.
'SIDES, I HAVE QUESTIONS FOR THE LADY.
SO, I GATHER HER UP--AN' SCOOT.

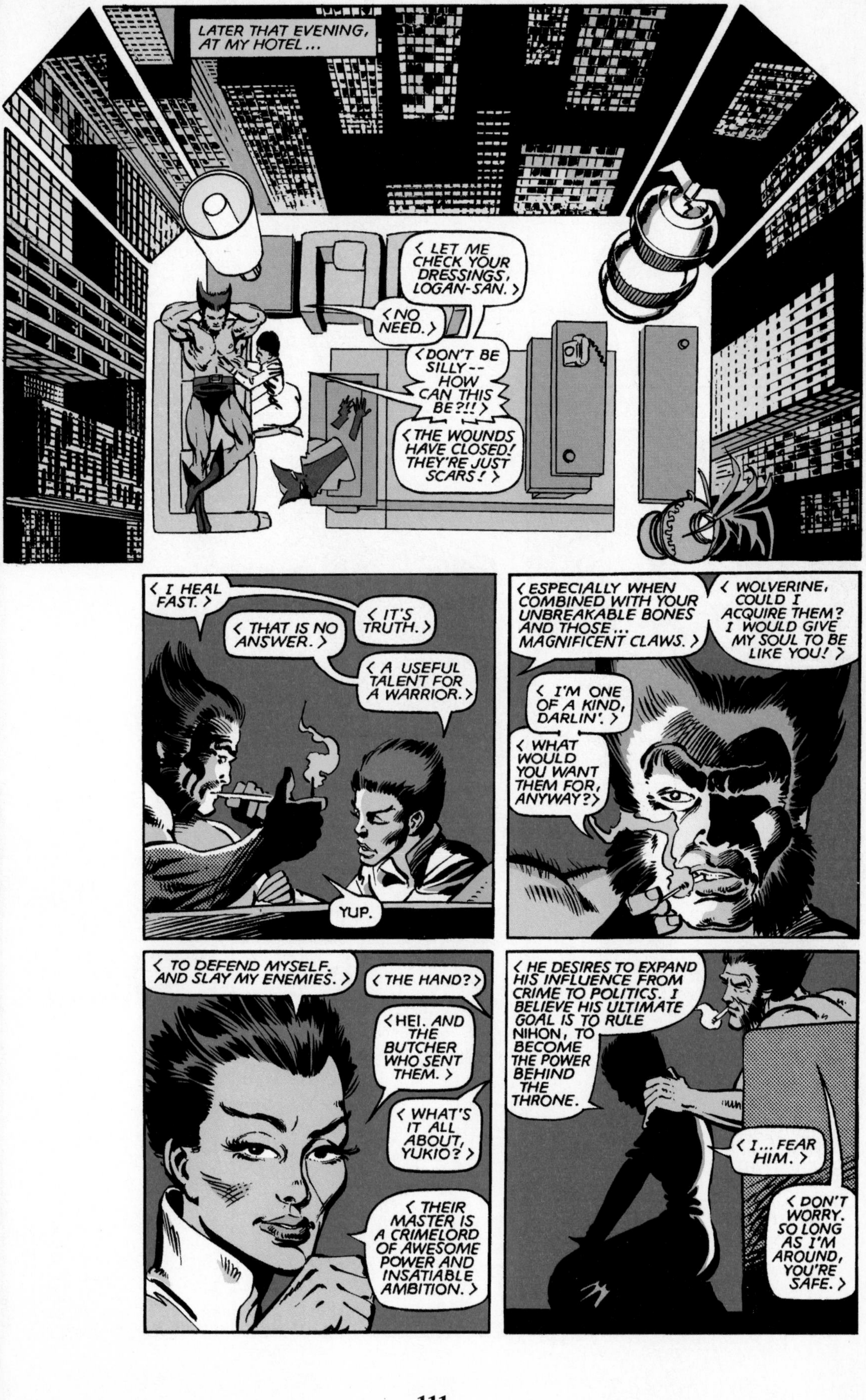
LATER THAT EVENING, AT MY HOTEL...
< LET ME CHECK YOUR DRESSINGS, LOGAN-SAN. >
< NO NEED. >
< DON'T BE SILLY -- HOW CAN THIS BE?!! >
< THE WOUNDS HAVE CLOSED! THEY'RE JUST SCARS! >
< I HEAL FAST. >
< IT'S TRUTH. >
< THAT IS NO ANSWER. >
< A USEFUL TALENT FOR A WARRIOR. >
YUP.
< ESPECIALLY WHEN COMBINED WITH YOUR UNBREAKABLE BONES AND THOSE... MAGNIFICENT CLAWS. >
< WOLVERINE, COULD I ACQUIRE THEM? I WOULD GIVE MY SOUL TO BE LIKE YOU! >
< I'M ONE OF A KIND, DARLIN'. >
< WHAT WOULD YOU WANT THEM FOR, ANYWAY? >
< TO DEFEND MYSELF. AND SLAY MY ENEMIES. >
< THE HAND? >
< HEI. AND THE BUTCHER WHO SENT THEM. >
< WHAT'S IT ALL ABOUT, YUKIO? >
< THEIR MASTER IS A CRIMELORD OF AWESOME POWER AND INSATIABLE AMBITION. >
< HE DESIRES TO EXPAND HIS INFLUENCE FROM CRIME TO POLITICS. I BELIEVE HIS ULTIMATE GOAL IS TO RULE NIHON, TO BECOME THE POWER BEHIND THE THRONE. >
< I... FEAR HIM. >
< DON'T WORRY. SO LONG AS I'M AROUND, YOU'RE SAFE. >

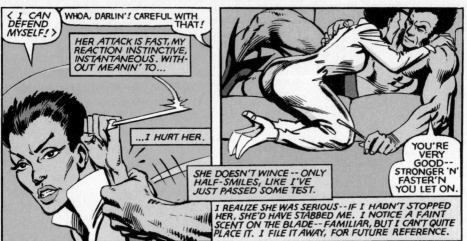

< I CAN DEFEND MYSELF! >

WHOA, DARLIN'! CAREFUL WITH THAT!

HER ATTACK IS FAST, MY REACTION INSTINCTIVE, INSTANTANEOUS. WITHOUT MEANIN' TO...

...I HURT HER.

SHE DOESN'T WINCE -- ONLY HALF-SMILES, LIKE I'VE JUST PASSED SOME TEST.

YOU'RE VERY GOOD-- STRONGER 'N' FASTER'N YOU LET ON.

I REALIZE SHE WAS SERIOUS--IF I HADN'T STOPPED HER, SHE'D HAVE STABBED ME. I NOTICE A FAINT SCENT ON THE BLADE-- FAMILIAR, BUT I CAN'T QUITE PLACE IT. I FILE IT AWAY, FOR FUTURE REFERENCE.

< I'M A TIGRESS, LOGAN. BUT IF YOU THINK ME SKILLED IN THE ARTS OF WAR...>

<... WAIT 'TIL YOU SEE ME PERFORM THOSE OF LOVE. >

< A WOMAN AFTER MY OWN HEART, eh ? >

< AMONG OTHER THINGS. >

THE CHEMISTRY IS PERFECT. BUT I CAN'T-- WON'T-- RESPOND.

MY EYES SEE YUKIO'S FACE...

... BUT MY BRAIN TRANSFORMS THE IMAGE INTO MARIKO'S.

LOGAN...

LATER, OKAY? I NEED SOME SACK-TIME.

< YOU WANT ME! YOU CANNOT DENY IT. WE ARE KINDRED SPIRITS, YOU AND I. DO NOT LEAVE. >

< MUST I BEG?! >

SHE HAS PRIDE, YET FOR ME SHE CHUCKS IT.

AND I... WALK AWAY.

< YOU WILL NOT DO SO AGAIN, LOGAN-CHAN. >

< SHINGEN'S DAUGHTER IS NOT WORTHY OF YOU. SHE WILL NOT HAVE YOU. >

< YOU ARE MINE! >

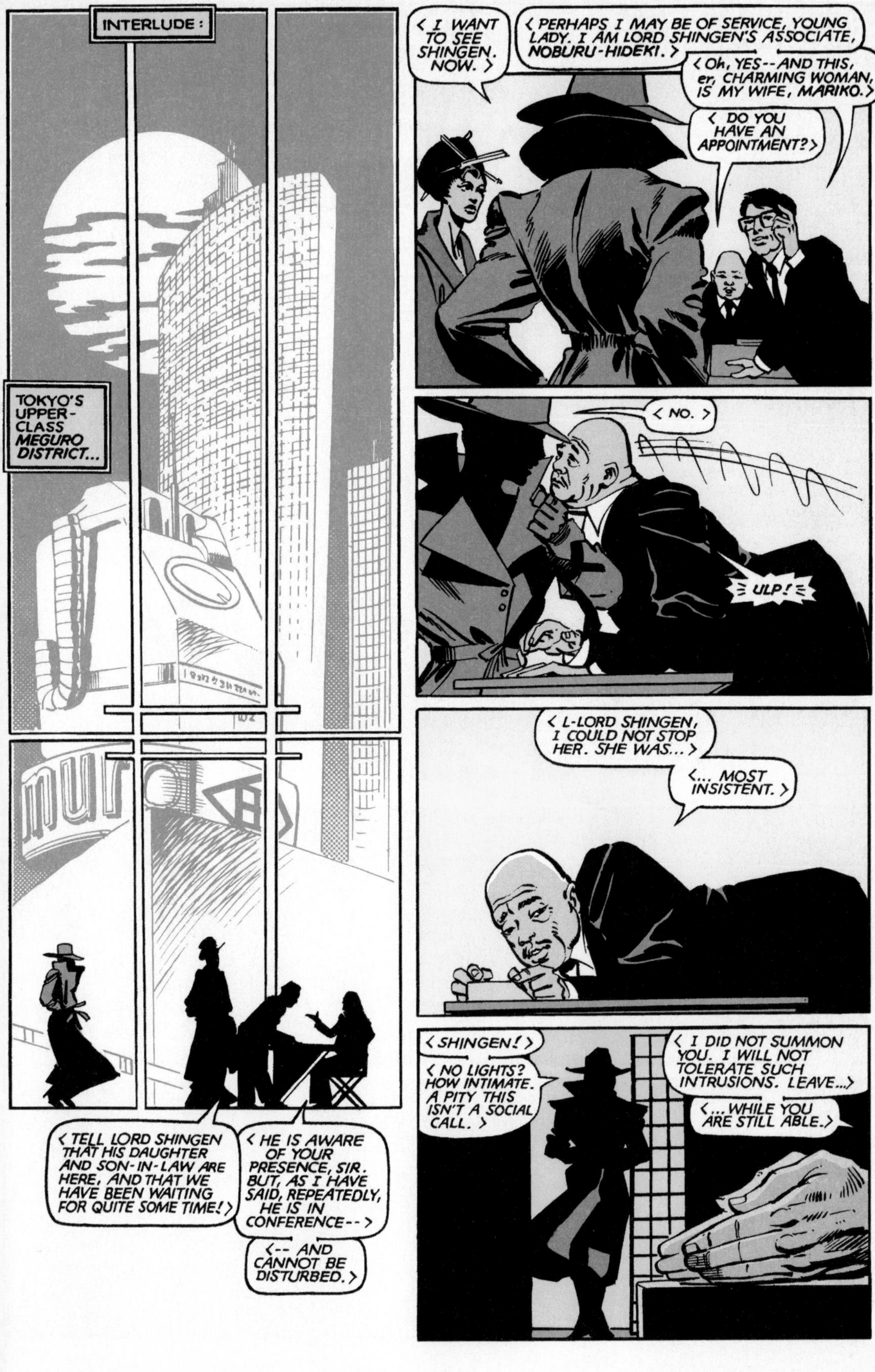
INTERLUDE:
TOKYO'S UPPER-CLASS MEGURO DISTRICT...
< TELL LORD SHINGEN THAT HIS DAUGHTER AND SON-IN-LAW ARE HERE, AND THAT WE HAVE BEEN WAITING FOR QUITE SOME TIME! >
< HE IS AWARE OF YOUR PRESENCE, SIR. BUT, AS I HAVE SAID, REPEATEDLY, HE IS IN CONFERENCE-- >
<-- AND CANNOT BE DISTURBED. >
< I WANT TO SEE SHINGEN. NOW. >
< PERHAPS I MAY BE OF SERVICE, YOUNG LADY. I AM LORD SHINGEN'S ASSOCIATE, NOBURU-HIDEKI. >
< DO YOU HAVE AN APPOINTMENT? >
< Oh, YES--AND THIS, er, CHARMING WOMAN, IS MY WIFE, MARIKO. >
< NO. >
ULP!
< L-LORD SHINGEN, I COULD NOT STOP HER. SHE WAS... >
<... MOST INSISTENT. >
< SHINGEN! >
< NO LIGHTS? HOW INTIMATE. A PITY THIS ISN'T A SOCIAL CALL. >
< I DID NOT SUMMON YOU. I WILL NOT TOLERATE SUCH INTRUSIONS. LEAVE... >
<... WHILE YOU ARE STILL ABLE. >

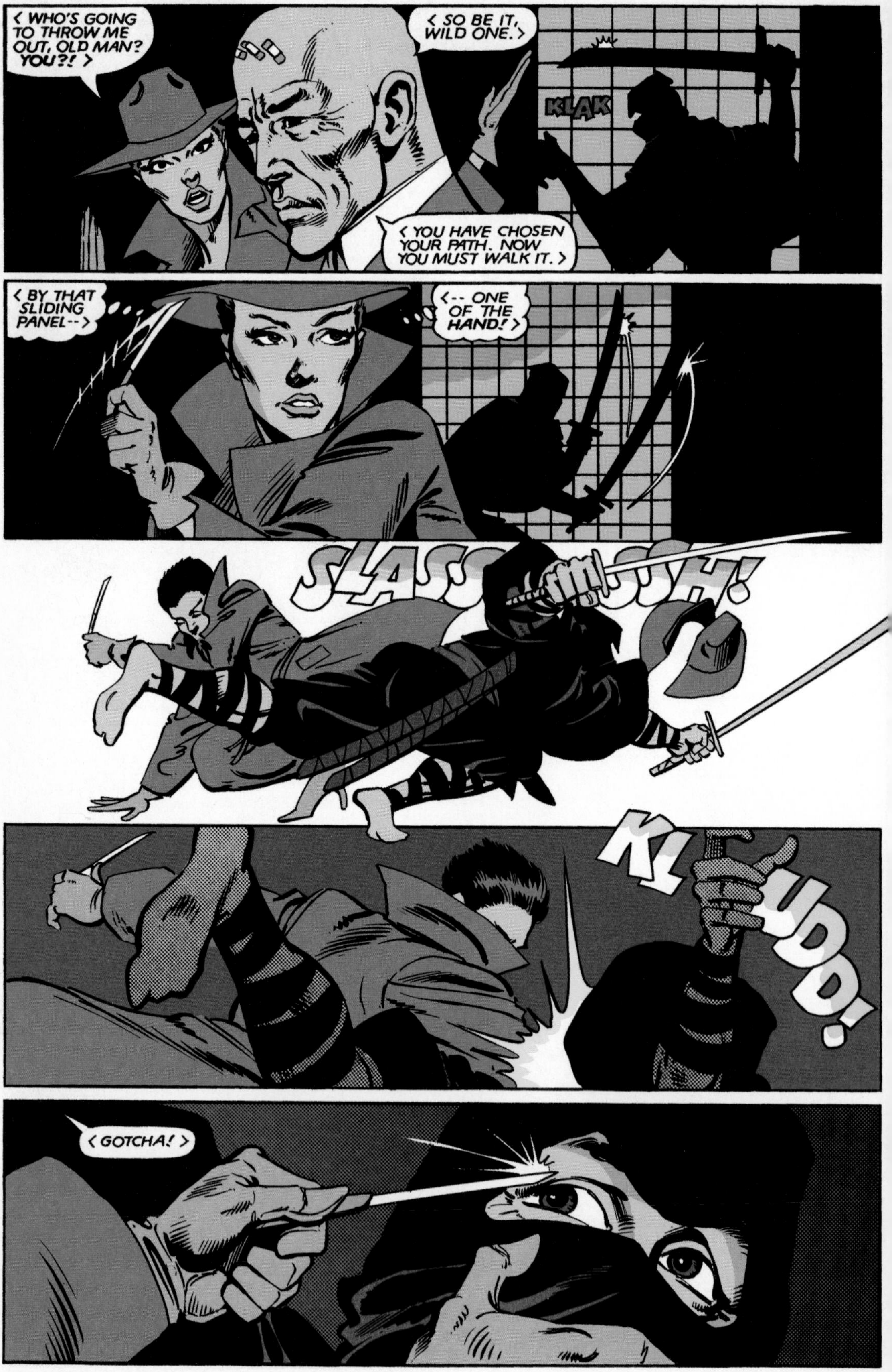

< WHO'S GOING TO THROW ME OUT, OLD MAN? YOU?! >
< SO BE IT, WILD ONE. >
KLAK
< YOU HAVE CHOSEN YOUR PATH. NOW YOU MUST WALK IT. >
< BY THAT SLIDING PANEL-- >
<-- ONE OF THE HAND! >
KI UDD!
< GOTCHA! >

< WHY DON'T YOU KILL HIM ? >

< WERE YOUR POSITIONS REVERSED, YOUR SOUL WOULD HAVE LONG SINCE DEPARTED TO JOIN THE GODDESS AMATERSU IN HEAVEN. >

< TRUE. BUT NOW HE HAS TO LIVE WITH THE MEMORY THAT I BEAT HIM. DEATH WOULD BE A MERCIFUL RELEASE. >

< I'VE SERVED YOU FAITHFULLY, SHINGEN, YET YOU SENT THE HAND TO KILL ME TONIGHT. THAT WAS SUPPOSED TO BE A DECEPTION-- TO WIN ME WOLVERINE'S SYMPATHY AND HIS AID-- BUT THE HAND WAS PLAYING FOR REAL! >

< BE VERY CAREFUL, DAIMYO. I AM A DANGEROUS LADY. YOU WOULDN'T LIKE ME FOR AN ENEMY. >

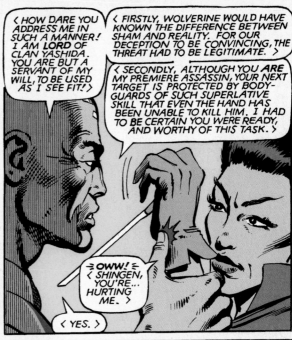

< HOW DARE YOU ADDRESS ME IN SUCH A MANNER! I AM LORD OF CLAN YASHIDA. YOU ARE BUT A SERVANT OF MY WILL, TO BE USED AS I SEE FIT! >

< FIRSTLY, WOLVERINE WOULD HAVE KNOWN THE DIFFERENCE BETWEEN SHAM AND REALITY. FOR OUR DECEPTION TO BE CONVINCING, THE THREAT HAD TO BE LEGITIMATE. >

< SECONDLY, ALTHOUGH YOU ARE MY PREMIERE ASSASSIN, YOUR NEXT TARGET IS PROTECTED BY BODY- GUARDS OF SUCH SUPERLATIVE SKILL THAT EVEN THE HAND HAS BEEN UNABLE TO KILL HIM. I HAD TO BE CERTAIN YOU WERE READY, AND WORTHY OF THIS TASK. >

≋ OWW! ≋ < SHINGEN, YOU'RE... HURTING ME. >

< YES. >

< I HAVE ARRANGED A "PEACE CONFERENCE" WITH KATSUYORI. MY REPRESENTATIVES WILL BE MARIKO AND NOBURU. HE BELIEVES I WILL NOT PLACE MY DAUGHTER IN JEOPARDY. HE WILL THINK HIMSELF SAFE. THEN AND THERE, YOU WILL STRIKE. >

< BUT SUPPOSE SOME- THING GOES WRONG? >

IF MARIKO COMES TO THE SLIGHTEST HARM, YOU WILL DIE.

< ONCE KATSUYORI HAS BEEN DEALT WITH, ELIMINATE WOLVERINE AS WELL. HE WILL HAVE SERVED HIS PURPOSE. >

< H-HEI, LORD. BOTH MEN ARE... ARE... >

< ...AS GOOD AS DEAD. >

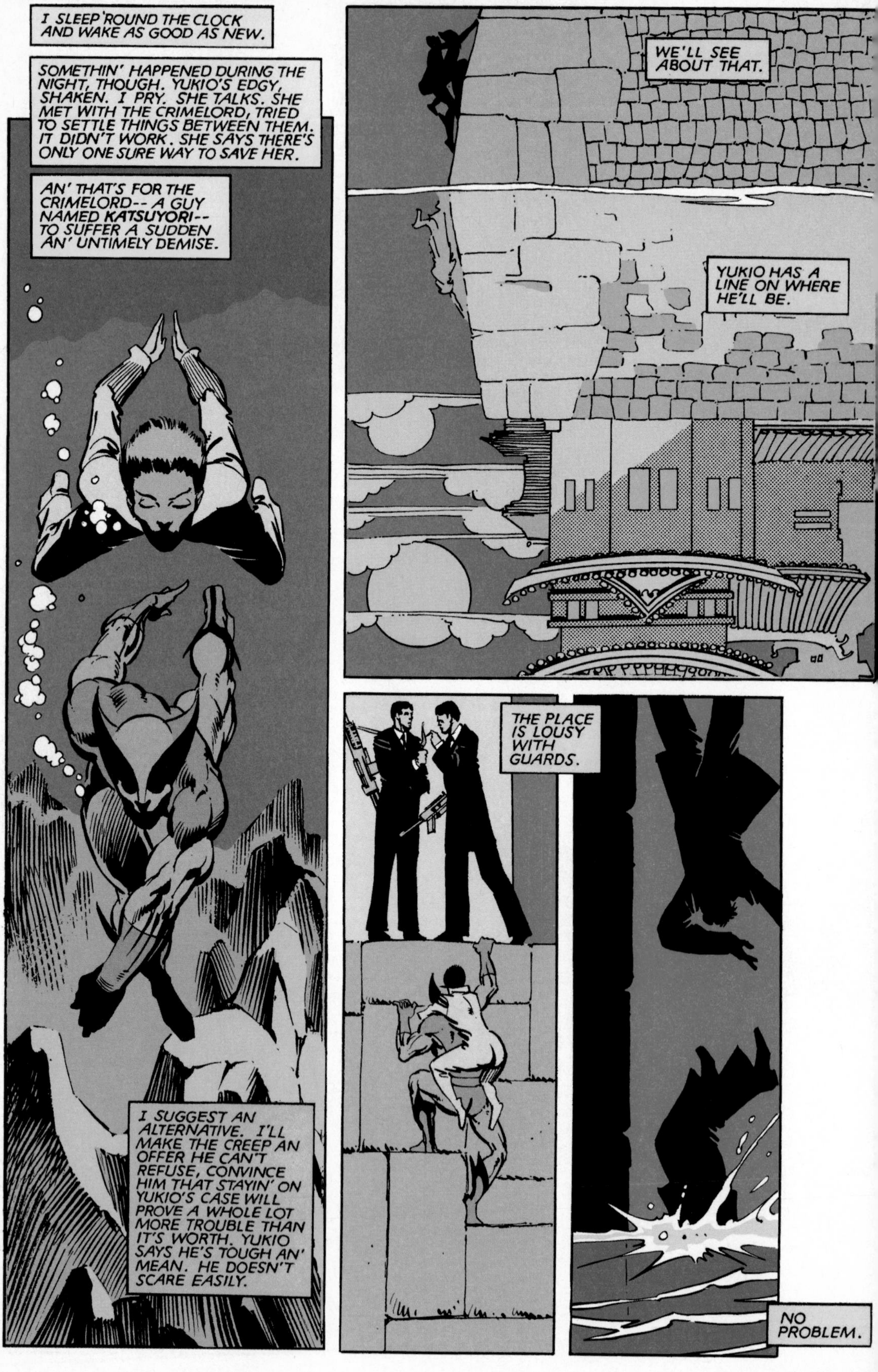
I SLEEP 'ROUND THE CLOCK AND WAKE AS GOOD AS NEW.
SOMETHIN' HAPPENED DURING THE NIGHT, THOUGH. YUKIO'S EDGY, SHAKEN. I PRY. SHE TALKS. SHE MET WITH THE CRIMELORD, TRIED TO SETTLE THINGS BETWEEN THEM. IT DIDN'T WORK. SHE SAYS THERE'S ONLY ONE SURE WAY TO SAVE HER.
AN' THAT'S FOR THE CRIMELORD-- A GUY NAMED KATSUYORI-- TO SUFFER A SUDDEN AN' UNTIMELY DEMISE.
I SUGGEST AN ALTERNATIVE. I'LL MAKE THE CREEP AN OFFER HE CAN'T REFUSE, CONVINCE HIM THAT STAYIN' ON YUKIO'S CASE WILL PROVE A WHOLE LOT MORE TROUBLE THAN IT'S WORTH. YUKIO SAYS HE'S TOUGH AN' MEAN. HE DOESN'T SCARE EASILY.
WE'LL SEE ABOUT THAT.
YUKIO HAS A LINE ON WHERE HE'LL BE.
THE PLACE IS LOUSY WITH GUARDS.
NO PROBLEM.

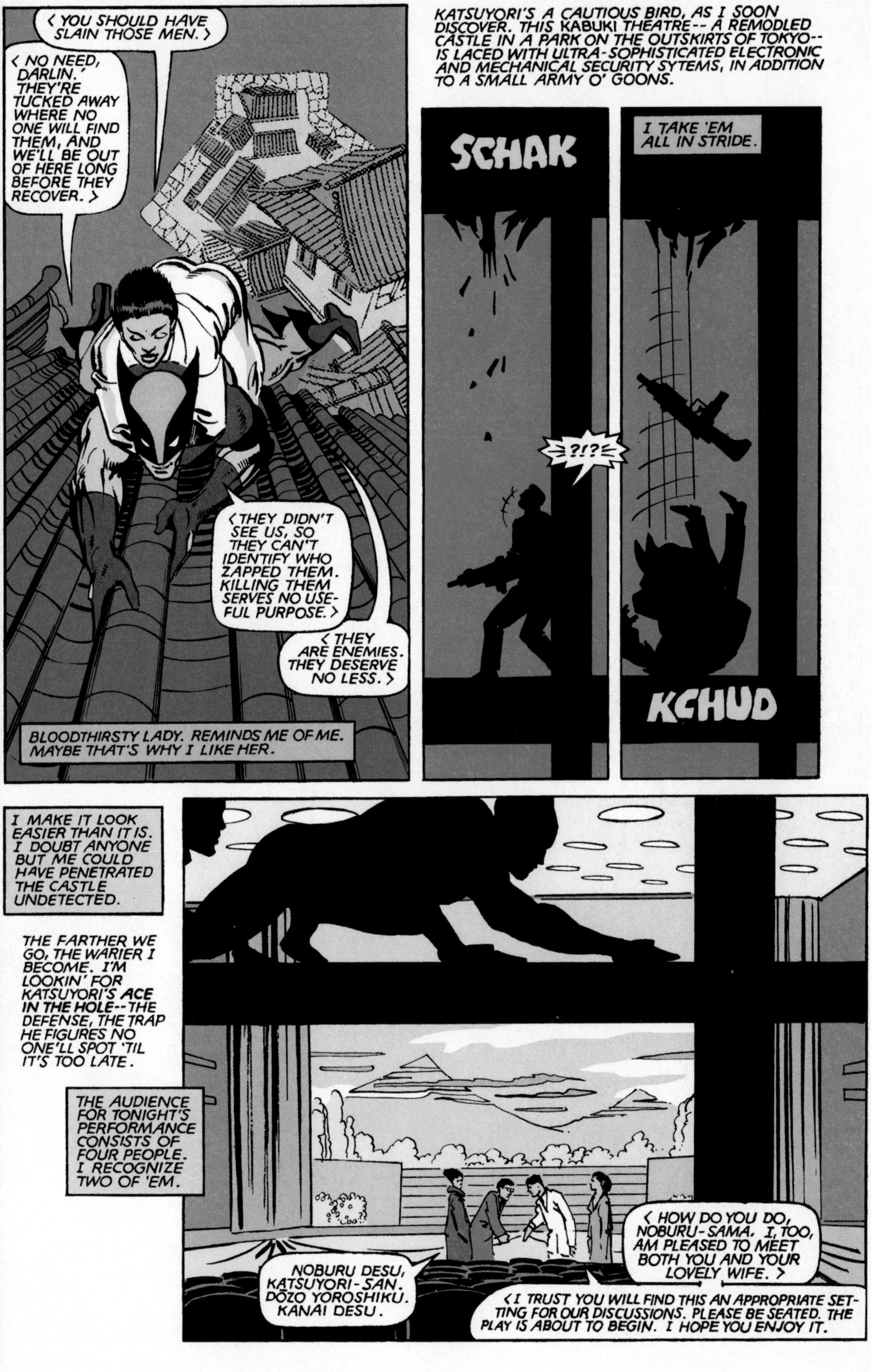

< YOU SHOULD HAVE SLAIN THOSE MEN. >
< NO NEED, DARLIN.' THEY'RE TUCKED AWAY WHERE NO ONE WILL FIND THEM, AND WE'LL BE OUT OF HERE LONG BEFORE THEY RECOVER. >
< THEY DIDN'T SEE US, SO THEY CAN'T IDENTIFY WHO ZAPPED THEM. KILLING THEM SERVES NO USEFUL PURPOSE. >
< THEY ARE ENEMIES. THEY DESERVE NO LESS. >
BLOODTHIRSTY LADY. REMINDS ME OF ME. MAYBE THAT'S WHY I LIKE HER.
KATSUYORI'S A CAUTIOUS BIRD, AS I SOON DISCOVER. THIS KABUKI THEATRE-- A REMODLED CASTLE IN A PARK ON THE OUTSKIRTS OF TOKYO-- IS LACED WITH ULTRA-SOPHISTICATED ELECTRONIC AND MECHANICAL SECURITY SYTEMS, IN ADDITION TO A SMALL ARMY O' GOONS.
SCHAK
?!?
I TAKE 'EM ALL IN STRIDE.
KCHUD
I MAKE IT LOOK EASIER THAN IT IS. I DOUBT ANYONE BUT ME COULD HAVE PENETRATED THE CASTLE UNDETECTED.
THE FARTHER WE GO, THE WARIER I BECOME. I'M LOOKIN' FOR KATSUYORI'S ACE IN THE HOLE--THE DEFENSE, THE TRAP HE FIGURES NO ONE'LL SPOT 'TIL IT'S TOO LATE.
THE AUDIENCE FOR TONIGHT'S PERFORMANCE CONSISTS OF FOUR PEOPLE. I RECOGNIZE TWO OF 'EM.
NOBURU DESU, KATSUYORI-SAN. DŌZO YOROSHIKU. KANAI DESU.
< HOW DO YOU DO, NOBURU-SAMA. I, TOO, AM PLEASED TO MEET BOTH YOU AND YOUR LOVELY WIFE. >
< I TRUST YOU WILL FIND THIS AN APPROPRIATE SETTING FOR OUR DISCUSSIONS. PLEASE BE SEATED. THE PLAY IS ABOUT TO BEGIN. I HOPE YOU ENJOY IT.

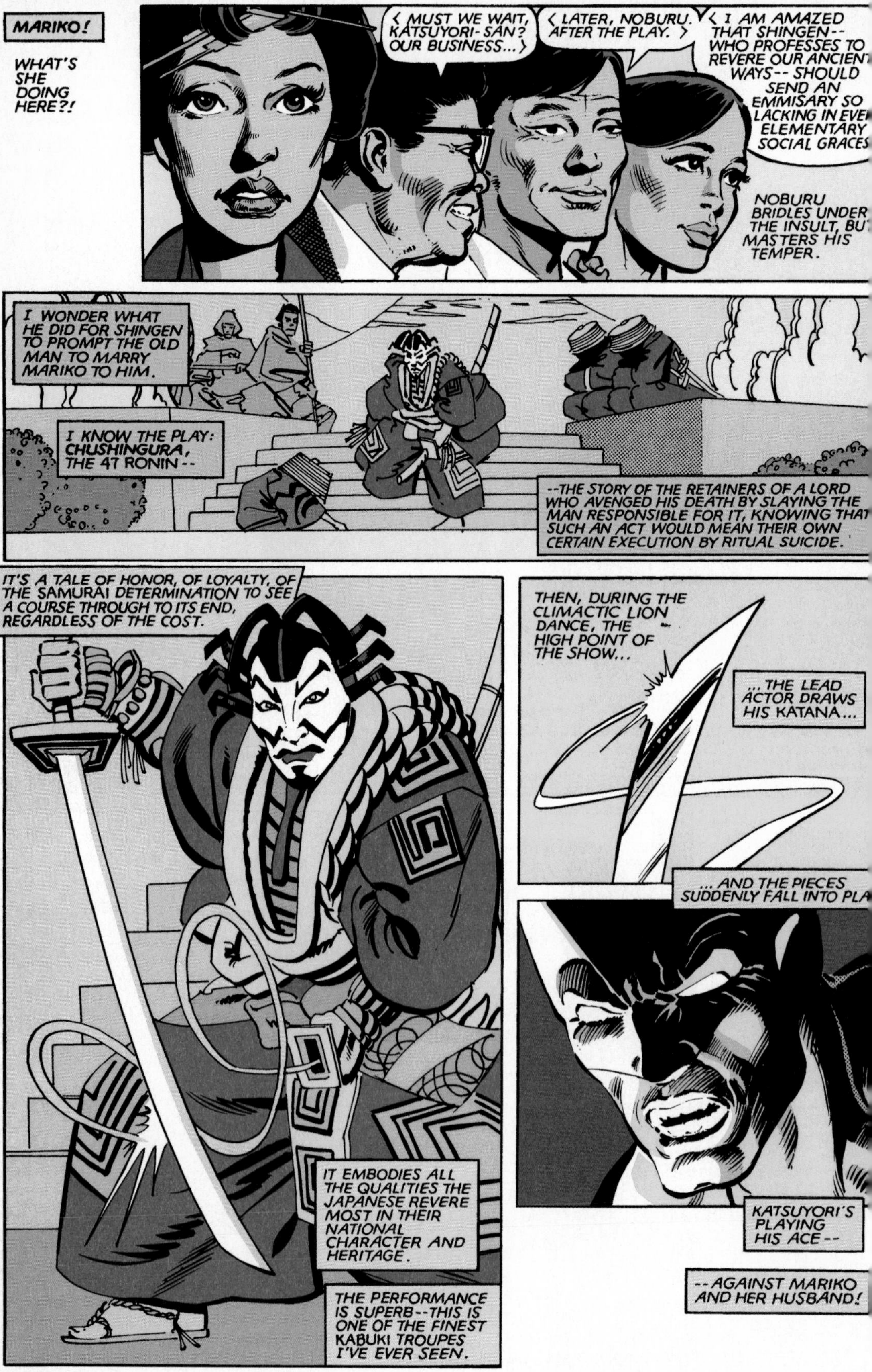

MARIKO!
WHAT'S SHE DOING HERE?!
< MUST WE WAIT, KATSUYORI-SAN? OUR BUSINESS... >
< LATER, NOBURU. AFTER THE PLAY. >
< I AM AMAZED THAT SHINGEN-- WHO PROFESSES TO REVERE OUR ANCIENT WAYS-- SHOULD SEND AN EMMISARY SO LACKING IN EVEN ELEMENTARY SOCIAL GRACES
NOBURU BRIDLES UNDER THE INSULT, BUT MASTERS HIS TEMPER.
I WONDER WHAT HE DID FOR SHINGEN TO PROMPT THE OLD MAN TO MARRY MARIKO TO HIM.
I KNOW THE PLAY: CHUSHINGURA, THE 47 RONIN--
--THE STORY OF THE RETAINERS OF A LORD WHO AVENGED HIS DEATH BY SLAYING THE MAN RESPONSIBLE FOR IT, KNOWING THAT SUCH AN ACT WOULD MEAN THEIR OWN CERTAIN EXECUTION BY RITUAL SUICIDE.
IT'S A TALE OF HONOR, OF LOYALTY, OF THE SAMURAI DETERMINATION TO SEE A COURSE THROUGH TO ITS END, REGARDLESS OF THE COST.
IT EMBODIES ALL THE QUALITIES THE JAPANESE REVERE MOST IN THEIR NATIONAL CHARACTER AND HERITAGE.
THE PERFORMANCE IS SUPERB--THIS IS ONE OF THE FINEST KABUKI TROUPES I'VE EVER SEEN.
THEN, DURING THE CLIMACTIC LION DANCE, THE HIGH POINT OF THE SHOW...
...THE LEAD ACTOR DRAWS HIS KATANA...
...AND THE PIECES SUDDENLY FALL INTO PLA
KATSUYORI'S PLAYING HIS ACE--
--AGAINST MARIKO AND HER HUSBAND!

I COUNTER THE ATTACK.

THE ACTOR'S A PRO, A MASTER OF HIS CRAFT.

WITHOUT MISSING A BEAT, HE SHIFTS TARGETS FROM MARIKO TO ME.

WE PASS IN MID-AIR, STAGELIGHTS FLASHING OFF SWORD AND CLAWS.

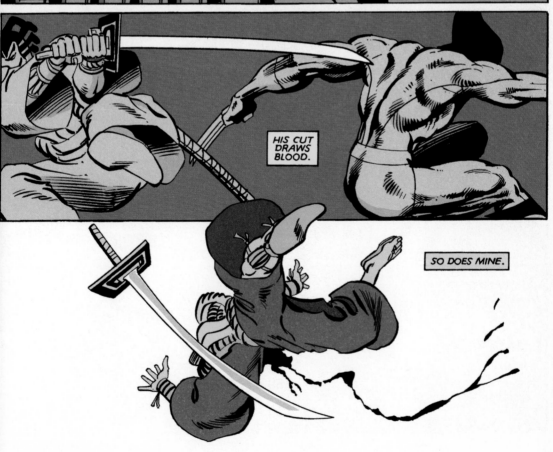

HIS CUT DRAWS BLOOD.

SO DOES MINE.

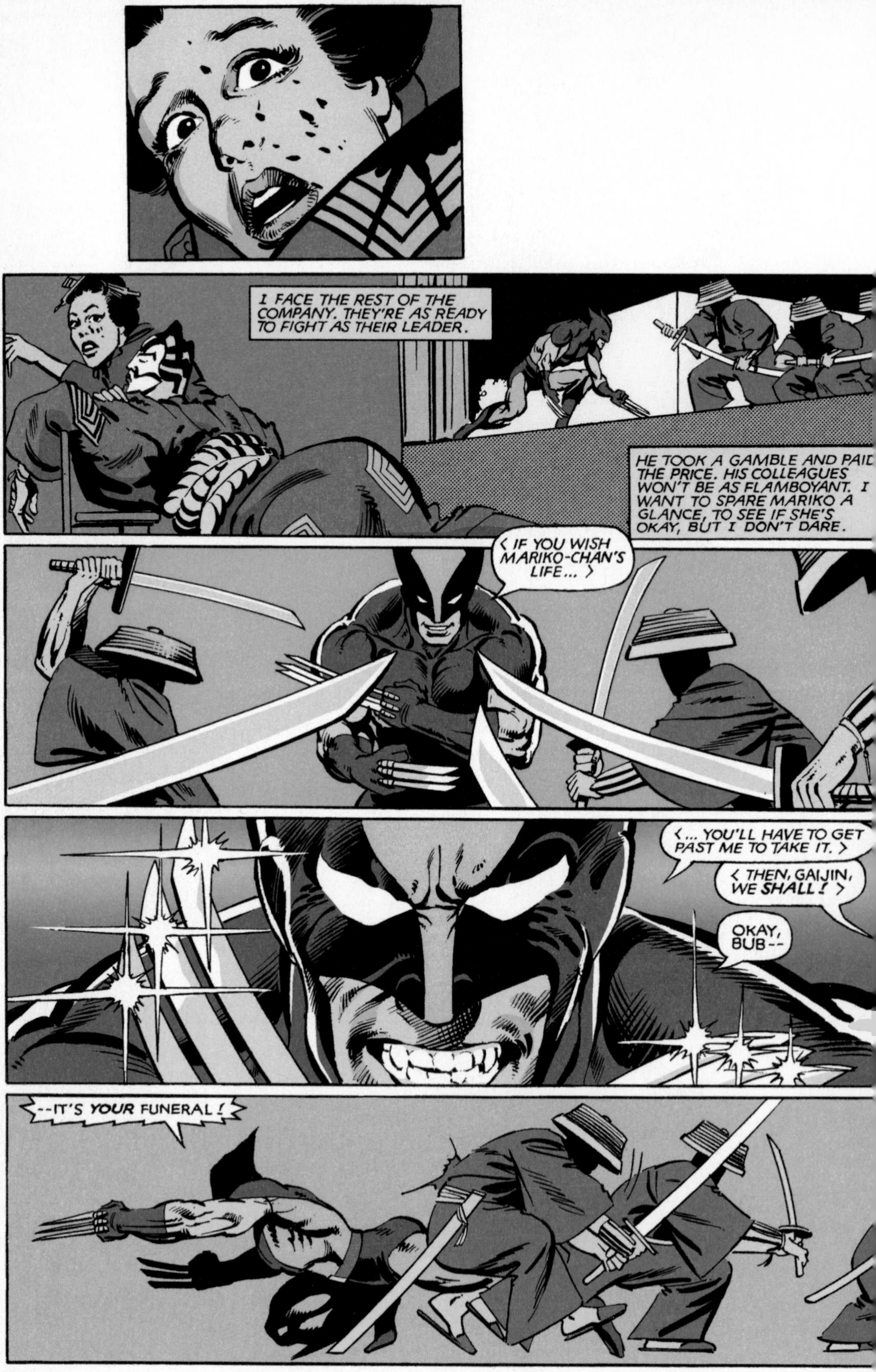
I FACE THE REST OF THE COMPANY. THEY'RE AS READY TO FIGHT AS THEIR LEADER.
HE TOOK A GAMBLE AND PAID THE PRICE. HIS COLLEAGUES WON'T BE AS FLAMBOYANT. I WANT TO SPARE MARIKO A GLANCE, TO SEE IF SHE'S OKAY, BUT I DON'T DARE.
‹ IF YOU WISH MARIKO-CHAN'S LIFE... ›
‹ ... YOU'LL HAVE TO GET PAST ME TO TAKE IT. ›
‹ THEN, GAIJIN, WE SHALL! ›
OKAY, BUB--
--IT'S YOUR FUNERAL!

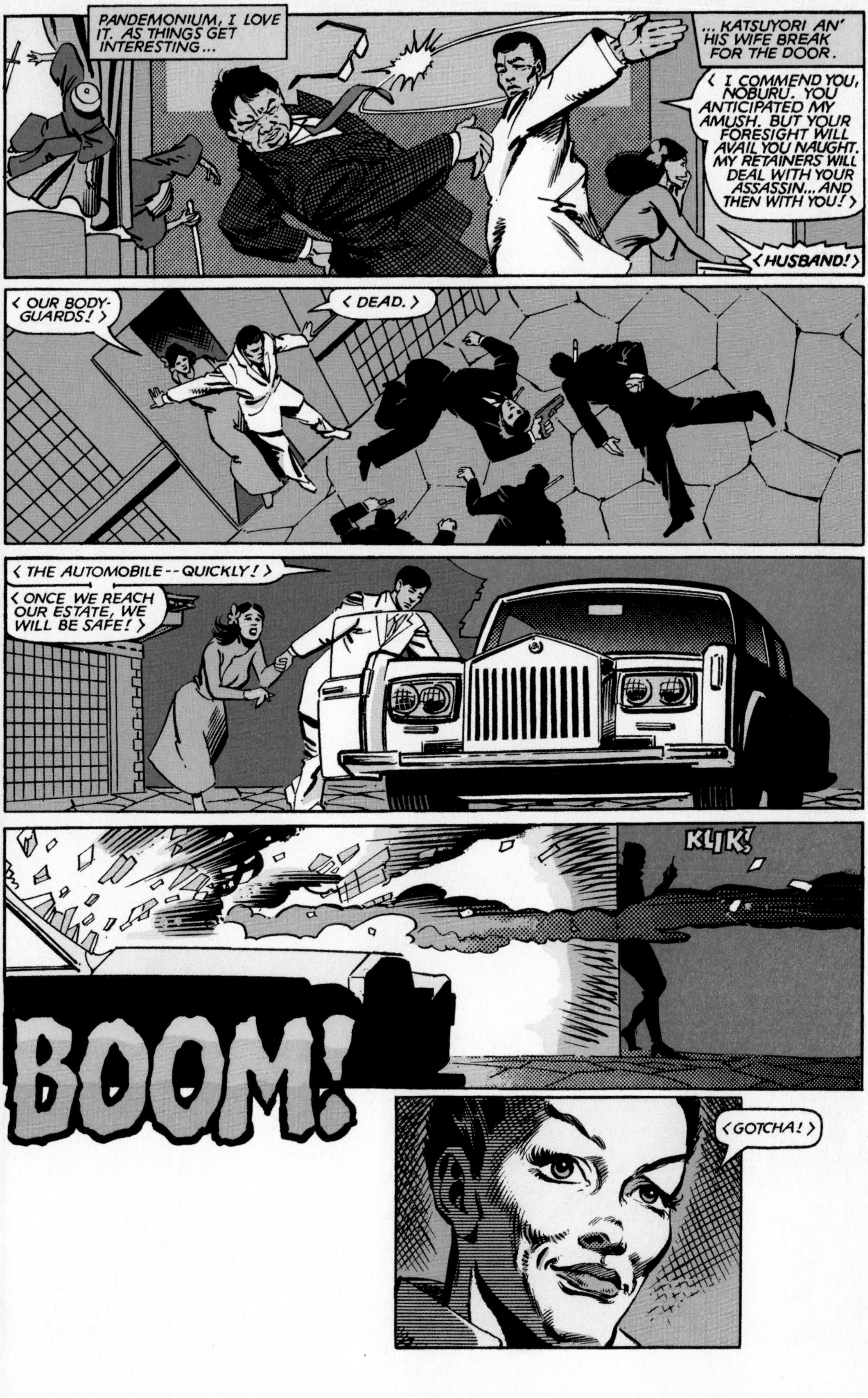
PANDEMONIUM, I LOVE IT. AS THINGS GET INTERESTING...
... KATSUYORI AN' HIS WIFE BREAK FOR THE DOOR.
< I COMMEND YOU, NOBURU. YOU ANTICIPATED MY AMUSH. BUT YOUR FORESIGHT WILL AVAIL YOU NAUGHT. MY RETAINERS WILL DEAL WITH YOUR ASSASSIN... AND THEN WITH YOU! >
< HUSBAND! >
< OUR BODY-GUARDS! >
< DEAD. >
< THE AUTOMOBILE -- QUICKLY! >
< ONCE WE REACH OUR ESTATE, WE WILL BE SAFE! >
KLIK!
BOOM!
< GOTCHA! >

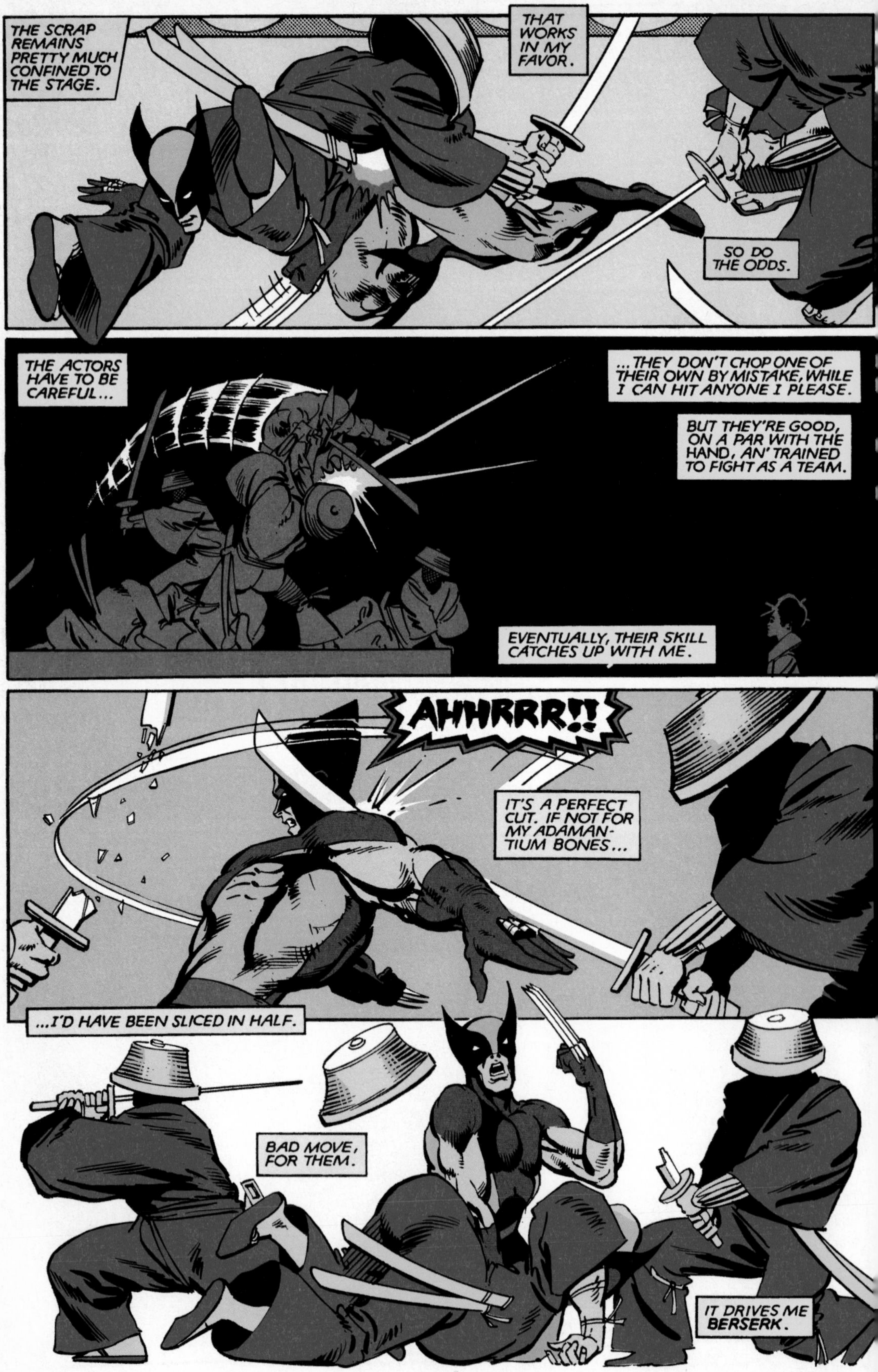
THE SCRAP REMAINS PRETTY MUCH CONFINED TO THE STAGE.
THAT WORKS IN MY FAVOR.
SO DO THE ODDS.
THE ACTORS HAVE TO BE CAREFUL...
...THEY DON'T CHOP ONE OF THEIR OWN BY MISTAKE, WHILE I CAN HIT ANYONE I PLEASE.
BUT THEY'RE GOOD, ON A PAR WITH THE HAND, AN' TRAINED TO FIGHT AS A TEAM.
EVENTUALLY, THEIR SKILL CATCHES UP WITH ME.
AHHRRR!!
IT'S A PERFECT CUT. IF NOT FOR MY ADAMAN-TIUM BONES...
...I'D HAVE BEEN SLICED IN HALF.
BAD MOVE, FOR THEM.
IT DRIVES ME BERSERK.

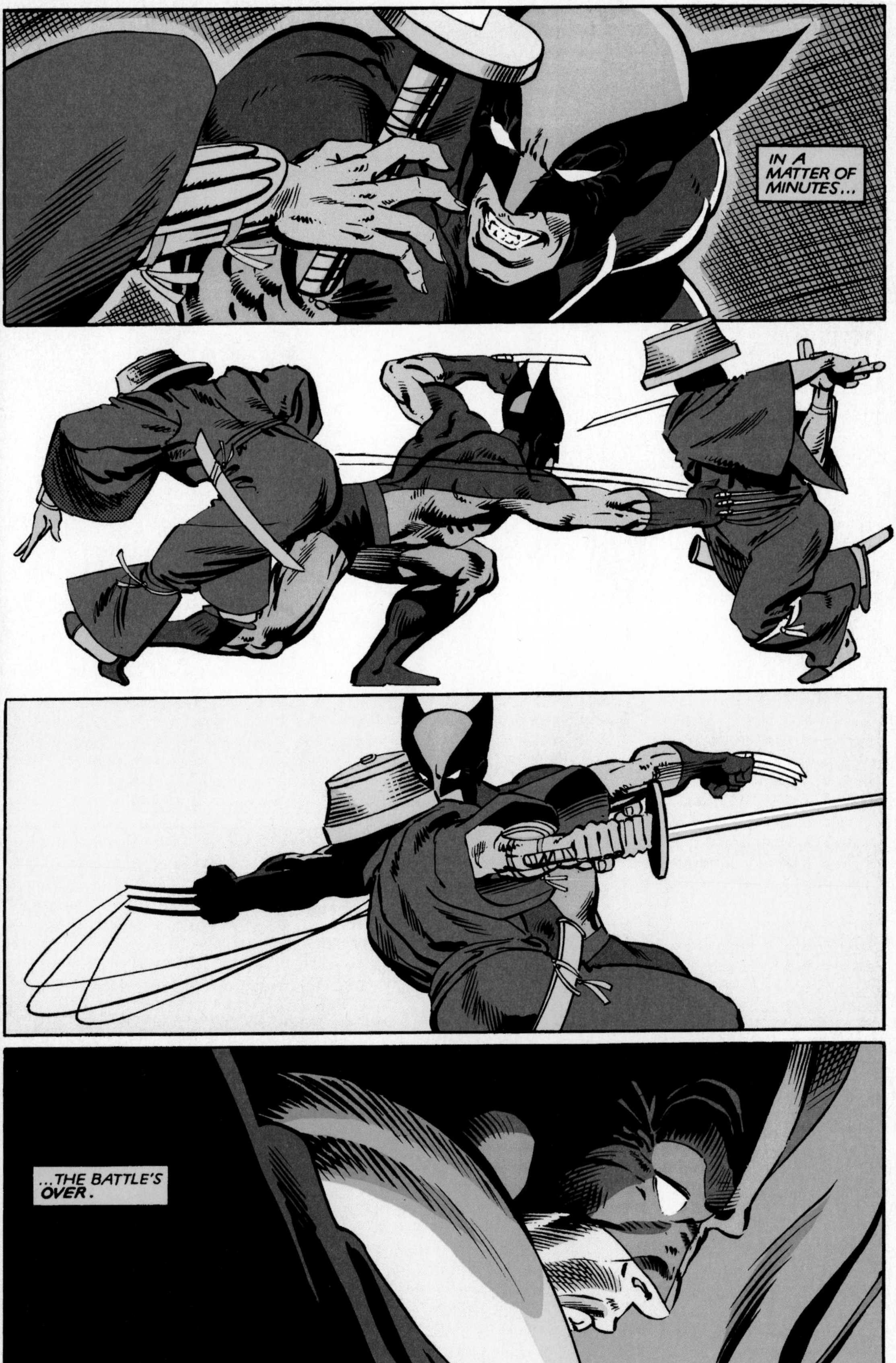
IN A MATTER OF MINUTES...
...THE BATTLE'S OVER.

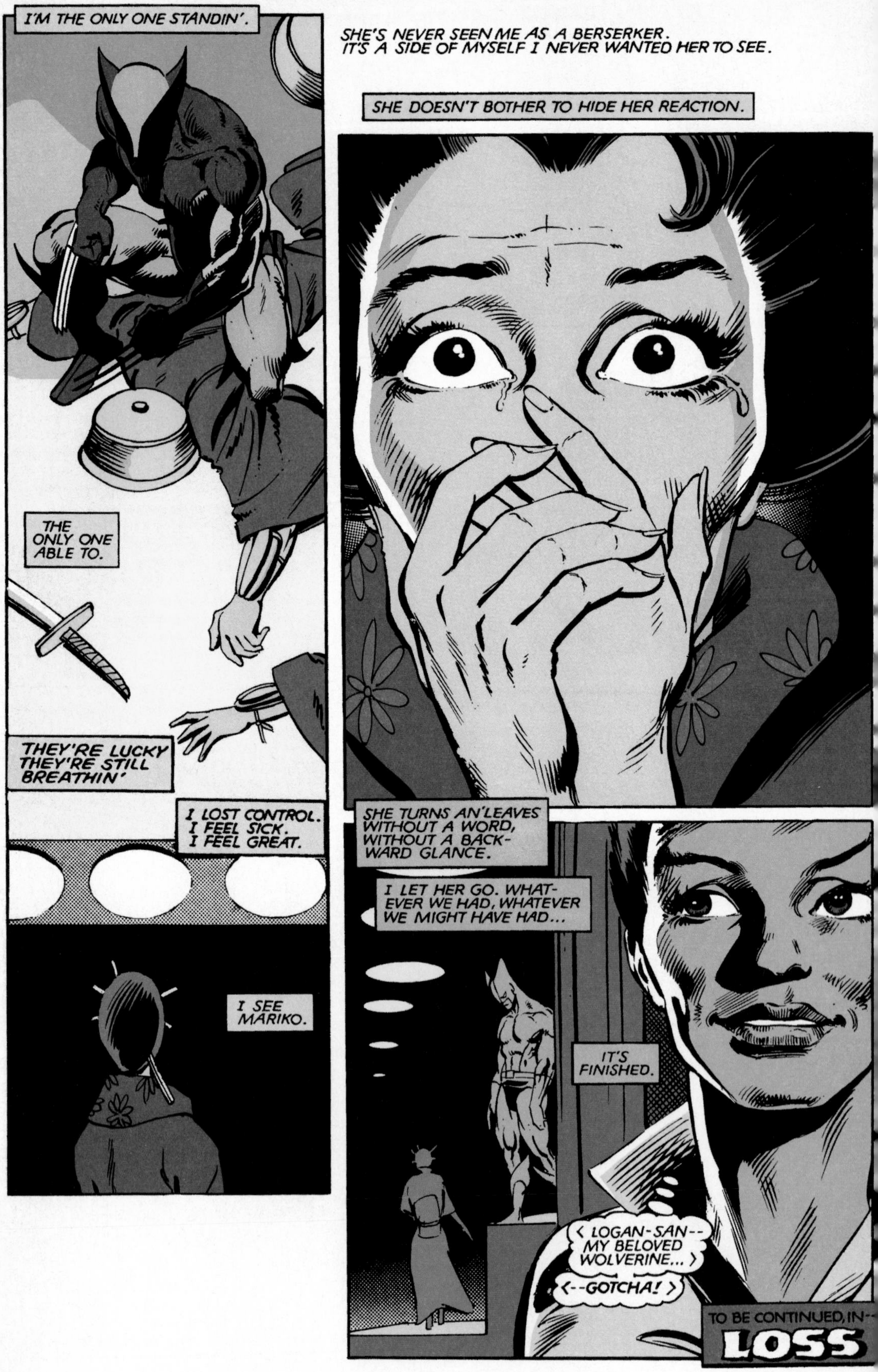
I'M THE ONLY ONE STANDIN'.
THE ONLY ONE ABLE TO.
THEY'RE LUCKY THEY'RE STILL BREATHIN'
I LOST CONTROL. I FEEL SICK. I FEEL GREAT.
I SEE MARIKO.
SHE'S NEVER SEEN ME AS A BERSERKER. IT'S A SIDE OF MYSELF I NEVER WANTED HER TO SEE.
SHE DOESN'T BOTHER TO HIDE HER REACTION.
SHE TURNS AN' LEAVES WITHOUT A WORD, WITHOUT A BACK-WARD GLANCE.
I LET HER GO. WHAT-EVER WE HAD, WHATEVER WE MIGHT HAVE HAD...
IT'S FINISHED.
‹ LOGAN-SAN-- MY BELOVED WOLVERINE... ›
‹--GOTCHA! ›
TO BE CONTINUED, IN--
LOSS

Can Wolverine win back Mariko's heart, defeat Lord Shingen, triumph over the villain's widespread criminal empire, and regain his honor? Find out in *Wolverine by Claremont & Miller HC!*

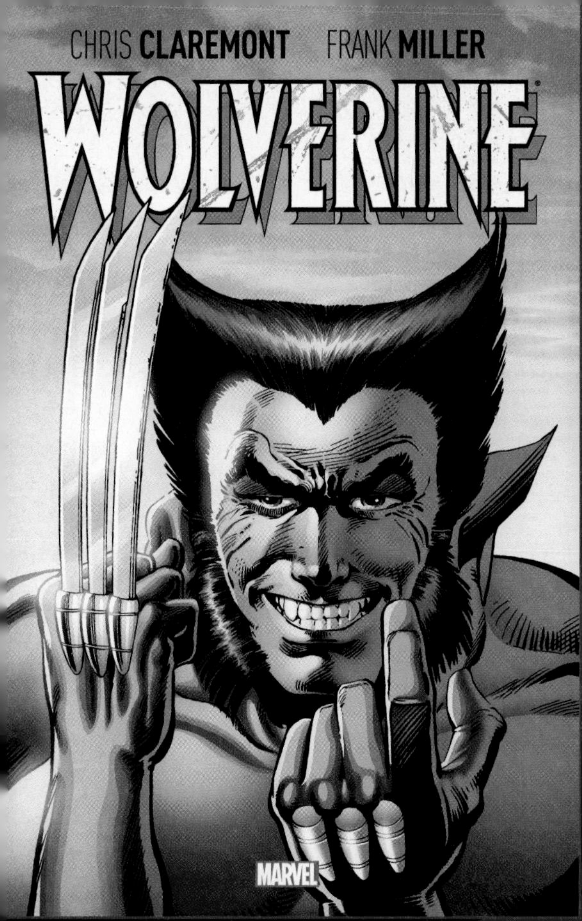
CHRIS CLAREMONT FRANK MILLER
WOLVERINE
MARVEL

The villainous Viper and Silver Samurai would go on to oppose Wolverine on many occasions. Though both have previously appeared elsewhere in the Marvel firmament, they make their debut as partners in crime in the following story.

One night in Manhattan, Spider-Man encounters a woman who looks exactly like the Black Widow, but who claims to be an amnesiac schoolteacher named Nancy Rushman. Suddenly, the two are attacked by a S.H.I.E.L.D. squadron and ambushed by Nick Fury — who shoots them both at point-blank range.

Get the full story in *Essential Marvel Team-Up Vol. 4!*

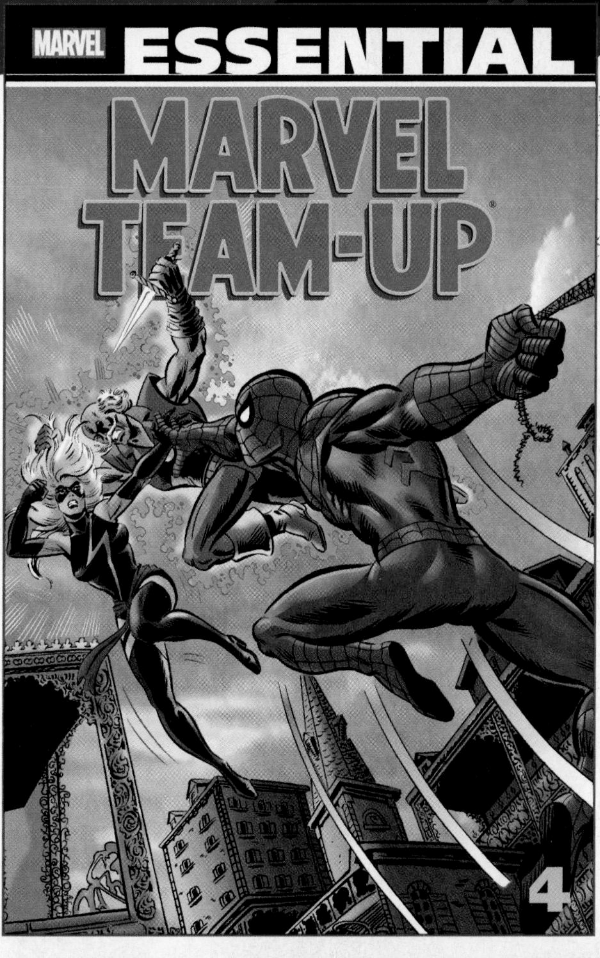
MARVEL ESSENTIAL
MARVEL TEAM-UP
4

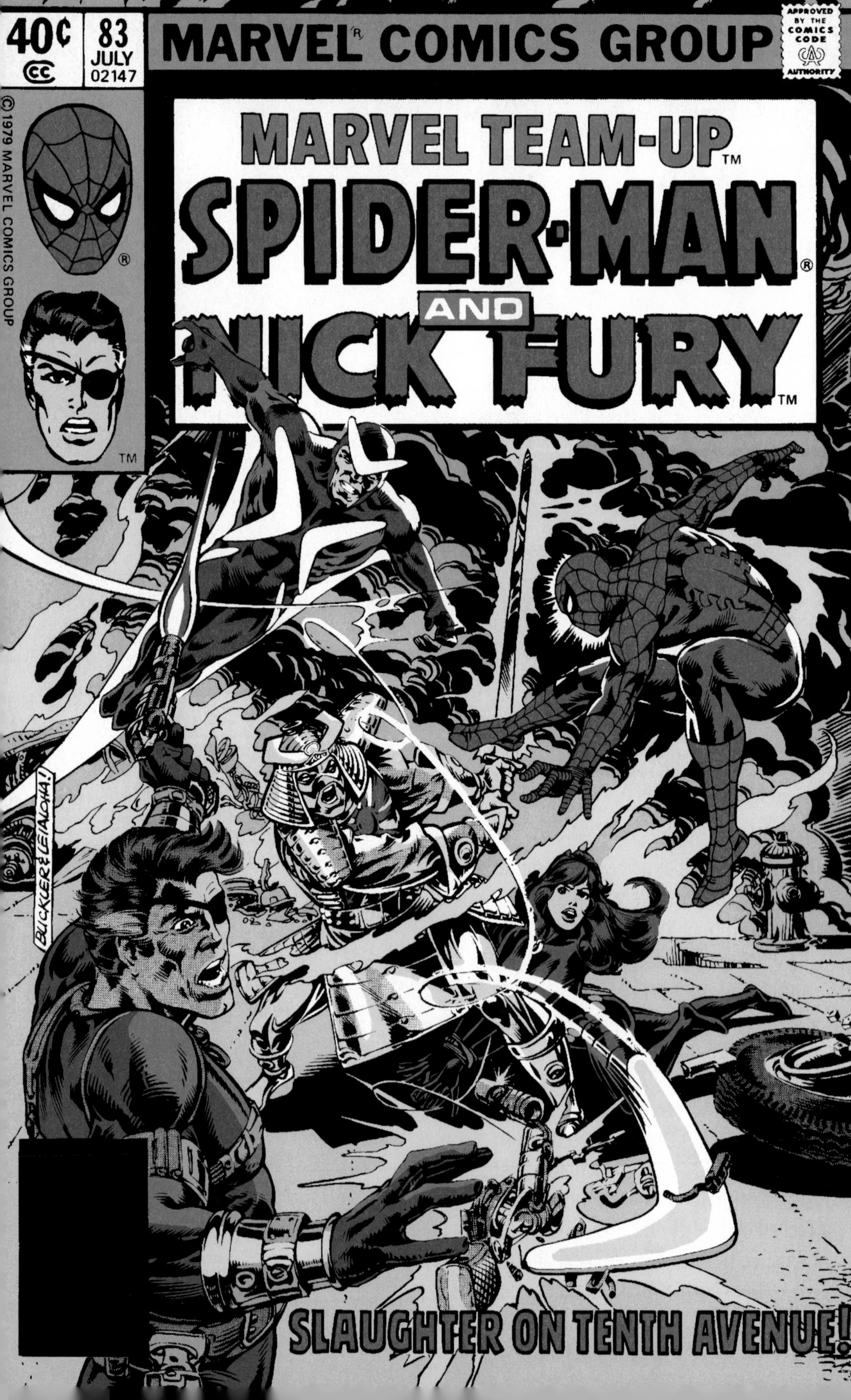
40¢
83
JULY
02147
CC
MARVEL COMICS GROUP
APPROVED BY THE COMICS CODE AUTHORITY
© 1979 MARVEL COMICS GROUP
MARVEL TEAM-UP™
SPIDER-MAN®
AND
NICK FURY™
BUCKLER & LEIALOHA!
SLAUGHTER ON TENTH AVENUE!

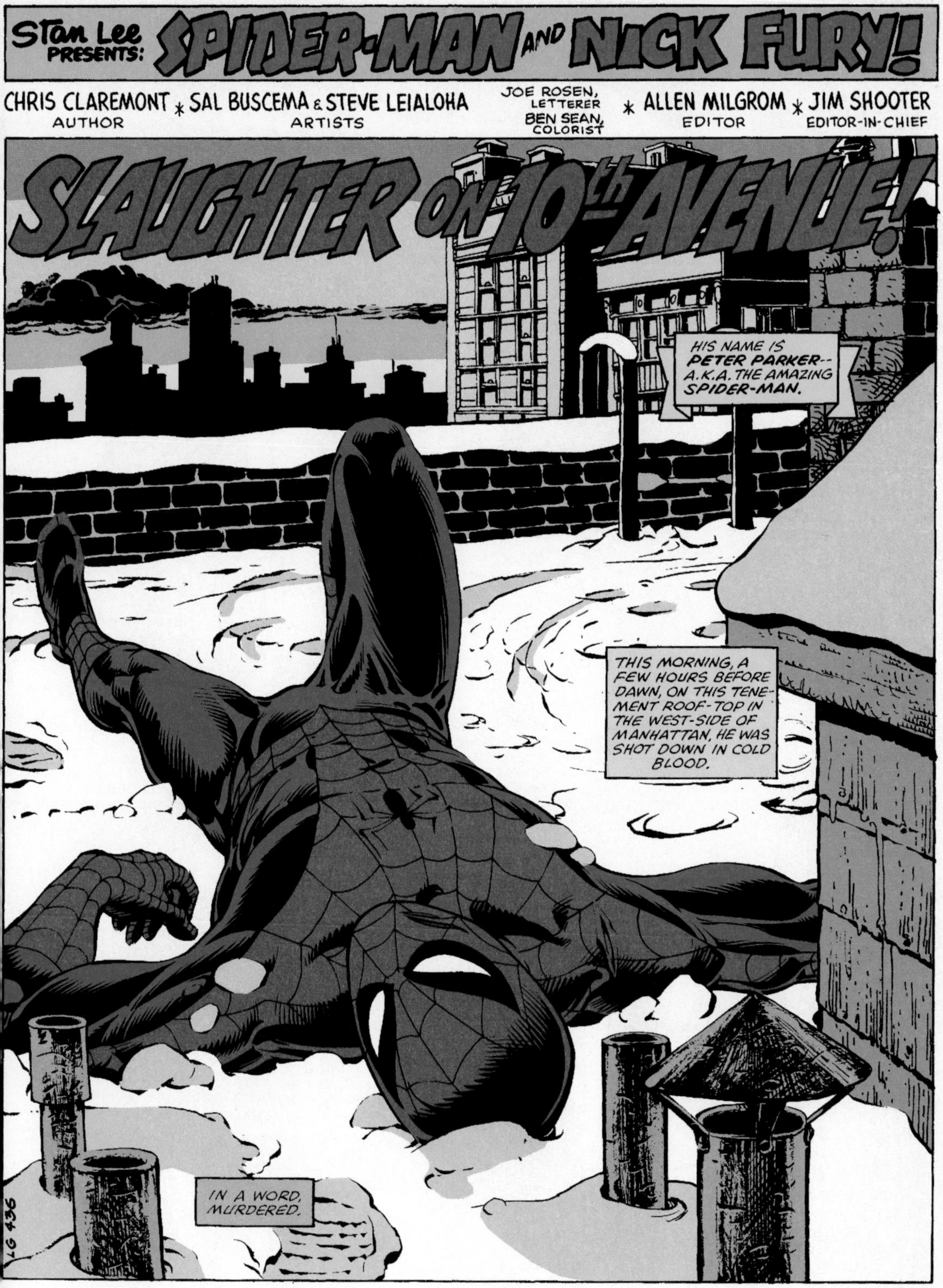
Stan Lee PRESENTS: SPIDER-MAN AND NICK FURY!
CHRIS CLAREMONT AUTHOR
SAL BUSCEMA & STEVE LEIALOHA ARTISTS
JOE ROSEN, LETTERER
BEN SEAN, COLORIST
ALLEN MILGROM EDITOR
JIM SHOOTER EDITOR-IN-CHIEF
SLAUGHTER ON 10th AVENUE!
HIS NAME IS PETER PARKER-- A.K.A. THE AMAZING SPIDER-MAN.
THIS MORNING, A FEW HOURS BEFORE DAWN, ON THIS TENEMENT ROOF-TOP IN THE WEST-SIDE OF MANHATTAN, HE WAS SHOT DOWN IN COLD BLOOD.
IN A WORD, MURDERED.

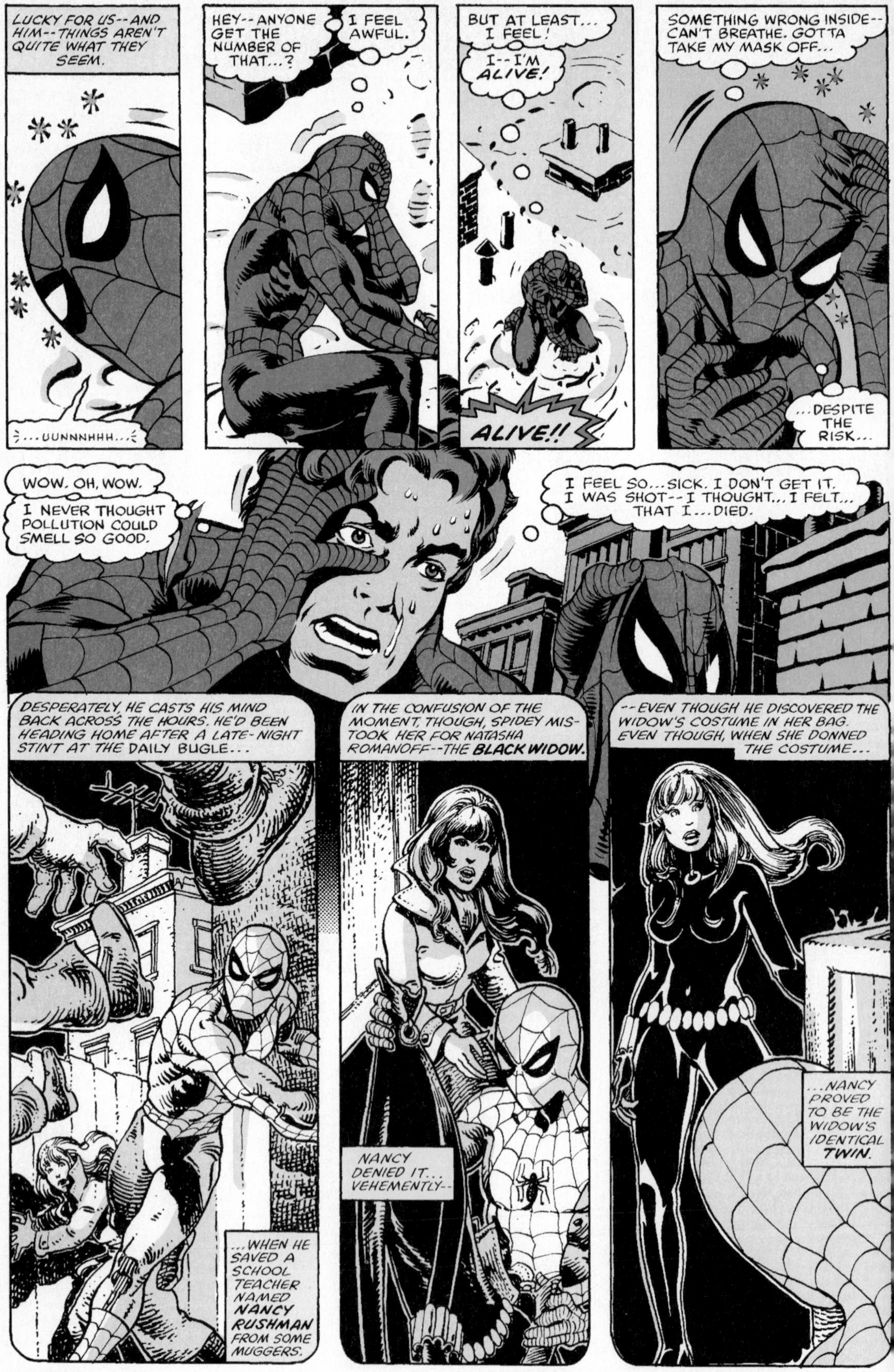
LUCKY FOR US--AND HIM--THINGS AREN'T QUITE WHAT THEY SEEM.
...UUNNNHHH...
HEY--ANYONE GET THE NUMBER OF THAT...?
I FEEL AWFUL.
BUT AT LEAST... I FEEL!
I--I'M ALIVE!
ALIVE!!
SOMETHING WRONG INSIDE--CAN'T BREATHE. GOTTA TAKE MY MASK OFF...
...DESPITE THE RISK...
WOW. OH, WOW.
I NEVER THOUGHT POLLUTION COULD SMELL SO GOOD.
I FEEL SO...SICK. I DON'T GET IT. I WAS SHOT--I THOUGHT... I FELT... THAT I...DIED.
DESPERATELY, HE CASTS HIS MIND BACK ACROSS THE HOURS. HE'D BEEN HEADING HOME AFTER A LATE-NIGHT STINT AT THE DAILY BUGLE...
...WHEN HE SAVED A SCHOOL TEACHER NAMED NANCY RUSHMAN FROM SOME MUGGERS.
IN THE CONFUSION OF THE MOMENT, THOUGH, SPIDEY MISTOOK HER FOR NATASHA ROMANOFF--THE BLACK WIDOW.
NANCY DENIED IT... VEHEMENTLY--
--EVEN THOUGH HE DISCOVERED THE WIDOW'S COSTUME IN HER BAG. EVEN THOUGH, WHEN SHE DONNED THE COSTUME...
...NANCY PROVED TO BE THE WIDOW'S IDENTICAL TWIN.

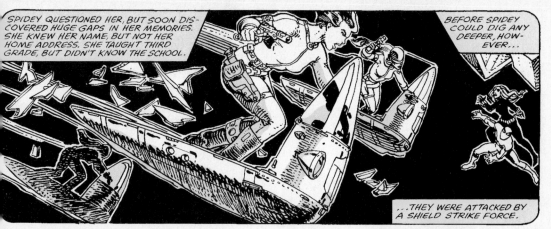

SPIDEY QUESTIONED HER, BUT SOON DISCOVERED HUGE GAPS IN HER MEMORIES. SHE KNEW HER NAME, BUT NOT HER HOME ADDRESS. SHE TAUGHT THIRD GRADE, BUT DIDN'T KNOW THE SCHOOL.

BEFORE SPIDEY COULD DIG ANY DEEPER, HOWEVER...

...THEY WERE ATTACKED BY A SHIELD STRIKE FORCE.

FOR SEEMINGLY NO REASON, SHIELD WANTED NANCY DEAD. BADLY OUTNUMBERED, SHE AND SPIDEY RAN.

BUT WHEN SPIDEY WAS WOUNDED, SHE SAVED HIM--SUDDENLY DISPLAYING ALL THE WIDOW'S LEGENDARY SKILL AND POWER.

THEN...

NICK FURY!

IN THE FLESH, WALL-CRAWLER.

YOU AN' ME HAVE KNOWN EACH OTHER A LONG TIME, WIDOW.

I WISH IT DIDN'T HAVE TO BE LIKE THIS.

BLAM!

I FELT BLOOD ON HER CHEST-- I THOUGHT HE'D KILLED HER, AND THEN, WHEN I WENT AFTER HIM, FURY SHOT ME.

HE MUST HAVE USED AN ANAESTHETIC BULLET.

FURY SHOT BOTH OF US WITH THE SAME GUN-- SO IF I'M ALIVE, I'LL BET NANCY IS, TOO.

I DON'T KNOW WHAT'S GOING ON, FURY, BUT I AIM TO FIND OUT.

AND, ALL THINGS CONSIDERED, I'M KIND OF HOPING YOU GET IN MY WAY.

ON THAT CUE, LET'S CUT CROSS-TOWN AND TO THE LEFT, TO A BRAND-NEW CORPORATE SKY-SCRAPER THAT ALSO HAPPENS TO BE SHIELD'S NEW YORK HEAD-QUARTERS.

COL. FURY, I DON'T UNDERSTAND.

ME NEITHER, SITWELL.

AN' THAT SCARES ME.

BUT I THOUGHT THE BLACK WIDOW'S LOYALTY WAS UNQUESTIONED?

IT IS. THE THING IS, JASPER-- LOYALTY TO **WHOM**?

HOW'S SHE DOIN', DOC?

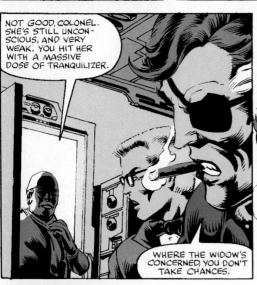

NOT GOOD, COLONEL. SHE'S STILL UNCON-SCIOUS, AND VERY WEAK. YOU HIT HER WITH A MASSIVE DOSE OF TRANQUILIZER.

WHERE THE WIDOW'S CONCERNED, YOU DON'T TAKE CHANCES.

I NEED HER AWAKE, DOC-- NOW.

IMPOSSIBLE.

I GOT QUESTIONS ONLY SHE CAN ANSWER, AMES-- AN' I CAN'T WAIT.

DO WHAT YOU HAVE TO DO, DOC, BUT HAVE HER READY FOR INTERROGATION BY SUNSET!

YOU FIGURE IT, SITWELL-- OUT OF THE BLUE, THE WIDOW CALLS IN A PANIC TO WARN ME OF SOME IMMINENT TERRIBLE DISASTER. THEN, SHE DISAPPEARS.

AN' WHEN WE FINALLY FIND HER, VAL DIS-OBEYS ORDERS AN', INSTEAD O' SIMPLY BRINGIN' HER IN, SHE TRIES TO KILL HER.

TOO MUCH HAS BEEN GOIN' WRONG WITH SHIELD LATELY, KID. AN' I GOT A NASTY FEELIN' THAT IF WE BOTCH THIS CAPER...

...NONE OF US WILL LIVE TO REGRET IT.

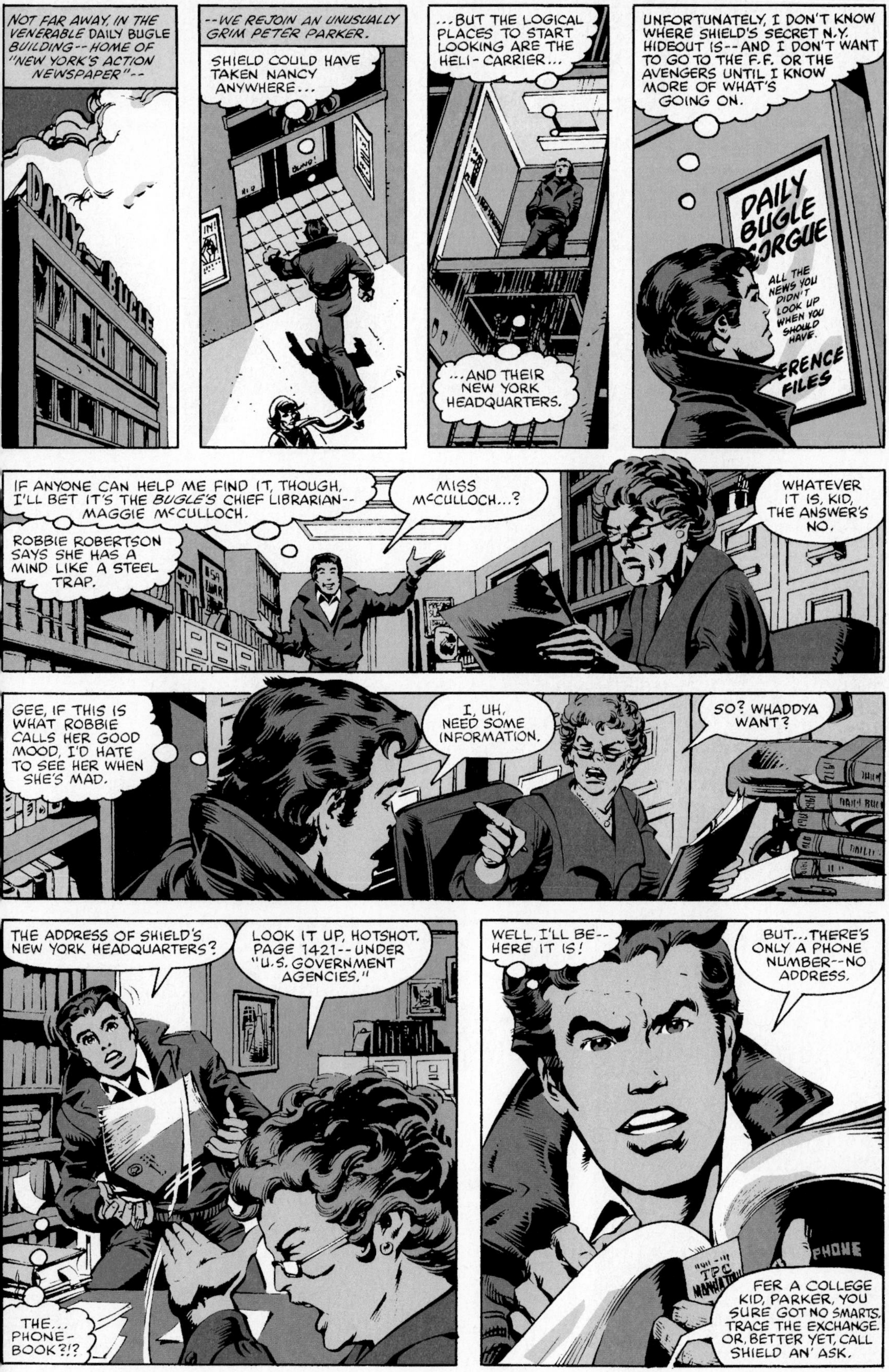
NOT FAR AWAY, IN THE VENERABLE DAILY BUGLE BUILDING--HOME OF "NEW YORK'S ACTION NEWSPAPER"--
--WE REJOIN AN UNUSUALLY GRIM PETER PARKER.
SHIELD COULD HAVE TAKEN NANCY ANYWHERE...
...BUT THE LOGICAL PLACES TO START LOOKING ARE THE HELI-CARRIER...
...AND THEIR NEW YORK HEADQUARTERS.
UNFORTUNATELY, I DON'T KNOW WHERE SHIELD'S SECRET N.Y. HIDEOUT IS--AND I DON'T WANT TO GO TO THE F.F. OR THE AVENGERS UNTIL I KNOW MORE OF WHAT'S GOING ON.
DAILY BUGLE MORGUE
ALL THE NEWS YOU DIDN'T LOOK UP WHEN YOU SHOULD HAVE.
ERENCE FILES
IF ANYONE CAN HELP ME FIND IT, THOUGH, I'LL BET IT'S THE BUGLE'S CHIEF LIBRARIAN--MAGGIE McCULLOCH.
ROBBIE ROBERTSON SAYS SHE HAS A MIND LIKE A STEEL TRAP.
MISS McCULLOCH...?
WHATEVER IT IS, KID, THE ANSWER'S NO.
GEE, IF THIS IS WHAT ROBBIE CALLS HER GOOD MOOD, I'D HATE TO SEE HER WHEN SHE'S MAD.
I, UH, NEED SOME INFORMATION.
SO? WHADDYA WANT?
THE ADDRESS OF SHIELD'S NEW YORK HEADQUARTERS?
LOOK IT UP, HOTSHOT. PAGE 1421--UNDER "U.S. GOVERNMENT AGENCIES."
THE... PHONE-BOOK?!?
WELL, I'LL BE--HERE IT IS!
BUT...THERE'S ONLY A PHONE NUMBER--NO ADDRESS.
PHONE
TPC MANHATTAN
FER A COLLEGE KID, PARKER, YOU SURE GOT NO SMARTS. TRACE THE EXCHANGE. OR, BETTER YET, CALL SHIELD AN' ASK.

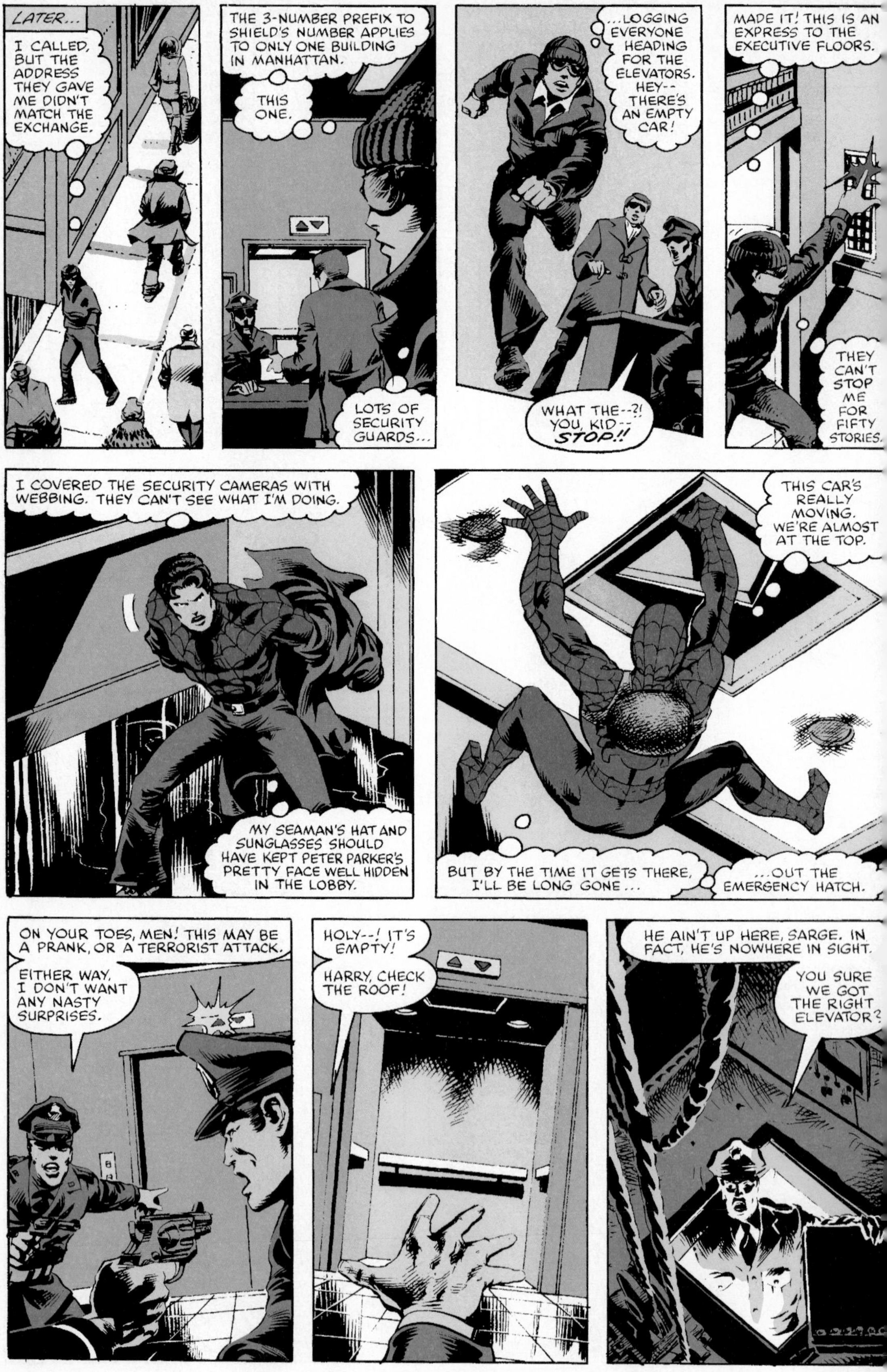
LATER...
I CALLED, BUT THE ADDRESS THEY GAVE ME DIDN'T MATCH THE EXCHANGE.
THE 3-NUMBER PREFIX TO SHIELD'S NUMBER APPLIES TO ONLY ONE BUILDING IN MANHATTAN.
THIS ONE.
LOTS OF SECURITY GUARDS...
...LOGGING EVERYONE HEADING FOR THE ELEVATORS. HEY-- THERE'S AN EMPTY CAR!
WHAT THE--?! YOU, KID-- STOP!!
MADE IT! THIS IS AN EXPRESS TO THE EXECUTIVE FLOORS.
THEY CAN'T STOP ME FOR FIFTY STORIES.
I COVERED THE SECURITY CAMERAS WITH WEBBING. THEY CAN'T SEE WHAT I'M DOING.
MY SEAMAN'S HAT AND SUNGLASSES SHOULD HAVE KEPT PETER PARKER'S PRETTY FACE WELL HIDDEN IN THE LOBBY.
THIS CAR'S REALLY MOVING. WE'RE ALMOST AT THE TOP.
BUT BY THE TIME IT GETS THERE, I'LL BE LONG GONE...
...OUT THE EMERGENCY HATCH.
ON YOUR TOES, MEN! THIS MAY BE A PRANK, OR A TERRORIST ATTACK.
EITHER WAY, I DON'T WANT ANY NASTY SURPRISES.
HOLY--! IT'S EMPTY!
HARRY, CHECK THE ROOF!
HE AIN'T UP HERE, SARGE. IN FACT, HE'S NOWHERE IN SIGHT.
YOU SURE WE GOT THE RIGHT ELEVATOR?

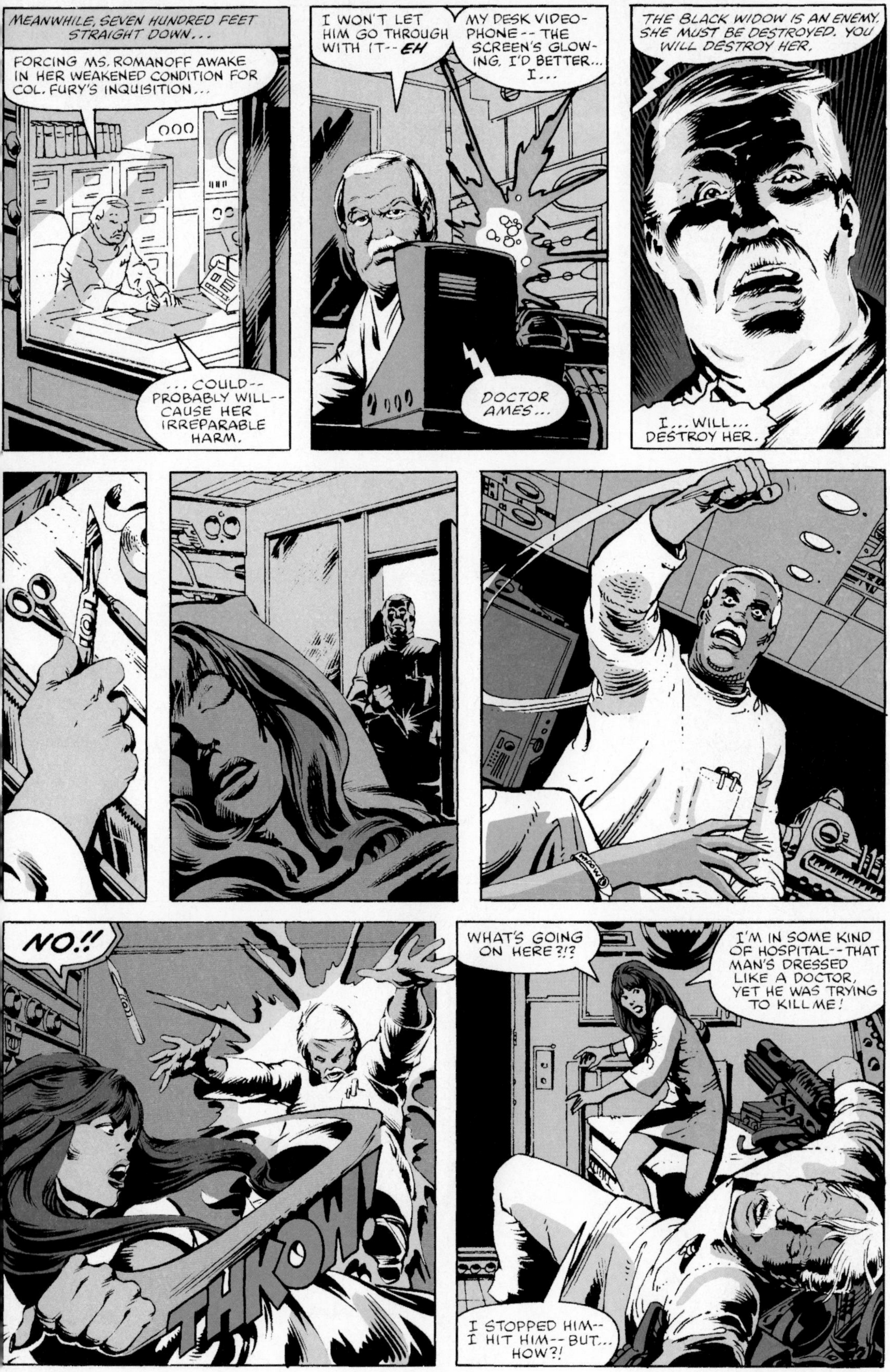
MEANWHILE, SEVEN HUNDRED FEET STRAIGHT DOWN...
FORCING MS. ROMANOFF AWAKE IN HER WEAKENED CONDITION FOR COL. FURY'S INQUISITION...
...COULD--PROBABLY WILL--CAUSE HER IRREPARABLE HARM.
I WON'T LET HIM GO THROUGH WITH IT--EH
MY DESK VIDEO-PHONE--THE SCREEN'S GLOWING. I'D BETTER... I...
DOCTOR AMES...
THE BLACK WIDOW IS AN ENEMY. SHE MUST BE DESTROYED. YOU WILL DESTROY HER.
I... WILL... DESTROY HER.
NO!!
THKOW!
WHAT'S GOING ON HERE?!?
I'M IN SOME KIND OF HOSPITAL--THAT MAN'S DRESSED LIKE A DOCTOR, YET HE WAS TRYING TO KILL ME!
I STOPPED HIM--I HIT HIM--BUT... HOW?!

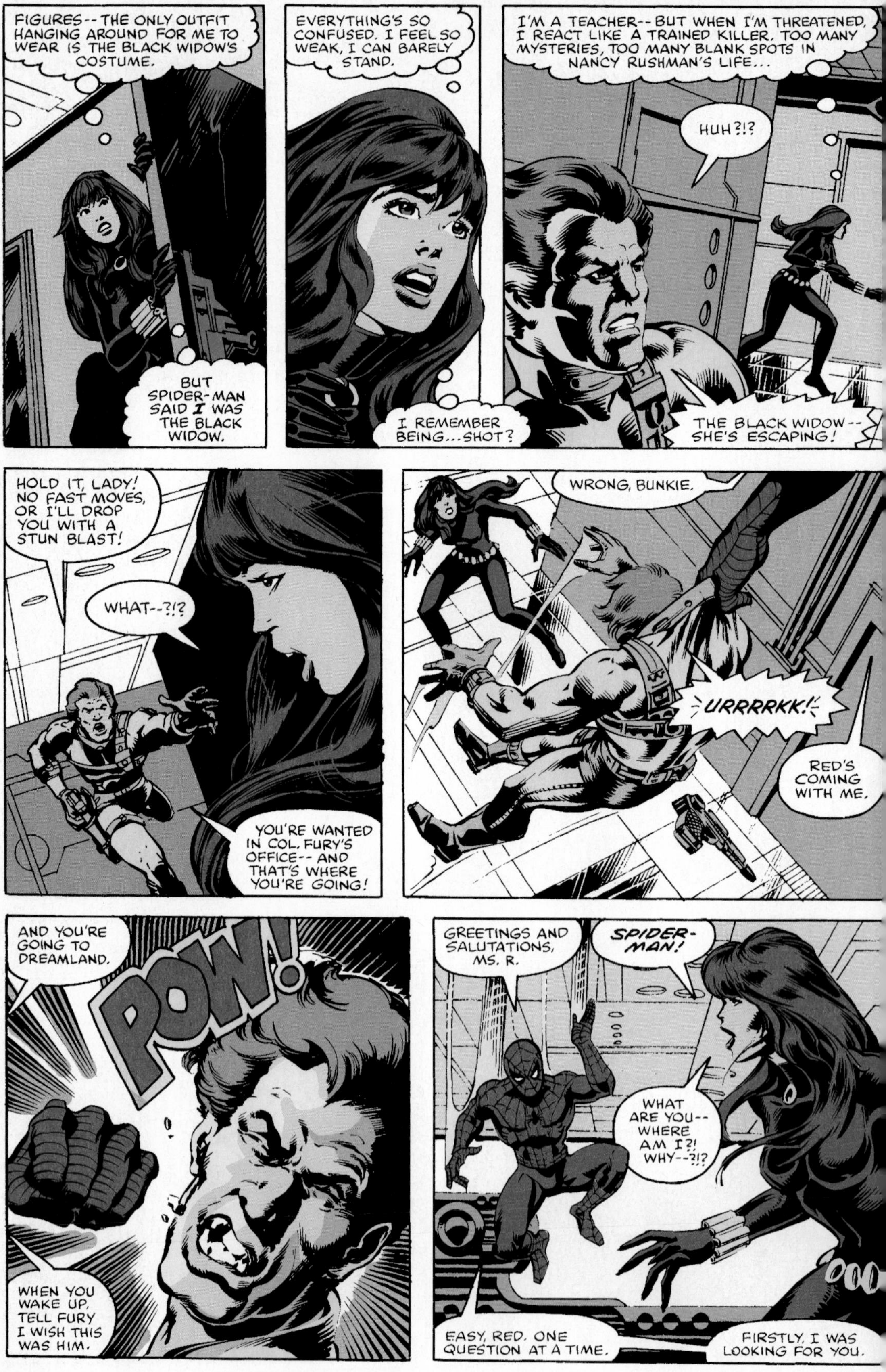

FIGURES--THE ONLY OUTFIT HANGING AROUND FOR ME TO WEAR IS THE BLACK WIDOW'S COSTUME.
BUT SPIDER-MAN SAID I WAS THE BLACK WIDOW.
EVERYTHING'S SO CONFUSED. I FEEL SO WEAK, I CAN BARELY STAND.
I REMEMBER BEING...SHOT?
I'M A TEACHER--BUT WHEN I'M THREATENED, I REACT LIKE A TRAINED KILLER. TOO MANY MYSTERIES, TOO MANY BLANK SPOTS IN NANCY RUSHMAN'S LIFE...
HUH?!?
THE BLACK WIDOW--SHE'S ESCAPING!
HOLD IT, LADY! NO FAST MOVES, OR I'LL DROP YOU WITH A STUN BLAST!
WHAT--?!?
YOU'RE WANTED IN COL. FURY'S OFFICE--AND THAT'S WHERE YOU'RE GOING!
WRONG, BUNKIE.
URRRRKK!
RED'S COMING WITH ME.
AND YOU'RE GOING TO DREAMLAND.
POW!
WHEN YOU WAKE UP, TELL FURY I WISH THIS WAS HIM.
GREETINGS AND SALUTATIONS, MS. R.
SPIDER-MAN!
WHAT ARE YOU--WHERE AM I?! WHY--?!?
EASY, RED. ONE QUESTION AT A TIME.
FIRSTLY, I WAS LOOKING FOR YOU.

SECONDLY, YOU'RE IN THE BASEMENT OF A MANHATTAN SKYSCRAPER; IT'S THE LOCAL SHIELD BASE.

UH-OH-- ALARMS!

N-NO! WHAT DO THEY MEAN?! WHY IS THIS *HAPPENING* TO ME?!

FURY'S DISCOVERED YOUR ESCAPE AND-- IF THOSE BOZOS ARE ANY INDICATION-- HE WANTS YOU BACK REAL BAD.

NANCY'S GOING TENSE-- SHE'S STARTING TO *PANIC!*

IF WE'RE GOING TO GET OUT OF HERE IN ONE PIECE, WE'LL HAVE TO MOVE LIKE GREASED LIGHTNING.

NANCY MAY HAVE THE WIDOW'S POWERS...

BOK!

...BUT SHE DOESN'T HAVE HER EXPERIENCE AND CONFIDENCE, SORRY ABOUT THIS, LADY, BUT IT'S FOR THE BEST.

AT LEAST, WHILE SHE'S UN-CONSCIOUS, I DON'T HAVE TO WORRY ABOUT HER MAKING A MISTAKE...

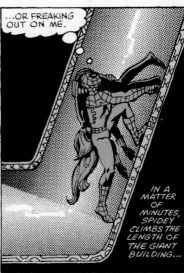

...OR FREAKING OUT ON ME.

IN A MATTER OF MINUTES, SPIDEY CLIMBS THE LENGTH OF THE GIANT BUILDING...

...FOLLOWING ITS VENTILATION DUCTS FROM SHIELD'S SUB-BASEMENT COMPLEX TO THE ROOF.

BEAUTIFUL-- NOT A SOUL IN SIGHT.

BUT THIS ESCAPE IS EASY COMPARED TO WHAT COMES NEXT.

SOMEONE'S BUILT A WALL SEPARATING NANCY FROM HER MEMORIES-- AND HER TRUE SELF.

I'VE GOT TO FIND A WAY THROUGH THAT WALL-- WHATEVER THE COST.

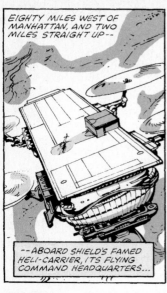

EIGHTY MILES WEST OF MANHATTAN, AND TWO MILES STRAIGHT UP--

--ABOARD SHIELD'S FAMED HELI-CARRIER, ITS FLYING COMMAND HEADQUARTERS...

REPORT ACKNOWLEDGED, NEW YORK-- THE WIDOW'S ON THE LOOSE. KEEP US POSTED ON ALL FURTHER DEVELOPMENTS, NO MATTER HOW TRIVIAL.

CLAY QUARTERMAIN, OUT.

THE WIDOW-- ESCAPED?

YES...COMMANDER. WITH...SPIDER-MAN'S HELP.

AMES FAILED-- I SHOULD HAVE EXPECTED THAT.

SILVER SAMURAI-- USE YOUR TELEPORT RING TO CARRY BOOMERANG TO MANHATTAN. BOOMERANG--FIND THE WIDOW AND SPIDER-MAN. KILL THEM BOTH.

COMMANDER, LET ME GO ALONE.

THE ARACHNID AND I HAVE... UNFINISHED BUSINESS.

NO, SAMURAI. YOU ARE NEEDED BY MY SIDE.

BUT THIS IS A MATTER OF HONOR!

HONOR MEANS NOTHING TO ME.

ALL THAT MATTERS IS THE PLAN.

NOW-- GO!

HE IS DEFIANT, BUT HE WILL OBEY. HE KNOWS THAT IN SINGLE COMBAT, HIS SKILL IS NOTHING COMPARED TO MINE.

...CBS MORNING NEWS--PRESIDENT CARTER WILL ADDRESS A JOINT SESSION OF CONGRESS THIS EVENING...

AND WHEN THAT SPEECH IS DONE, FOOL...

...THE WORLD WILL NEVER BE THE SAME AGAIN.

TEK!

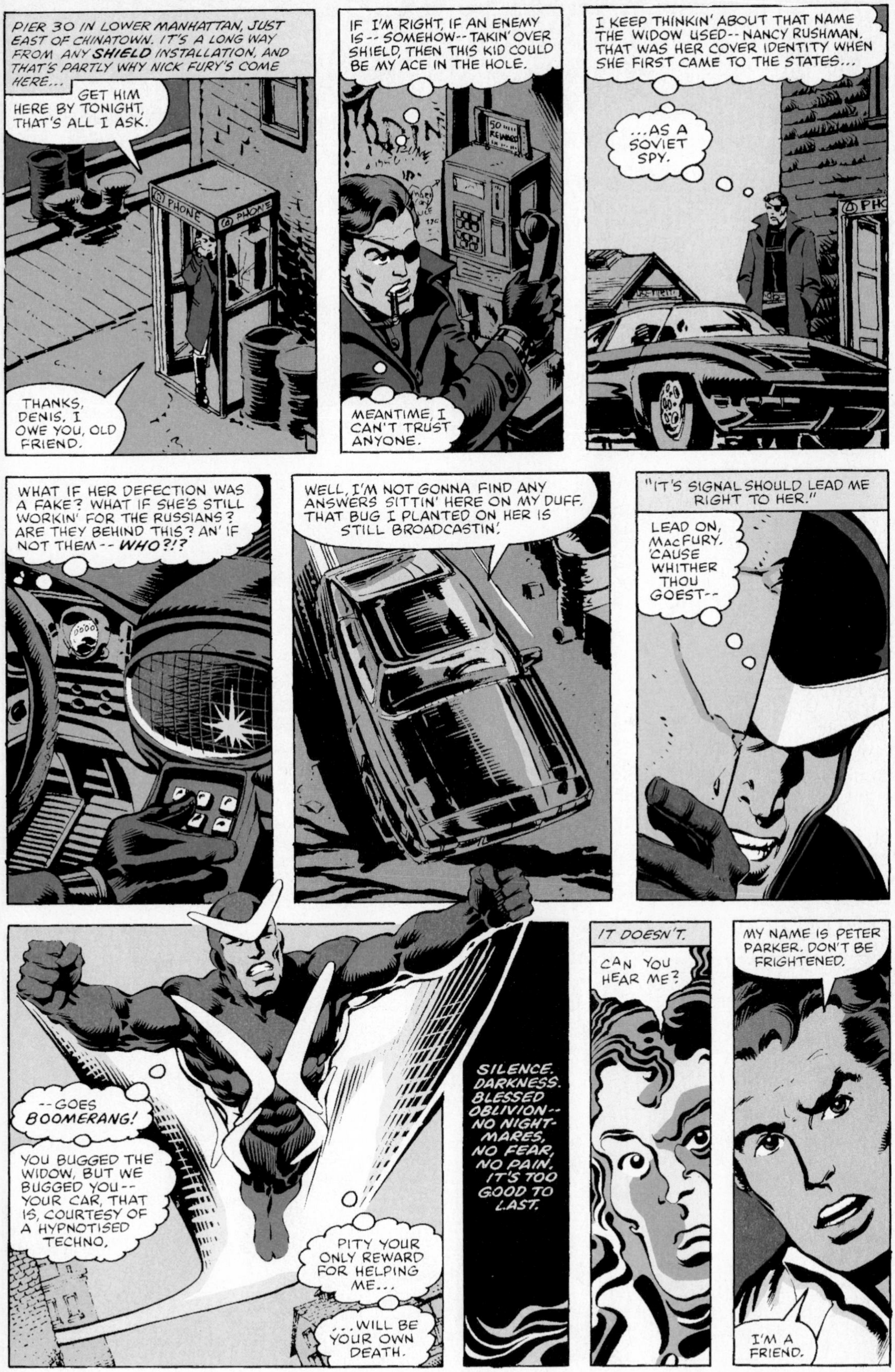
PIER 30 IN LOWER MANHATTAN, JUST EAST OF CHINATOWN. IT'S A LONG WAY FROM ANY SHIELD INSTALLATION, AND THAT'S PARTLY WHY NICK FURY'S COME HERE...
GET HIM HERE BY TONIGHT, THAT'S ALL I ASK.
PHONE
PHONE
THANKS, DENIS, I OWE YOU, OLD FRIEND.
IF I'M RIGHT, IF AN ENEMY IS--SOMEHOW--TAKIN' OVER SHIELD, THEN THIS KID COULD BE MY ACE IN THE HOLE.
MEANTIME, I CAN'T TRUST ANYONE.
I KEEP THINKIN' ABOUT THAT NAME THE WIDOW USED--NANCY RUSHMAN. THAT WAS HER COVER IDENTITY WHEN SHE FIRST CAME TO THE STATES...
...AS A SOVIET SPY.
WHAT IF HER DEFECTION WAS A FAKE? WHAT IF SHE'S STILL WORKIN' FOR THE RUSSIANS? ARE THEY BEHIND THIS? AN' IF NOT THEM--WHO?!?
WELL, I'M NOT GONNA FIND ANY ANSWERS SITTIN' HERE ON MY DUFF. THAT BUG I PLANTED ON HER IS STILL BROADCASTIN'.
"IT'S SIGNAL SHOULD LEAD ME RIGHT TO HER."
LEAD ON, MacFURY. 'CAUSE WHITHER THOU GOEST--
--GOES BOOMERANG!
YOU BUGGED THE WIDOW, BUT WE BUGGED YOU--YOUR CAR, THAT IS, COURTESY OF A HYPNOTISED TECHNO.
PITY YOUR ONLY REWARD FOR HELPING ME...
...WILL BE YOUR OWN DEATH.
SILENCE. DARKNESS. BLESSED OBLIVION--NO NIGHTMARES, NO FEAR, NO PAIN. IT'S TOO GOOD TO LAST.
IT DOESN'T.
CAN YOU HEAR ME?
MY NAME IS PETER PARKER. DON'T BE FRIGHTENED.
I'M A FRIEND.

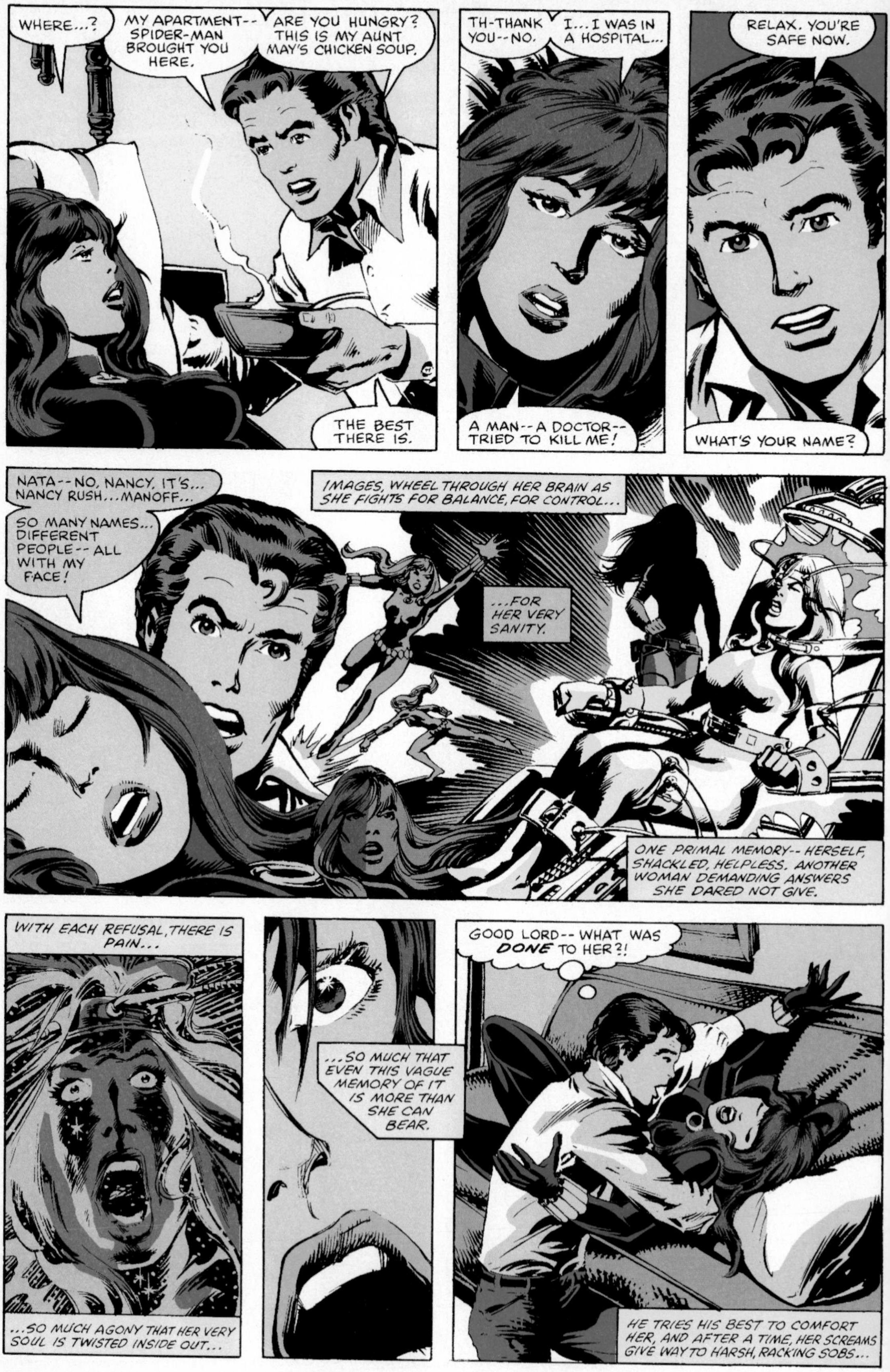
WHERE...?
MY APARTMENT-- SPIDER-MAN BROUGHT YOU HERE.
ARE YOU HUNGRY? THIS IS MY AUNT MAY'S CHICKEN SOUP.
THE BEST THERE IS.
TH-THANK YOU--NO.
I... I WAS IN A HOSPITAL...
A MAN--A DOCTOR-- TRIED TO KILL ME!
RELAX. YOU'RE SAFE NOW.
WHAT'S YOUR NAME?
NATA--NO, NANCY. IT'S... NANCY RUSH...MANOFF...
SO MANY NAMES... DIFFERENT PEOPLE--ALL WITH MY FACE!
IMAGES, WHEEL THROUGH HER BRAIN AS SHE FIGHTS FOR BALANCE, FOR CONTROL...
...FOR HER VERY SANITY.
ONE PRIMAL MEMORY--HERSELF, SHACKLED, HELPLESS. ANOTHER WOMAN DEMANDING ANSWERS SHE DARED NOT GIVE.
WITH EACH REFUSAL, THERE IS PAIN...
...SO MUCH AGONY THAT HER VERY SOUL IS TWISTED INSIDE OUT...
...SO MUCH THAT EVEN THIS VAGUE MEMORY OF IT IS MORE THAN SHE CAN BEAR.
GOOD LORD--WHAT WAS DONE TO HER?!
HE TRIES HIS BEST TO COMFORT HER, AND AFTER A TIME, HER SCREAMS GIVE WAY TO HARSH, RACKING SOBS...

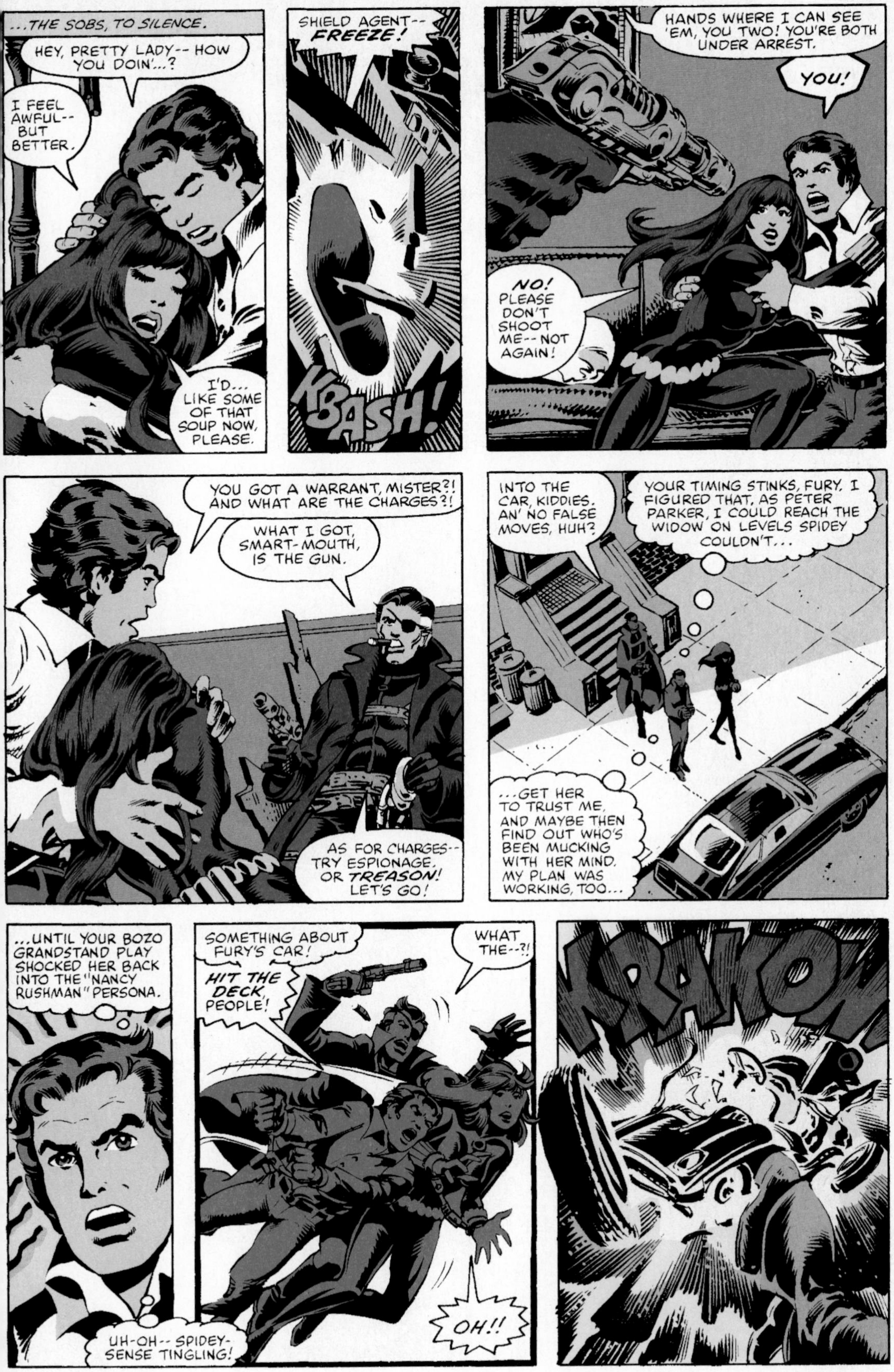
...THE SOBS, TO SILENCE.
HEY, PRETTY LADY-- HOW YOU DOIN'...?
I FEEL AWFUL-- BUT BETTER.
I'D... LIKE SOME OF THAT SOUP NOW, PLEASE.
SHIELD AGENT-- FREEZE!
KBASH!
HANDS WHERE I CAN SEE 'EM, YOU TWO! YOU'RE BOTH UNDER ARREST.
YOU!
NO! PLEASE DON'T SHOOT ME-- NOT AGAIN!
YOU GOT A WARRANT, MISTER?! AND WHAT ARE THE CHARGES?!
WHAT I GOT, SMART-MOUTH, IS THE GUN.
AS FOR CHARGES-- TRY ESPIONAGE, OR TREASON! LET'S GO!
INTO THE CAR, KIDDIES. AN' NO FALSE MOVES, HUH?
YOUR TIMING STINKS, FURY. I FIGURED THAT, AS PETER PARKER, I COULD REACH THE WIDOW ON LEVELS SPIDEY COULDN'T...
...GET HER TO TRUST ME, AND MAYBE THEN FIND OUT WHO'S BEEN MUCKING WITH HER MIND. MY PLAN WAS WORKING, TOO...
...UNTIL YOUR BOZO GRANDSTAND PLAY SHOCKED HER BACK INTO THE "NANCY RUSHMAN" PERSONA.
UH-OH-- SPIDEY-SENSE TINGLING!
SOMETHING ABOUT FURY'S CAR!
HIT THE DECK, PEOPLE!
WHAT THE--?!
OH!!
KRAKOW

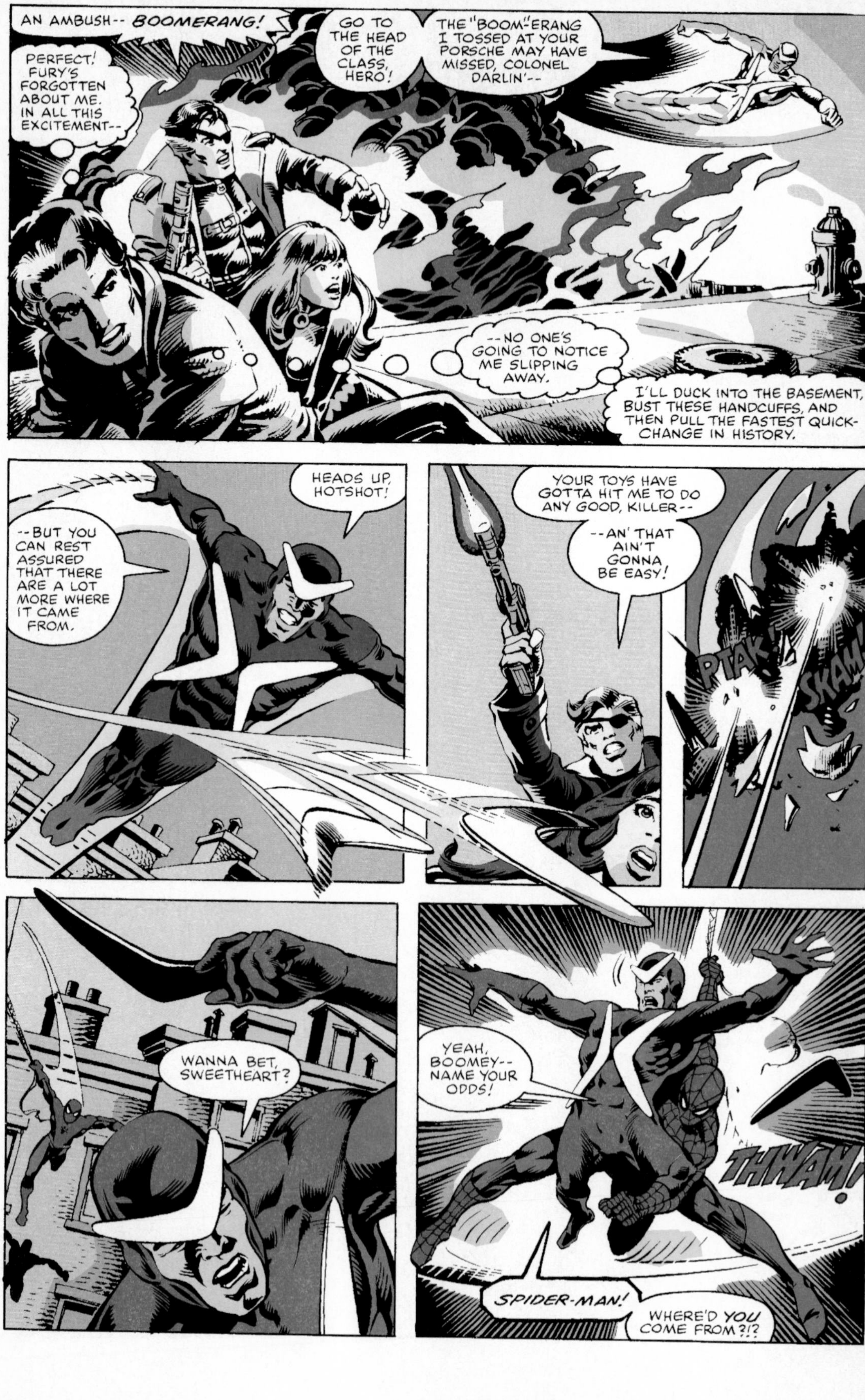
AN AMBUSH-- BOOMERANG!
PERFECT! FURY'S FORGOTTEN ABOUT ME. IN ALL THIS EXCITEMENT--
GO TO THE HEAD OF THE CLASS, HERO!
THE "BOOM"-ERANG I TOSSED AT YOUR PORSCHE MAY HAVE MISSED, COLONEL DARLIN'--
--NO ONE'S GOING TO NOTICE ME SLIPPING AWAY.
I'LL DUCK INTO THE BASEMENT, BUST THESE HANDCUFFS, AND THEN PULL THE FASTEST QUICK-CHANGE IN HISTORY.
--BUT YOU CAN REST ASSURED THAT THERE ARE A LOT MORE WHERE IT CAME FROM.
HEADS UP, HOTSHOT!
YOUR TOYS HAVE GOTTA HIT ME TO DO ANY GOOD, KILLER--
--AN' THAT AIN'T GONNA BE EASY!
PTAK!
SKAM!
WANNA BET, SWEETHEART?
YEAH, BOOMEY-- NAME YOUR ODDS!
THWAM!
SPIDER-MAN!
WHERE'D YOU COME FROM?!?

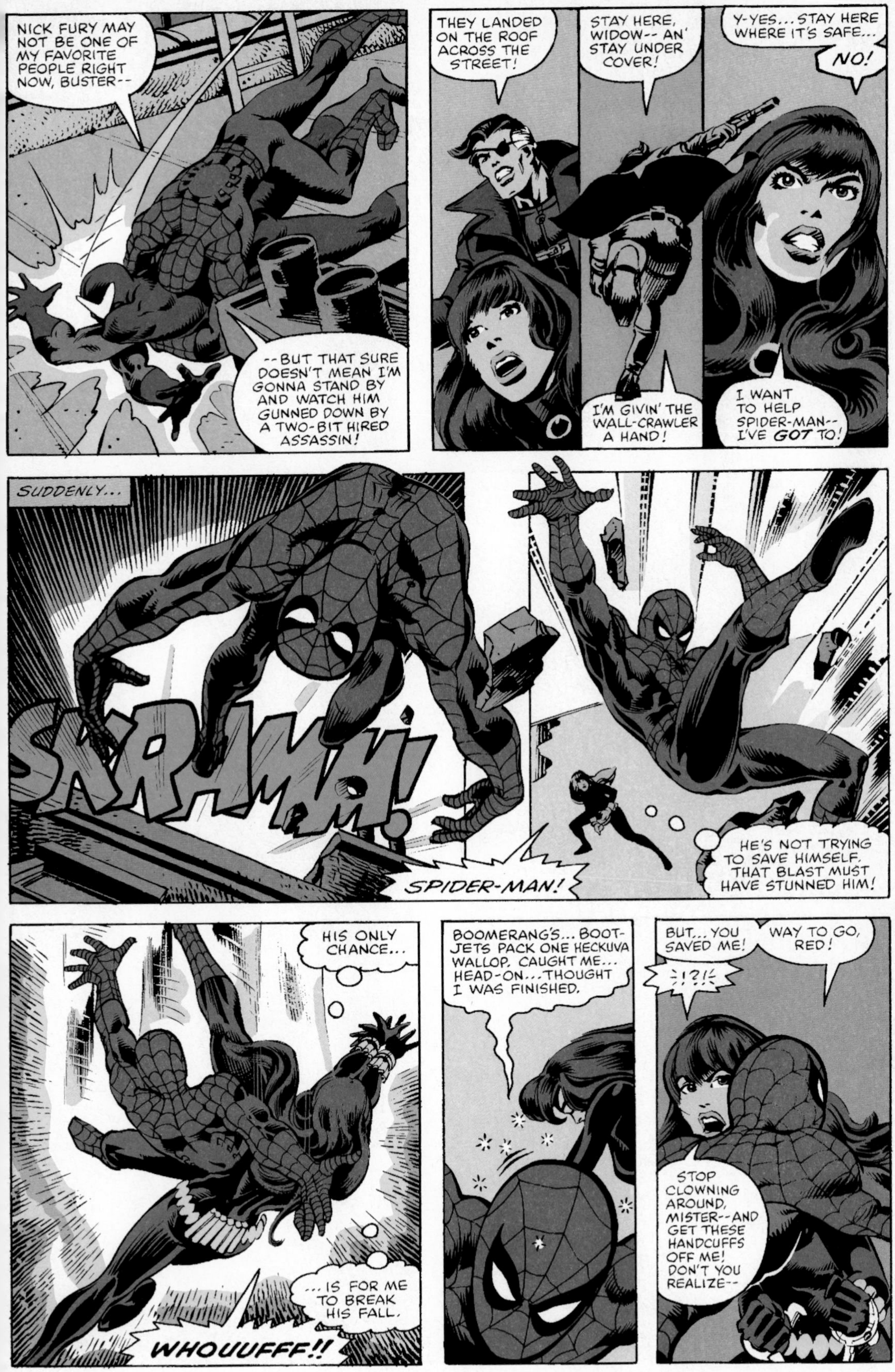
NICK FURY MAY NOT BE ONE OF MY FAVORITE PEOPLE RIGHT NOW, BUSTER--
--BUT THAT SURE DOESN'T MEAN I'M GONNA STAND BY AND WATCH HIM GUNNED DOWN BY A TWO-BIT HIRED ASSASSIN!
THEY LANDED ON THE ROOF ACROSS THE STREET!
STAY HERE, WIDOW-- AN' STAY UNDER COVER!
I'M GIVIN' THE WALL-CRAWLER A HAND!
Y-YES... STAY HERE WHERE IT'S SAFE...
NO!
I WANT TO HELP SPIDER-MAN-- I'VE GOT TO!
SUDDENLY...
SKRAMM!
SPIDER-MAN!
HE'S NOT TRYING TO SAVE HIMSELF. THAT BLAST MUST HAVE STUNNED HIM!
HIS ONLY CHANCE...
...IS FOR ME TO BREAK HIS FALL.
WHOUUFFF!!
BOOMERANG'S... BOOT-JETS PACK ONE HECKUVA WALLOP. CAUGHT ME... HEAD-ON... THOUGHT I WAS FINISHED.
BUT... YOU SAVED ME!
WAY TO GO, RED!
!?!
STOP CLOWNING AROUND, MISTER--AND GET THESE HANDCUFFS OFF ME! DON'T YOU REALIZE--

Panel 1: "--NICK FURY'S ON THAT ROOF-TOP FIGHTING BOOMERANG ALONE!"

Panel 2: NOT FOR LONG, LADY! NANCY'S VOICE, HER BEARING--SUDDENLY EVERYTHING'S CHANGED. SHE'S SOUNDING AND ACTING LIKE THE *BLACK WIDOW.*

Panel 3: DOES THAT MEAN SHE'S GETTING BETTER-- OR CURED, BACK TO NORMAL? PART OF ME HOPES SO... ...YET PART OF ME DOESN'T, I REALLY *LIKED* NANCY RUSHMAN. HOLD THAT POSE, BOOMEY-- --AND SAY HELLO TO DREAMLAND.

Panel 4: YIKES!

Panel 5: THAT FLASH OF LIGHT BEHIND BOOMERANG, I'VE SEEN IT BEFORE! OH, NO!

Panel 6: OH, YES, ARACHNID. IT SEEMS WE MEET AGAIN. AND IF THE FATES ARE KIND TO ME-- --THIS TIME SHALL BE THE LAST!

Panel 7: THE *SILVER SAMURAI!* AND HE'S WEARING THAT CRAZY *TELEPORT* RING HE STOLE OFF JOHN BELUSHI. *

*SEE THE LEGENDARY MTU #74 --AL.

142

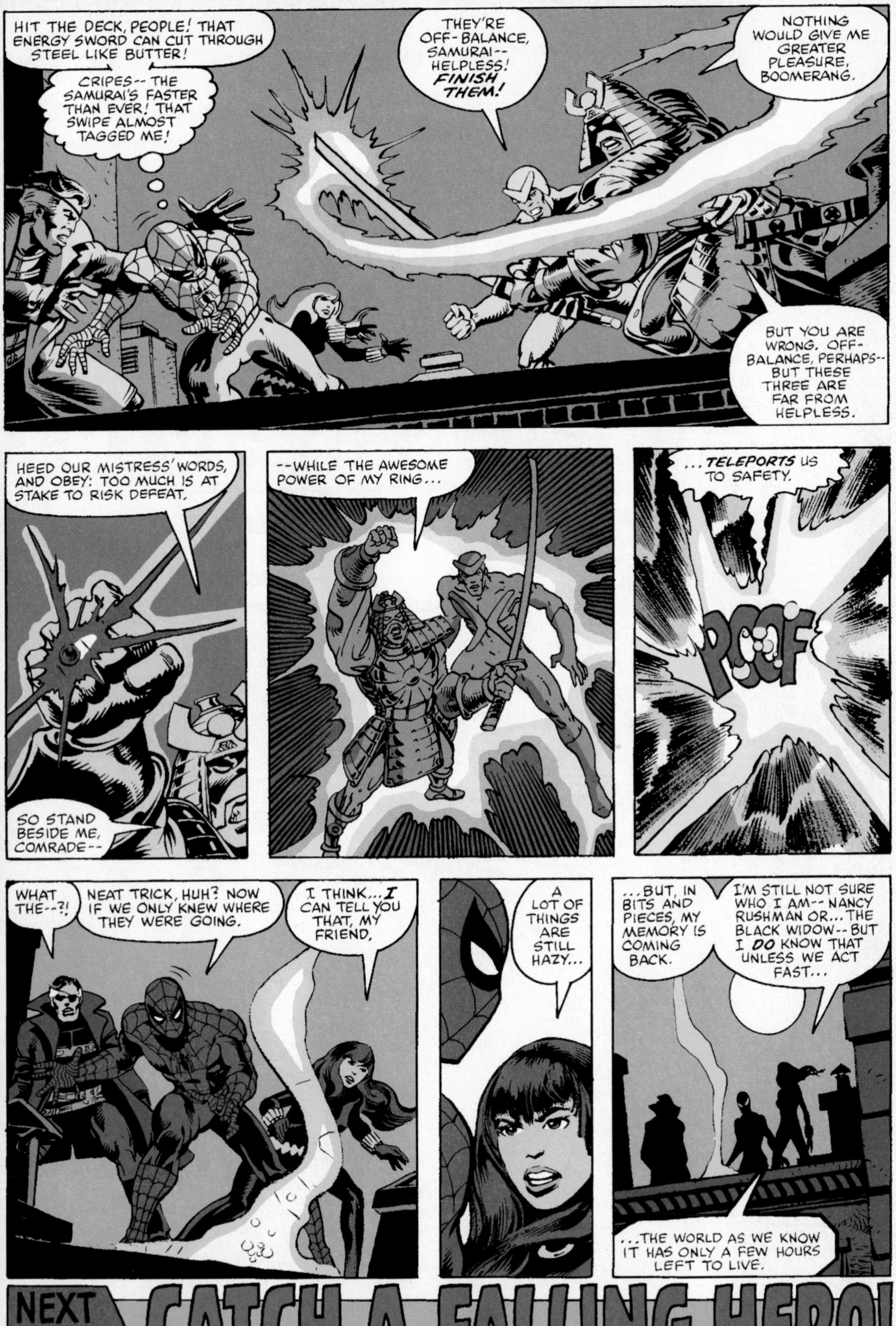
HIT THE DECK, PEOPLE! THAT ENERGY SWORD CAN CUT THROUGH STEEL LIKE BUTTER!
CRIPES-- THE SAMURAI'S FASTER THAN EVER! THAT SWIPE ALMOST TAGGED ME!
THEY'RE OFF-BALANCE, SAMURAI-- HELPLESS! FINISH THEM!
NOTHING WOULD GIVE ME GREATER PLEASURE, BOOMERANG.
BUT YOU ARE WRONG. OFF-BALANCE, PERHAPS-- BUT THESE THREE ARE FAR FROM HELPLESS.
HEED OUR MISTRESS' WORDS, AND OBEY: TOO MUCH IS AT STAKE TO RISK DEFEAT.
SO STAND BESIDE ME, COMRADE--
--WHILE THE AWESOME POWER OF MY RING...
...TELEPORTS US TO SAFETY.
POOF
WHAT THE--?!
NEAT TRICK, HUH? NOW IF WE ONLY KNEW WHERE THEY WERE GOING.
I THINK... I CAN TELL YOU THAT, MY FRIEND.
A LOT OF THINGS ARE STILL HAZY...
...BUT, IN BITS AND PIECES, MY MEMORY IS COMING BACK.
I'M STILL NOT SURE WHO I AM-- NANCY RUSHMAN OR... THE BLACK WIDOW-- BUT I DO KNOW THAT UNLESS WE ACT FAST...
...THE WORLD AS WE KNOW IT HAS ONLY A FEW HOURS LEFT TO LIVE.
NEXT ISSUE: CATCH A FALLING HERO!

40¢
84
AUG
02147
MARVEL® COMICS GROUP
APPROVED BY THE COMICS CODE AUTHORITY
© 1979 MARVEL COMICS GROUP
MARVEL TEAM-UP™
SPIDER-MAN®
AND SHANG CHI..
MASTER OF KUNG FU
TM
LEI ALOHA -79-

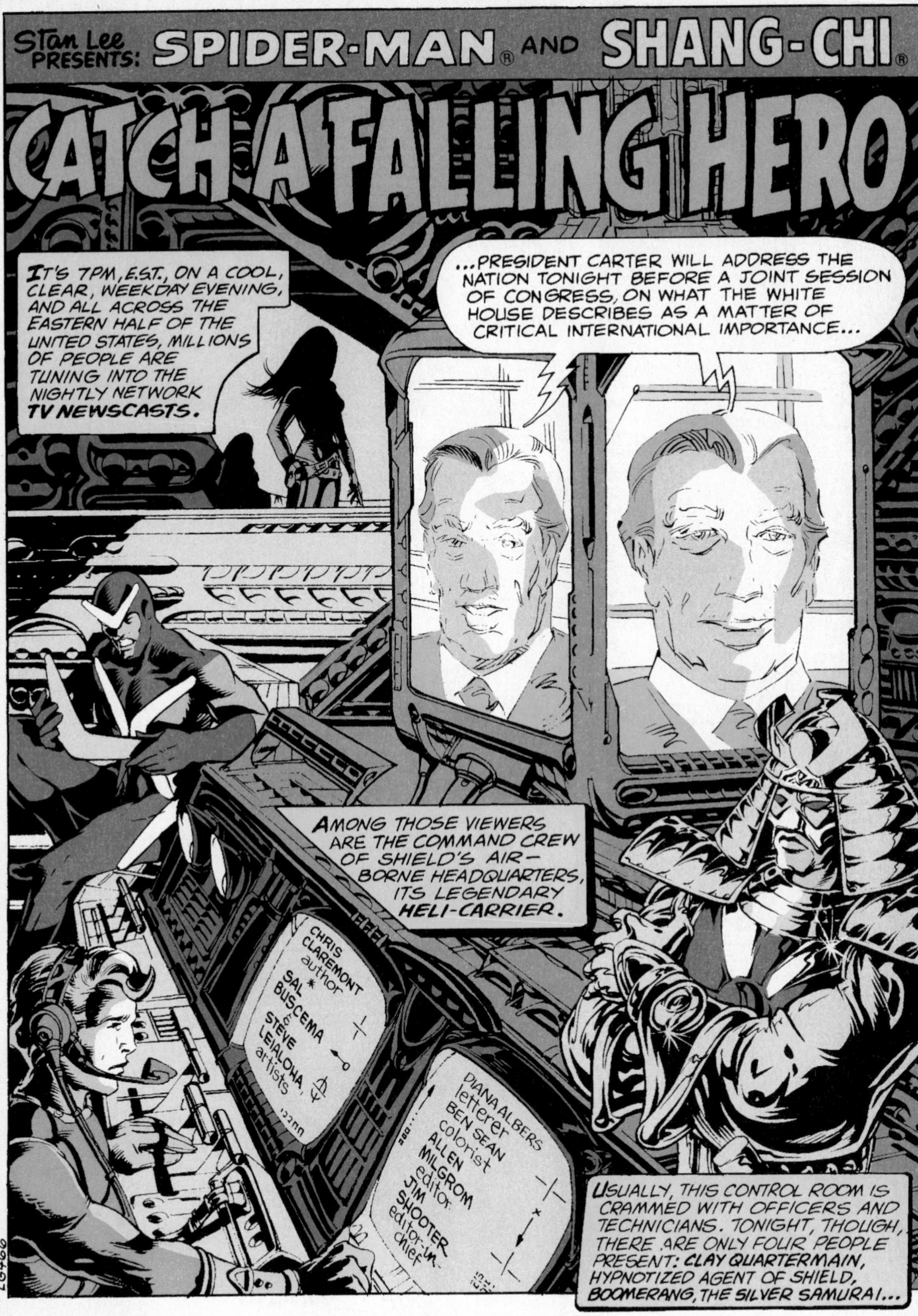

Stan Lee PRESENTS: SPIDER-MAN® AND SHANG-CHI®
CATCH A FALLING HERO
IT'S 7PM, E.S.T., ON A COOL, CLEAR, WEEKDAY EVENING, AND ALL ACROSS THE EASTERN HALF OF THE UNITED STATES, MILLIONS OF PEOPLE ARE TUNING INTO THE NIGHTLY NETWORK TV NEWSCASTS.
...PRESIDENT CARTER WILL ADDRESS THE NATION TONIGHT BEFORE A JOINT SESSION OF CONGRESS, ON WHAT THE WHITE HOUSE DESCRIBES AS A MATTER OF CRITICAL INTERNATIONAL IMPORTANCE...
AMONG THOSE VIEWERS ARE THE COMMAND CREW OF SHIELD'S AIR-BORNE HEADQUARTERS, ITS LEGENDARY HELI-CARRIER.
CHRIS CLAREMONT author * SAL BUSCEMA & STEVE LEIALOHA, artists
DIANA ALBERS letterer BEN SEAN colorist ALLEN MILGROM editor JIM SHOOTER editor-in-chief
USUALLY, THIS CONTROL ROOM IS CRAMMED WITH OFFICERS AND TECHNICIANS. TONIGHT, THOUGH, THERE ARE ONLY FOUR PEOPLE PRESENT: CLAY QUARTERMAIN, HYPNOTIZED AGENT OF SHIELD, BOOMERANG, THE SILVER SAMURAI...

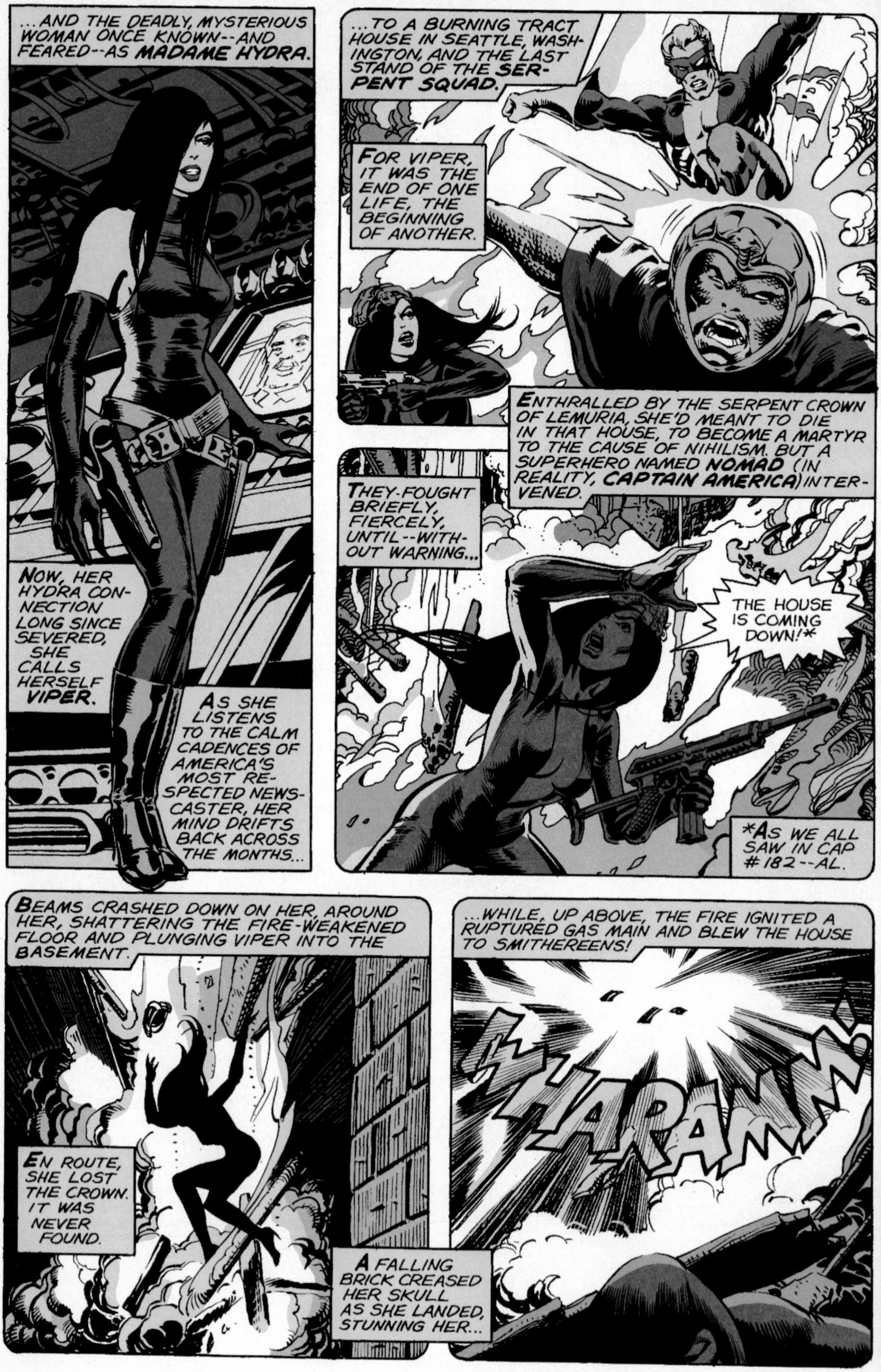
...AND THE DEADLY, MYSTERIOUS WOMAN ONCE KNOWN--AND FEARED--AS MADAME HYDRA.
NOW, HER HYDRA CONNECTION LONG SINCE SEVERED, SHE CALLS HERSELF VIPER.
AS SHE LISTENS TO THE CALM CADENCES OF AMERICA'S MOST RESPECTED NEWSCASTER, HER MIND DRIFTS BACK ACROSS THE MONTHS...
...TO A BURNING TRACT HOUSE IN SEATTLE, WASHINGTON, AND THE LAST STAND OF THE SERPENT SQUAD.
FOR VIPER, IT WAS THE END OF ONE LIFE, THE BEGINNING OF ANOTHER.
ENTHRALLED BY THE SERPENT CROWN OF LEMURIA, SHE'D MEANT TO DIE IN THAT HOUSE, TO BECOME A MARTYR TO THE CAUSE OF NIHILISM. BUT A SUPERHERO NAMED NOMAD (IN REALITY, CAPTAIN AMERICA) INTERVENED.
THEY FOUGHT BRIEFLY, FIERCELY, UNTIL--WITHOUT WARNING...
THE HOUSE IS COMING DOWN!*
*AS WE ALL SAW IN CAP #182--AL.
BEAMS CRASHED DOWN ON HER, AROUND HER, SHATTERING THE FIRE-WEAKENED FLOOR AND PLUNGING VIPER INTO THE BASEMENT.
EN ROUTE, SHE LOST THE CROWN. IT WAS NEVER FOUND.
A FALLING BRICK CREASED HER SKULL AS SHE LANDED, STUNNING HER...
...WHILE, UP ABOVE, THE FIRE IGNITED A RUPTURED GAS MAIN AND BLEW THE HOUSE TO SMITHEREENS!
WHAPAMM!

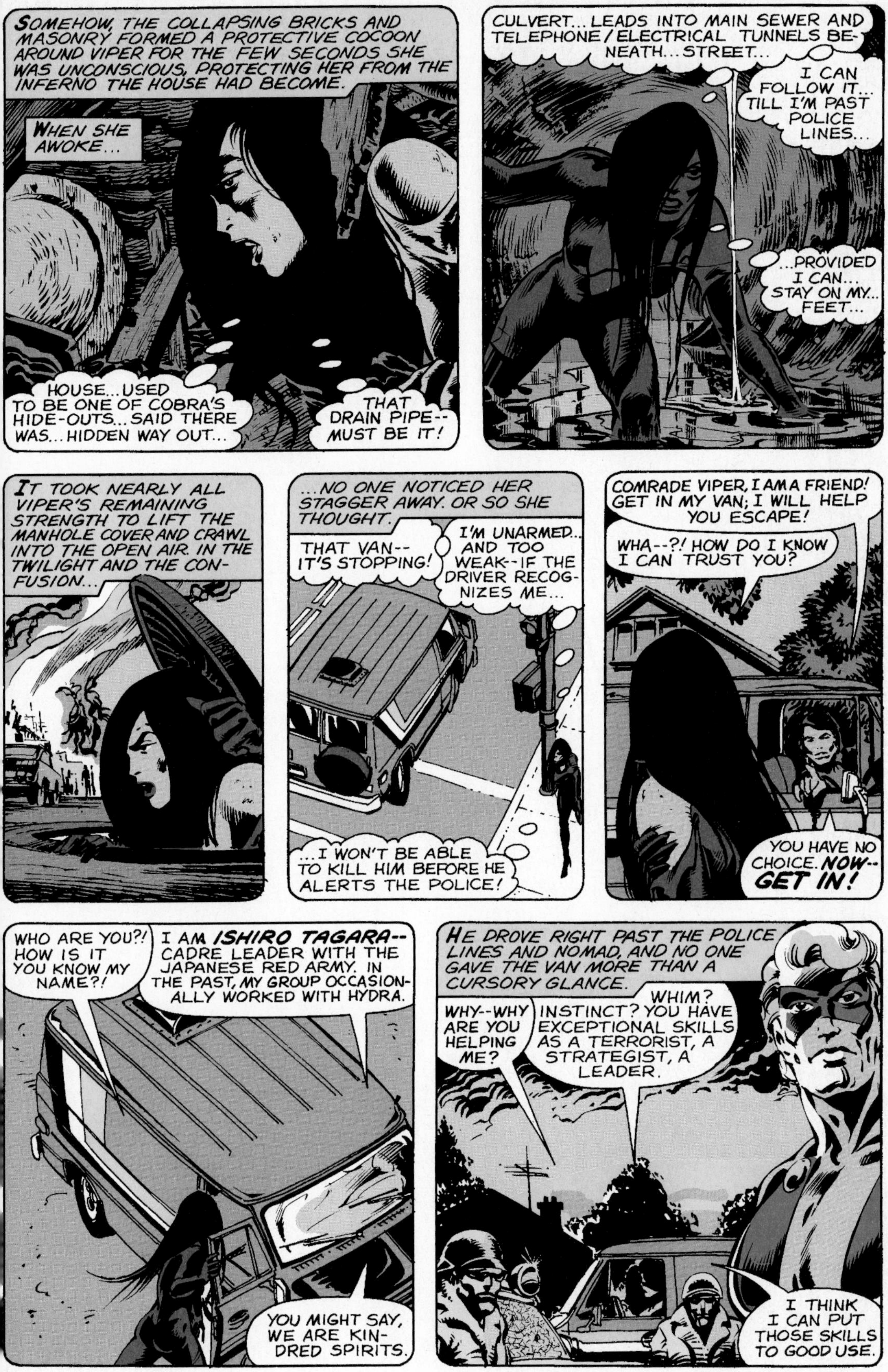
SOMEHOW, THE COLLAPSING BRICKS AND MASONRY FORMED A PROTECTIVE COCOON AROUND VIPER FOR THE FEW SECONDS SHE WAS UNCONSCIOUS, PROTECTING HER FROM THE INFERNO THE HOUSE HAD BECOME.
WHEN SHE AWOKE...
HOUSE... USED TO BE ONE OF COBRA'S HIDE-OUTS... SAID THERE WAS... HIDDEN WAY OUT...
THAT DRAIN PIPE-- MUST BE IT!
CULVERT... LEADS INTO MAIN SEWER AND TELEPHONE / ELECTRICAL TUNNELS BENEATH... STREET...
I CAN FOLLOW IT... TILL I'M PAST POLICE LINES...
...PROVIDED I CAN... STAY ON MY... FEET...
IT TOOK NEARLY ALL VIPER'S REMAINING STRENGTH TO LIFT THE MANHOLE COVER AND CRAWL INTO THE OPEN AIR. IN THE TWILIGHT AND THE CONFUSION...
...NO ONE NOTICED HER STAGGER AWAY. OR SO SHE THOUGHT.
THAT VAN-- IT'S STOPPING!
I'M UNARMED... AND TOO WEAK--IF THE DRIVER RECOGNIZES ME...
...I WON'T BE ABLE TO KILL HIM BEFORE HE ALERTS THE POLICE!
COMRADE VIPER, I AM A FRIEND! GET IN MY VAN; I WILL HELP YOU ESCAPE!
WHA--?! HOW DO I KNOW I CAN TRUST YOU?
YOU HAVE NO CHOICE. NOW-- GET IN!
WHO ARE YOU?! HOW IS IT YOU KNOW MY NAME?!
I AM ISHIRO TAGARA-- CADRE LEADER WITH THE JAPANESE RED ARMY. IN THE PAST, MY GROUP OCCASIONALLY WORKED WITH HYDRA.
YOU MIGHT SAY, WE ARE KINDRED SPIRITS.
HE DROVE RIGHT PAST THE POLICE LINES AND NOMAD, AND NO ONE GAVE THE VAN MORE THAN A CURSORY GLANCE.
WHY--WHY ARE YOU HELPING ME?
WHIM? INSTINCT? YOU HAVE EXCEPTIONAL SKILLS AS A TERRORIST, A STRATEGIST, A LEADER.
I THINK I CAN PUT THOSE SKILLS TO GOOD USE.

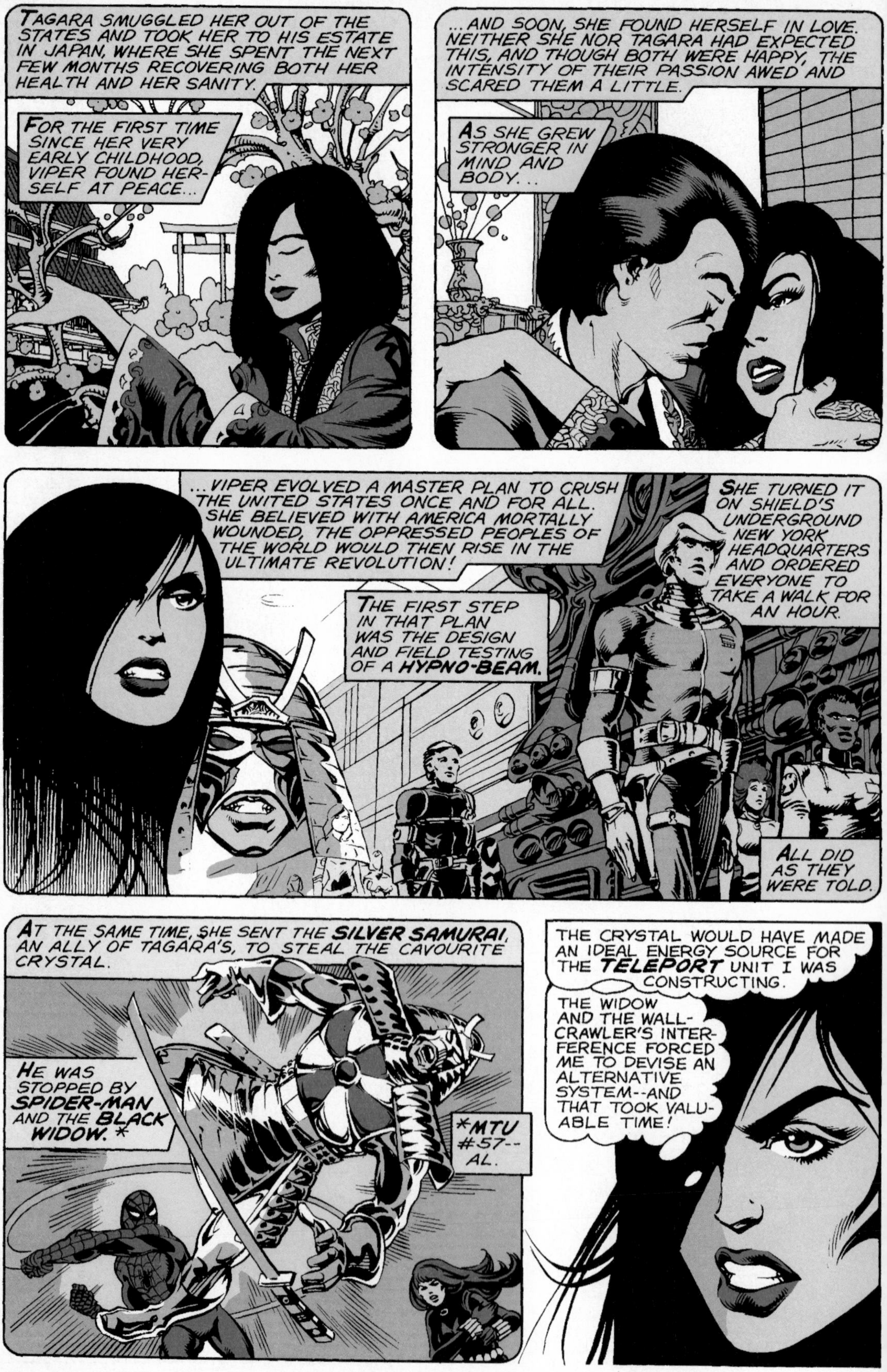

TAGARA SMUGGLED HER OUT OF THE STATES AND TOOK HER TO HIS ESTATE IN JAPAN, WHERE SHE SPENT THE NEXT FEW MONTHS RECOVERING BOTH HER HEALTH AND HER SANITY.
FOR THE FIRST TIME SINCE HER VERY EARLY CHILDHOOD, VIPER FOUND HERSELF AT PEACE...
...AND SOON, SHE FOUND HERSELF IN LOVE. NEITHER SHE NOR TAGARA HAD EXPECTED THIS, AND THOUGH BOTH WERE HAPPY, THE INTENSITY OF THEIR PASSION AWED AND SCARED THEM A LITTLE.
AS SHE GREW STRONGER IN MIND AND BODY...
...VIPER EVOLVED A MASTER PLAN TO CRUSH THE UNITED STATES ONCE AND FOR ALL. SHE BELIEVED WITH AMERICA MORTALLY WOUNDED, THE OPPRESSED PEOPLES OF THE WORLD WOULD THEN RISE IN THE ULTIMATE REVOLUTION!
THE FIRST STEP IN THAT PLAN WAS THE DESIGN AND FIELD TESTING OF A HYPNO-BEAM.
SHE TURNED IT ON SHIELD'S UNDERGROUND NEW YORK HEADQUARTERS AND ORDERED EVERYONE TO TAKE A WALK FOR AN HOUR.
ALL DID AS THEY WERE TOLD.
AT THE SAME TIME, SHE SENT THE SILVER SAMURAI, AN ALLY OF TAGARA'S, TO STEAL THE CAVOURITE CRYSTAL.
HE WAS STOPPED BY SPIDER-MAN AND THE BLACK WIDOW.*
*MTU #57--AL.
THE CRYSTAL WOULD HAVE MADE AN IDEAL ENERGY SOURCE FOR THE TELEPORT UNIT I WAS CONSTRUCTING.
THE WIDOW AND THE WALL-CRAWLER'S INTERFERENCE FORCED ME TO DEVISE AN ALTERNATIVE SYSTEM--AND THAT TOOK VALUABLE TIME!

HER PLAN WAS SIMPLICITY ITSELF. UNFORTUNATELY, IT REQUIRED THAT VIPER TAKE OVER SHIELD'S HELI-CARRIER, A SEEMINGLY IMPOSSIBLE FEAT.

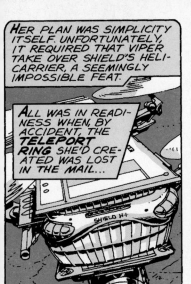

ALL WAS IN READINESS WHEN, BY ACCIDENT, THE TELEPORT RING SHE'D CREATED WAS LOST IN THE MAIL...

...AND MIS-DELIVERED TO A TELEVISION COMEDY ACTOR. SHE SENT THE SAMURAI (WHOM SHE'D FREED FROM PRISON) TO GET IT BACK.*

*FROM JOHN BELU-SHI, IN THE NOW-LEGENDARY MTU #74 -- AL.

THIS TIME, HE SUC-CEEDED.

TOGETHER, HE AND VIPER TELEPORTED UP TO THE HELI-CARRIER.

WHILE THE NEW YORK BASE HAD BEEN DESERTED, VIPER HAD LOOTED ITS COMPUTERS OF THE COMPLETE SCHEMATIC LAYOUTS OF THE CARRIER, SO SHE KNEW EXACTLY WHERE TO STRIKE.

THEY MATERIALIZED IN THE VESSEL'S SICK BAY, IN THE WEE HOURS OF THE MORNING WHEN MOST OF THE CREW WERE ASLEEP. NONE SAW THEM ARRIVE.

THEY REPLACED THE DOCTOR'S VIDEO-PHONE WITH ONE MODIFIED TO PROJECT A HYPNO-BEAM (VIPER HAVING DISCOVERED THAT THESE PHONE UNITS AFFORDED HER MORE COMPLETE CONTROL OVER SUBJECTS THAN THE BROADEST BEAM).

FIRST, THEY ENSNARED THE DOCTOR, THEN, WHENEVER HE SUMMONED A CREWPERSON TO SICK BAY...

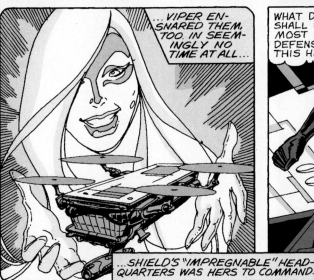

...VIPER EN-SNARED THEM, TOO. IN SEEM-INGLY NO TIME AT ALL...

...SHIELD'S "IMPREGNABLE" HEAD-QUARTERS WAS HERS TO COMMAND.

WHAT DELICIOUS IRONY. I SHALL USE AMERICA'S MOST TRUSTED DEFENSIVE SYSTEM-- THIS HELI-CARRIER--

--TO EXPUNGE ITS ENTIRE GOVERN-MENT!

PRESI-DENT, VICE-PRESIDENT, CABINET, CONGRESS, THE SU-PREME COURT, THE JOINT CHIEFS--TONIGHT, ALL WILL DIE!!

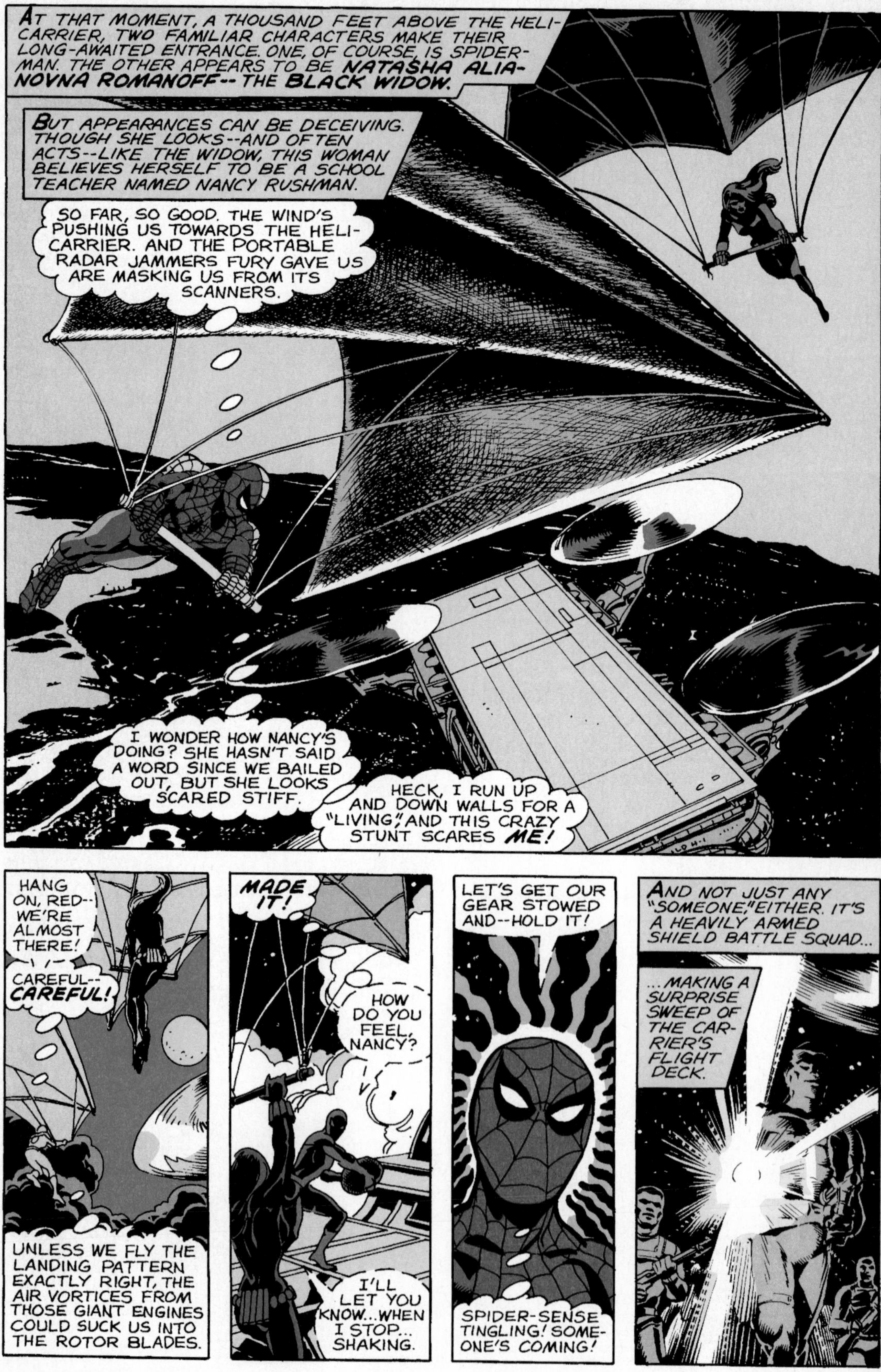
AT THAT MOMENT, A THOUSAND FEET ABOVE THE HELI-CARRIER, TWO FAMILIAR CHARACTERS MAKE THEIR LONG-AWAITED ENTRANCE. ONE, OF COURSE, IS SPIDER-MAN. THE OTHER APPEARS TO BE NATASHA ALIANOVNA ROMANOFF-- THE BLACK WIDOW.
BUT APPEARANCES CAN BE DECEIVING. THOUGH SHE LOOKS--AND OFTEN ACTS--LIKE THE WIDOW, THIS WOMAN BELIEVES HERSELF TO BE A SCHOOL TEACHER NAMED NANCY RUSHMAN.
SO FAR, SO GOOD. THE WIND'S PUSHING US TOWARDS THE HELI-CARRIER. AND THE PORTABLE RADAR JAMMERS FURY GAVE US ARE MASKING US FROM ITS SCANNERS.
I WONDER HOW NANCY'S DOING? SHE HASN'T SAID A WORD SINCE WE BAILED OUT, BUT SHE LOOKS SCARED STIFF.
HECK, I RUN UP AND DOWN WALLS FOR A "LIVING," AND THIS CRAZY STUNT SCARES ME!
HANG ON, RED-- WE'RE ALMOST THERE!
CAREFUL-- CAREFUL!
UNLESS WE FLY THE LANDING PATTERN EXACTLY RIGHT, THE AIR VORTICES FROM THOSE GIANT ENGINES COULD SUCK US INTO THE ROTOR BLADES.
MADE IT!
HOW DO YOU FEEL, NANCY?
I'LL LET YOU KNOW...WHEN I STOP... SHAKING.
LET'S GET OUR GEAR STOWED AND--HOLD IT!
SPIDER-SENSE TINGLING! SOME-ONE'S COMING!
AND NOT JUST ANY "SOMEONE," EITHER. IT'S A HEAVILY ARMED SHIELD BATTLE SQUAD...
...MAKING A SURPRISE SWEEP OF THE CAR-RIER'S FLIGHT DECK.

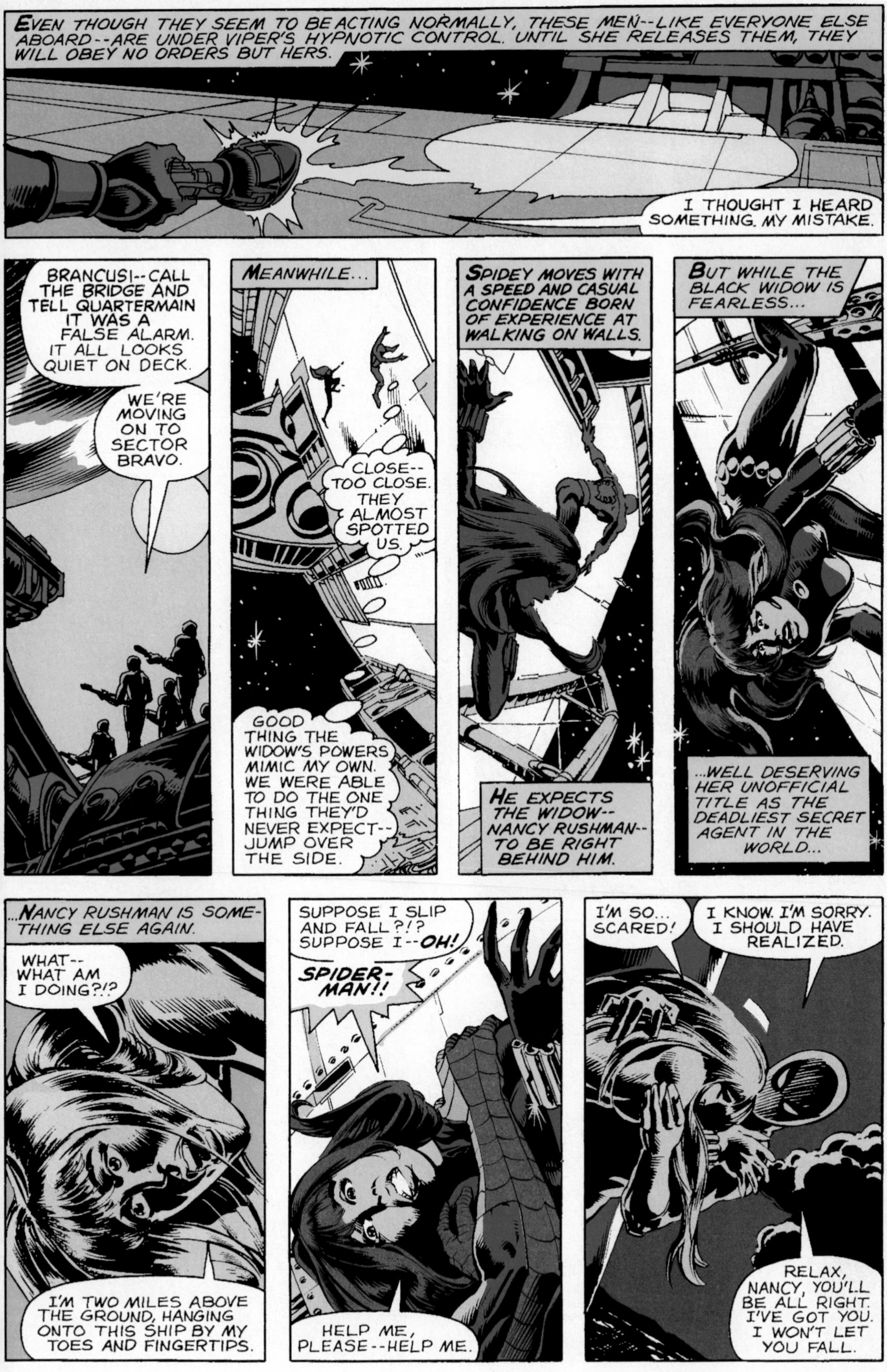
EVEN THOUGH THEY SEEM TO BE ACTING NORMALLY, THESE MEN--LIKE EVERYONE ELSE ABOARD--ARE UNDER VIPER'S HYPNOTIC CONTROL. UNTIL SHE RELEASES THEM, THEY WILL OBEY NO ORDERS BUT HERS.
I THOUGHT I HEARD SOMETHING. MY MISTAKE.
BRANCUSI--CALL THE BRIDGE AND TELL QUARTERMAIN IT WAS A FALSE ALARM. IT ALL LOOKS QUIET ON DECK.
WE'RE MOVING ON TO SECTOR BRAVO.
MEANWHILE...
CLOSE--TOO CLOSE. THEY ALMOST SPOTTED US.
GOOD THING THE WIDOW'S POWERS MIMIC MY OWN. WE WERE ABLE TO DO THE ONE THING THEY'D NEVER EXPECT--JUMP OVER THE SIDE.
SPIDEY MOVES WITH A SPEED AND CASUAL CONFIDENCE BORN OF EXPERIENCE AT WALKING ON WALLS.
HE EXPECTS THE WIDOW--NANCY RUSHMAN--TO BE RIGHT BEHIND HIM.
BUT WHILE THE BLACK WIDOW IS FEARLESS...
...WELL DESERVING HER UNOFFICIAL TITLE AS THE DEADLIEST SECRET AGENT IN THE WORLD...
...NANCY RUSHMAN IS SOMETHING ELSE AGAIN.
WHAT--WHAT AM I DOING?!?
I'M TWO MILES ABOVE THE GROUND, HANGING ONTO THIS SHIP BY MY TOES AND FINGERTIPS.
SUPPOSE I SLIP AND FALL?!? SUPPOSE I--OH!
SPIDER-MAN!!
HELP ME, PLEASE--HELP ME.
I'M SO... SCARED!
I KNOW. I'M SORRY. I SHOULD HAVE REALIZED.
RELAX, NANCY, YOU'LL BE ALL RIGHT. I'VE GOT YOU. I WON'T LET YOU FALL.

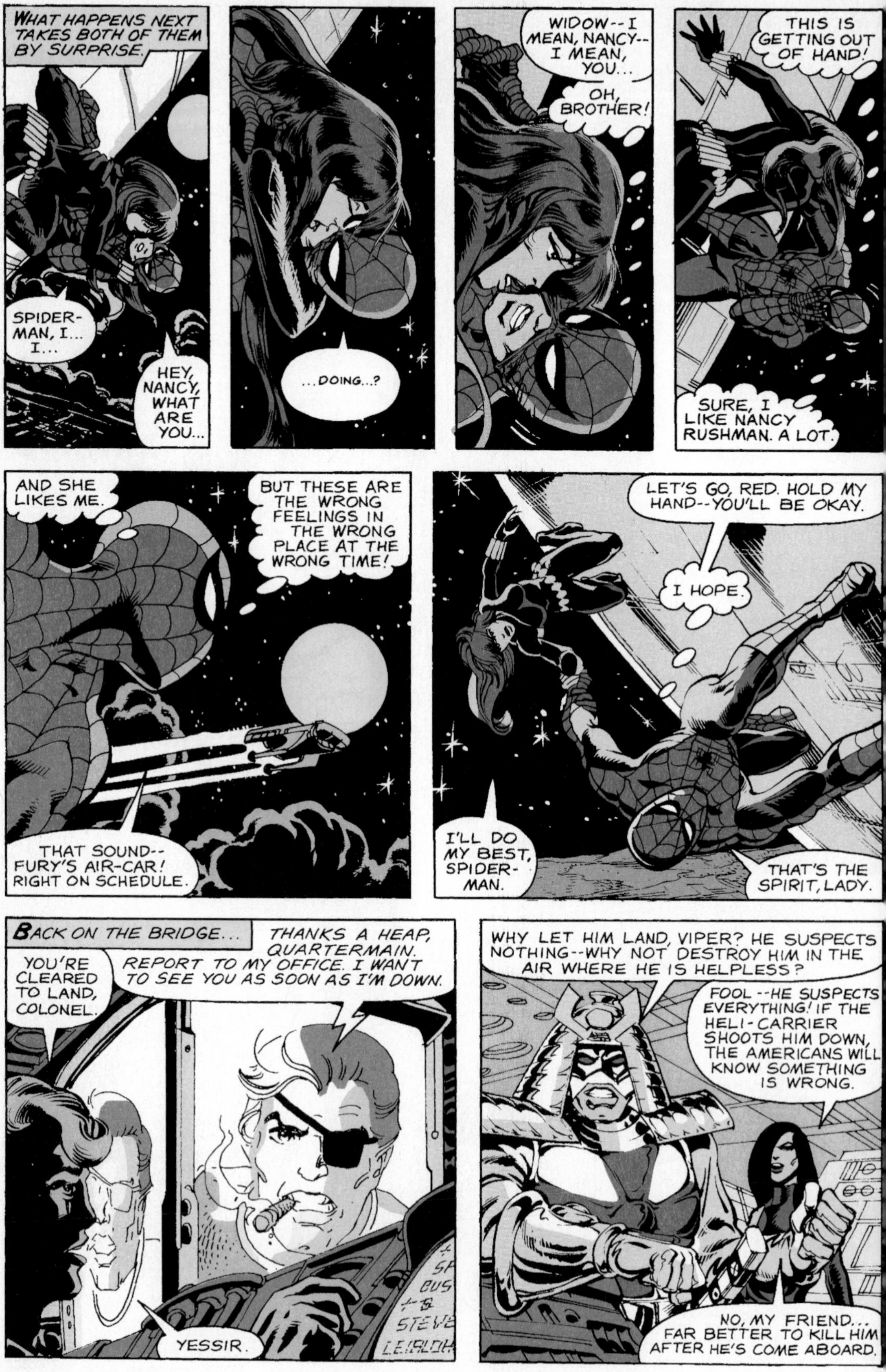
WHAT HAPPENS NEXT TAKES BOTH OF THEM BY SURPRISE.
SPIDER-MAN, I... I...
HEY, NANCY, WHAT ARE YOU...
...DOING...?
WIDOW--I MEAN, NANCY--I MEAN, YOU...
OH, BROTHER!
THIS IS GETTING OUT OF HAND!
SURE, I LIKE NANCY RUSHMAN. A LOT.
AND SHE LIKES ME.
BUT THESE ARE THE WRONG FEELINGS IN THE WRONG PLACE AT THE WRONG TIME!
THAT SOUND--FURY'S AIR-CAR! RIGHT ON SCHEDULE.
LET'S GO, RED. HOLD MY HAND--YOU'LL BE OKAY.
I HOPE.
I'LL DO MY BEST, SPIDER-MAN.
THAT'S THE SPIRIT, LADY.
BACK ON THE BRIDGE...
YOU'RE CLEARED TO LAND, COLONEL.
THANKS A HEAP, QUARTERMAIN. REPORT TO MY OFFICE. I WANT TO SEE YOU AS SOON AS I'M DOWN.
YESSIR.
WHY LET HIM LAND, VIPER? HE SUSPECTS NOTHING--WHY NOT DESTROY HIM IN THE AIR WHERE HE IS HELPLESS?
FOOL--HE SUSPECTS EVERYTHING! IF THE HELI-CARRIER SHOOTS HIM DOWN, THE AMERICANS WILL KNOW SOMETHING IS WRONG.
NO, MY FRIEND... FAR BETTER TO KILL HIM AFTER HE'S COME ABOARD.

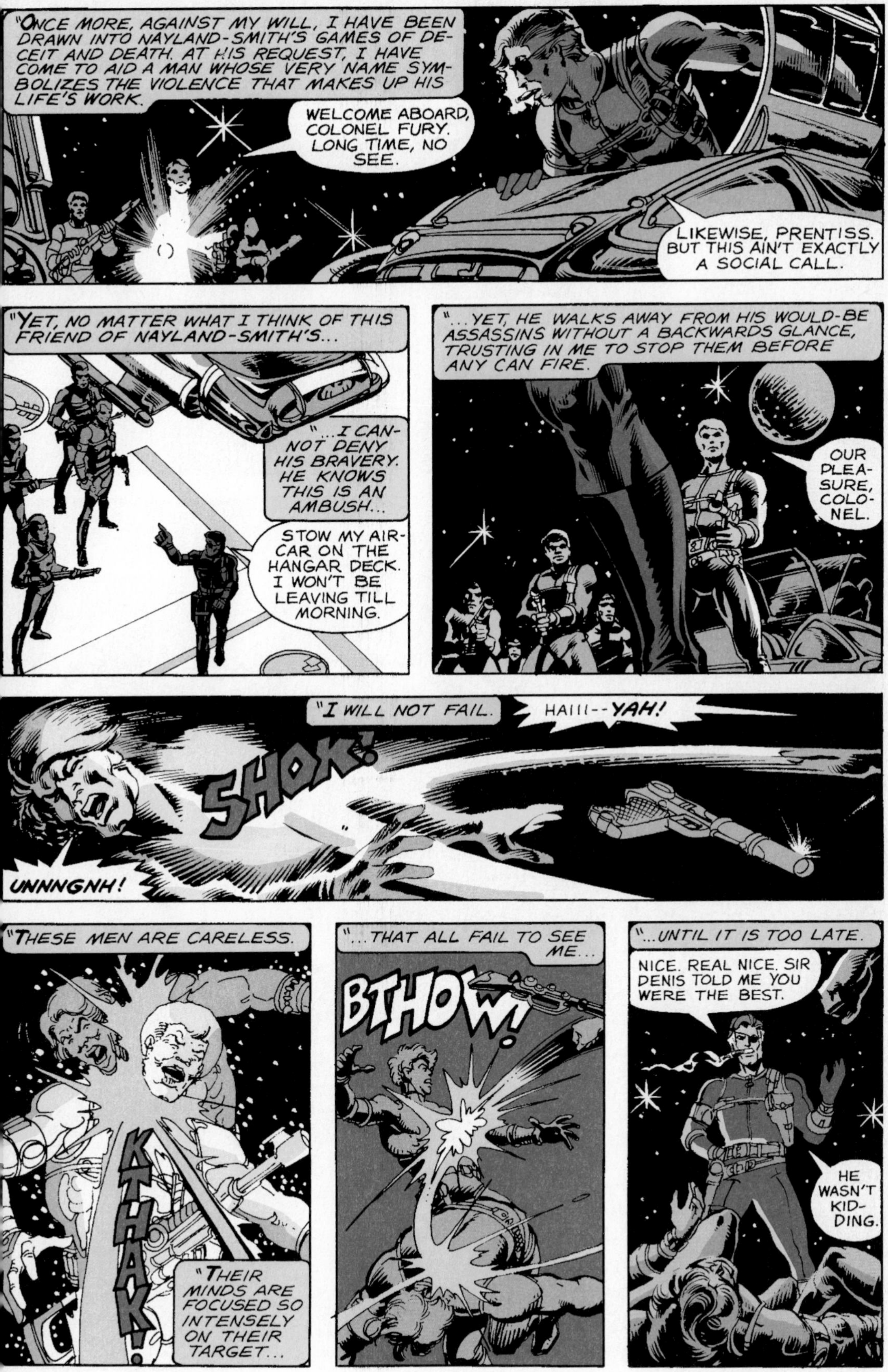
"ONCE MORE, AGAINST MY WILL, I HAVE BEEN DRAWN INTO NAYLAND-SMITH'S GAMES OF DECEIT AND DEATH. AT HIS REQUEST, I HAVE COME TO AID A MAN WHOSE VERY NAME SYMBOLIZES THE VIOLENCE THAT MAKES UP HIS LIFE'S WORK.
WELCOME ABOARD, COLONEL FURY. LONG TIME, NO SEE.
LIKEWISE, PRENTISS. BUT THIS AIN'T EXACTLY A SOCIAL CALL.
"YET, NO MATTER WHAT I THINK OF THIS FRIEND OF NAYLAND-SMITH'S...
"...I CANNOT DENY HIS BRAVERY. HE KNOWS THIS IS AN AMBUSH...
STOW MY AIR-CAR ON THE HANGAR DECK. I WON'T BE LEAVING TILL MORNING.
"...YET, HE WALKS AWAY FROM HIS WOULD-BE ASSASSINS WITHOUT A BACKWARDS GLANCE, TRUSTING IN ME TO STOP THEM BEFORE ANY CAN FIRE.
OUR PLEASURE, COLONEL.
"I WILL NOT FAIL.
HAIII--YAH!
SHOK!
UNNNGNH!
"THESE MEN ARE CARELESS.
KTHAK!
"THEIR MINDS ARE FOCUSED SO INTENSELY ON THEIR TARGET...
"...THAT ALL FAIL TO SEE ME...
BTHOW!
"...UNTIL IT IS TOO LATE.
NICE. REAL NICE. SIR DENIS TOLD ME YOU WERE THE BEST.
HE WASN'T KIDDING.

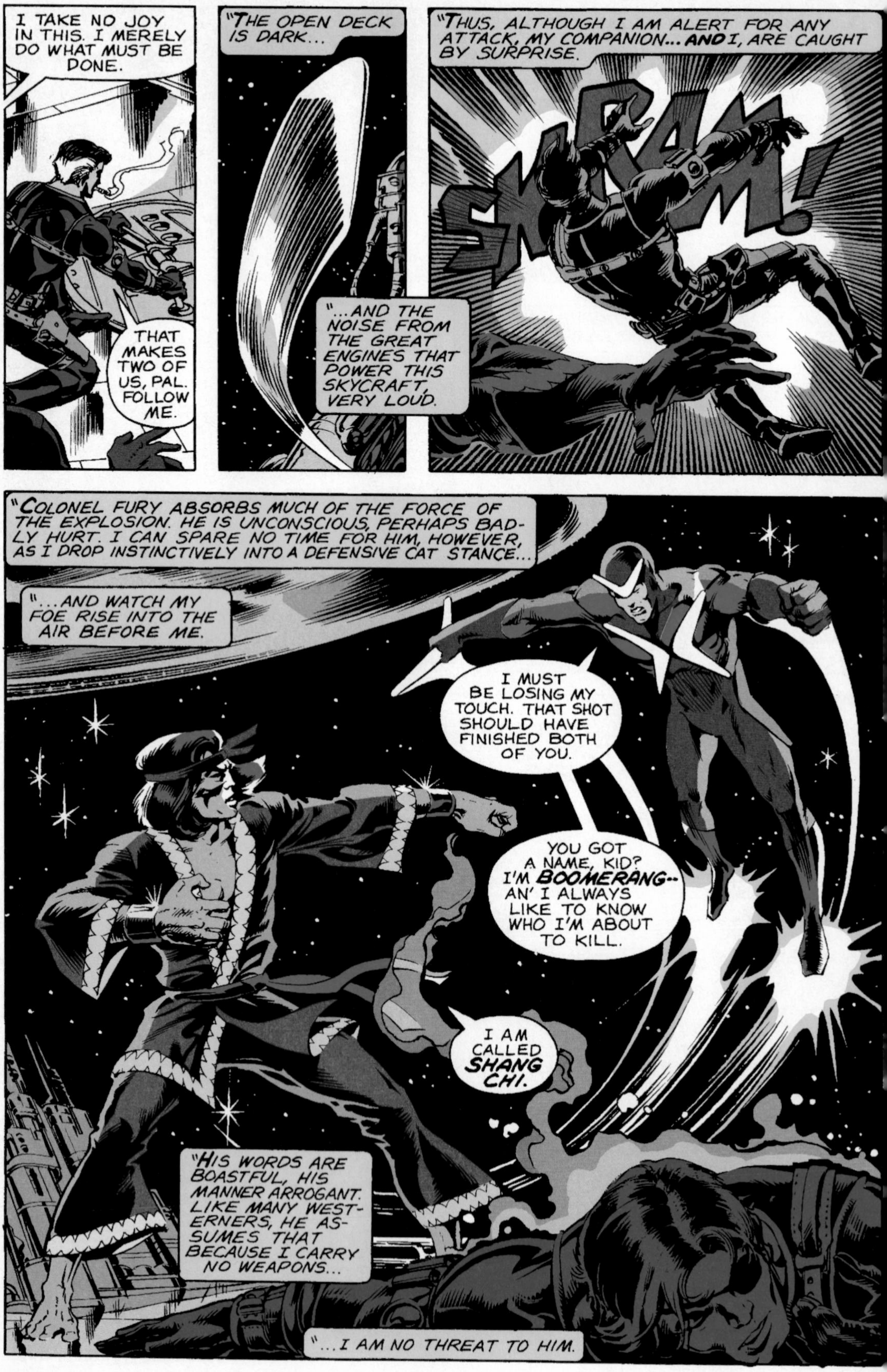
I TAKE NO JOY IN THIS. I MERELY DO WHAT MUST BE DONE.
THAT MAKES TWO OF US, PAL. FOLLOW ME.
"THE OPEN DECK IS DARK...
"...AND THE NOISE FROM THE GREAT ENGINES THAT POWER THIS SKYCRAFT, VERY LOUD.
"THUS, ALTHOUGH I AM ALERT FOR ANY ATTACK, MY COMPANION... AND I, ARE CAUGHT BY SURPRISE.
SKRAM!
"COLONEL FURY ABSORBS MUCH OF THE FORCE OF THE EXPLOSION. HE IS UNCONSCIOUS, PERHAPS BADLY HURT. I CAN SPARE NO TIME FOR HIM, HOWEVER, AS I DROP INSTINCTIVELY INTO A DEFENSIVE CAT STANCE...
"...AND WATCH MY FOE RISE INTO THE AIR BEFORE ME.
I MUST BE LOSING MY TOUCH. THAT SHOT SHOULD HAVE FINISHED BOTH OF YOU.
YOU GOT A NAME, KID? I'M BOOMERANG-- AN' I ALWAYS LIKE TO KNOW WHO I'M ABOUT TO KILL.
I AM CALLED SHANG CHI.
"HIS WORDS ARE BOASTFUL, HIS MANNER ARROGANT. LIKE MANY WESTERNERS, HE ASSUMES THAT BECAUSE I CARRY NO WEAPONS...
"...I AM NO THREAT TO HIM.

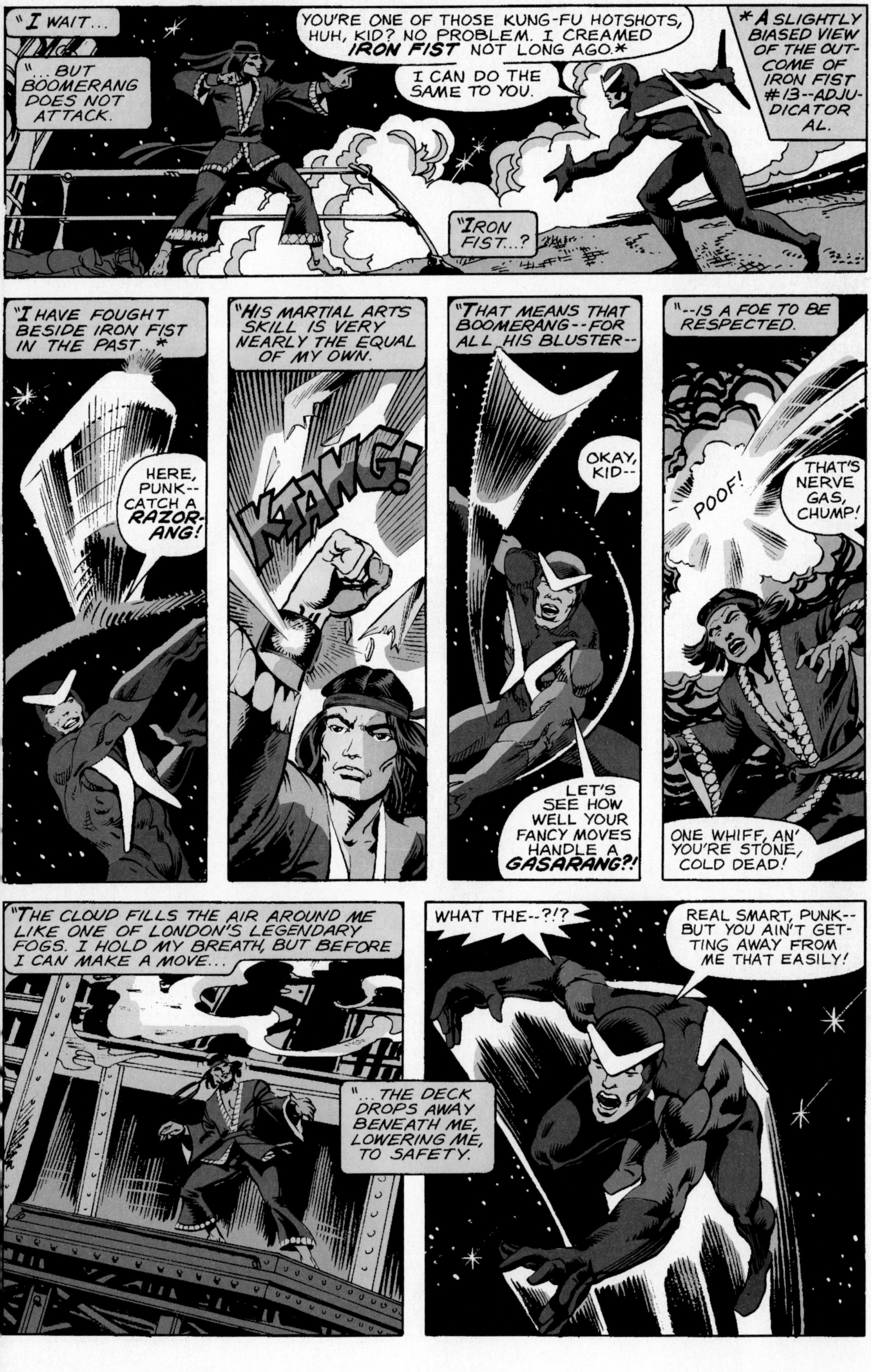
"I WAIT...
"...BUT BOOMERANG DOES NOT ATTACK.
YOU'RE ONE OF THOSE KUNG-FU HOTSHOTS, HUH, KID? NO PROBLEM. I CREAMED IRON FIST NOT LONG AGO.*
I CAN DO THE SAME TO YOU.
*A SLIGHTLY BIASED VIEW OF THE OUTCOME OF IRON FIST #13--ADJUDICATOR AL.
"IRON FIST...?
"I HAVE FOUGHT BESIDE IRON FIST IN THE PAST...*
HERE, PUNK--CATCH A RAZOR-ANG!
"HIS MARTIAL ARTS SKILL IS VERY NEARLY THE EQUAL OF MY OWN.
KTANG!
"THAT MEANS THAT BOOMERANG--FOR ALL HIS BLUSTER--
OKAY, KID--
LET'S SEE HOW WELL YOUR FANCY MOVES HANDLE A GASARANG?!
"--IS A FOE TO BE RESPECTED.
POOF!
THAT'S NERVE GAS, CHUMP!
ONE WHIFF, AN' YOU'RE STONE, COLD DEAD!
"THE CLOUD FILLS THE AIR AROUND ME LIKE ONE OF LONDON'S LEGENDARY FOGS. I HOLD MY BREATH, BUT BEFORE I CAN MAKE A MOVE...
"...THE DECK DROPS AWAY BENEATH ME, LOWERING ME, TO SAFETY.
WHAT THE--?!?
REAL SMART, PUNK--BUT YOU AIN'T GETTING AWAY FROM ME THAT EASILY!

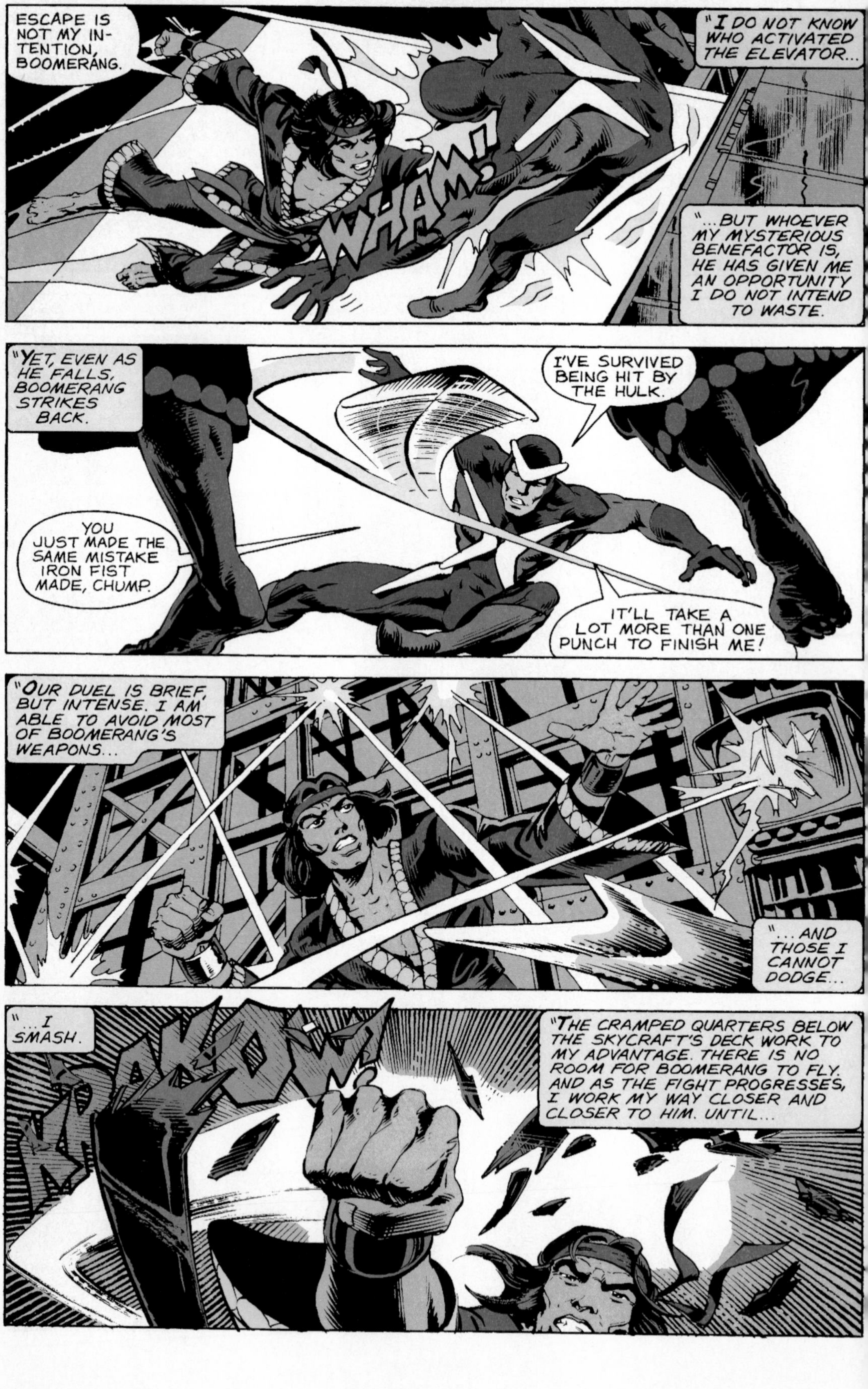
ESCAPE IS NOT MY IN-TENTION, BOOMERANG.
"I DO NOT KNOW WHO ACTIVATED THE ELEVATOR...
WHAM!
"...BUT WHOEVER MY MYSTERIOUS BENEFACTOR IS, HE HAS GIVEN ME AN OPPORTUNITY I DO NOT INTEND TO WASTE.
"YET, EVEN AS HE FALLS, BOOMERANG STRIKES BACK.
I'VE SURVIVED BEING HIT BY THE HULK.
YOU JUST MADE THE SAME MISTAKE IRON FIST MADE, CHUMP.
IT'LL TAKE A LOT MORE THAN ONE PUNCH TO FINISH ME!
"OUR DUEL IS BRIEF, BUT INTENSE. I AM ABLE TO AVOID MOST OF BOOMERANG'S WEAPONS...
"...AND THOSE I CANNOT DODGE...
"...I SMASH.
"THE CRAMPED QUARTERS BELOW THE SKYCRAFT'S DECK WORK TO MY ADVANTAGE. THERE IS NO ROOM FOR BOOMERANG TO FLY. AND AS THE FIGHT PROGRESSES, I WORK MY WAY CLOSER AND CLOSER TO HIM. UNTIL...

"I HAVE PLAYED MY GAMBIT WELL.

"MY SUDDEN ATTACK CATCHES BOOMERANG OFF-BALANCE.

THAK

KAAAA--!

"MY EARLIER ESTIMATION OF HIM WAS CORRECT. THOUGH VERY STRONG AND VERY FAST--AND SUPREMELY GIFTED IN THE USE OF HIS UNIQUE WEAPONS--

CHNNKK!

HAIII--!

"--BOOMERANG'S KNOWLEDGE OF THE MARTIAL ARTS IS MINIMAL.

APOM!

YAHHH!!

YOU ARE BEATEN, BOOMERANG. SURRENDER, AND SPARE YOURSELF FURTHER, UNNECESSARY PAIN.

I MAY BE DOWN, KID--

--BUT I AIN'T OUT.

NOT WHILE I'VE A BOOMERANG LEFT TO THROW!

KRAKOOM!

157

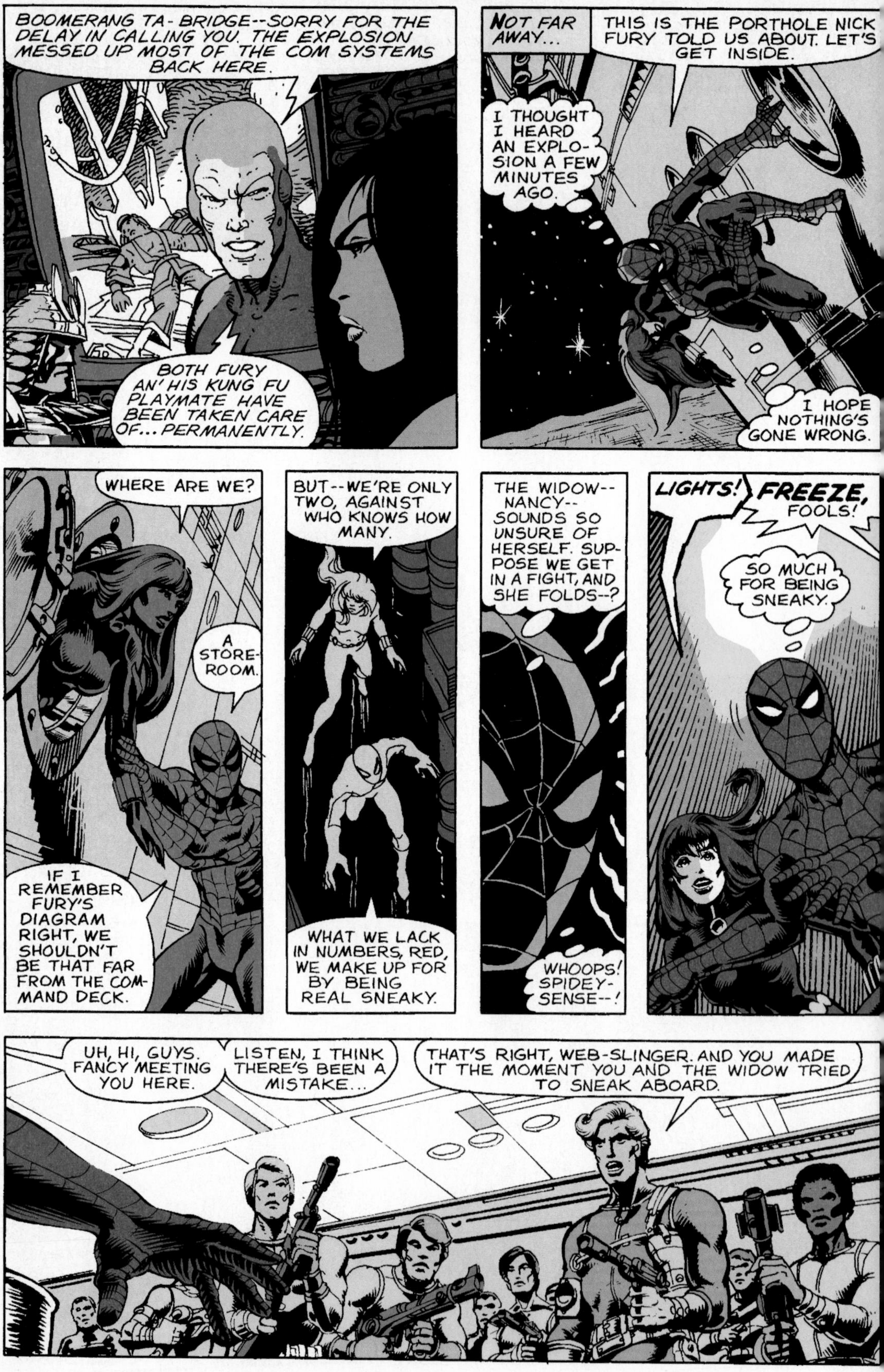
BOOMERANG TA- BRIDGE--SORRY FOR THE DELAY IN CALLING YOU. THE EXPLOSION MESSED UP MOST OF THE COM SYSTEMS BACK HERE.
BOTH FURY AN' HIS KUNG FU PLAYMATE HAVE BEEN TAKEN CARE OF... PERMANENTLY.
NOT FAR AWAY...
THIS IS THE PORTHOLE NICK FURY TOLD US ABOUT. LET'S GET INSIDE.
I THOUGHT I HEARD AN EXPLO-SION A FEW MINUTES AGO.
I HOPE NOTHING'S GONE WRONG.
WHERE ARE WE?
A STORE-ROOM.
IF I REMEMBER FURY'S DIAGRAM RIGHT, WE SHOULDN'T BE THAT FAR FROM THE COM-MAND DECK.
BUT--WE'RE ONLY TWO, AGAINST WHO KNOWS HOW MANY.
WHAT WE LACK IN NUMBERS, RED, WE MAKE UP FOR BY BEING REAL SNEAKY.
THE WIDOW--NANCY--SOUNDS SO UNSURE OF HERSELF. SUP-POSE WE GET IN A FIGHT, AND SHE FOLDS--?
WHOOPS! SPIDEY-SENSE--!
LIGHTS!
FREEZE, FOOLS!
SO MUCH FOR BEING SNEAKY.
UH, HI, GUYS. FANCY MEETING YOU HERE.
LISTEN, I THINK THERE'S BEEN A MISTAKE...
THAT'S RIGHT, WEB-SLINGER. AND YOU MADE IT THE MOMENT YOU AND THE WIDOW TRIED TO SNEAK ABOARD.

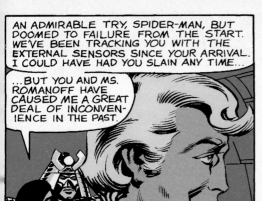

AN ADMIRABLE TRY, SPIDER-MAN, BUT DOOMED TO FAILURE FROM THE START. WE'VE BEEN TRACKING YOU WITH THE EXTERNAL SENSORS SINCE YOUR ARRIVAL. I COULD HAVE HAD YOU SLAIN ANY TIME...

...BUT YOU AND MS. ROMANOFF HAVE CAUSED ME A GREAT DEAL OF INCONVENIENCE IN THE PAST.

I WANTED TO BE PRESENT FOR YOUR EXECUTION.

Y-YOU--I KNOW YOU.

YOU'RE THE FIGURE FROM MY NIGHTMARES!

I TRIED... SO HARD TO FORGET... BECAUSE TO REMEMBER MEANT...MORE PAIN THAN I COULD STAND!

BUT NOW, SEEING YOU--I... DO...REMEMBER...I...

AARRGH.

THAT SCREAM--

--WHAT IN HEAVEN'S NAME DID YOU DO TO HER?!?

I ASKED QUESTIONS.

THE BLACK WIDOW REFUSED TO ANSWER.

TIME GROWS SHORT, HOWEVER, AND THERE IS MUCH TO DO BEFORE ZERO HOUR.

KILL THEM, QUARTERMAIN.

YES, MA'AM.

HOLD IT, FELLA!

I BROUGHT YOU A PRESENT, VIPER-- FURY'S SURPRISE ACE IN THE HOLE. HE'S A BRUCE LEE CLONE NAMED CHANG-SHI.

I THOUGHT YOU MIGHT WANT TO QUESTION HIM, LIKE YOU DID THE WIDOW.

CRETIN! I DO NOT PAY YOU TO THINK, ONLY TO DO AS YOU'RE TOLD!

YOU TRY MY PATIENCE WITH YOUR CONTINUAL BUMBLING, BOOMERANG.

PUT YOUR PRISONER WITH THE OTHERS AND KILL THEM ALL--AT ONCE!

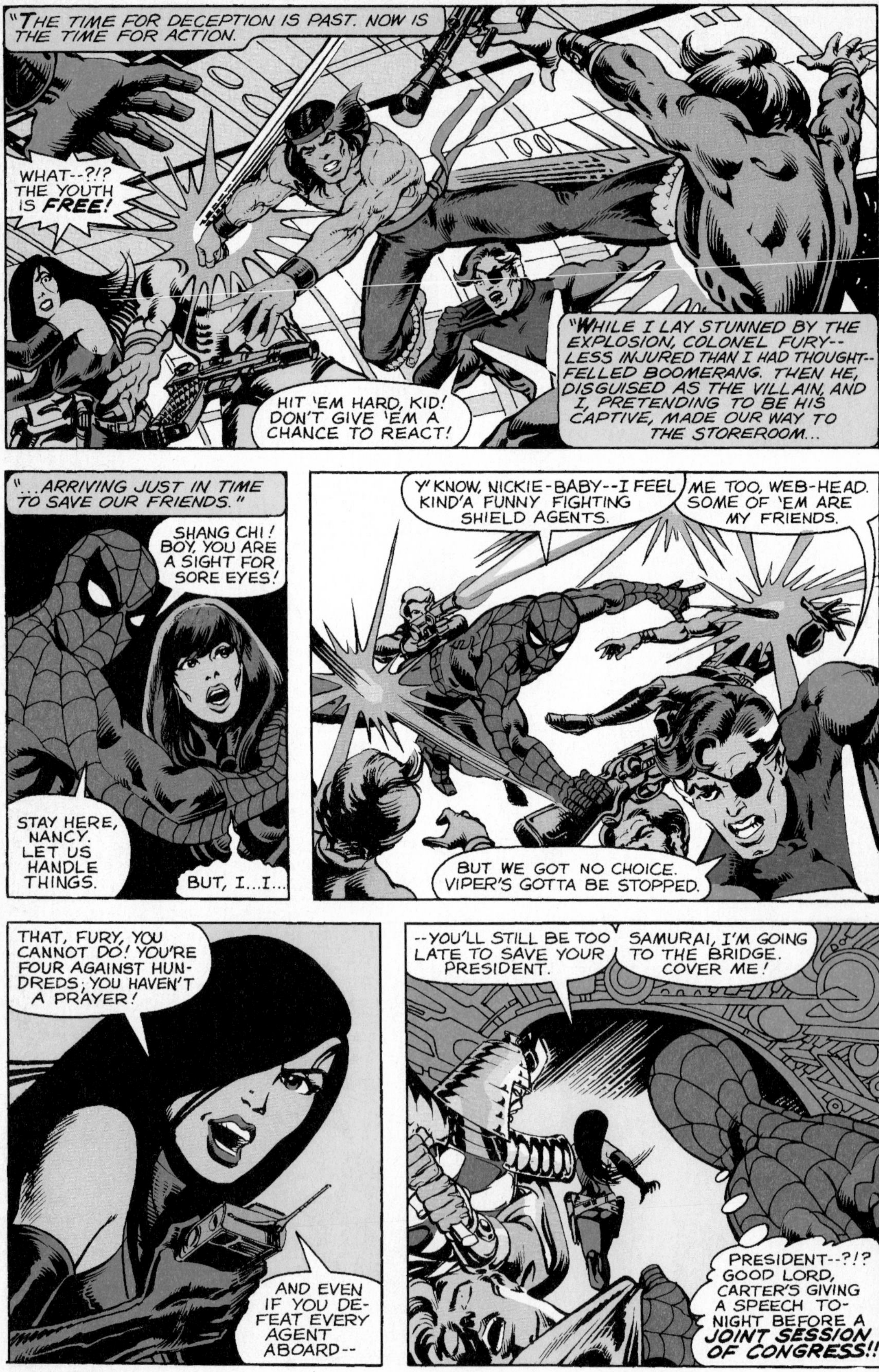
"THE TIME FOR DECEPTION IS PAST. NOW IS THE TIME FOR ACTION.
WHAT--?!? THE YOUTH IS FREE!
"WHILE I LAY STUNNED BY THE EXPLOSION, COLONEL FURY--LESS INJURED THAN I HAD THOUGHT--FELLED BOOMERANG. THEN HE, DISGUISED AS THE VILLAIN, AND I, PRETENDING TO BE HIS CAPTIVE, MADE OUR WAY TO THE STOREROOM...
HIT 'EM HARD, KID! DON'T GIVE 'EM A CHANCE TO REACT!
"...ARRIVING JUST IN TIME TO SAVE OUR FRIENDS."
SHANG CHI! BOY, YOU ARE A SIGHT FOR SORE EYES!
STAY HERE, NANCY. LET US HANDLE THINGS.
BUT, I...I...
Y'KNOW, NICKIE-BABY--I FEEL KIND'A FUNNY FIGHTING SHIELD AGENTS.
ME TOO, WEB-HEAD. SOME OF 'EM ARE MY FRIENDS.
BUT WE GOT NO CHOICE. VIPER'S GOTTA BE STOPPED.
THAT, FURY, YOU CANNOT DO! YOU'RE FOUR AGAINST HUNDREDS; YOU HAVEN'T A PRAYER!
AND EVEN IF YOU DEFEAT EVERY AGENT ABOARD--
--YOU'LL STILL BE TOO LATE TO SAVE YOUR PRESIDENT.
SAMURAI, I'M GOING TO THE BRIDGE. COVER ME!
PRESIDENT--?!? GOOD LORD, CARTER'S GIVING A SPEECH TONIGHT BEFORE A JOINT SESSION OF CONGRESS!!

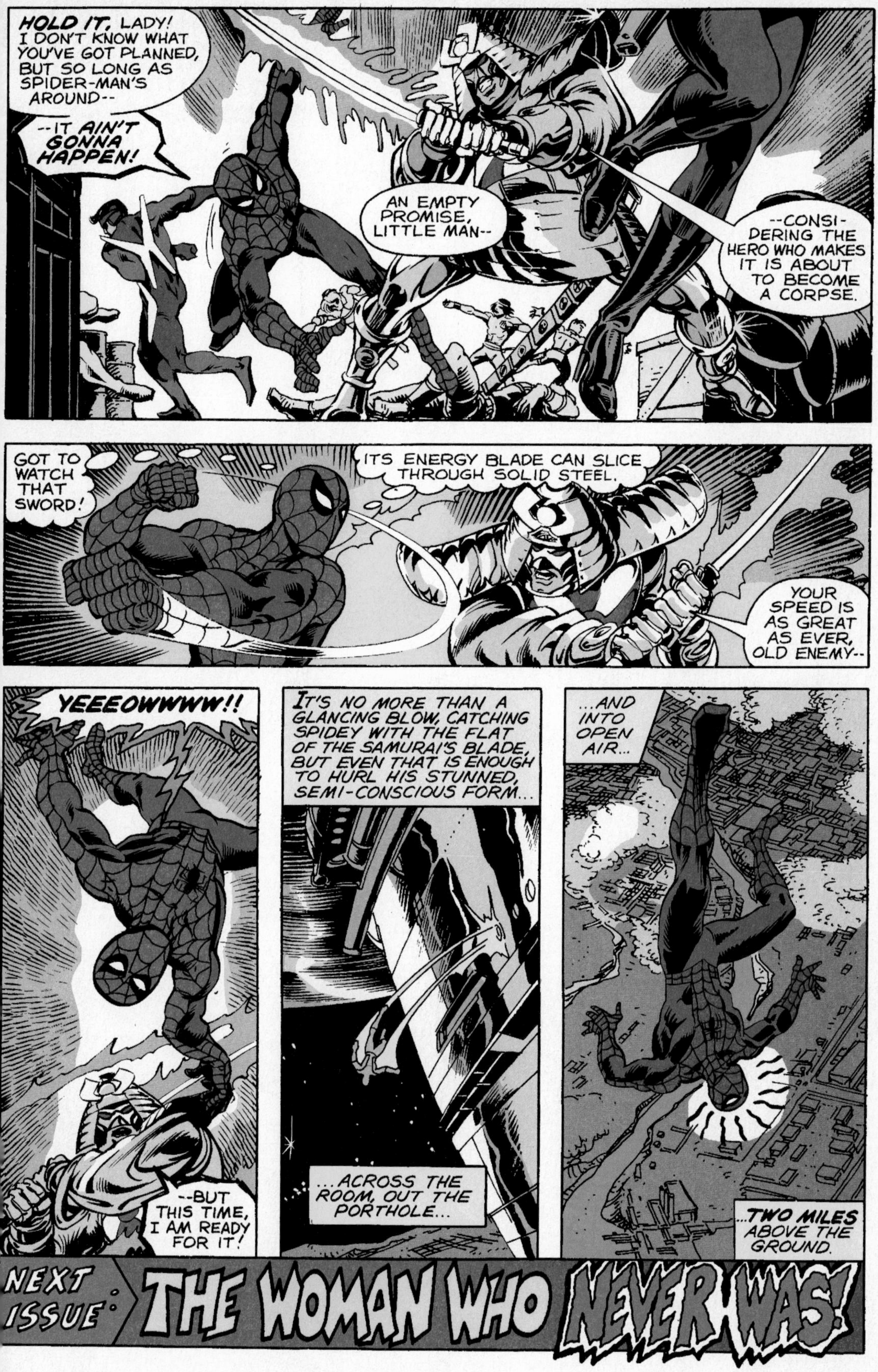
HOLD IT, LADY! I DON'T KNOW WHAT YOU'VE GOT PLANNED, BUT SO LONG AS SPIDER-MAN'S AROUND--
--IT AIN'T GONNA HAPPEN!
AN EMPTY PROMISE, LITTLE MAN--
--CONSIDERING THE HERO WHO MAKES IT IS ABOUT TO BECOME A CORPSE.
GOT TO WATCH THAT SWORD!
ITS ENERGY BLADE CAN SLICE THROUGH SOLID STEEL.
YOUR SPEED IS AS GREAT AS EVER, OLD ENEMY--
YEEEOWWWW!!
--BUT THIS TIME, I AM READY FOR IT!
IT'S NO MORE THAN A GLANCING BLOW, CATCHING SPIDEY WITH THE FLAT OF THE SAMURAI'S BLADE, BUT EVEN THAT IS ENOUGH TO HURL HIS STUNNED, SEMI-CONSCIOUS FORM...
...ACROSS THE ROOM, OUT THE PORTHOLE...
...AND INTO OPEN AIR...
...TWO MILES ABOVE THE GROUND.
NEXT ISSUE: THE WOMAN WHO NEVER WAS!

40¢
CC
85
SEPT
02147
MARVEL COMICS GROUP
APPROVED BY THE COMICS CODE AUTHORITY
©1979 MARVEL COMICS GROUP
MARVEL TEAM-UP
SPIDER-MAN
SHANG-CHI, THE BLACK WIDOW AND NICK FURY
THE SPIDER-MAN WHO FELL TO EARTH!

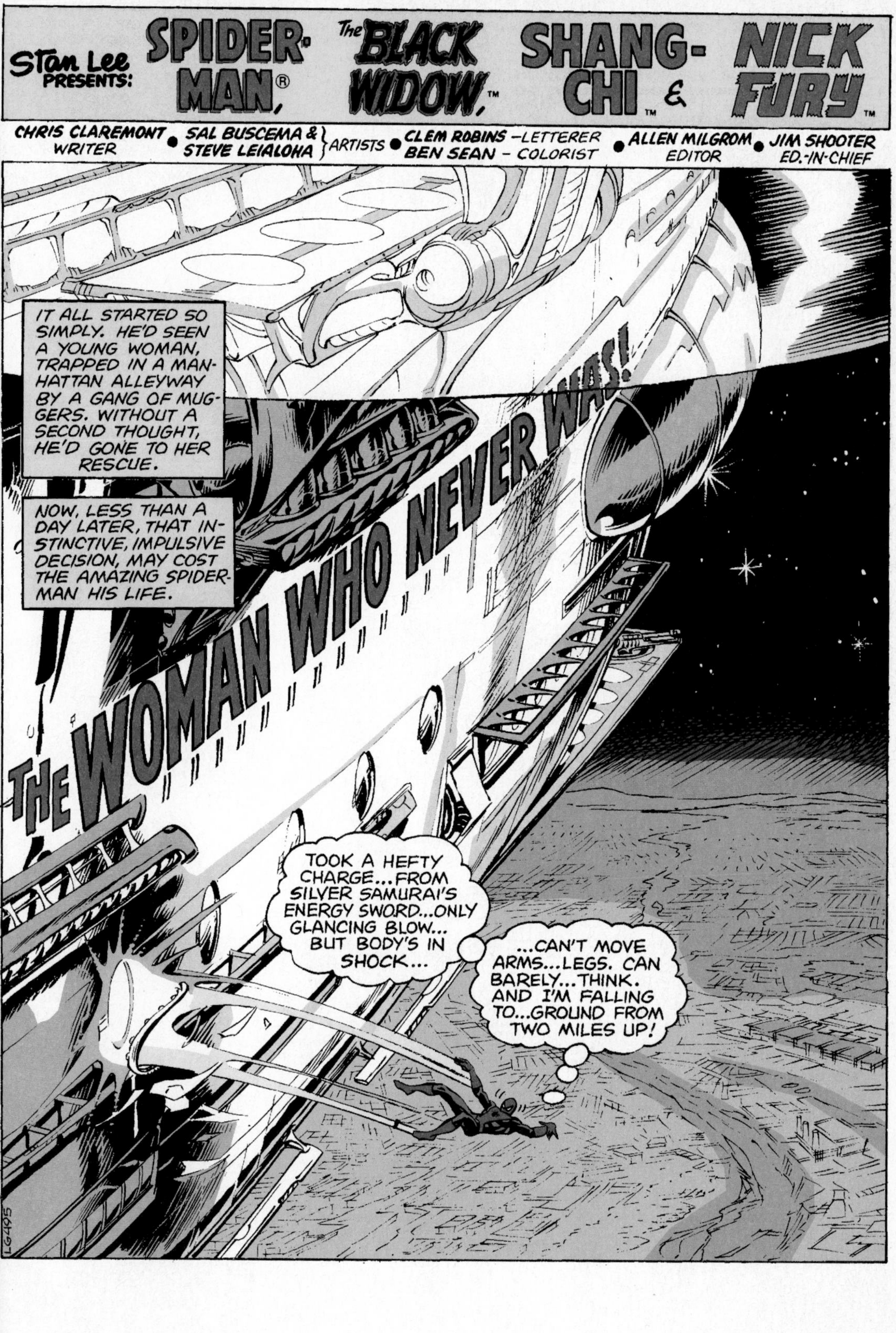

Stan Lee PRESENTS: SPIDER-MAN®, The BLACK WIDOW,™ SHANG-CHI™ & NICK FURY™
CHRIS CLAREMONT WRITER • SAL BUSCEMA & STEVE LEIALOHA ARTISTS • CLEM ROBINS - LETTERER BEN SEAN - COLORIST • ALLEN MILGROM EDITOR • JIM SHOOTER ED.-IN-CHIEF
IT ALL STARTED SO SIMPLY. HE'D SEEN A YOUNG WOMAN, TRAPPED IN A MANHATTAN ALLEYWAY BY A GANG OF MUGGERS. WITHOUT A SECOND THOUGHT, HE'D GONE TO HER RESCUE.
NOW, LESS THAN A DAY LATER, THAT INSTINCTIVE, IMPULSIVE DECISION, MAY COST THE AMAZING SPIDER-MAN HIS LIFE.
THE WOMAN WHO NEVER WAS!
TOOK A HEFTY CHARGE...FROM SILVER SAMURAI'S ENERGY SWORD...ONLY GLANCING BLOW... BUT BODY'S IN SHOCK...
...CAN'T MOVE ARMS...LEGS. CAN BARELY...THINK. AND I'M FALLING TO...GROUND FROM TWO MILES UP!

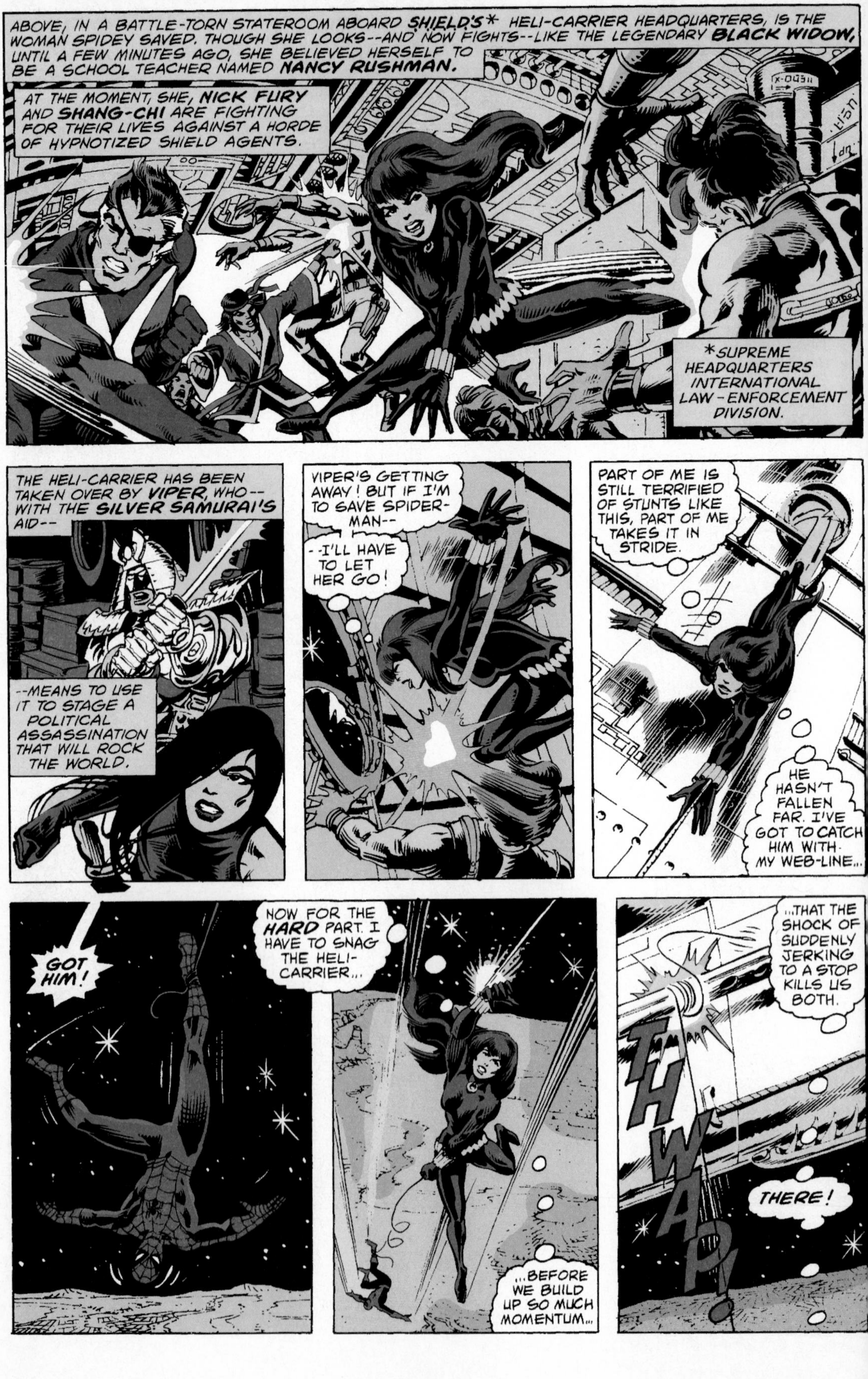

ABOVE, IN A BATTLE-TORN STATEROOM ABOARD SHIELD'S* HELI-CARRIER HEADQUARTERS, IS THE WOMAN SPIDEY SAVED. THOUGH SHE LOOKS--AND NOW FIGHTS--LIKE THE LEGENDARY BLACK WIDOW, UNTIL A FEW MINUTES AGO, SHE BELIEVED HERSELF TO BE A SCHOOL TEACHER NAMED NANCY RUSHMAN.
AT THE MOMENT, SHE, NICK FURY AND SHANG-CHI ARE FIGHTING FOR THEIR LIVES AGAINST A HORDE OF HYPNOTIZED SHIELD AGENTS.
*SUPREME HEADQUARTERS INTERNATIONAL LAW-ENFORCEMENT DIVISION.
THE HELI-CARRIER HAS BEEN TAKEN OVER BY VIPER, WHO--WITH THE SILVER SAMURAI'S AID--
--MEANS TO USE IT TO STAGE A POLITICAL ASSASSINATION THAT WILL ROCK THE WORLD.
VIPER'S GETTING AWAY! BUT IF I'M TO SAVE SPIDER-MAN--
--I'LL HAVE TO LET HER GO!
PART OF ME IS STILL TERRIFIED OF STUNTS LIKE THIS, PART OF ME TAKES IT IN STRIDE.
HE HASN'T FALLEN FAR. I'VE GOT TO CATCH HIM WITH MY WEB-LINE...
GOT HIM!
NOW FOR THE HARD PART. I HAVE TO SNAG THE HELI-CARRIER...
...BEFORE WE BUILD UP SO MUCH MOMENTUM...
...THAT THE SHOCK OF SUDDENLY JERKING TO A STOP KILLS US BOTH.
THWAP!
THERE!

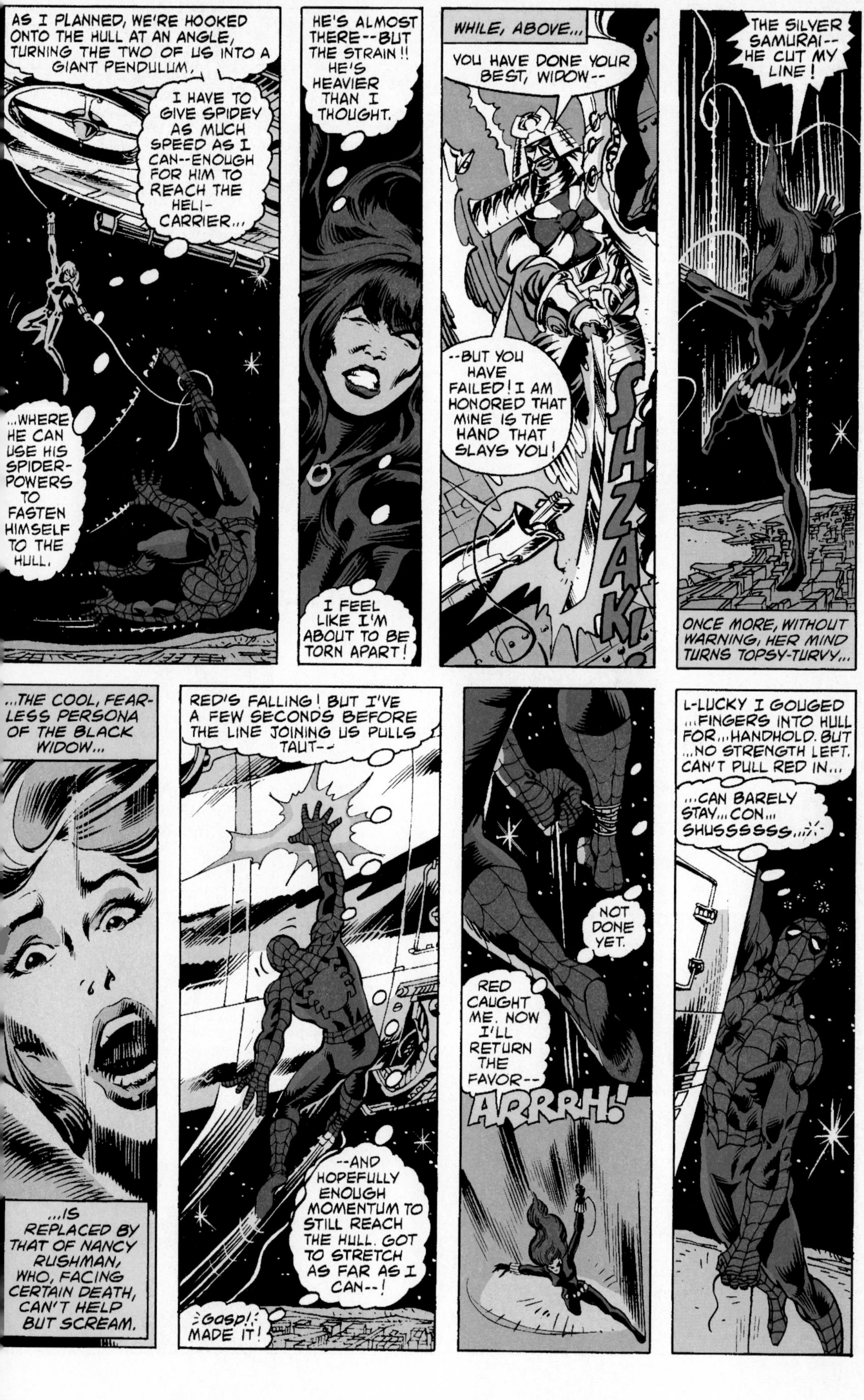

AS I PLANNED, WE'RE HOOKED ONTO THE HULL AT AN ANGLE, TURNING THE TWO OF US INTO A GIANT PENDULUM.
I HAVE TO GIVE SPIDEY AS MUCH SPEED AS I CAN--ENOUGH FOR HIM TO REACH THE HELI-CARRIER...
...WHERE HE CAN USE HIS SPIDER-POWERS TO FASTEN HIMSELF TO THE HULL.
HE'S ALMOST THERE--BUT THE STRAIN!! HE'S HEAVIER THAN I THOUGHT.
I FEEL LIKE I'M ABOUT TO BE TORN APART!
WHILE, ABOVE...
YOU HAVE DONE YOUR BEST, WIDOW--
--BUT YOU HAVE FAILED! I AM HONORED THAT MINE IS THE HAND THAT SLAYS YOU!
SHZAK!
THE SILVER SAMURAI--HE CUT MY LINE!
ONCE MORE, WITHOUT WARNING, HER MIND TURNS TOPSY-TURVY...
...THE COOL, FEARLESS PERSONA OF THE BLACK WIDOW...
...IS REPLACED BY THAT OF NANCY RUSHMAN, WHO, FACING CERTAIN DEATH, CAN'T HELP BUT SCREAM.
RED'S FALLING! BUT I'VE A FEW SECONDS BEFORE THE LINE JOINING US PULLS TAUT--
--AND HOPEFULLY ENOUGH MOMENTUM TO STILL REACH THE HULL. GOT TO STRETCH AS FAR AS I CAN--!
Gasp! MADE IT!
NOT DONE YET.
RED CAUGHT ME. NOW I'LL RETURN THE FAVOR--
ARRRH!
L-LUCKY I GOUGED ...FINGERS INTO HULL FOR...HANDHOLD. BUT ...NO STRENGTH LEFT. CAN'T PULL RED IN...
...CAN BARELY STAY...CON... SHUSSSSSS...

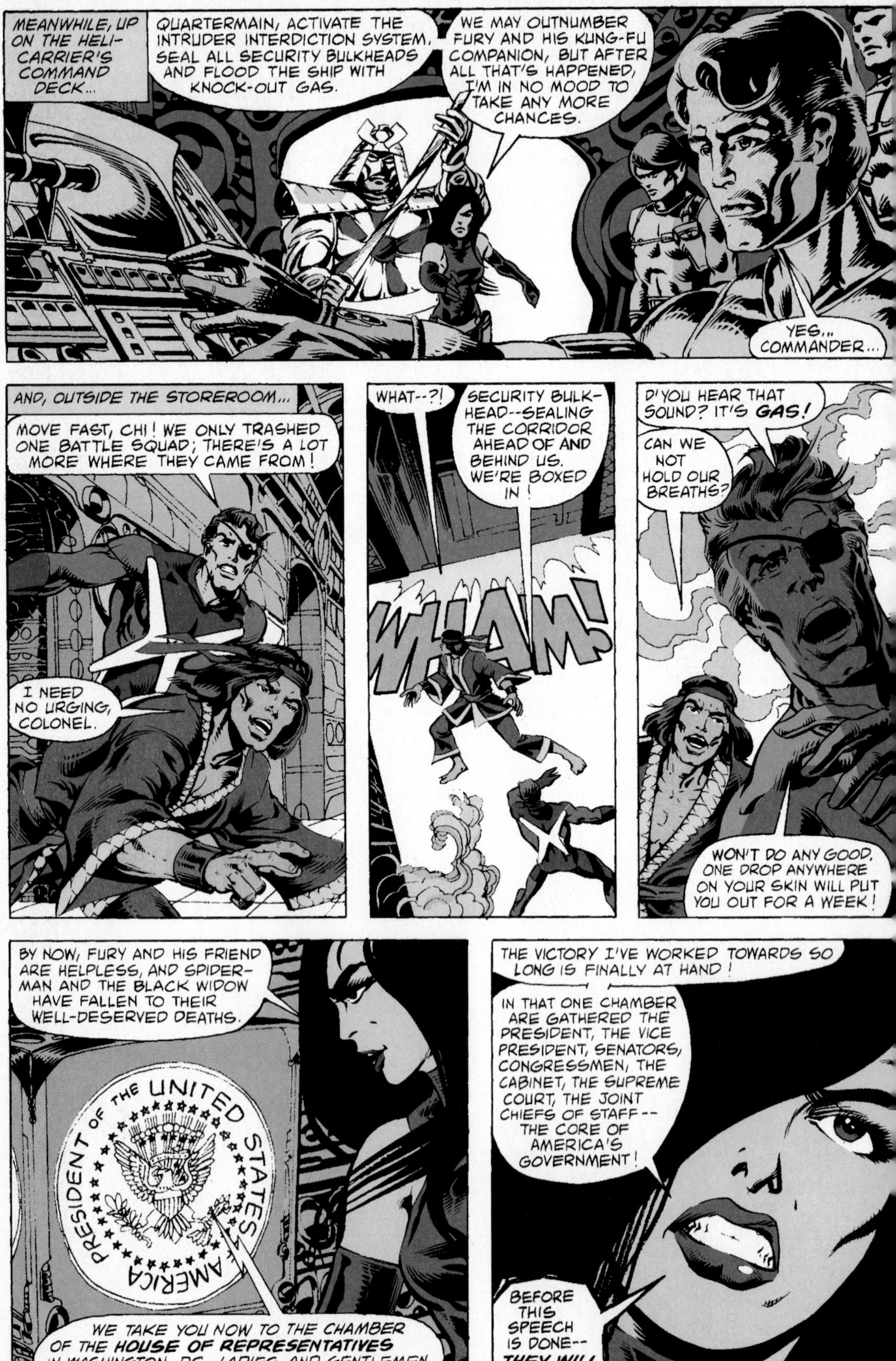
MEANWHILE, UP ON THE HELI-CARRIER'S COMMAND DECK...
QUARTERMAIN, ACTIVATE THE INTRUDER INTERDICTION SYSTEM. SEAL ALL SECURITY BULKHEADS AND FLOOD THE SHIP WITH KNOCK-OUT GAS.
WE MAY OUTNUMBER FURY AND HIS KUNG-FU COMPANION, BUT AFTER ALL THAT'S HAPPENED, I'M IN NO MOOD TO TAKE ANY MORE CHANCES.
YES... COMMANDER...
AND, OUTSIDE THE STOREROOM...
MOVE FAST, CHI! WE ONLY TRASHED ONE BATTLE SQUAD; THERE'S A LOT MORE WHERE THEY CAME FROM!
I NEED NO URGING, COLONEL.
WHAT--?!
SECURITY BULK-HEAD--SEALING THE CORRIDOR AHEAD OF AND BEHIND US. WE'RE BOXED IN!
WHAM!
D'YOU HEAR THAT SOUND? IT'S GAS!
CAN WE NOT HOLD OUR BREATHS?
WON'T DO ANY GOOD. ONE DROP ANYWHERE ON YOUR SKIN WILL PUT YOU OUT FOR A WEEK!
BY NOW, FURY AND HIS FRIEND ARE HELPLESS, AND SPIDER-MAN AND THE BLACK WIDOW HAVE FALLEN TO THEIR WELL-DESERVED DEATHS.
PRESIDENT OF THE UNITED STATES OF AMERICA
WE TAKE YOU NOW TO THE CHAMBER OF THE HOUSE OF REPRESENTATIVES IN WASHINGTON, DC--LADIES AND GENTLEMEN, THE PRESIDENT OF THE UNITED STATES.
THE VICTORY I'VE WORKED TOWARDS SO LONG IS FINALLY AT HAND!
IN THAT ONE CHAMBER ARE GATHERED THE PRESIDENT, THE VICE PRESIDENT, SENATORS, CONGRESSMEN, THE CABINET, THE SUPREME COURT, THE JOINT CHIEFS OF STAFF -- THE CORE OF AMERICA'S GOVERNMENT!
BEFORE THIS SPEECH IS DONE-- THEY WILL ALL DIE!

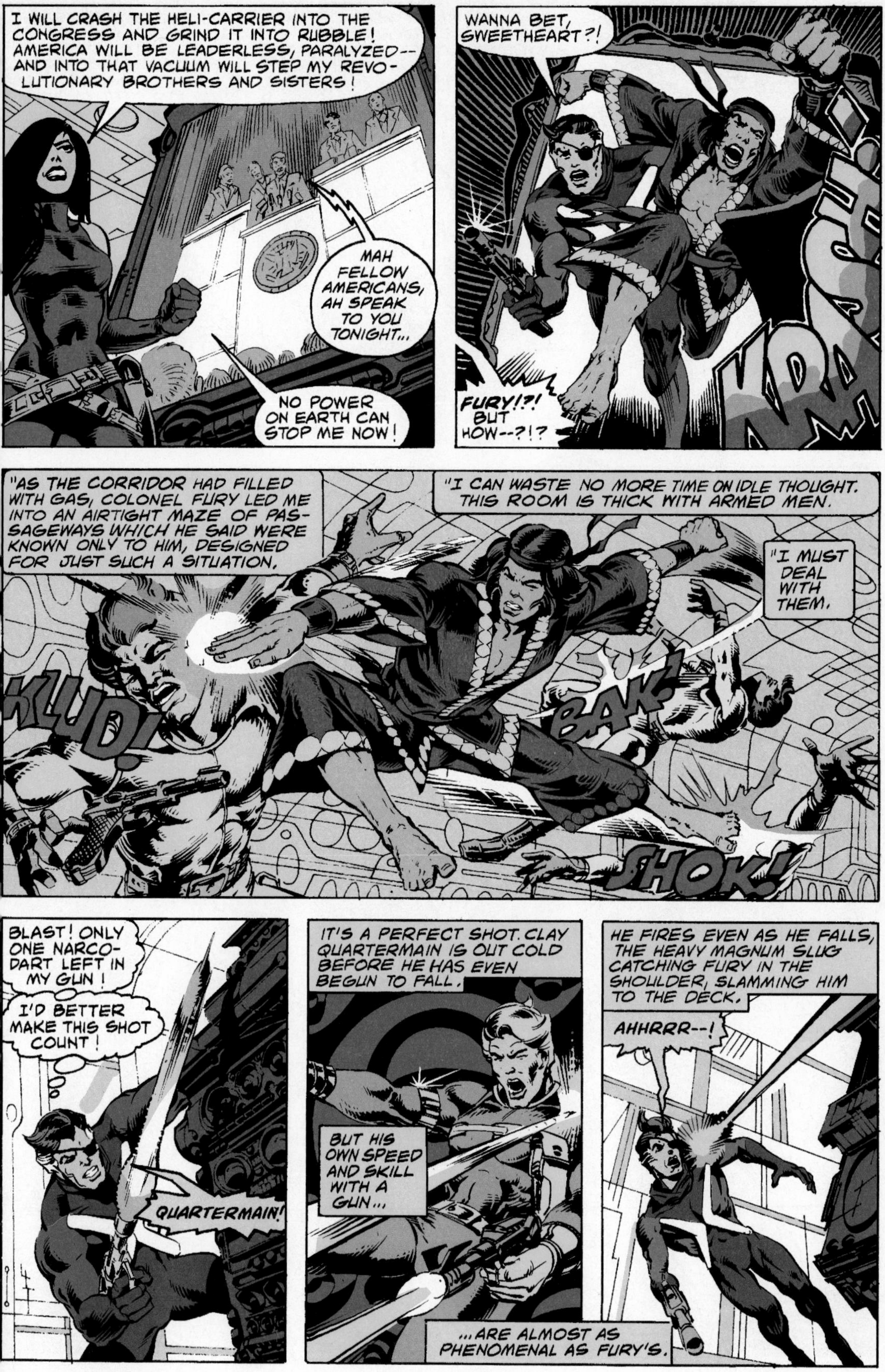

I WILL CRASH THE HELI-CARRIER INTO THE CONGRESS AND GRIND IT INTO RUBBLE! AMERICA WILL BE LEADERLESS, PARALYZED-- AND INTO THAT VACUUM WILL STEP MY REVOLUTIONARY BROTHERS AND SISTERS!
MAH FELLOW AMERICANS, AH SPEAK TO YOU TONIGHT...
NO POWER ON EARTH CAN STOP ME NOW!
WANNA BET, SWEETHEART?!
FURY!?! BUT HOW--?!?
KRA
"AS THE CORRIDOR HAD FILLED WITH GAS, COLONEL FURY LED ME INTO AN AIRTIGHT MAZE OF PASSAGEWAYS WHICH HE SAID WERE KNOWN ONLY TO HIM, DESIGNED FOR JUST SUCH A SITUATION.
"I CAN WASTE NO MORE TIME ON IDLE THOUGHT. THIS ROOM IS THICK WITH ARMED MEN.
"I MUST DEAL WITH THEM.
KLUD!
BAK!
SHOK!
BLAST! ONLY ONE NARCO-DART LEFT IN MY GUN!
I'D BETTER MAKE THIS SHOT COUNT!
QUARTERMAIN!
IT'S A PERFECT SHOT. CLAY QUARTERMAIN IS OUT COLD BEFORE HE HAS EVEN BEGUN TO FALL.
BUT HIS OWN SPEED AND SKILL WITH A GUN...
...ARE ALMOST AS PHENOMENAL AS FURY'S.
HE FIRES EVEN AS HE FALLS, THE HEAVY MAGNUM SLUG CATCHING FURY IN THE SHOULDER, SLAMMING HIM TO THE DECK.
AHHRRR--!

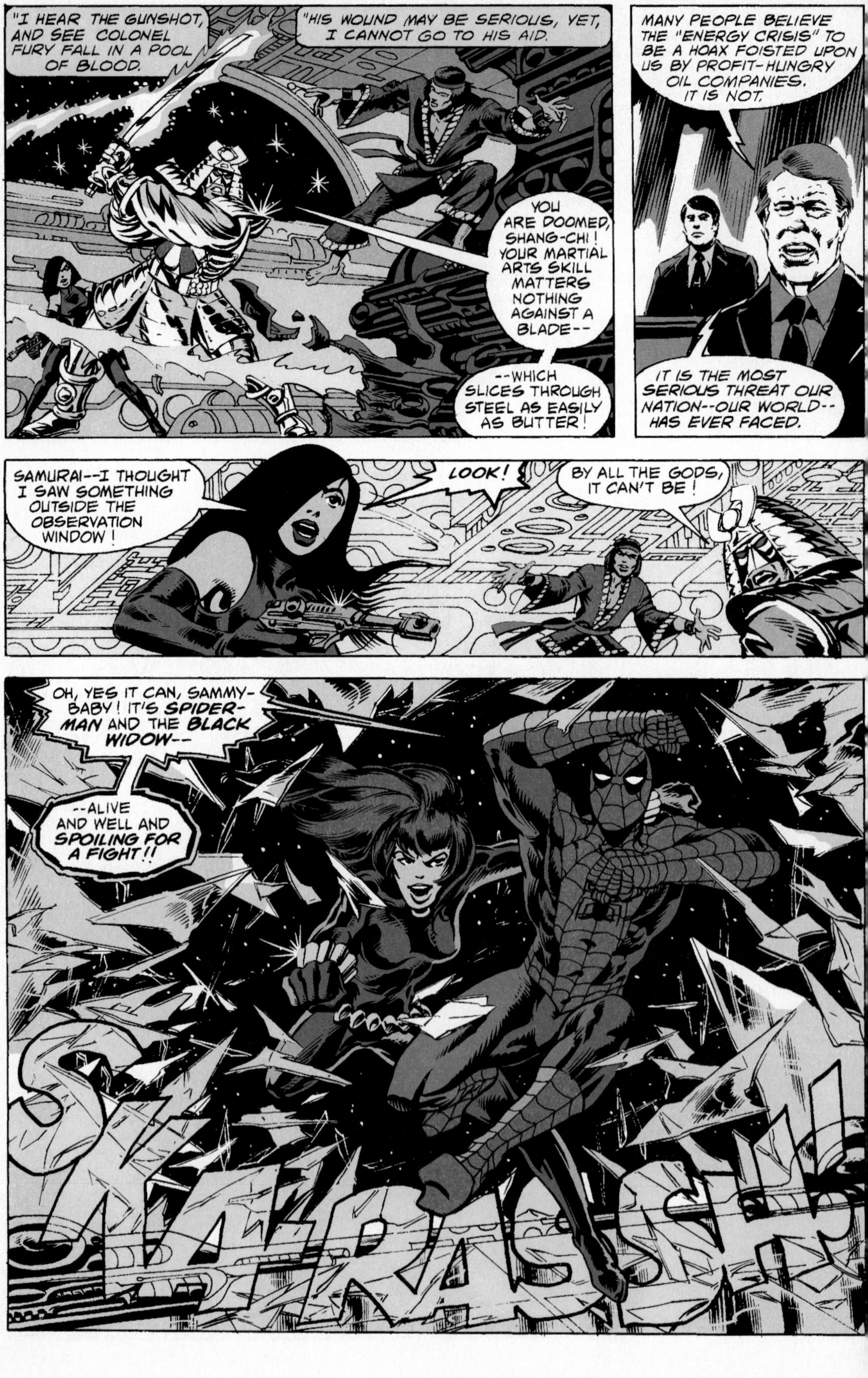
"I HEAR THE GUNSHOT, AND SEE COLONEL FURY FALL IN A POOL OF BLOOD.
"HIS WOUND MAY BE SERIOUS, YET, I CANNOT GO TO HIS AID.
YOU ARE DOOMED, SHANG-CHI! YOUR MARTIAL ARTS SKILL MATTERS NOTHING AGAINST A BLADE--
--WHICH SLICES THROUGH STEEL AS EASILY AS BUTTER!
MANY PEOPLE BELIEVE THE "ENERGY CRISIS" TO BE A HOAX FOISTED UPON US BY PROFIT-HUNGRY OIL COMPANIES. IT IS NOT.
IT IS THE MOST SERIOUS THREAT OUR NATION--OUR WORLD--HAS EVER FACED.
SAMURAI--I THOUGHT I SAW SOMETHING OUTSIDE THE OBSERVATION WINDOW!
LOOK!
BY ALL THE GODS, IT CAN'T BE!
OH, YES IT CAN, SAMMY-BABY! IT'S SPIDER-MAN AND THE BLACK WIDOW--
--ALIVE AND WELL AND SPOILING FOR A FIGHT!!

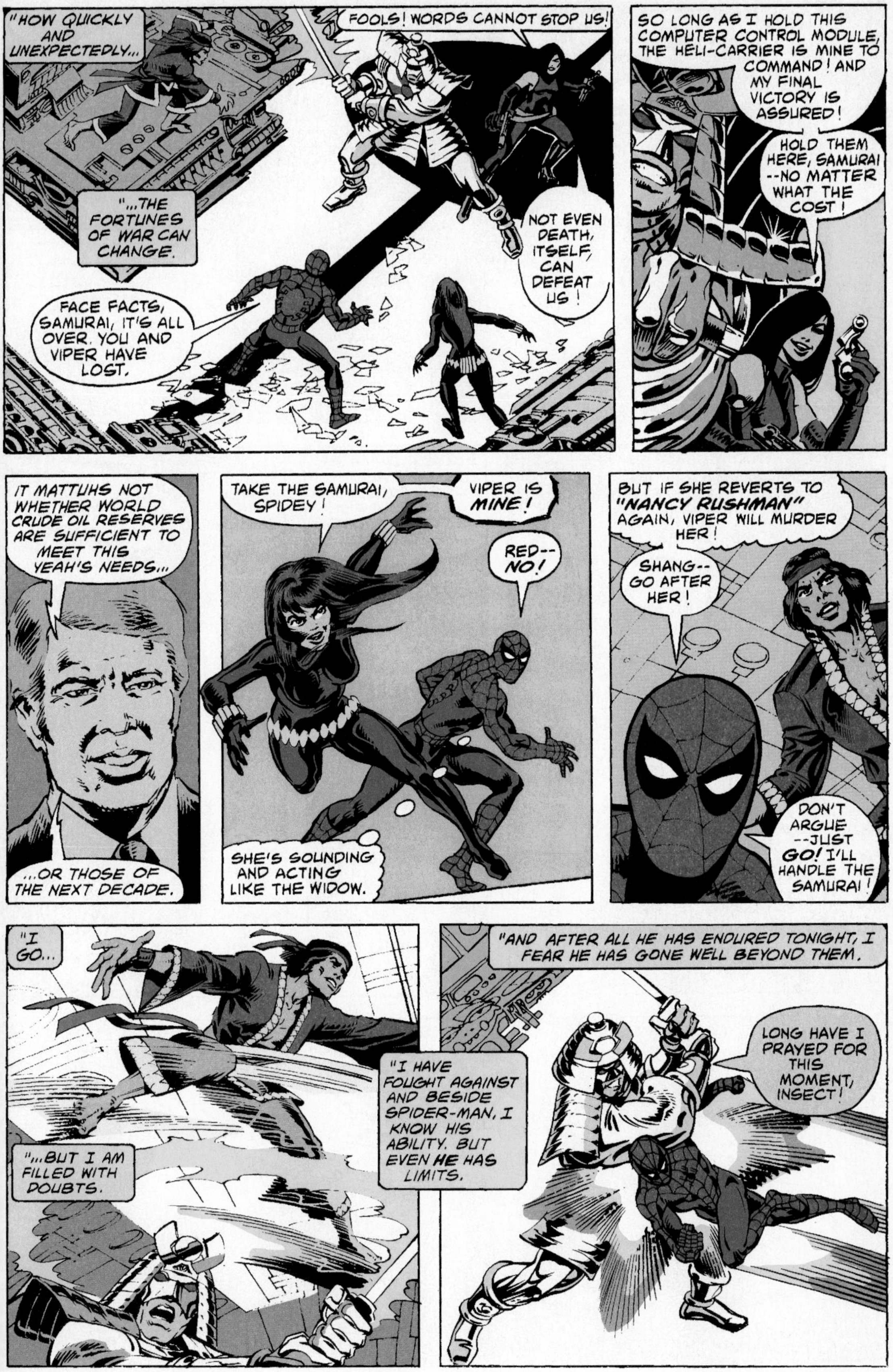
"HOW QUICKLY AND UNEXPECTEDLY...
FOOLS! WORDS CANNOT STOP US!
"...THE FORTUNES OF WAR CAN CHANGE.
NOT EVEN DEATH, ITSELF, CAN DEFEAT US!
FACE FACTS, SAMURAI, IT'S ALL OVER. YOU AND VIPER HAVE LOST.
SO LONG AS I HOLD THIS COMPUTER CONTROL MODULE, THE HELI-CARRIER IS MINE TO COMMAND! AND MY FINAL VICTORY IS ASSURED!
HOLD THEM HERE, SAMURAI --NO MATTER WHAT THE COST!
IT MATTUHS NOT WHETHER WORLD CRUDE OIL RESERVES ARE SUFFICIENT TO MEET THIS YEAH'S NEEDS...
...OR THOSE OF THE NEXT DECADE.
TAKE THE SAMURAI, SPIDEY!
VIPER IS MINE!
RED-- NO!
SHE'S SOUNDING AND ACTING LIKE THE WIDOW.
BUT IF SHE REVERTS TO "NANCY RUSHMAN" AGAIN, VIPER WILL MURDER HER!
SHANG-- GO AFTER HER!
DON'T ARGUE --JUST GO! I'LL HANDLE THE SAMURAI!
"I GO...
"...BUT I AM FILLED WITH DOUBTS.
"I HAVE FOUGHT AGAINST AND BESIDE SPIDER-MAN. I KNOW HIS ABILITY. BUT EVEN HE HAS LIMITS.
"AND AFTER ALL HE HAS ENDURED TONIGHT, I FEAR HE HAS GONE WELL BEYOND THEM.
LONG HAVE I PRAYED FOR THIS MOMENT, INSECT!

AT LAST, WE MEET IN SINGLE-COMBAT!
WHAMMO!
UNNNGNH!
A DUEL TO THE DEATH THAT I WILL WIN!
THIS TIME, NO MATTER HOW HARD YOU TRY--
--YOU WILL NOT ESCAPE!
SKRAM!
SOONER OR LATER, OIL--AND ALL FOSSIL FUELS--WILL RUN OUT. WE MUST RECOGNIZE, ONCE AND FOAH ALL...
...THAT OUR PLANET'S RESOURCES ARE FINITE.
ESCAPE, SAMMY? PERISH THE THOUGHT!
THAK
NUTS! HIS ARMOR BLUNTS THE FORCE OF MY PUNCHES!
MY BIG EDGE IS SPEED.
HIS IS THAT FERSHLUGGINER SWORD. WHOOPS!
AND, BOY, DOES HE KNOW HOW TO USE IT! I'LL BET HE COULD GIVE TOSHIRO MIFUNE A HARD TIME.

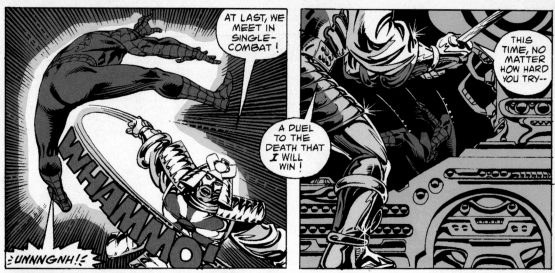

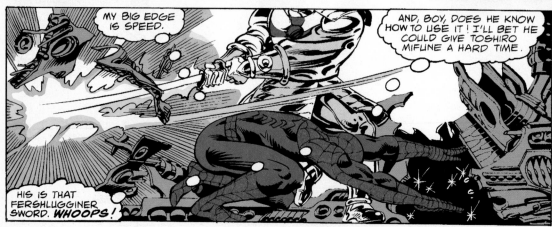

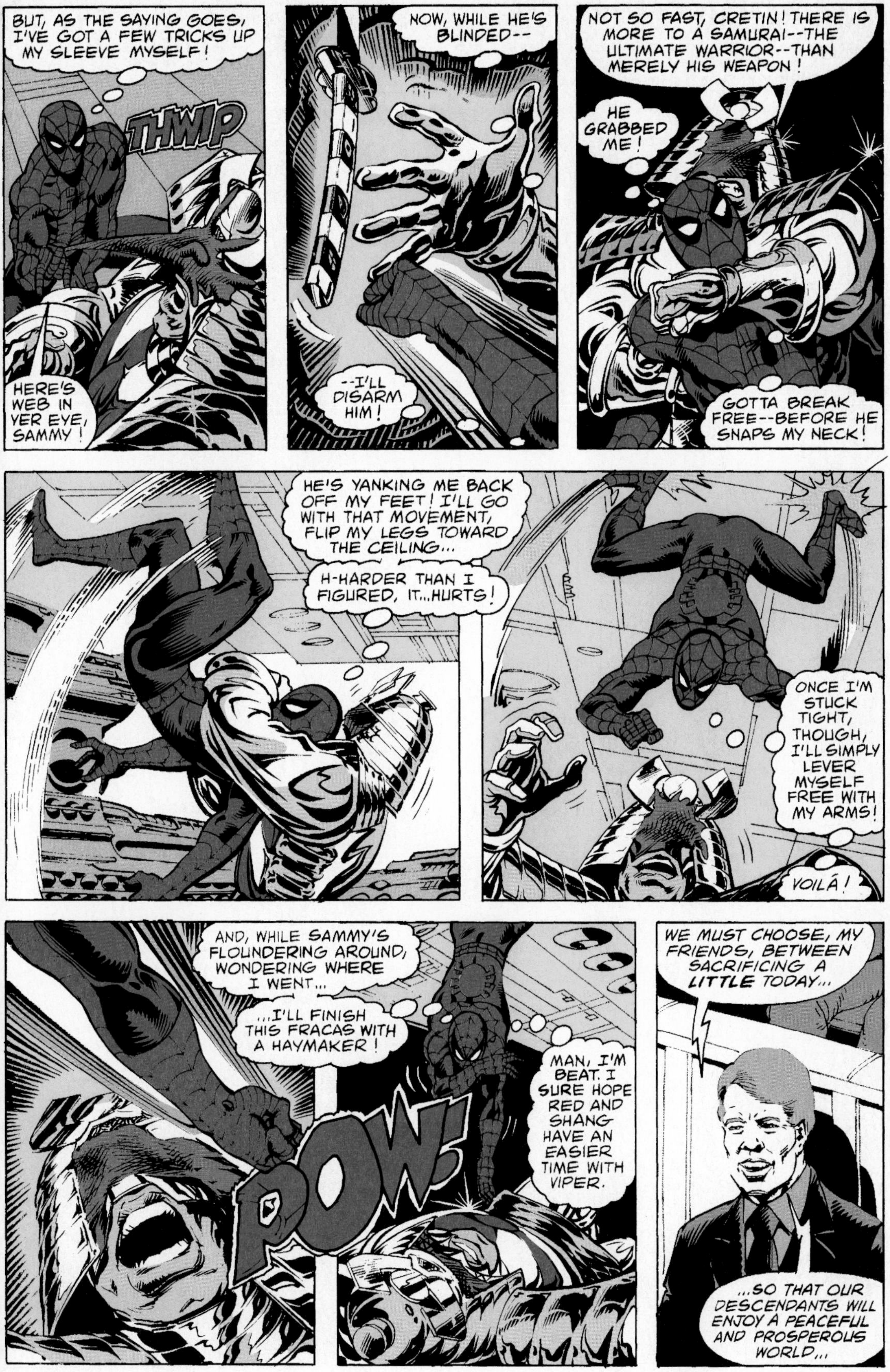
BUT, AS THE SAYING GOES, I'VE GOT A FEW TRICKS UP MY SLEEVE MYSELF!
THWIP
HERE'S WEB IN YER EYE, SAMMY!
NOW, WHILE HE'S BLINDED--
--I'LL DISARM HIM!
NOT SO FAST, CRETIN! THERE IS MORE TO A SAMURAI--THE ULTIMATE WARRIOR--THAN MERELY HIS WEAPON!
HE GRABBED ME!
GOTTA BREAK FREE--BEFORE HE SNAPS MY NECK!
HE'S YANKING ME BACK OFF MY FEET! I'LL GO WITH THAT MOVEMENT, FLIP MY LEGS TOWARD THE CEILING...
H-HARDER THAN I FIGURED, IT...HURTS!
ONCE I'M STUCK TIGHT, THOUGH, I'LL SIMPLY LEVER MYSELF FREE WITH MY ARMS!
VOILÀ!
AND, WHILE SAMMY'S FLOUNDERING AROUND, WONDERING WHERE I WENT...
...I'LL FINISH THIS FRACAS WITH A HAYMAKER!
POW!
MAN, I'M BEAT. I SURE HOPE RED AND SHANG HAVE AN EASIER TIME WITH VIPER.
WE MUST CHOOSE, MY FRIENDS, BETWEEN SACRIFICING A LITTLE TODAY...
...SO THAT OUR DESCENDANTS WILL ENJOY A PEACEFUL AND PROSPEROUS WORLD...

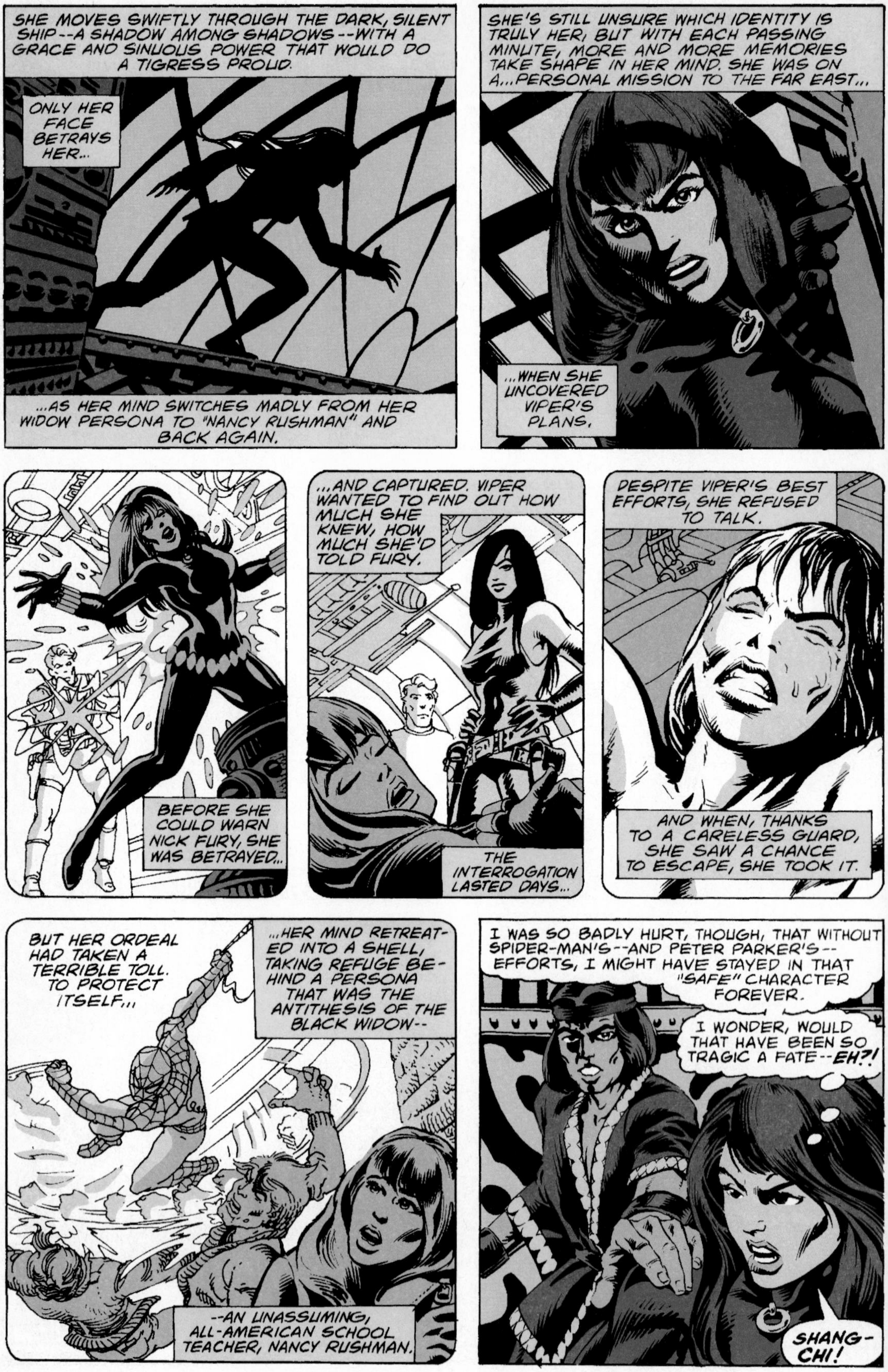
SHE MOVES SWIFTLY THROUGH THE DARK, SILENT SHIP--A SHADOW AMONG SHADOWS--WITH A GRACE AND SINUOUS POWER THAT WOULD DO A TIGRESS PROUD.
ONLY HER FACE BETRAYS HER...
...AS HER MIND SWITCHES MADLY FROM HER WIDOW PERSONA TO "NANCY RUSHMAN" AND BACK AGAIN.
SHE'S STILL UNSURE WHICH IDENTITY IS TRULY HER, BUT WITH EACH PASSING MINUTE, MORE AND MORE MEMORIES TAKE SHAPE IN HER MIND. SHE WAS ON A...PERSONAL MISSION TO THE FAR EAST...
...WHEN SHE UNCOVERED VIPER'S PLANS.
BEFORE SHE COULD WARN NICK FURY, SHE WAS BETRAYED...
...AND CAPTURED. VIPER WANTED TO FIND OUT HOW MUCH SHE KNEW, HOW MUCH SHE'D TOLD FURY.
THE INTERROGATION LASTED DAYS...
DESPITE VIPER'S BEST EFFORTS, SHE REFUSED TO TALK.
AND WHEN, THANKS TO A CARELESS GUARD, SHE SAW A CHANCE TO ESCAPE, SHE TOOK IT.
BUT HER ORDEAL HAD TAKEN A TERRIBLE TOLL. TO PROTECT ITSELF...
...HER MIND RETREATED INTO A SHELL, TAKING REFUGE BEHIND A PERSONA THAT WAS THE ANTITHESIS OF THE BLACK WIDOW--
--AN UNASSUMING, ALL-AMERICAN SCHOOL TEACHER, NANCY RUSHMAN.
I WAS SO BADLY HURT, THOUGH, THAT WITHOUT SPIDER-MAN'S--AND PETER PARKER'S--EFFORTS, I MIGHT HAVE STAYED IN THAT "SAFE" CHARACTER FOREVER.
I WONDER, WOULD THAT HAVE BEEN SO TRAGIC A FATE--EH?!
SHANG-CHI!

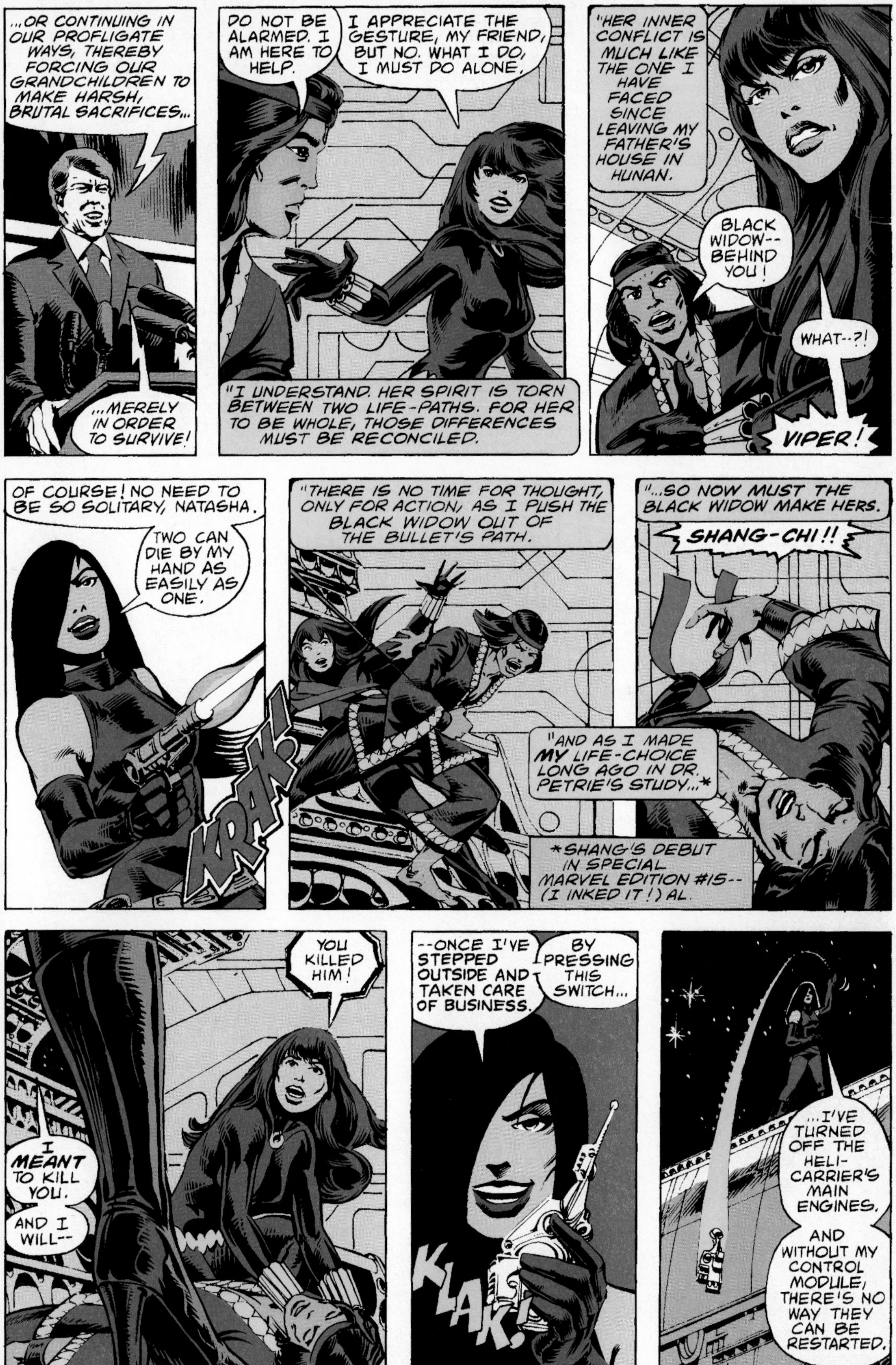
...OR CONTINUING IN OUR PROFLIGATE WAYS, THEREBY FORCING OUR GRANDCHILDREN TO MAKE HARSH, BRUTAL SACRIFICES...
...MERELY IN ORDER TO SURVIVE!
DO NOT BE ALARMED. I AM HERE TO HELP.
I APPRECIATE THE GESTURE, MY FRIEND, BUT NO. WHAT I DO, I MUST DO ALONE.
"I UNDERSTAND. HER SPIRIT IS TORN BETWEEN TWO LIFE-PATHS. FOR HER TO BE WHOLE, THOSE DIFFERENCES MUST BE RECONCILED.
"HER INNER CONFLICT IS MUCH LIKE THE ONE I HAVE FACED SINCE LEAVING MY FATHER'S HOUSE IN HUNAN.
BLACK WIDOW-- BEHIND YOU!
WHAT--?!
VIPER!
OF COURSE! NO NEED TO BE SO SOLITARY, NATASHA.
TWO CAN DIE BY MY HAND AS EASILY AS ONE.
KRAK!
"THERE IS NO TIME FOR THOUGHT, ONLY FOR ACTION, AS I PUSH THE BLACK WIDOW OUT OF THE BULLET'S PATH.
"AND AS I MADE MY LIFE-CHOICE LONG AGO IN DR. PETRIE'S STUDY...*
"...SO NOW MUST THE BLACK WIDOW MAKE HERS.
SHANG-CHI!!
*SHANG'S DEBUT IN SPECIAL MARVEL EDITION #15-- (I INKED IT!) AL.
YOU KILLED HIM!
I MEANT TO KILL YOU.
AND I WILL--
BY PRESSING THIS SWITCH...
--ONCE I'VE STEPPED OUTSIDE AND TAKEN CARE OF BUSINESS.
KLAK!
...I'VE TURNED OFF THE HELI-CARRIER'S MAIN ENGINES.
AND WITHOUT MY CONTROL MODULE, THERE'S NO WAY THEY CAN BE RESTARTED.

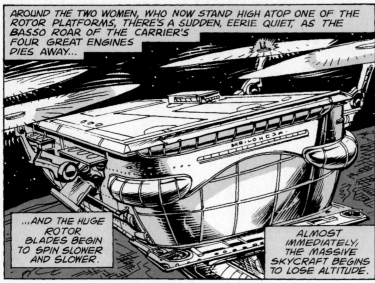

AROUND THE TWO WOMEN, WHO NOW STAND HIGH ATOP ONE OF THE ROTOR PLATFORMS, THERE'S A SUDDEN, EERIE QUIET, AS THE BASSO ROAR OF THE CARRIER'S FOUR GREAT ENGINES DIES AWAY...

...AND THE HUGE ROTOR BLADES BEGIN TO SPIN SLOWER AND SLOWER.

ALMOST IMMEDIATELY, THE MASSIVE SKYCRAFT BEGINS TO LOSE ALTITUDE.

EASY, COLONEL, I'M NO DOCTOR, AND THAT BULLET DID A LOT OF DAMAGE...

SHUT UP, WILLYA-- AN' LISTEN!

TO WHAT?! HEY--THE ENGINES!

THEY'VE BEEN SHUT DOWN. THAT MUST'A BEEN WHAT VIPER'S CONTROL MODULE WAS FOR.

CAN WE START 'EM UP AGAIN?

FROM THE LOOKS O' THINGS, VIPER GIM-MICKED ALL THE BRIDGE COMMAND SYSTEMS-- PROBABLY BOOBY-TRAPPED EVERYTHING, TOO!

SHE EVEN KNOCKED OUT THE VORTEX BEAM.

OUR ONLY CHANCE...

...IS TO REWIRE THE MAIN TRUNK LINES. THEY'RE BEHIND THIS WALL. IT'S REINFORCED STEEL--CAN YOU PEEL IT BACK?

WATCH ME!

HOW MUCH TIME DO WE HAVE?

NOT MUCH.

RRRAKT!

CAREFUL, KID! THE SMALLEST LINE IN THERE CARRIES OVER A THOUSAND VOLTS!

NOW HE TELLS ME!

MY LEFT ARM'S USELESS, AN' THE REST OF ME IS SHAKY FROM SHOCK. YOU'LL HAVE TO DO MOST OF THE WORK.

JUST FOLLOW MY LEAD...

...AN' PRAY.

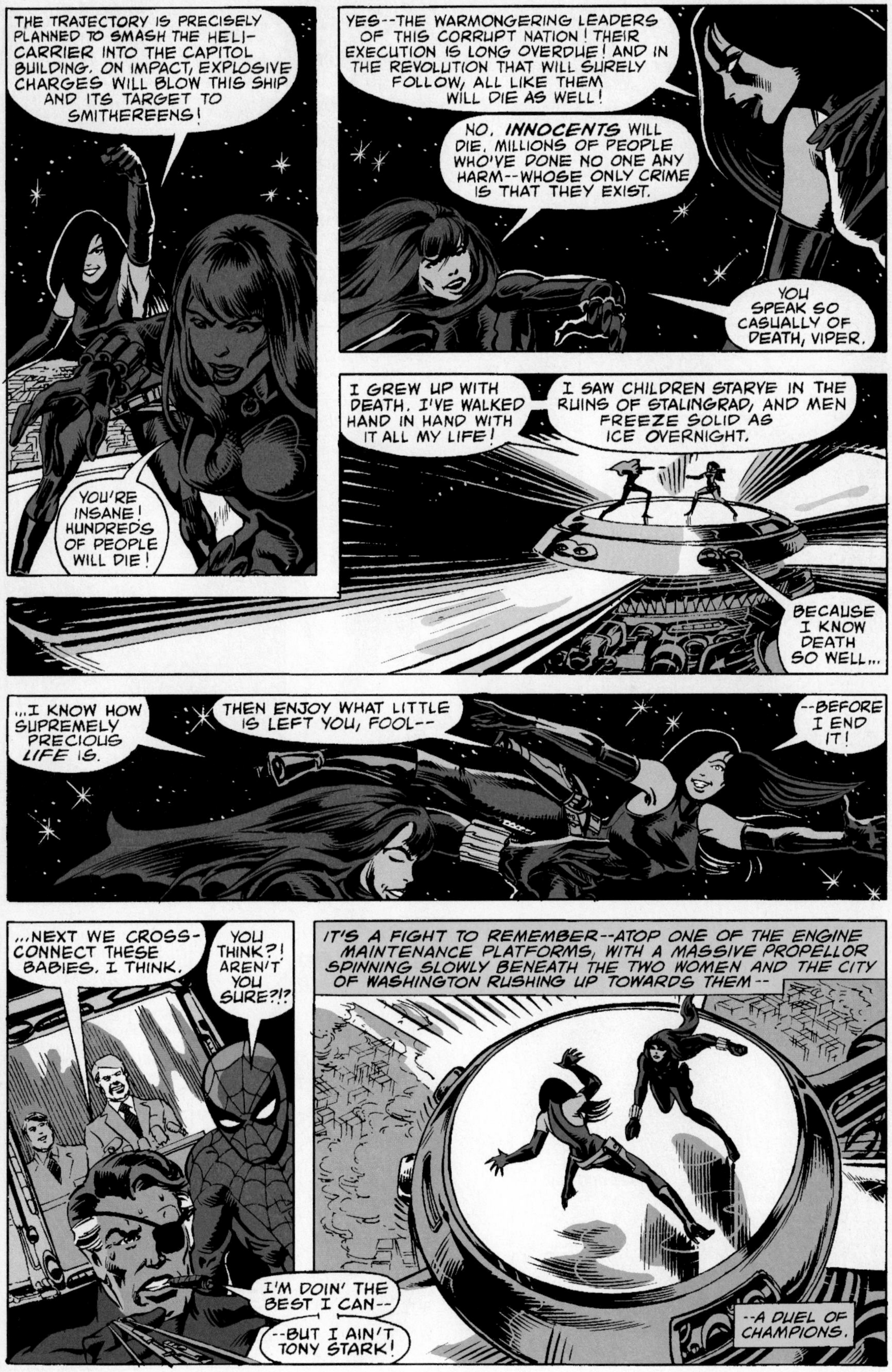

THE TRAJECTORY IS PRECISELY PLANNED TO SMASH THE HELI-CARRIER INTO THE CAPITOL BUILDING. ON IMPACT, EXPLOSIVE CHARGES WILL BLOW THIS SHIP AND ITS TARGET TO SMITHEREENS!
YOU'RE INSANE! HUNDREDS OF PEOPLE WILL DIE!
YES--THE WARMONGERING LEADERS OF THIS CORRUPT NATION! THEIR EXECUTION IS LONG OVERDUE! AND IN THE REVOLUTION THAT WILL SURELY FOLLOW, ALL LIKE THEM WILL DIE AS WELL!
NO. INNOCENTS WILL DIE. MILLIONS OF PEOPLE WHO'VE DONE NO ONE ANY HARM--WHOSE ONLY CRIME IS THAT THEY EXIST.
YOU SPEAK SO CASUALLY OF DEATH, VIPER.
I GREW UP WITH DEATH. I'VE WALKED HAND IN HAND WITH IT ALL MY LIFE!
I SAW CHILDREN STARVE IN THE RUINS OF STALINGRAD, AND MEN FREEZE SOLID AS ICE OVERNIGHT.
BECAUSE I KNOW DEATH SO WELL...
...I KNOW HOW SUPREMELY PRECIOUS LIFE IS.
THEN ENJOY WHAT LITTLE IS LEFT YOU, FOOL--
--BEFORE I END IT!
...NEXT WE CROSS-CONNECT THESE BABIES. I THINK.
YOU THINK?! AREN'T YOU SURE?!?
I'M DOIN' THE BEST I CAN--
--BUT I AIN'T TONY STARK!
IT'S A FIGHT TO REMEMBER--ATOP ONE OF THE ENGINE MAINTENANCE PLATFORMS, WITH A MASSIVE PROPELLOR SPINNING SLOWLY BENEATH THE TWO WOMEN AND THE CITY OF WASHINGTON RUSHING UP TOWARDS THEM--
--A DUEL OF CHAMPIONS.

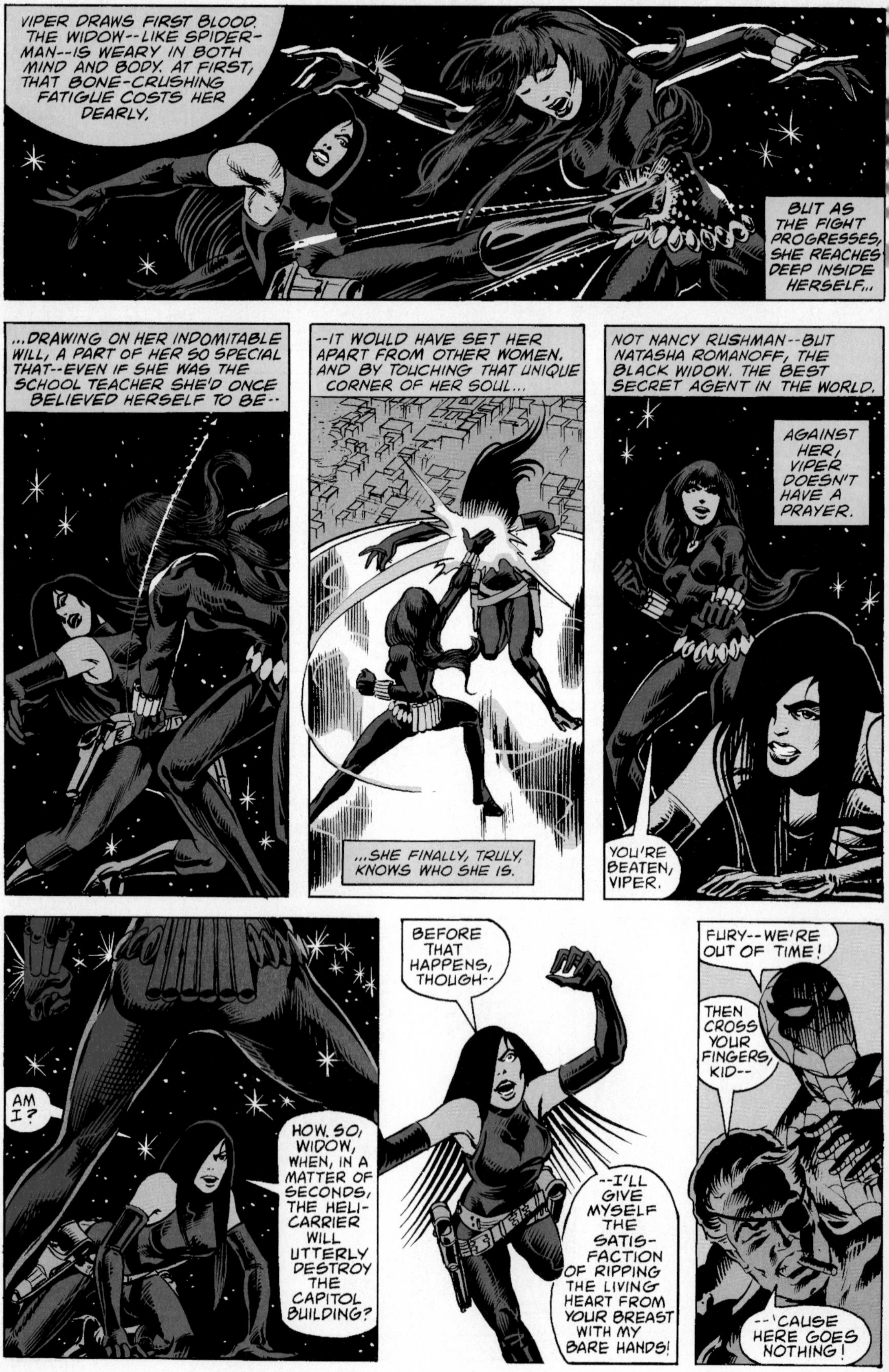
VIPER DRAWS FIRST BLOOD. THE WIDOW--LIKE SPIDER-MAN--IS WEARY IN BOTH MIND AND BODY. AT FIRST, THAT BONE-CRUSHING FATIGUE COSTS HER DEARLY.
BUT AS THE FIGHT PROGRESSES, SHE REACHES DEEP INSIDE HERSELF...
...DRAWING ON HER INDOMITABLE WILL, A PART OF HER SO SPECIAL THAT--EVEN IF SHE WAS THE SCHOOL TEACHER SHE'D ONCE BELIEVED HERSELF TO BE--
--IT WOULD HAVE SET HER APART FROM OTHER WOMEN. AND BY TOUCHING THAT UNIQUE CORNER OF HER SOUL...
...SHE FINALLY, TRULY, KNOWS WHO SHE IS.
NOT NANCY RUSHMAN--BUT NATASHA ROMANOFF, THE BLACK WIDOW. THE BEST SECRET AGENT IN THE WORLD.
AGAINST HER, VIPER DOESN'T HAVE A PRAYER.
YOU'RE BEATEN, VIPER.
AM I?
HOW. SO, WIDOW, WHEN, IN A MATTER OF SECONDS, THE HELI-CARRIER WILL UTTERLY DESTROY THE CAPITOL BUILDING?
BEFORE THAT HAPPENS, THOUGH--
--I'LL GIVE MYSELF THE SATIS-FACTION OF RIPPING THE LIVING HEART FROM YOUR BREAST WITH MY BARE HANDS!
FURY--WE'RE OUT OF TIME!
THEN CROSS YOUR FINGERS, KID--
--'CAUSE HERE GOES NOTHING!

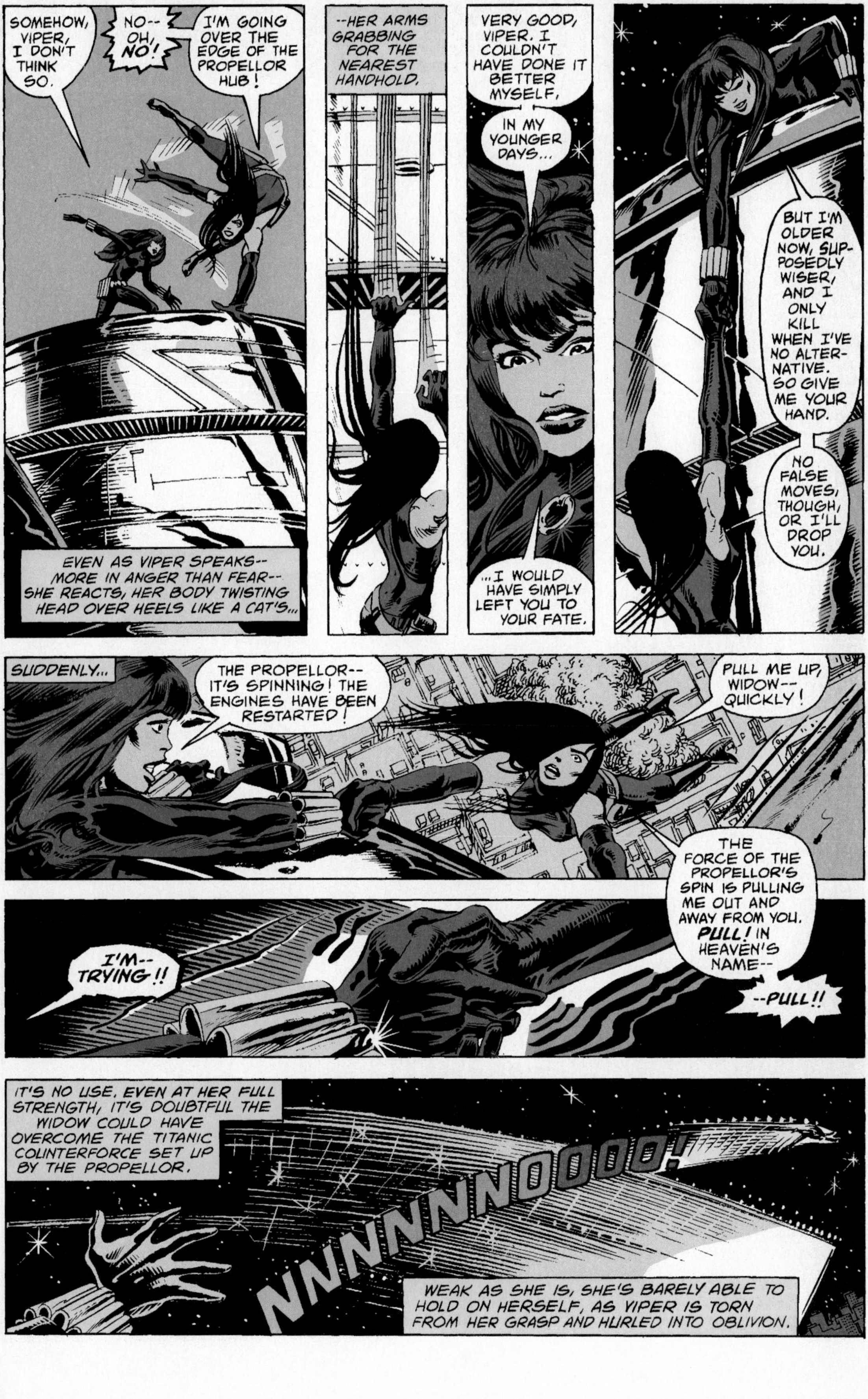
SOMEHOW, VIPER, I DON'T THINK SO.
NO-- OH, NO!
I'M GOING OVER THE EDGE OF THE PROPELLOR HUB!
EVEN AS VIPER SPEAKS-- MORE IN ANGER THAN FEAR-- SHE REACTS, HER BODY TWISTING HEAD OVER HEELS LIKE A CAT'S...
--HER ARMS GRABBING FOR THE NEAREST HANDHOLD.
VERY GOOD, VIPER. I COULDN'T HAVE DONE IT BETTER MYSELF,
IN MY YOUNGER DAYS...
...I WOULD HAVE SIMPLY LEFT YOU TO YOUR FATE.
BUT I'M OLDER NOW, SUPPOSEDLY WISER, AND I ONLY KILL WHEN I'VE NO ALTERNATIVE. SO GIVE ME YOUR HAND.
NO FALSE MOVES, THOUGH, OR I'LL DROP YOU.
SUDDENLY...
THE PROPELLOR-- IT'S SPINNING! THE ENGINES HAVE BEEN RESTARTED!
PULL ME UP, WIDOW-- QUICKLY!
THE FORCE OF THE PROPELLOR'S SPIN IS PULLING ME OUT AND AWAY FROM YOU. PULL! IN HEAVEN'S NAME--
I'M-- TRYING!!
--PULL!!
IT'S NO USE. EVEN AT HER FULL STRENGTH, IT'S DOUBTFUL THE WIDOW COULD HAVE OVERCOME THE TITANIC COUNTERFORCE SET UP BY THE PROPELLOR.
NNNNNNNOOOOO!
WEAK AS SHE IS, SHE'S BARELY ABLE TO HOLD ON HERSELF, AS VIPER IS TORN FROM HER GRASP AND HURLED INTO OBLIVION.

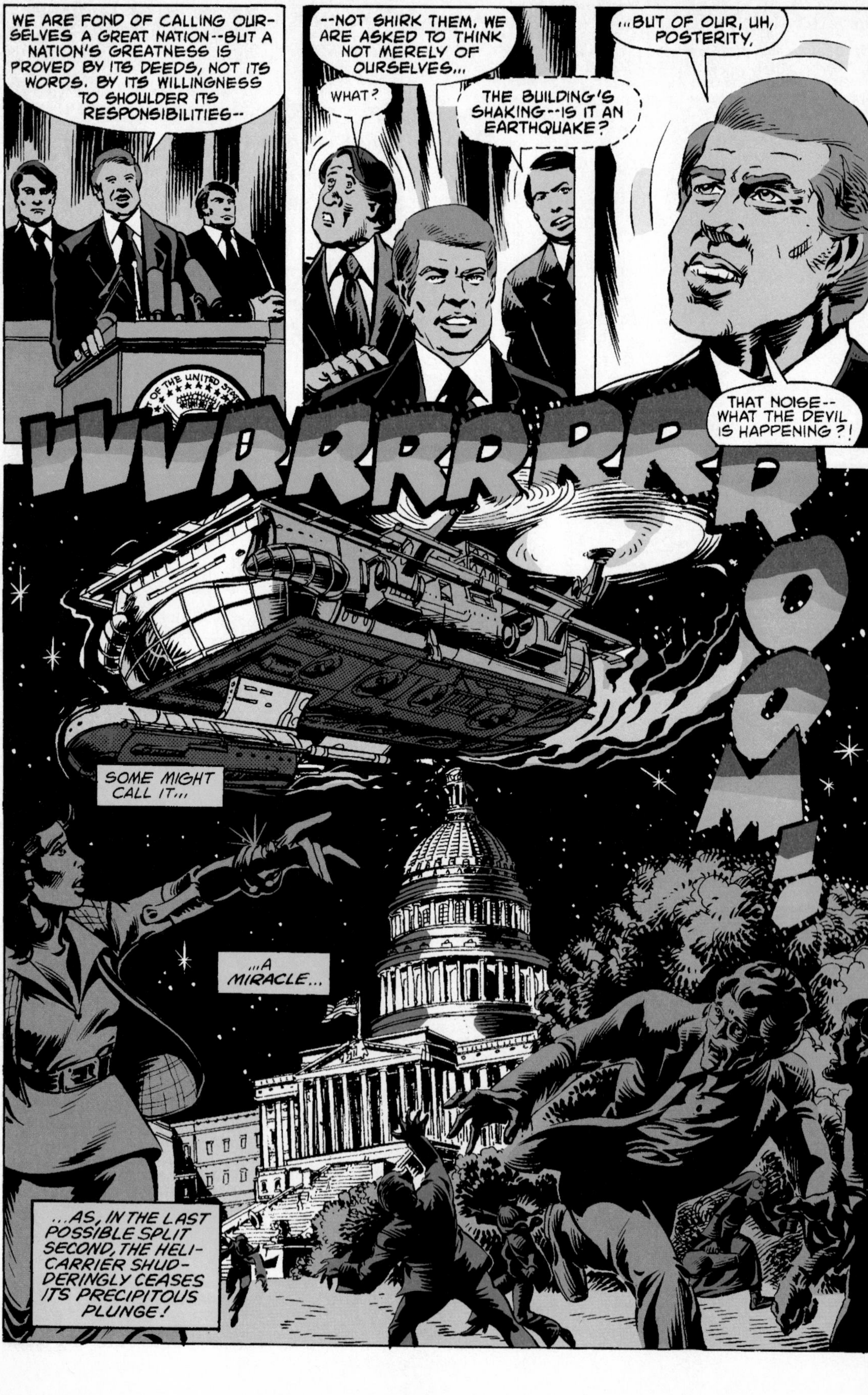
WE ARE FOND OF CALLING OURSELVES A GREAT NATION--BUT A NATION'S GREATNESS IS PROVED BY ITS DEEDS, NOT ITS WORDS. BY ITS WILLINGNESS TO SHOULDER ITS RESPONSIBILITIES--
--NOT SHIRK THEM. WE ARE ASKED TO THINK NOT MERELY OF OURSELVES...
WHAT?
THE BUILDING'S SHAKING--IS IT AN EARTHQUAKE?
...BUT OF OUR, UH, POSTERITY,
THAT NOISE-- WHAT THE DEVIL IS HAPPENING?!
VVVRRRRRRROOOM!
SOME MIGHT CALL IT...
...A MIRACLE...
...AS, IN THE LAST POSSIBLE SPLIT SECOND, THE HELI-CARRIER SHUDDERINGLY CEASES ITS PRECIPITOUS PLUNGE!

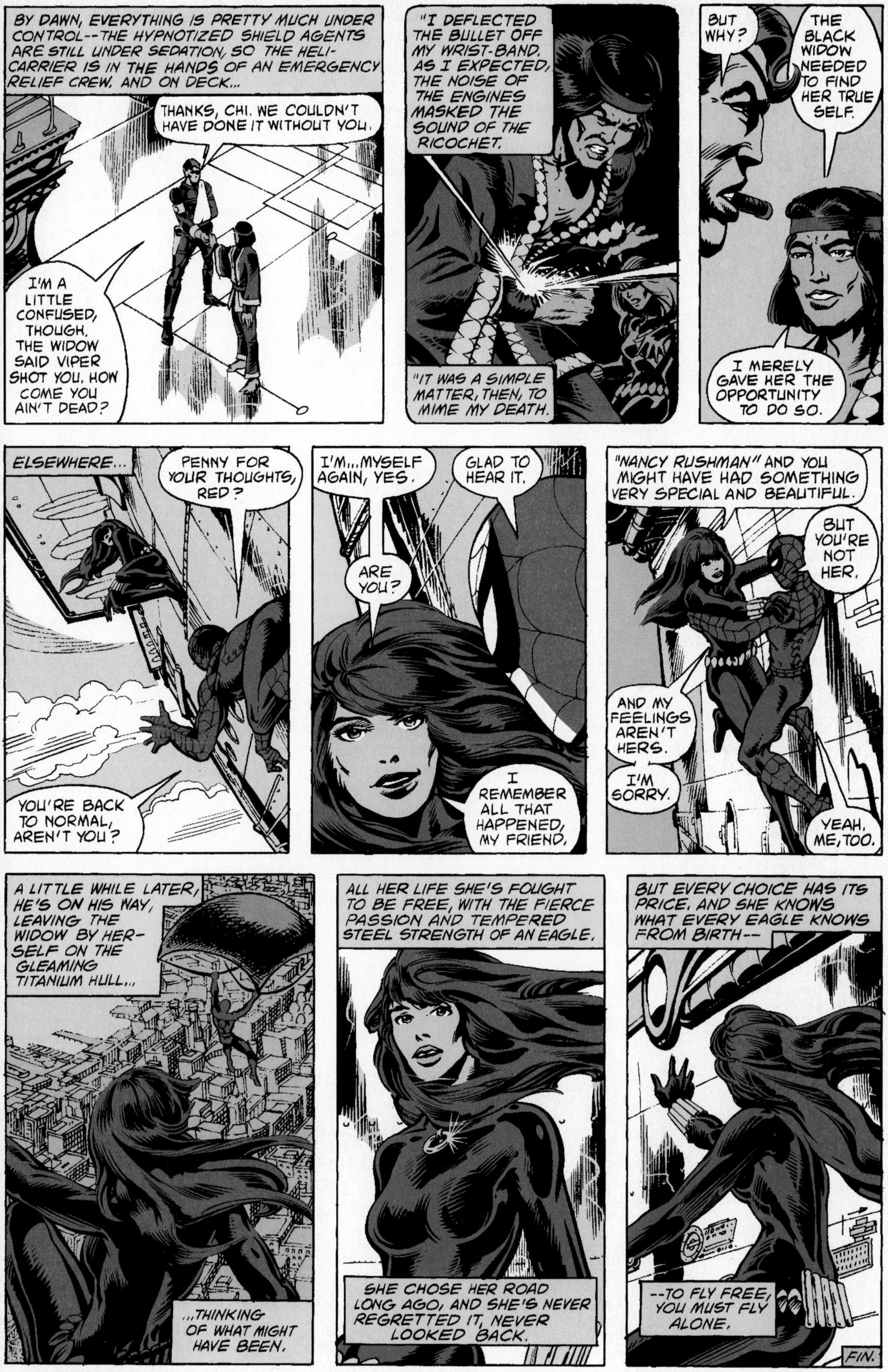

BY DAWN, EVERYTHING IS PRETTY MUCH UNDER CONTROL--THE HYPNOTIZED SHIELD AGENTS ARE STILL UNDER SEDATION, SO THE HELI-CARRIER IS IN THE HANDS OF AN EMERGENCY RELIEF CREW, AND ON DECK...
THANKS, CHI. WE COULDN'T HAVE DONE IT WITHOUT YOU.
I'M A LITTLE CONFUSED, THOUGH. THE WIDOW SAID VIPER SHOT YOU. HOW COME YOU AIN'T DEAD?
"I DEFLECTED THE BULLET OFF MY WRIST-BAND, AS I EXPECTED, THE NOISE OF THE ENGINES MASKED THE SOUND OF THE RICOCHET.
"IT WAS A SIMPLE MATTER, THEN, TO MIME MY DEATH.
BUT WHY?
THE BLACK WIDOW NEEDED TO FIND HER TRUE SELF.
I MERELY GAVE HER THE OPPORTUNITY TO DO SO.
ELSEWHERE...
PENNY FOR YOUR THOUGHTS, RED?
YOU'RE BACK TO NORMAL, AREN'T YOU?
I'M...MYSELF AGAIN, YES.
GLAD TO HEAR IT.
ARE YOU?
I REMEMBER ALL THAT HAPPENED, MY FRIEND.
"NANCY RUSHMAN" AND YOU MIGHT HAVE HAD SOMETHING VERY SPECIAL AND BEAUTIFUL.
BUT YOU'RE NOT HER.
AND MY FEELINGS AREN'T HERS.
I'M SORRY.
YEAH, ME, TOO.
A LITTLE WHILE LATER, HE'S ON HIS WAY, LEAVING THE WIDOW BY HER-SELF ON THE GLEAMING TITANIUM HULL...
...THINKING OF WHAT MIGHT HAVE BEEN.
ALL HER LIFE SHE'S FOUGHT TO BE FREE, WITH THE FIERCE PASSION AND TEMPERED STEEL STRENGTH OF AN EAGLE.
SHE CHOSE HER ROAD LONG AGO, AND SHE'S NEVER REGRETTED IT, NEVER LOOKED BACK.
BUT EVERY CHOICE HAS ITS PRICE, AND SHE KNOWS WHAT EVERY EAGLE KNOWS FROM BIRTH--
--TO FLY FREE, YOU MUST FLY ALONE.
FIN.

LORD SHINGEN

REAL NAME: Shingen Harada
ALIASES: Shingen Yashida
IDENTITY: No dual identity
OCCUPATION: Former Clan Yashida oyabun, professional criminal
CITIZENSHIP: Japan
PLACE OF BIRTH: Presumably the Yashida ancestral stronghold near Agarashima, Japan
KNOWN RELATIVES: Mariko Yashida (daughter, deceased), Kenuichio Harada (Silver Samurai, son, deceased), Shingen "Shin" Harada (Silver Samurai, grandson), Saburo and Tomo Yoshida (cousins, deceased), Shiro Yoshida (Sunfire, first cousin once removed), Leyu Yoshida (Sunpyre, first cousin once removed, deceased), Yoshi's unidentified mother (possible first cousin), Yoshi (last name unrevealed, possible first cousin once removed, deceased), Ichiro and Fukuko (last name unrevealed, possible niece and nephew), Rikuto (last name unrevealed, possible first grandnephew, deceased), Hoken Yashida (ancestor, deceased), Noburu-Hideki (son-in-law, deceased)
GROUP AFFILIATION: Clan Yashida, Yakuza
EDUCATION: Unrevealed
FIRST APPEARANCE: (Mentioned, unidentified) Daredevil #111 (1974); (full) Wolverine #1 (1982)

HISTORY: Shingen Harada was the head of Clan Yashida, a powerful, 2000-year old Japanese family. Believing his family's claim on the Imperial throne was as legitimate as the Emperor's, he joined the Yakuza intending to unite Japan's criminal underworld and control Japan. Presumably to facilitate this, Shingen disappeared during his daughter Mariko's childhood and was believed dead, though he maintained contact with his illegitimate son, Kenuichio, to whom Shingen promised clan control; a mutant, Kenuichio eventually became the Silver Samurai. Over a few decades, Shingen eliminated rival crimelords, using Hand ninjas and the mercenary assassin Yukio. At some point he incurred a debt to the criminal Mandrill (Jerome Beechman) that the Silver Samurai later repaid, perhaps at Shingen's behest.

Ultimately, Shingen's sole remaining rivals were the elderly grand oyabun ("father") Nabatone Yokuse, who Shingen felt no need to slay, and the well-protected Katsuyori. The now-adult Mariko was romantically involved with Canadian mutant Wolverine (Logan/James Howlett), and Shingen, believing Logan could get to Katsuyori if suitably motivated, reclaimed his leadership of Clan Yashida and insisted Mariko marry the abusive Noburu-Hideki, allegedly to clear another obligation Shingen had incurred. When Mariko ended their relationship without

explanation, Logan snuck into the Yashida Clan's stronghold and learned of her plight, but was rendered unconscious with poisoned shuriken by the unseen Yukio. When Logan awoke, Shingen challenged him to a duel to prove Logan unworthy of his daughter. Shingen chose bokken, wooden training swords, for the battle, but targeted Logan's nerve clusters, giving Logan the impression Shingen was fighting lethally. As anticipated, Logan unsheathed his Adamantium claws before realizing the observing Mariko, unaware of Shingen's lethal efforts, believed Logan had dishonored himself, resorting to deadly force simply because he was losing. Easily defeating the drugged and disheartened Logan, Shingen cast him out, then sent Yukio to befriend him. Unaware of Yukio's employment, Logan defended her from Shingen-sent Hand ninjas, and fell for her claim that Katsuyori had sent the ninjas. Shingen then lured Katsuyori to a peace conference, sending Mariko and Noburu as his envoys; though willing to place his daughter in jeopardy, Shingen warned Yukio of dire consequences should Mariko be harmed. Katsuyori also broke the truce, and while Logan protected Mariko from Katsuyori's assassins, Yukio slew Katsuyori. Having fallen in love with Logan, Yukio declined Shingen's order to slay him and defeated more Shingen-sent Hand agents. However, Logan then uncovered Yukio's true alliance, and she fled. Having learned of Shingen's criminal ambitions, Logan targeted his operations, knowing the gangs would not follow a leader they neither feared nor respected. To redeem herself in Logan's eyes, Yukio tried to kill Shingen, but he easily defeated her; Logan's timely arrival to fight Shingen anew saved her life. Though Shingen delivered better strikes, Logan's Adamantium protected him until he stabbed Shingen's face, killing him. Meanwhile, Yukio slew Noburu while aiding Logan; realizing her father's deceptions and Logan's true honor, Mariko resumed her relationship with Logan.

Logan subsequently encountered Shingen's spirit leading Logan's slain foes in a purgatory-like realm. Later, after she too came into conflict with Logan, Hand priestess Phaedra apparently resurrected Shingen and became his lover. Shingen battled Logan when he tracked Phaedra, but Logan again stabbed Shingen's face and slew Phaedra; but after he departed, Shingen rose to his feet and took the protective helmet from Shogun, a suit of armor Phaedra had previously animated with a stolen fragment of Logan's soul. Despite this, when Logan was later temporarily sent to an unidentified Hell realm, he again encountered Shingen amidst an army of his former foes.

NOTE: *Lord Shingen has been intermittently referred to as both Shingen Harada and Shingen Yashida; it is believed that Shingen Harada is his true name, and Shingen Yashida an alias, though explanations/arguments exist for both this and vice versa. Though Logan has twice met what appears to be Shingen's spirit, he may have been hallucinating, facing shapeshifting demons or their illusions, or he may have encountered soul fragments, broken off from the main soul by near-death experiences.*

CLAN YASHIDA CREST

HEIGHT: 5' 10"
WEIGHT: 185 lbs.
EYES: Brown
HAIR: Bald (formerly black)

ABILITIES/ACCESSORIES: Shingen was a master swordsman and martial artist, able to target nerve clusters to paralyze or kill. He was at least bilingual, speaking both his native Japanese and flawless English, and was a cunning manipulator.

POWER GRID	1	2	3	4	5	6	7
INTELLIGENCE							
STRENGTH							
SPEED							
DURABILITY							
ENERGY PROJECTION							
FIGHTING SKILLS							

ART BY HOWARD CHAYKIN

HISTORY: The mutant son of Japanese crimelord Shingen Harada, Kenuichio Harada mastered the fighting techniques and honor code of the Japanese samurai, but instead became a criminal when he found himself forced to repay an unspecified honor debt his father owed the criminal Mandrill (Jerome Beechman). Harada was next employed in various plots by the terrorist Viper (Ophelia Sarkissian), starting a long professional and personal relationship with her. After learning of his father's death, and that his half-sister Mariko had become Clan Yashida's oyabun ("father") — a title Harada sought himself — he and Viper tried to seize control of the Clan, but after clashes with the ronin Yukio and Mariko's lover Wolverine (Logan/James Howlett), Mariko declared Harada an unworthy criminal. Despite repeated attempts to take over the Clan, Harada was eventually forgiven by Mariko and accepted as her heir. Harada worked with Wolverine on a few occasions and became master of Muramasa's Black Blade, a sword mystically imbued with its creator's madness; Harada was somehow unaffected by this curse. When Mariko sought to divest Clan Yashida of its criminal holdings, an attack from Matsuo Tsurayaba's Hand sect forced Harada to ally with Wolverine and his fellow X-Man Gambit (Remy LeBeau) to repel them, but they were unable to stop Matsuo from fatally poisoning Mariko; Harada subsequently became Clan leader. In exchange for the Clan's Honor Sword, Harada ensured the welfare of Wolverine's ward Amiko Kobayashi.

After briefly leading Japanese super-team Big Hero 6, Harada temporarily lost control of Clan Yashida to the Mongolian Kaishek family. A disgraced Harada returned to mercenary life and sought status and power among the criminal underworld. When the mutant Blindspot erased his memories, Harada renamed himself the Silver Shogun and slew the heads of Tokyo's Yakuza clans as part of his plan to become Tokyo's new oyabun. Later, the peacekeeping agency SHIELD kidnapped Harada (calling himself the Silver Samurai again) from his private plane and imprisoned him in the super-villain prison the Raft, but he escaped during a mass break-out and reunited with Viper, who sought an alliance between her terrorist Hydra organization and the Hand ninja clan; Harada declined to become involved with either group. After aiding X-Man Kitty Pryde and the Japanese Department of Supernatural Sciences (JDSS) in defeating the Path of Destiny ninja cult, Harada's left hand was severed during a conflict with Wolverine. Sometime later, Harada briefly stood with the heroic Avengers in opposition to the Hand, and, though she still loved him,

SILVER SAMURAI

REAL NAME: Kenuichio "Ken" Harada
ALIASES: Silver Shogun, Samurai, "Sammy," "Kenny"
IDENTITY: Known to some Japanese government officials and international law enforcement agencies
OCCUPATION: Former Clan Yashida oyabun, bodyguard, government operative, mercenary
CITIZENSHIP: Japan, international criminal record
PLACE OF BIRTH: Agarashima, Japan
KNOWN RELATIVES: Shingen "Shin" Harada (son), Shingen Harada (father, deceased), Mariko Yashida (half-sister, deceased), Ichiro and Fukuko (last name unrevealed, possible first cousins), Rikuto (last name unrevealed, possible first cousin once removed, deceased), Saburo and Tomo Yoshida (first cousins once removed, deceased), Yoshi's unidentified mother (possible first cousin once removed), Yoshi (last name unrevealed, possible second cousin, deceased), Shiro Yoshida (Sunfire, second cousin), Leyu Yoshida (Sunpyre, second cousin, deceased), Hoken Yashida (ancestor, deceased), Noboru-Hideki (brother-in-law, deceased)
GROUP AFFILIATION: Japanese government, Clan Yashida; formerly Big Hero 6, Legion Accursed; former ally of Viper/Madame Hydra, Mandrill's Black Spectre
EDUCATION: Unspecified undergraduate degree
FIRST APPEARANCE: Daredevil #111 (1974)

Viper left Harada to honor her ties with Hydra and blackmailed Clan Yashida into an alliance by abducting their families. With Wolverine's aid, Harada later ended Clan Yashida's ongoing dealings with the Hand then trained Wolverine in sword combat in return. Harada was later fatally attacked by the Black Samurai, a group sent by Wolverine's vengeful Red Right Hand (RRH) enemies, and died at Mariko's grave. Later, in an unidentified Hell realm, the "Devil" crushed Harada's soul when he tried to aid Wolverine, whose soul the RRH had temporarily sent there during their plot to murder those Wolverine cared for. Harada's son, Shin, continues the Silver Samurai's legacy.

HEIGHT: 6'6"   **EYES:** Brown
WEIGHT: 250 lbs.; (armored) 310 lbs.   **HAIR:** Black

ABILITIES/ACCESSORIES: The Silver Samurai generated a tachyon energy field from within his body that he typically focused through his sword, allowing it to cut through almost any substance except Adamantium. He was a master of kenjutsu (Japanese swordsmanship), an expert in bushidō (the history and customs of the samurai class), and was also a highly skilled martial arts master. He wore a suit of lightweight steel alloy plate body armor, designed to resemble ancient samurai garb and with enough articulation so as to not impede his movements. He wielded a traditional samurai long sword (katana) as well as a companion sword (wakizashi), and has previously wielded both Muramasa's Black Blade and Clan Yashida's Honor Sword. On occasion he used shuriken and other traditional samurai weaponry. He previously employed a teleportation ring given to him by Viper that was activated when twisted.

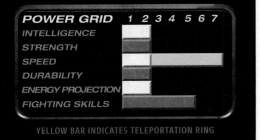

POWER GRID	1	2	3	4	5	6	7
INTELLIGENCE							
STRENGTH							
SPEED							
DURABILITY							
ENERGY PROJECTION							
FIGHTING SKILLS							

YELLOW BAR INDICATES TELEPORTATION RING

ART BY DEREC DONOVAN WITH PAUL SMITH (INSET)

VIPER

REAL NAME: Ophelia Sarkissian
ALIASES: Madame Hydra, Madame Viper, White Warrior Princess, White Princess, Leona Hiss, Mrs. Smith, Meriem Drew, Supreme Hydra
IDENTITY: Secret
OCCUPATION: Terrorist, subversive, mercenary; former ruler, smuggler
CITIZENSHIP: Hungary; internationally wanted criminal with record in USA and Bulgaria
PLACE OF BIRTH: Székesfehérvár, Hungary
KNOWN RELATIVES: Unidentified parents (deceased), unidentified sisters (presumably deceased), Logan/James Howlett (Wolverine, ex-husband)
GROUP AFFILIATION: Hydra; formerly HAMMER, Hellfire Club Inner Circle, her own terrorist organization, Secret Empire, Fangs, Save Our Society, Serpent Society, two Serpent Squads
EDUCATION: Unrevealed
FIRST APPEARANCE: (Madame Hydra) Captain America #110 (1969); (Viper) Captain America #180 (1974)

HISTORY: Ophelia Sarkissian survived a nightmarish youth in Hungary, where her parents died and her sisters were defiled and discarded during a revolution, but an accident severely scarred the right side of her face as she escaped across the border; she began hiding this side of her face under her hair and learned to not fear death. During adolescence she trained under Hydra's Kraken (Thomas Whitehall), lived by her wits and excelled at crime, becoming the freelance mercenary Viper. Mentored by diminutive adventurer Seraph of the crime-ridden island nation Madripoor, Viper aided Seraph and Logan (James Howlett; later Wolverine) against the mutant Sabretooth (Victor Creed) who grievously wounded Seraph, though Viper got her allies home. Seemingly dying, Seraph made Logan promise to fulfill a future wish of Viper's. A leading international espionage criminal by age thirty, Viper joined the terrorist group Hydra. After Viper arranged for Hydra founder Baron (Wolfgang) von Strucker and his elite to die during Hydra Island's destruction, Viper eliminated her remaining superiors and became Supreme Hydra, aka Madame Hydra, leader of Hydra's New York operations. She adopted green costuming and

cosmetics symbolizing her Hydra leadership. Madame Hydra clashed with adventurers such as Captain America (Steve Rogers) and his fellow Avengers until time-spanning Immortus' shape-shifting operative the Space Phantom trapped Madame Hydra in timeless Limbo and replaced her as the new Supreme Hydra. Eventually returning to Earth, the shaken former Madame Hydra now wanted to destroy the world rather than rule it. She agreed to help Atlantean warlord Krang and serpentine Elder God Set conquer Earth and she reassembled the snake-inspired criminal group Serpent Squad, killing its founder Viper (Jordan Dixon/ Stryke) and reclaiming the Viper identity. The Nomad (Steve Rogers in a brief alternate identity) foiled their plans. Japanese Red Army cadre leader Ishiro Tagara recruited Viper and became her first love, then helped her form her own terrorist army. Tagara soon introduced her to the Silver Samurai (Kenuichio Harada), who became her enforcer and confidant.

Viper later clashed with the peacekeeping agency SHIELD, the mutant X-Men (whose numbers included Wolverine) and other heroes, notably ex-Hydra agent Spider-Woman (Jessica Drew). A spell cast by Drew's foe Morgan Le Fay tricked Viper into believing she was Drew's mother. These false memories wore off but Viper has shown continued interest in Spider-Woman, repeatedly trying to recruit her back into Hydra. At some point, Viper apparently underwent cosmetic surgery or began using technology to appear unscarred and gradually turned from nihilism to pursuit of power. She later used Seraph's dying wish to make Wolverine marry her, but soon after she became Madripoor's ruler, Wolverine forced her to grant him a divorce. Avenger Iron Man (Tony Stark) helped rival crime lord Tyger Tiger overthrow Viper and replace her as Madripoor's ruler. Again leading a Hydra faction, Viper reluctantly cooperated with fellow factional leaders including a new Madame Hydra (Valentina de Fontaine), who betrayed the organization and fatally shot Viper. Apparently resurrected by Hydra's monstrous Hive and bonded with a squid-like creature in the process, Viper reclaimed the Madame Hydra alias. Corrupt politician Norman Osborn soon re-formed his disbanded intelligence agency HAMMER, while backed by factions of the anarchistic AIM (Advanced Idea Mechanics), the ninja Hand and Hydra, the latter led by Madame Hydra, HAMMER scientists Superia (Dr. Deidre Wentworth) and Dr. Carolina Washington removed the squid-like entity from Madame Hydra, restoring her normal appearance. HAMMER tried to take over the USA, but the Avengers defeated them. Having anticipated the unstable Osborn's downfall, Madame Hydra escaped and expanded her Hydra faction using HAMMER resources, notably genetically modified super-soldiers. She has since clashed with SHIELD, the Avengers and the X-Men.

BATTLE ARMOR

HEIGHT: 5'9"	**EYES:** Green	
WEIGHT: 140 lbs.	**HAIR:** Black (usually dyed green)	

ABILITIES/ACCESSORIES: Viper is an Olympic-level athlete, a formidable martial artist and a skilled marksman proficient with firearms, knives and whips. A gifted intellect, actress, master of disguise, strategist, combat tactician and organizer, she is also a charismatic leader. She uses paralytic and/or lethal snake venoms in darts, lipstick and her own fang-capped canine teeth, having developed immunity to such venoms herself. Her high-tech arsenal includes body armor, energy pistols, force fields and her personal teleportation ring; she has access to Hydra's extensive weaponry and technology.

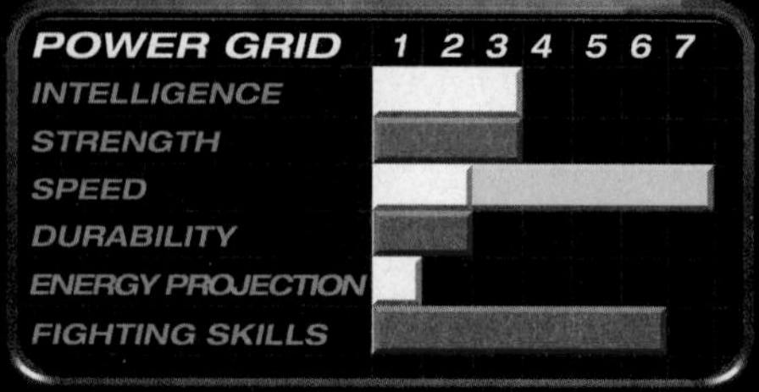

POWER GRID	1	2	3	4	5	6	7
INTELLIGENCE							
STRENGTH							
SPEED							
DURABILITY							
ENERGY PROJECTION							
FIGHTING SKILLS							

YELLOW BAR INDICATES TELEPORTATION RING

ART BY DAVID FINCH WITH DAVID MARQUEZ (INSET)

HISTORY: Born to Canadians John and Elizabeth Howlett toward the end of the 19th century, sickly and frail James Howlett was often neglected by his mother, who had been traumatized due to the death of her first son; James grew up unaware that his mother's brothers (the Hudsons) secretly served shadowy millennia-old crimelord Romulus. As a child, James befriended a young girl named Rose O'Hara, and Dog, son of groundskeeper Thomas Logan; James was unaware Thomas was also his true father. When Thomas killed John in front of James, the shock triggered James' mutant claws to manifest. In a fury, James killed Thomas and slashed Dog's face. Driven away by Elizabeth, James and Rose fled; James' healing factor repressed his traumatic memories, leaving him partially amnesiac. The two found work at a quarry, where Rose gave James the alias "Logan." James gradually fell in love with Rose but became more violent as his healing factor, heightened senses and agility manifested; the quarry workers nicknamed him "Wolverine." Years later, when Dog confronted Logan, Rose was killed when she was accidentally impaled on Logan's claws. A grief-stricken Logan lived in the wilderness in a feral state for a time, his mind retreating deeper into amnesia, possibly enhanced by the mental manipulations of Romulus, who desired Logan as a pawn.

Over time, Logan largely reclaimed his humanity and reentered civilization, unknowingly constantly observed by Romulus. While working as a mercenary in Japan, Logan first encountered Sabretooth (Victor Creed), a similarly empowered mutant Romulus operative; the two earned each other's enmity. However, sometime later, amnesiac once more and living in Canada with a young Blackfoot woman named Silver Fox, Logan befriended Sabretooth, who, presumably under Romulus' orders, raped and seemingly murdered Silver Fox on Logan's birthday. A subsequent battle left Logan near-death and mentally manipulated by Romulus to believe anyone Logan ever loved would die horribly. Logan then fought in World War I, traveled through Canada, Japan and Mexico, and was a criminal throughout the 1920s.

ART BY JOHN CASSADAY

In the 1930s, Wolverine romanced the diminutive Seraph and trained for years as a samurai under sorcerer and soldier Ogun in Japan. Logan began suspecting others around him, including Seraph, reported to a singular authority, but did not investigate further. After serving in the Spanish Civil War and studying espionage for two years, Logan joined the Canadian military to fight in World War II, all the while being directed by Seraph, who secretly served Romulus. During the war, Logan encountered Captain America (Steve Rogers) and Bucky (James Barnes). Following the war, Logan found peace when he married a Japanese woman named Itsu, who was expecting their first child when Bucky, now the brainwashed Winter Soldier, murdered Itsu under orders from Romulus. Unknown to Logan, the child survived but fell under Romulus' influence. This child, called later "Daken," meaning "Mongrel," was fed lies about Logan for years, resulting in deep loathing toward the father he'd never known.

Logan returned to mercenary work but, possibly under Romulus' orders, eventually joined Weapon X (the tenth iteration of the Captain America-creating Weapon Plus Program)'s Team X and began using the Wolverine codename. Sabretooth and Silver Fox joined as well; Weapon X removed their memories of each other and mentally manipulated them. Fox soon betrayed the team to join the terrorist Hydra organization; Sabretooth began a macabre "tradition" of attacking Wolverine on his birthday. Shot with Carbonadium bullets to slow his healing factor so either Romulus or Weapon X could determine lethal failsafes against him, Wolverine briefly regained many of his memories.

ART BY FRANK CHO

WOLVERINE

REAL NAME: James Howlett

ALIASES: Logan, "Wolvie," "Runt"; formerly Patient X, Death, Weapon Ten, Patch, "Canucklehead," Weapon X, Experiment X, many others

IDENTITY: Known to certain government agencies

OCCUPATION: Adventurer, headmaster; former instructor, spy, government operative, mercenary, bartender, bouncer, criminal, enforcer, fur trapper, soldier, sailor, miner, many others

CITIZENSHIP: Canada, possible dual citizenship in Japan and/or Madripoor

PLACE OF BIRTH: Alberta, Canada

KNOWN RELATIVES: Itsu (wife, deceased), Akihiro (Daken, son, deceased), William Downing (Gunhawk, son, deceased), Cannonfoot, Saw Fist (real names unrevealed, sons, deceased), Fire Knives, Shadow Stalker (real names unrevealed, daughters, deceased), Erista (son), unborn child by Native (presumed deceased), Amiko Kobayashi (foster daughter), Thomas Logan (father, deceased), Elizabeth Hudson Howlett (mother, deceased), John Howlett Sr. (adoptive father, deceased), John Howlett Jr. (half-brother, deceased), Dog Logan (half-brother), two unidentified uncles (deceased), unidentified paternal grandparents (deceased), unidentified maternal grandparents (deceased), Elias Hudson, Frederick Hudson (uncles, deceased), Frederick Hudson II, Truett Hudson, Victor Hudson (cousins, deceased), James Hudson (Guardian, cousin), Heather Hudson (Vindicator, cousin), Claire MacNeil Hudson (cousin once removed), Folkbern Logan (alleged ancestor, deceased), X-23 (Laura Kinney, clone), Shogun (soul fragment, deceased), Ophelia Sarkissian (Viper/Madame Hydra, ex-wife), others

GROUP AFFILIATION: Avengers, X-Men; formerly X-Force (clandestine), X-Force (X-Men strikeforce), Clan Yashida, Department H, Flight, Department K, Team X, Weapon X, Romulus' criminal empire, others

EDUCATION: Privately tutored as a child, extensive training in multiple disciplines

FIRST APPEARANCE: Incredible Hulk #180 (1974); (as Patch, unidentified) Marvel Comics Presents #1 (1988); (as Patch, identified) Marvel Comics Presents #9 (1988); (as Death) Astonishing X-Men #1 (1999)

ORIGINAL
DEPT. H
COSTUME

ART BY PACO DIAZ LUQUE

Wolverine eventually resigned from Team X and joined the Canadian Defense Ministry, where he worked for years. He briefly teamed with Sabretooth to gather and tutor young mutants, but the US Government's prototype Sentinels wiped out this ad hoc group, depressing Wolverine deeply.

Following his Ministry partner Neil Langram's death, Wolverine fell further into depression, turning to drugs and alcohol. Soon after, he was captured by Weapon X, where Truett Hudson (aka Professor Andre Thorton, secretly Logan's cousin), possibly under orders from Romulus, subjected Wolverine to inhumane experimentation to turn him into a "killing machine" by bonding the indestructible Adamantium metal to his bones and claws and brainwashing him further. After brutal testing and research, Wolverine broke free and in a fury, slew nearly everyone at the Weapon X facility. In a feral state, Wolverine lived in the Canadian Rockies for months, cohabitating with a female Weapon X escapee called Native; at some point, Weapon X secretly used Wolverine's DNA to clone him, creating X-23 (Laura Kinney), a female assassin. Wolverine was eventually found by James and Heather Hudson and returned to humanity, both men unaware they were cousins. However, Wolverine was horrified by his Adamantium claws, memories of his natural claws lost in his amnesia. He later joined Department H, the superhuman-oriented government agency Hudson headed. Dept. H helped restore much of Wolverine's memories, but many holes remained. As Weapon X, Wolverine returned to espionage.

In recent years, Wolverine was asked to lead the Flight, a public super-team, and was given his distinctive yellow-and-blue costume for the role. When Seraph was seemingly fatally wounded by Sabretooth, her dying wish was that Wolverine promise to help her student Viper (Ophelia Sarkissian) in the future, no questions asked; Wolverine agreed. When the Hulk (Bruce Banner) arrived in Canada, Wolverine was instructed by Romulus to battle the Hulk alone, but he was soundly defeated. Eventually, fighting romantic feelings for Heather, Wolverine resigned to accept Professor Charles Xavier's offer to join a new iteration of his mutant X-Men; a request Romulus had anticipated even prior to Wolverine's battle with the Hulk. After joining the X-Men, Xavier telepathically broke Romulus' hold on Wolverine without ever learning Romulus' identity. The brusque Wolverine repeatedly clashed with X-Men leader Cyclops (Scott Summers), secretly fell deeply in love with Cyclops' lover Jean Grey, became close with his teammates, especially Nightcrawler (Kurt Wagner) and Storm (Ororo Munroe), and grew to believe in the X-Men's goal of human/mutant coexistence. In Japan with the X-Men, Wolverine met Mariko Yashida and gradually fell in love with her. After a battle-suited Hudson and Alpha Flight (formerly the Flight) unsuccessfully attempted to retrieve Wolverine,

Jean Grey was supposedly killed, devastating Wolverine and the X-Men. Wolverine soon made peace with Alpha Flight.

When Wolverine learned Mariko's crimelord father and Clan Yashida leader, Lord Shingen Harada, had forced her to marry criminal Noburu-Hideki, a prolonged series of confrontations between Shingen, his hired assassin Yukio and Wolverine ultimately resulted in Shingen and Noburu dead; Mariko declared Wolverine her champion and the two became engaged. However, X-Men foe Mastermind (Jason Wyngarde) mentally manipulated Mariko into calling off the wedding and renewing the clan's criminal ties. When she regained her senses, Wolverine offered to break those ties, but Mariko insisted on accomplishing this herself so she could regain her honor and be worthy of marrying Wolverine; the two later became foster parents to a Japanese girl named Amiko Kobayashi when a battle left her mother dead. When Wolverine's sensei Ogun, now corrupted by black magic, tried to mystically corrupt young X-Man Kitty Pryde, Wolverine instructed her in Samurai training, establishing a deep bond between the two; Wolverine was forced to kill Ogun to save Pryde. When Wolverine caught Jean Grey's scent, he feared he was going insane, but later learned of her true survival. After a televised battle left the world believing them dead, the X-Men went underground for a time. During a visit to the Savage Land, Wolverine romanced tribeswoman Gahck, who later gave birth to Erista, Wolverine's son.

Sometime later, when cyborg Reavers captured and tortured Wolverine, he was rescued by teen mutant Jubilee (Jubilation Lee), who became his constant sidekick. After numerous X-Men and solo operations, Wolverine returned to Japan to assist Mariko against assaults on her clan from within and without. When she was poisoned with fatal blowfish toxin, Mariko begged Wolverine for a quick death, which he reluctantly granted her with his claws; Wolverine eventually entrusted Amiko to now-ally Yukio. Not long after, Wolverine encountered Silver Fox again, this time remembering her, shortly before she was killed by Sabretooth. During a battle between the X-Men and their archenemy Magneto (Max Eisenhardt), Wolverine's Adamantium was forcibly extracted, a painful event that helped Wolverine rediscover his bone claws; a later forcible attempt to return the metal to his skeleton left him feral for a time. Viper returned to Wolverine's life, demanding he marry her so she could use her married status to gain the throne of the island nation Madripoor; Wolverine later forced her to divorce him. X-Men foe Apocalypse (En Sabah Nur) forcibly re-grafted the Adamantium to Wolverine's bones and brainwashed him into becoming his servant Death until the X-Men helped him regain his identity and rejoin the team. But when Jean Grey was slain in battle, Wolverine was devastated once more. After this, Wolverine and Native conceived a child, but Sabretooth apparently killed her to spite Wolverine; presumably the embryo did not survive as well. Wolverine soon met his clone, X-23, ultimately becoming a mentor to her when she attended Charles Xavier's school for mutants.

When Hand ninjas and terrorist Hydra organization killed and resurrected Wolverine as a mind-controlled assassin, Hand mystic Phaedra secretly retained a fragment of Wolverine's soul. After committing a series of bloody attacks on the superhuman community, Wolverine was captured and gradually freed from the brainwashing; after which, needing someone to cross lines they could not, Earth's premiere super-team, the Avengers, recruited Wolverine into their ranks. Following a reality manipulation by the insane Scarlet Witch (Wanda Maximoff), Wolverine's complete memories were restored; additionally, all but a few hundred mutants were stripped of their mutant abilities. Horrified by the memories of the pain inflicted on him by others, but still unaware of Romulus' identity, Wolverine began investigating the man who had manipulated him his entire life. X-Men telepath Emma Frost learned of Daken's existence and told Wolverine, who vowed to find him and help free him of Romulus' influence. During the resulting clash, Wolverine learned much of Romulus' operations but was unable to free Daken from his anger toward Wolverine.

Phaedra soon attacked Wolverine with his own soul fragment, now a warrior named Shogun, and a briefly resurrected Lord Shingen Harada, but Wolverine defeated his foes and reclaimed his soul fragment. Soon after, Cyclops appointed Wolverine the leader of a covert X-Men strikeforce named X-Force, which carried out lethal preemptive strikes against mutantkind's enemies; around this time, the X-Men relocated to San Francisco, California. Working with the Winter Soldier (now freed from his brainwashing), Wolverine had Daken shot in the head with Carbonadium, slowing his healing factor enough for Wolverine to capture him. However, Daken awoke in an amnesiac state, enabling Professor Xavier to mentally free Daken from Romulus' influence; corrupt tycoon Norman Osborn soon recruited Daken into his own Avengers team as "Wolverine."

Romulus finally revealed himself to Wolverine, and declared his intent for Wolverine to become his empire's heir. As the two fought, Romulus taunted Wolverine by suggesting that Daken would be a viable substitute; unwilling to see his son further corrupted, Wolverine defeated Romulus. After she helped him with information gathering, Wolverine began dating human reporter Melita Garner. During a siege on mutantkind by Sentinel Bastion's forces, X-Force's existence came to light, creating a rift between Wolverine and the X-Men (particularly Storm); Wolverine disbanded X-Force but secretly recreated the team without Cyclops' knowledge.

ART BY PAUL SMITH

Soon after Wolverine helped Jubilee cope with her unwilling transformation into a vampire, the Red Right Hand (RRH) — an organization of those who believed themselves wronged by Wolverine — worked with Daken to send Wolverine's soul to an unrevealed Hell dimension and used his demon-possessed body to attack his loved ones. After apparently encountering the souls of many enemies (and Mariko), Wolverine escaped the realm and reclaimed his body, then tracked the RRH and killed their five super-powered henchmen, the Mongrels. However, a pre-recorded message left after the RRH committed suicide identified the Mongrels as Wolverine's previously unknown illegitimate children, devastating him; after an extended period of wandering in the wilderness alone, Wolverine's friends and teammates convinced him to return to civilization.

Later, Wolverine's philosophical disagreement with Cyclops over allowing mutant children to fight in battle irrevocably divided the X-Men. With half of the X-Men as staff and Kitty Pryde as co-headmaster, Wolverine opened the Jean Grey School for Higher Learning on the site of the X-Men's former New York headquarters. There, dozens of mutant youth receive formal education and safely

learn to use their powers while remaining out of combat; Wolverine is particularly challenged in his dealings with anarchist psychic student Kid Omega (Quentin Quire). Wolverine bested Romulus in another battle and had him imprisoned in superhuman penitentiary the Raft. Soon after, longtime Wolverine enemy Mystique (Raven Darkholme)'s machinations caused Garner to leave Wolverine, and in a confrontation with Daken, Wolverine apparently killed his son through drowning to prevent Daken from harming Grey School students. When a massive worldwide war erupted between the Avengers and X-Men over Cyclops' belief that the deadly cosmic Phoenix Force could reinstate mutantkind's depowered numbers, Wolverine sided with the Avengers because he believed the Force would ultimately corrupt any host it took. The war ended with mutantkind restored, but also with Xavier's death at the hands of a Phoenix Force-possessed Cyclops, who was briefly imprisoned before escaping to become an underground mutant revolutionary. After a century of separation, Wolverine was shocked when he was attacked by his now time-traveling brother Dog, who wanted to prove his value by beating his brother in battle and claiming his students. After his students rejected Dog and Wolverine refused to fight him, a self-doubting Dog departed.

After Kitty Pryde stepped down to mentor five time-traveling teenaged X-Men, whose ranks included a young Cyclops, Wolverine shared the Grey School's headmaster duties with Storm. Wolverine and Storm are exploring romantic feelings for one another while they protect mutantkind with the X-Men, and Wolverine also serves on the Avengers' Unity Squad, a public mutant/human cooperative force.

HEIGHT: 5'3"
WEIGHT: 300 lbs.; (without Adamantium skeleton) 195 lbs.
EYES: Blue
HAIR: Black

ABILITIES/ACCESSORIES: Wolverine can regenerate damaged or destroyed areas of his cellular structure rapidly, is virtually immune to poisons, most drugs and diseases and is partially immune to exertion-induced fatigue poisons which grants him great endurance. His aging is greatly slowed and his agility and reflexes are similarly enhanced. All of Wolverine senses are superhumanly acute, enabling him to recognize people and objects by scent, which, combined with combat and stealth training, makes him one of the world's foremost trackers. His skeleton includes six retractable, slightly curved, foot-long bone claws, three in each arm, beneath the skin and muscle of his forearms. The claws are naturally sharp and tougher than bone, allowing them to penetrate most types of natural materials. Wolverine's entire skeletal structure and claws are bonded to the nearly indestructible metal Adamantium, rendering his bones virtually unbreakable and his claws capable of penetrating almost any substance. His healing factor prevents the Adamantium from interfering with his bones' normal generation of blood cells, and his reinforced skeleton enables him to withstand heavy physical pressure, allowing him to briefly lift 800 pounds or more. Wolverine is an extraordinary hand-to-hand combatant, having mastered virtually every fighting style on Earth, as well as a trained expert in multiple weapons (including bladed weapons and firearms), vehicles, computer systems, explosives and assassination techniques. He is fluent in numerous languages and has undergone extensive training as samurai, soldier, spy and other disciplines; he frequently travels by motorcycle.

POWER GRID	1	2	3	4	5	6	7
INTELLIGENCE							
STRENGTH							
SPEED							
DURABILITY							
ENERGY PROJECTION							
FIGHTING SKILLS							

MARIKO YASHIDA

REAL NAME: Mariko Yashida
ALIASES: None
IDENTITY: No dual identity
OCCUPATION: Former businesswoman, Clan Yashida oyabun
CITIZENSHIP: Japan
PLACE OF BIRTH: Agarashima, Japan
KNOWN RELATIVES: Noburu-Hideki (husband, deceased), Amiko Kobayashi (foster daughter), Shingen Harada (father), Kenuichio Harada (Silver Samurai, half-brother), Shingen "Shin" Harada (Silver Samurai, nephew), Saburo and Tomo Yashida (first cousins once removed, deceased), Yoshi's unidentified mother (possible first cousin once removed), Yoshi (last name unrevealed, possible second cousin, deceased), Shiro Yoshida (Sunfire, second cousin), Leyu Yoshida (Sunpyre, second cousin, deceased), Ichiro and Fukuko (last name unrevealed, possible first cousins), Rikuto (last name unrevealed, possible first cousin once removed, deceased), Hoken Yashida (ancestor, deceased)
GROUP AFFILIATION: Clan Yashida, Yakuza
EDUCATION: Unrevealed
FIRST APPEARANCE: X-Men #118 (1979)

HISTORY: Born to a 2000-year old Japanese family, Mariko Yashida's crimelord father, Shingen Harada, disappeared during her childhood and was believed dead. As an adult, Mariko met Wolverine (Logan/James Howlett) when he and his fellow X-Men sought her cousin Sunfire (Shiro Yoshida)'s help. Initially frightened of the intimidating mutant, she was drawn to his courage and respect for Japanese ways, while he was charmed by her beauty and manner. While he was in Japan, Mariko and Wolverine fell in love; despite her sheltered upbringing, she later visited America to spend more time with him. Shingen resurfaced, summoned her home and allegedly repaid an obligation to a criminal associate, the abusive Noburu-Hideki, by giving him Mariko's hand in marriage; Mariko felt honor bound to obey Shingen, even though she believed his criminal activities disgraced their family name. When Wolverine traveled to Japan to confront her, Shingen secretly had him drugged, then manipulated him into a duel with wooden swords; Shingen's seemingly harmless blows

were potentially fatal pressure point strikes, leading Wolverine to unsheathe his Adamantium claws, shocking Mariko, whose dismay disheartened Wolverine, enabling Shingen to defeat him. Mariko subsequently accompanied Hideki to a negotiation with Shingen's rival Katsuyori; Katsuyori deployed assassins, but Wolverine intervened while his ally Yukio killed Katsuyori. Wolverine killed the assassins in a berserker rage, horrifying Mariko. Later, Mariko resolved to kill her father for dishonoring Clan Yashida, and then kill herself to expiate patricide. When Wolverine directly attacked the Clan during a prolonged campaign against Shingen's forces, Hideki threatened to kill Mariko unless allowed to escape, but Yukio slew him as Wolverine killed Shingen in a duel, which Mariko considered just punishment. She and Wolverine became engaged, but preparations were disrupted by terrorist Viper (Ophelia Sarkissian) and Mariko's half-brother Silver Samurai (Kenuichio Harada), seeking control of Clan Yashida. While the visiting X-Men were distracted, their enemy Mastermind (Jason Wyngarde) mentally manipulated Mariko to cancel the wedding and strengthen Clan Yashida's criminal ties. Mastermind's involvement was soon uncovered, but Mariko, vowing to break Clan Yashida's underworld ties, felt she could not marry Wolverine until she had done so. To the surprise of many, she became a formidable underworld force.

When crimelord Tatsu'o the Dragon Lord sent his super-powered Cybersamurai to abduct his American granddaughter, Opal Tanaka, so he could force her to bear an heir with one of his Cybersamurai, Opal's boyfriend Iceman (Bobby Drake) and his X-Factor teammates obtained Mariko's help in rescuing Opal. Later, Mariko encountered US super-team the New Warriors when founder Night Thrasher (Dwayne Taylor) obtained her help in his efforts to divest his Taylor Foundation business of Yakuza ties. Despite challenges for rule by Silver Samurai, Mariko was close to cutting Clan Yashida's criminal ties when the Hand ninja organization, under Matsuo Tsurayaba and allied with Hydra's Silver Fox, besieged her. While Wolverine and allies were distracted by Hand ninjas and the cyborg Cylla, Tsurayaba's employee Reiko claimed Tsurayaba would buy Clan Yashida's criminal enterprises and dissolve them, cleansing Mariko of dishonor if, in payment, she observed Yakuza tradition by severing one of her fingers. Mariko did so, but the knife was coated with lethal blowfish poison. Learning Mariko was betrothed to Wolverine, Reiko, who felt she owed Wolverine a great debt, committed suicide. Rather than undergo prolonged suffering, Mariko asked Wolverine to grant her a quick death, which he reluctantly did, stabbing her with his claws. Much later, Wolverine refused to spare Hand agent Phaedra's life in battle in exchange for the resurrection of Mariko, believing Mariko would feel dishonored by the exchange. Later still, while escaping from an unidentified Hell realm after being trapped there by his enemies the Right Red Hand (RRH), Wolverine apparently encountered Mariko, who refused to leave because she felt she deserved to be there due to her Clan's criminal past; the RRH also stole Mariko's corpse, but Wolverine later had her reinterred.

HEIGHT: 5'		**EYES:** Brown	
WEIGHT: 100 lbs.		**HAIR:** Black	

ABILITIES/ACCESSORIES: Mariko Yashida was an accomplished and, when necessary, ruthless businesswoman and leader in both corporate and criminal arenas. She had access to the vast resources of Clan Yashida. Near the end of her life, she wielded the Yashida Clan's 800-year-old Honor Sword.

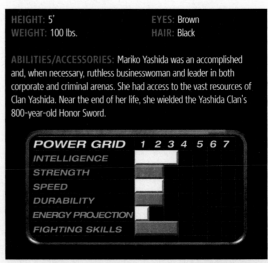

POWER GRID	1	2	3	4	5	6	7
INTELLIGENCE							
STRENGTH							
SPEED							
DURABILITY							
ENERGY PROJECTION							
FIGHTING SKILLS							

ART BY PAUL SMITH WITH MICHAL DUTKIEWICZ (INSET)

HISTORY: In her youth, Yukio trained under multiple martial arts masters and declared herself a ronin, or masterless ninja, dedicated to risk and adventure. As a thief, she sometimes worked with future X-Man Gambit (Remy LeBeau), her frequently exclaimed "gotcha" when accomplishing tasks and life-threatening stunts often provoking others to think her insane. After several British heists, Yukio told police officer Alexandra Davies of Gambit's theft of a French painting stolen years before by Nazis, presuming Gambit would be blamed for her thefts. Gambit in turn tipped off Davies, who arrested Yukio. Back in Japan, she encountered Goro the Poisoner, who had escaped from the Hand ninjas' Valley of Mercy and Wrath stronghold; before dying, Goro revealed its location to Yukio, who explored a hidden entrance; subsequent events are unrevealed. Eventually, Yukio turned to mercenary and assassination work, again clashing with Gambit in Singapore, Italy and elsewhere. Yukio became a hired assassin to Clan Yashida's Lord Shingen Harada. When Wolverine (Logan/James Howlett) visited Japan to investigate his beloved Mariko Yashida's (Shingen's daughter) forced marriage, Yukio surreptitiously poisoned him, enabling Shingen to shame him in battle. During a staged Hand attack, she befriended Wolverine, whom she persuaded to attack gangster Katsuyori, Shingen's rival; Wolverine was kept busy with Hand assassins while Yukio slew Katsuyori and his wife. Although drawn to Yukio, Wolverine remained in love with Mariko, to Yukio's chagrin. When intelligence agent Asano Kimura investigated Shingen, Yukio killed him, revealing her true loyalties. To atone, she helped Wolverine decimate Shingen's forces, although Shingen brutally beat her. When Mariko's husband, Noburu-Hideki, took Mariko hostage, Yukio rescued her, killing Hideki. After Wolverine slew Shingen, he and Mariko became engaged, and later, Viper (Ophelia Sarkissian) and Mariko's half-brother Silver Samurai sought to claim Clan Yashida. Yukio penetrated Viper's defenses, fighting Silver Samurai while Wolverine's X-Men teammate Storm (Ororo Munroe) rescued Mariko from Viper. Yukio and Storm became close friends, Yukio's extroverted personality influencing Storm. Months later, Wolverine's teammate Kitty Pryde was brainwashed by his ex-mentor, ninja-sorcerer Ogun; Yukio helped rescue Kitty and allied with her against Ogun's gangster ally Heiji Shigematsu.

Months later, Yukio rescued Wolverine's friend Jubilee (Jubilation Lee) from the Hand, but failed to prevent Mariko from being fatally poisoned by Hydra's Silver Fox and the Yakuza's Matsuo Tsurayaba. By then, Yukio had joined Professor X's Mutant Underground, a covert mutant rights organization; her activities attracted the X-Men's techno-organic enemies the Phalanx, whose members pursued her for weeks before she fled to Manhattan where Storm and Gambit (now an X-Man) helped defeat her pursuers. Returning to Japan, she rescued a weakened Wolverine, troubled by increasingly bestial impulses, from Hand ninjas. Wolverine entrusted Yukio with his foster daughter

YUKIO

REAL NAME: Yukiko (full name unrevealed)
ALIASES: Wild One
IDENTITY: Full name secret
OCCUPATION: Ronin/adventurer, mercenary; former assassin, professional criminal
CITIZENSHIP: Japan with a criminal record
PLACE OF BIRTH: Presumably Japan
KNOWN RELATIVES: Amiko Kobayashi (foster daughter)
GROUP AFFILIATION: Formerly Mutant Underground
EDUCATION: Unrevealed
FIRST APPEARANCE: Wolverine #1 (1982)

Amiko Kobayashi, whom Yukio vowed to raise as her own, occasionally entrusting her to the Kuan family when her mercenary work took her away from Japan; at some point, Wolverine and Yukio began a casual physical relationship. After helping Havok (Alex Summers)'s X-Factor against Dark Beast's hired assassin Fatale, Yukio helped Wolverine prevent the robot Red Ronin's theft. When filmmaker Akatora's Hand faction abducted Yukio and Amiko, Wolverine rescued the pair, neither he nor Yukio realizing the Hand had brainwashed Amiko. When Yukio assisted Elektra Natchios against the Hand, Amiko warned the group. Amiko's brainwashing was eventually reversed, and Yukio trained her in fighting techniques should she again be targeted. Yukio was also briefly brainwashed by Viper against Wolverine.

When Wolverine again visited Japan, criminal Gom Kaishek abducted Yukio and Amiko to force Wolverine into killing Gom's brother and rival Haan. After Haan slew Gom, their sister Kia seized the hostages, and Wolverine accompanied her to meet with Haan; Yukio and Amiko escaped, freeing Wolverine to attack both sides. After killing Haan, Kia fled to Mongolia to kill her father Yolyn; Yukio followed, and the two women fought, Kia almost killing Yukio until Wolverine intervened. Weeks later, Wolverine's enemies Lady Deathstrike (Yuriko Oyama) and Omega Red (Arkady Rossovich) crippled Yukio and abducted Amiko. Wolverine yet again saved Amiko, and although prepared to die rather than live as a paraplegic, Yukio made a miraculous recovery. Yukio helped Storm infiltrate Masque's mutant combat Arena, then stole the Mark of Mana necklace, unaware demon Ryuki was imprisoned within. When Wolverine inadvertently released him, Ryuki abducted Yukio and Amiko, but Wolverine and mystic guardian Mana freed them. Sometime after Wolverine ended their physical trysts to focus on a new relationship, Yukio again lost the use of her legs when a temporarily soulless, demon-possessed Wolverine attacked her upon orders of Wolverine's enemies the Red Right Hand. Despite being confined to a wheelchair, Yukio remains a highly capable warrior.

HEIGHT: 5'9" **EYES:** Brown
WEIGHT: 130 lbs. **HAIR:** Black

ABILITIES/ACCESSORIES: Yukio is an accomplished thief, exceptional athlete, acrobat, and hand-to-hand combatant trained in multiple martial arts; she is resilient enough to fight despite multiple bullet wounds. Possessing an encyclopedic knowledge of ninja lore, she is also an expert with bladed weapons and has employed knives, darts, and shuriken, sometimes poisoned.

POWER GRID	1	2	3	4	5	6	7
INTELLIGENCE							
STRENGTH							
SPEED							
DURABILITY							
ENERGY PROJECTION							
FIGHTING SKILLS							

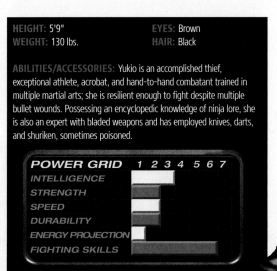

ART BY LEINIL FRANCIS YU WITH RON GARNEY (INSET)

CURRENT APPEARANCE

WOLVERINE

The most popular X-Man of all time in classic solo action!

Wolverine: Origin TPB
Wolverine: Origin #1-6
Paul Jenkins & Andy Kubert
The story that could never be told… until now!
DEC082436 • 978-0-7851-3727-6

WOLVERINE
ORIGIN

X-MEN
WOLVERINE/
GAMBIT
LOEB · SALE

X-Men: Wolverine/Gambit MPHC
Wolverine/Gambit: Victims #1-4
Jeph Loeb & Tim Sale
Two outlaw heroes face the retur of Jack the Ripper!
MAY090584 • 978-0-7851-3802-0

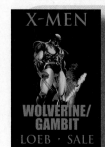

Wolverine: Weapon X TPB
Marvel Comics Presents #72-84
Barry Windsor-Smith
Modern classic that set the mold for Wolverine origins!
JAN092592 • 978-0-7851-3726-9

WOLVERINE
WEAPON
X

WOLVERINE
NOT DEAD YET
ELLIS · YU

Wolverine: Not Dead Yet MPHC
Wolverine (1988) #119-122
Warren Ellis & Leinil Francis Yu
Stirring Wolverine tale by writer Ellis!
NOV082448 • 978-0-7851-3766-5

Wolverine by Miller & Claremont TPB
Wolverine (1982) #1-4 & Uncanny X-Men #172-173
Chris Claremont, Frank Miller & Paul Smith
Wolverine heads to Japan for big adventure and bigger trouble!
JAN092591 • 978-0-7851-3724-5

WOLVERINE
CLAREMONT
MILLER

WOLVERINE
GREG RUCKA
ULTIMATE
COLLECTION

Wolverine by Greg Rucka Ultimate Collection TPB
Wolverine (2003) #1-19
Greg Rucka, Leandro Fernande Darick Robertson
Rucka's razor-sharp series reboot complete in one volume!
OCT110732 • 978-0-7851-5845-5

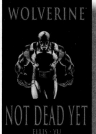

X-Men: Kitty Pryde & Wolverine MPHC
Kitty Pryde & Wolverine #1-6
Chris Claremont & Al Milgrom
Kitty heads to Japan and gets mixed up with Wolverine's sensei, Ogun!
MAR082260 • 978-0-7851-3089-5

X-MEN
KITTY PRYDE
& WOLVERINE

WOLVERINE
CAPTAIN AMERICA

Wolverine & Captain Ameri TPB
Wolverine/Captain America #1-4 & more
R.A. Jones, Thomas Derenick, T DeFalco & Denys Cowan
Cap and Wolverine vs. the crimin Contingency!
DEC110751 • 978-0-7851-5942-1

Wolverine & Nick Fury: Scorpio TPB
Wolverine/Nick Fury: The Scorpio Connection, Wolverine: Bloody Choices & Wolverine & Nick Fury: Scorpio Rising
Howard Chaykin, John Buscema & Shawn McManus
Logan and Fury in action as both allies and adversaries!
JAN120762 • 978-0-7851-5348-1

WOLVERINE · NICK FURY

WOLVERINE
ENEMY
OF THE STATE
MILLAR · ROMITA JR.

Wolverine: Enemy of the State Ultimate Collection T
Wolverine (2003) #20-32
Mark Millar & John Romita Jr.
The mind-blowing epic complete one volume!
APR082366 • 978-0-7851-3301-8

**use of M: Wolverine, Iron
n & Hulk HC**

*lverine (2003) #33-35,
edible Hulk #83-87* & more

iiel Way, Javier Saltares &
ers

*lverine is an Agent of S.H.I.E.L.D.
he House of M!*

V090535 • 978-0-7851-3882-2

HOUSE OF M
WOLVERINE, IRON MAN & HULK

WOLVERINE
THE DEATH OF WOLVERINE
GUGGENHEIM • AARON • CHAYKIN

**Wolverine: The Death of
Wolverine MPHC/TPB**

Wolverine (2003) #56-61

Marc Guggenheim, Jason Aaron &
Howard Chaykin

*Wolverine is the best there is…at
dying!*

HC: FEB082288 • 978-0-7851-2611-9
TPB: MAY082371 • 978-0-7851-2612-6

**lverine: Origins & Endings
B**

lverine (2003) #36-40

iiel Way, Javier Saltares & Mark
eira

*memories are back. Now it is
e for vengeance!*

T062221 • 978-0-7851-1979-1

WOLVERINE
ORIGINS & ENDINGS

WOLVERINE:
LOGAN
VAUGHAN • RISSO

Wolverine: Logan MPHC/TPB

Logan #1-3

Brian K. Vaughan & Eduardo Risso

*With memories intact, Wolverine
settles an old score!*

HC: JUN082418 • 978-0-7851-3425-1
TPB: FEB092645 • 978-0-7851-3414-5

lverine: Civil War TPB

lverine (2003) #42-48

rc Guggenheim & Humberto
nos

*rching for the secrets behind
mford.*

R072149 • 978-0-7851-1980-7

WOLVERINE
A MARVEL COMICS EVENT
CIVIL WAR

WOLVERINE
OLD MAN LOGAN
MARK MILLAR • STEVE McNIVEN

**Wolverine: Old Man Logan
HC/TPB**

*Wolverine (2003) #66-72 & Giant-
Size Wolverine: Old Man Logan #1*

Mark Millar & Steve McNiven

*Civil War tandem reunite for all-time
Wolverine classic!*

HC: AUG090551 • 978-0-7851-3159-5
TPB: JUL100692 • 978-0-7851-3172-4

**lverine: Blood & Sorrow
B**

*lverine (2003) #41, 49, Giant-
ed Wolverine #1 & X-Men
imited #12*

art Moore, David Lapham,
rence Campbell, David Aja &
ers

*-contained stories starring
lverine!*

R072372 • 978-0-7851-2607-2

WOLVERINE
BLOOD & SORROW

**lverine: Evolution MPHC/
B**

lverine (2003) #50-55

h Loeb & Simone Bianchi

*retooth is back for another
hday surprise!*

AUG072297 • 978-0-7851-2837-3
: DEC072275 • 978-0-7851-2256-2

WOLVERINE
EVOLUTION

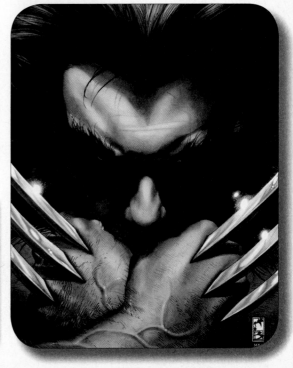

WOLVERINE by JASON AARON

Wolverine: Get Mystique TPB

Wolverine (2003) #62-65

Jason Aaron & Ron Garney

Mystique action yarn that will leave you breathless!

JUN082433 • 978-0-7851-2963-9

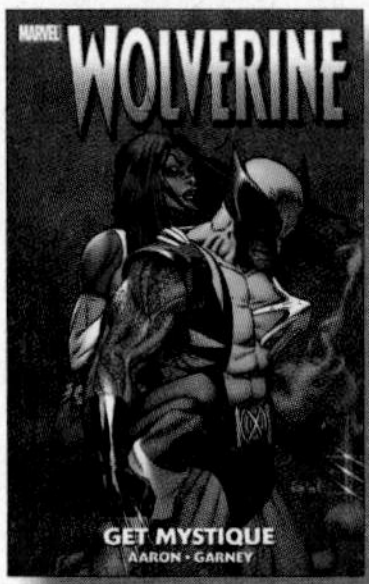
WOLVERINE
GET MYSTIQUE
AARON • GARNEY

X-Men: Manifest Destiny HC/TPB

Wolverine: Manifest Destiny #1-4, X-Men: Manifest Destiny: Nightcrawler #1 and more

Jason Aaron, Stephen Segovia, Mike Carey & others

Wolverine takes over San Francisco's Chinatown!

HC: FEB092606 • 978-0-7851-3817-4
TPB: SEP090538 • 978-0-7851-3951-5

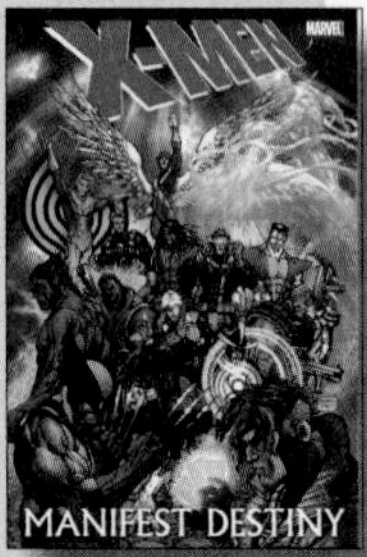
X-MEN
MANIFEST DESTINY

Wolverine Weapon X Vol. 1: Adamantium Men MPHC/TPB

Wolverine: Weapon X #1-5 & *Wolverine (2003) #73-74*

Jason Aaron & Ron Garney

Someone is building Adamantium-laced super-soldiers like Wolverine!

HC: SEP090511 • 978-0-7851-4017-7
TPB: FEB100624 • 978-0-7851-4111-2

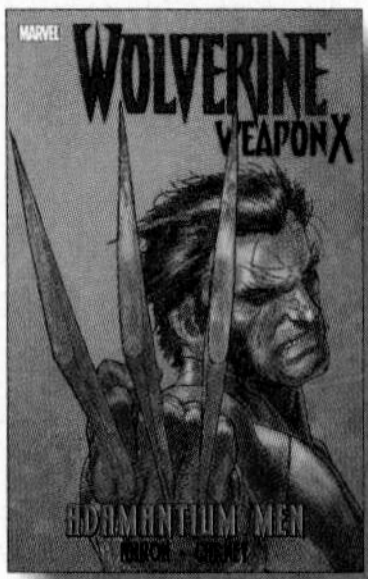
WOLVERINE
WEAPON X
ADAMANTIUM MEN

Wolverine Weapon X Vol. 2: Insane in the Brain MPHC/TPB

Wolverine: Weapon X #6-10

Jason Aaron & Yanick Paquette

Welcome to Dunwich Sanatorium, Wolverine!

HC: JAN100657 • 978-0-7851-4018-4
TPB: APR100684 • 978-0-7851-4112-9

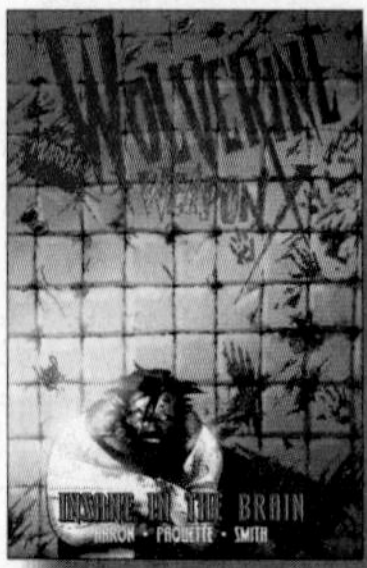
WOLVERINE
WEAPON X
INSANE IN THE BRAIN

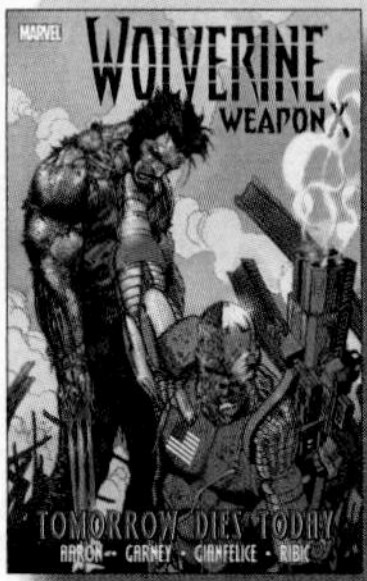
WOLVERINE
WEAPON X
TOMORROW DIES TODAY

Wolverine Weapon X Vol. 3 Tomorrow Dies Today MPH TPB

Wolverine: Weapon X #11-16 & *Dark Reign: The List – Wolverine*

Jason Aaron, Ron Garney & Esa Ribic

Killer cyborgs come from the futu to kill the heroes of today!

HC: AUG100685 • 978-0-7851-465
TPB: JAN110850 • 978-0-7851-465

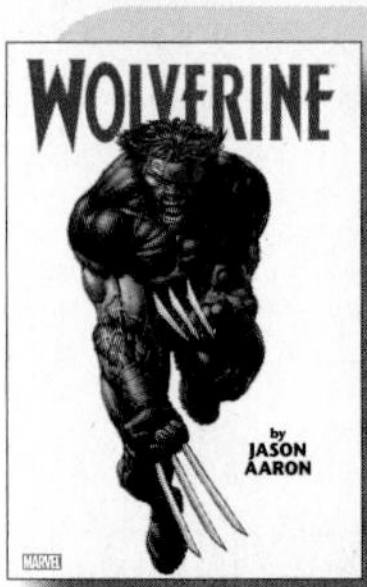
WOLVERINE
by
JASON
AARON

Wolverine by Jason Aaron Omnibus Vol. 1 HC

Wolverine #56, 62-65, Wolverin Manifest Destiny #1-4, Wolverine Weapon X #1-16 & more

MAY110713 • 978-0-7851-5639-0

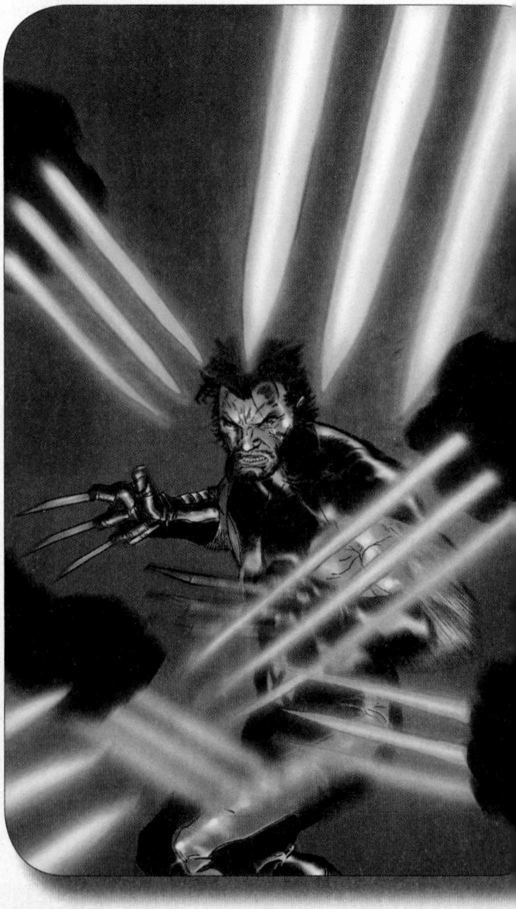